Innovation and Growth in the Global Economy

Innovation and Growth in the Global Economy

Gene M. Grossman and
Elhanan Helpman

The MIT Press
Cambridge, Massachusetts
London, England

This book was set in Palatino by Asco Trade Typesetting Ltd., Hong Kong and was printed and bound in the United States of America.

Library of Congress Cataloging-in-Publication Data

Grossman, Gene M.
Innovation and growth in the global economy / Gene M. Grossman and Elhanan Helpman.
p. cm.
Includes bibliographical references and index.
ISBN 0-262-07136-3
1. Technological innovations—Economic aspects. 2. Economic development. 3. International trade. 4. Economic history—1945– I. Helpman, Elhanan. II. Title.
HC79.T4G697 1991
338.9—dc20 91-15795
CIP

To the women in our lives:
Jean, Shari, and Dina
Ruthi, Limor, and Liat

Contents

Preface

Countries vary greatly in their growth performances. Standards of living in Japan, for example, have risen dramatically in the post-World War II period, while residents of many African nations continue to languish in poverty. A substantial body of evidence suggests moreover that these differences in experience are not simply the outcome of a random process. High growth rates correlate systematically with a number of variables that describe the economic and political environment. It is the job of the social scientist to uncover the mechanisms that link structural and policy conditions to realized growth performance.

A casual reading of recent economic history suggests two important trends in the world economy. First, technological innovations are becoming an ever more important contributor to economic well-being. Second, the nations in the world economy are becoming increasingly open and increasingly interdependent. The two are not unrelated. Rapid communication and close contacts among innovators in different countries facilitate the process of invention and the spread of new ideas. And rapid changes in technology intensify the motives for trade and the consequences of integration into the world trading system. It is not surprising therefore to find that increasing attention is being paid to issues of productivity and technology, on the one hand, and to international competitiveness and the world trading system, on the other, as commentators seek to understand recent growth experiences and to develop scenarios for the future.

This book attempts to integrate the theory of international trade with the theory of economic growth. As growth theory, it focuses on the economic determinants of technological progress. As trade theory, it deals with the dynamic evolution of comparative advantage and the consequences of international trade in a world of global technological competition. Our premise in writing this book is that new technologies stem from the intentional actions of economic agents responding to market incentives. In an open world economy these incentives invariably reflect aspects of the international trade environment. Thus we concentrate on mechanisms that link the growth performance and the trade performance of nations in the world economy.

Our work has antecedents in both the literatures on international trade and economic growth. On the trade side, we draw heavily on recent analyses of international trade with imperfect competition. Paul Krugman, Kelvin Lancaster, Avinash Dixit, Victor Norman, and Wilfred Ethier, among others, have shown how approaches developed in the field of industrial organization can be incorporated into a general-equilibrium framework to provide a static theory of trade in differentiated products. These static models provide the building blocks for our treatment of imperfectly competitive world markets for innovative products. On the growth side, Paul Romer, Phillipe Aghion, and Peter Howitt have applied similar tools from the theory of industrial organization, and their extensions in trade theory to general-equilibrium settings, to develop aggregate models of ongoing investments in new technologies. Their insights have been useful to us in extending the static trade models to a dynamic setting.

In the light of the dual focus of our book and the dual nature of its intellectual origins, we believe that it will be of interest both to macroeconomists concerned with the mechanisms of aggregate growth and to international economists concerned with the evolution of trading patterns and with the dynamic effects of trade policies. We regard the book as too circumscribed in its focus to serve as a primary text in a regular graduate course. However, we hope that it will find use as a supplementary text in both macroeconomics and international trade classes, with some chapters being adopted by courses on industrial organization as well. Industrial organization economists may benefit from our general-equilibrium treatment of technological competition in chapters 3 and 4. For a macro course the first five chapters offer a self-contained discussion of the mechanisms of growth in a closed economy. These chapters provide evidence on the role of technology in growth, a discussion of the relationship between the traditional growth theory based on factor accumulation and our own approach based on industrial innovation, and a thorough analysis of two distinct but related models of endogenous technological progress. Students of macroeconomics may also wish to refer to chapter 9, which addresses the interdependencies in the growth processes in different countries and which can be read immediately following chapter 5 without loss of comprehension. Students of international trade will want to read (at least) chapters 3 and 4 for background, and then could skip to chapter 6 which begins our treatment of open economy issues. Chapters 7 through 10 form the corps of our discussion of technological competition between advanced industrial countries. The first two of these chapters concern the determination of patterns of specialization and trade in a dynamic setting of endogenous comparative advantage, while the last two treat the link between the trade environment (including the policy environment) and growth. Finally, chapters 11 and 12 study North–South trade in a setting in which firms in the South imitate technological developments in the North.

Some of the chapters in this book build on material that we have published in professional journals and conference volumes. The interested reader may wish to refer to some of the following articles: (1) "Growth, Technological Progress, and Trade" (*Empirica–Austrian Economic Papers* 15, March 1988, pp. 5–25); (2) "Product Development and International Trade" (*Journal of Political Economy* 97, December 1989, pp. 1261–1282); (3) "Trade, Innovation, and Growth" (*American Economic Review* 80, Papers and Proceedings, May 1990, pp. 86–91); (4) "Explaining Japan's Innovation and Trade" (*Bank of Japan Monetary and Economic Studies* 8, September 1990, pp. 75–100); (5) "Comparative Advantage and Long-Run Growth," (*American Economic Review* 80, September 1990, pp. 796–815); (6) "Quality Ladders in the Theory of Growth" (*Review of Economic Studies* 58, January 1991, pp. 43–61); (7) "Growth and Welfare in a Small Open Economy" (in E. Helpman and A. Razin, eds., *International Trade and Trade Policy*, MIT Press, 1991); (8) "Quality Ladders and Product Cycles" (*Quarterly Journal of Economics* 106, May 1991, pp. 557–586); (9) "Trade, Knowledge Spillovers, and Growth" (*European Economic Review* 35, Papers and Proceedings, 1991, forthcoming); and (10) "Endogenous Product Cycles" (*The Economic Journal* 101, September, 1991, forthcoming).

During the course of our collaboration on the subject of this book, we have received financial support from the National Science Foundation, the Institute for Advanced Studies at the Hebrew University in Jerusalem, the Bank of Sweden Tercentenary Foundation, the International Monetary Fund, the World Bank, the Bank of Japan Institute for Monetary and Economic Studies, the MITI Research Institute, the Haas School of Business of the University of California at Berkeley (where Grossman was visiting professor in the B. T. Rocca Chair in International Trade), and the Board of Governors of the Federal Reserve System. Support for the writing of this book has been generously provided by the National Science Foundation in the form of a grant to the National Bureau of Economic Research, by the Pew Charitable Trusts in the form of a grant to the Center for International Studies at Princeton University, and by the U.S.–Israel Binational Science

Foundation in the form of a grant to Tel Aviv University. We are grateful to all of these organizations, which of course bear no responsibility for any of the opinions expressed herein.

Many people have provided helpful comments on drafts of some of these chapters. We thank Eitan Berglas, Ben Bernanke, Avinash Dixit, Chaim Fershtman, Alex Galetovic, Zvi Griliches, Jean Baldwin Grossman, Jim Levinsohn, Kiminori Matsuyama, David Pines, Torsten Persson, Jim Rauch, Paul Romer, Manuel Trachtenberg, and Alwyn Young. We are also grateful to Kellett Hannah, a research assistant at the International Monetary Fund, who helped us to perform some computer simulations, and to Robert Barro, Alan Krueger, and Lars Svensson, who aided in the preparation of some of the figures. John Martin, at the OECD, provided the data for figure 1.2 at very short notice. Finally, Arijit Sen, a graduate student in the doctoral program at Princeton University, deserves special mention. He tirelessly read all of the manuscript, reviewed the logic of our arguments, and checked our algebra. We thank him warmly, while absolving him of any blame for remaining errors.

Innovation and Growth in the Global Economy

1 Growth and Technology

1.1 Facts about Growth

Two facts about the economic growth experience of the world economy beg for an explanation. First, growth in per capita income has been sustained at positive and apparently nondeclining rates in many countries for prolonged periods of time. Second, dynamic performance has varied greatly across different countries in a given time period, and across different historical periods in a given country. Moreover realized growth rates seem not to be the outcome of a random process but rather relate systematically to observable features of the economies, including their government policies.

Kaldor (1961) observed as one of his celebrated "stylized facts" about growth that output per worker rises continually and productivity growth rates show no tendency to decline. More recent evidence is provided by Romer (1986, 1989a) and Scott (1989). In his 1986 paper Romer (following Maddison 1979) reported that in four successive periods of several decades or longer since 1700, the rate of growth of output per person-hour in the world's highest productivity country has increased relative to the growth rate of the technological leader in the preceding period. He also calculated using data from Maddison (1979) that, in a sample of decade-long growth rates of per capita GDP for eleven industrialized countries, the proportion of observations in which a country's growth rate was higher than that in the previous decade varied between 0.58 (for Sweden) and 0.81 (for Norway). Romer's 1989a paper addresses the perception that growth has been slowing in the United States in recent years, and concludes that the last few annual observations on labor productivity growth seemingly represent an aberration in a generally upward trend. Scott (1989) provides evidence that growth rates of nonresidential business output have been roughly constant in the United States, the United Kingdom, and Japan within ten to thirty year periods since the late nineteenth century. He also corroborates the view that productivity growth rates in these countries have shown no tendency to decline.

Concerning the cross-country variation in growth performances (which was another of Kaldor's "stylized facts"), the data from the Summers and Heston (1988) international comparison project can be used to compute growth rates of real per capita income in 114 countries for the period from 1960 to 1985. Figure 1.1 plots these growth rates, which ranged from a low of −2.8 percent per annum in Chad to a high of 7.5 percent per annum in Singapore (with a mean annual growth rate of 2.2 percent), against the level of per capita income in 1960.[1] The figure reveals the great dispersion in realized growth rates in the sample and suggests the absence of any strong correlation between beginning of period levels of income and growth during the period.

Many studies have identified correlates of output and productivity growth. Investment-to-output ratios typically correlate positively with real GDP growth in cross-sectional studies (Dowrik and Nguyen 1989), as do various proxies for the stock of human capital, such as the literacy rate (Azariades and Drazen 1990; Romer 1989b) and the school enrollment rate (Baumol et al. 1989; Barro 1989b). Countries that export a large share of their output seem to grow faster than others (Michaely 1977; Feder 1982; Romer 1989c), as do countries with a low rate of population growth (Baumol et al. 1989). Romer (1989c) finds a positive correlation between the number of scientists and engineers employed in research and the growth rate of output in a sample of 22 of the most developed economies. Finally, a number of authors writing on the industrialization process in the less developed countries find a significant association between the rate of productivity growth and both the size of an economy and the share of its GDP generated by the manufacturing sector (e.g., see the survey article by Syrquin and Chenery 1989).

Historical data also link various government policies with exceptional growth performance. Countries with high shares of government consumption in GDP have grown on average more slowly than others (Landau 1983; Barro 1989a, b), whereas those with high rates of government investment have tended to grow more rapidly. High marginal tax rates are associated with slow growth in output, holding constant the average

1. This type of figure was first presented by Romer (1987). Ours is identical to figure 1 in Barro (1989a), except that the sample has been augmented to include all countries in the Summers-Heston data set, save a few of the centrally planned economies. We thank Robert Barro for his help in preparing this figure.

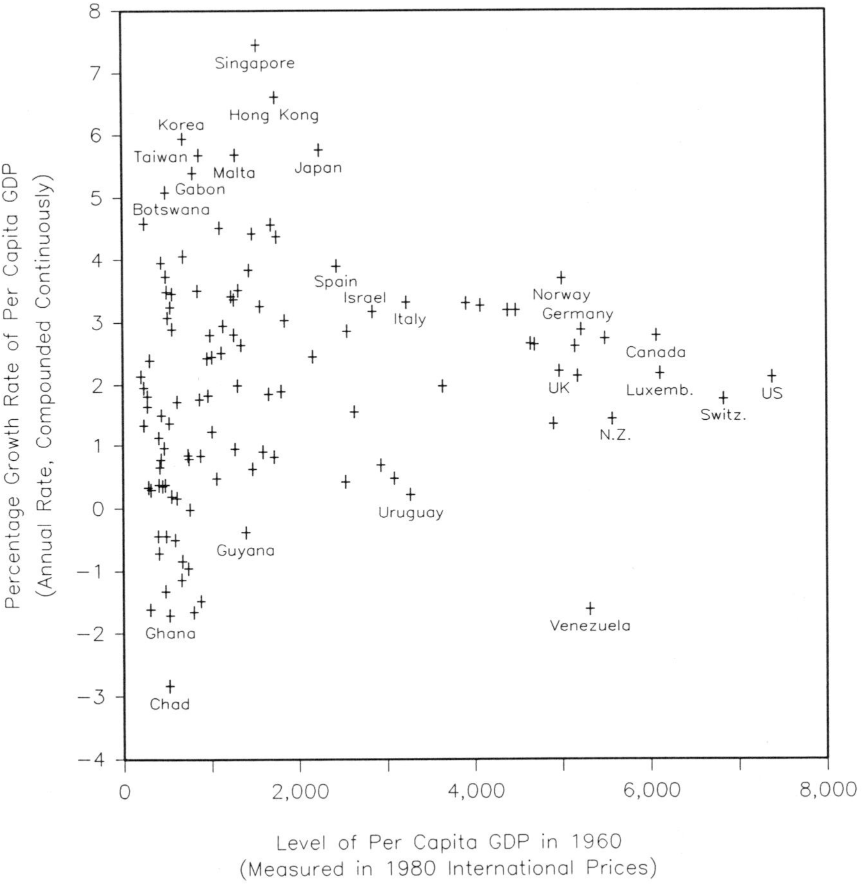

Figure 1.1
Growth rates for 114 countries between 1960 and 1985. Source: Summers and Heston (1988).

rate of taxation (Koester and Kormendi 1989). Kuznets (1988) tries to identify the common features in the successful growth performances of Japan, Taiwan, and South Korea and concludes that all three countries have pursued a policy of encouraging the corporate sector and of removing regulatory restrictions on business activity. Finally, several researchers find a strong relationship between a country's trade policy regime and its dynamic performance. Syrquin and Chenery (1989) report that in a sample of over one hundred countries, those with an outward orientation achieved an average output growth rate of 5.22 percent per annum from 1952 to 1983, and average growth in total factor productivity of 2.2 percent per annum, while those with an inward orientation grew at an average rate of 4.28 percent per annum during the same period and experienced average productivity growth of only 1.6 percent per year. This general finding of a positive association between "openness" and growth rates is corroborated by the more detailed case studies of individual countries reported in, for example, Krueger (1978), Corbo et al. (1985), and Kuznets (1988).

How do the facts that positive growth rates have been sustained for long periods and that growth rates vary systematically from country to country bear upon the theorist's attempt to understand and explain the process of economic growth? Classical writers such as Mill and Marx speculated that standards of living could not rise indefinitely unless advances in technology served to augment the productivity of resources. This proposition received analytical support from the neoclassical growth theorists, who elaborated a model of growth based on capital accumulation. As we shall discuss in chapter 2, if production of output is characterized by diminishing returns to the accumulated factors, the incentive to invest may disappear in the long run in the absence of productivity gains. The fact that investment has continued for more than two hundred years since the industrial revolution suggests that technical change has played a major role in the growth process.

The systematic relationship between output and productivity growth rates and a number of economic variables suggests moreover that technological progress probably is not a purely random process but rather one guided by market forces. Early writers on the sources of technological change saw scientific discoveries as the primary, stimulating force behind innovation. Since scientific advances largely reflect the interests and resources of a community of researchers operating outside the profit sector of the economy, a scientific basis for most industrial innovation would remove technological progress from the realm of economic analysis. But

Schmookler (1966) took exception to this view of the way that technologies evolve in his influential study of almost a thousand inventions in four different industries.

> Despite the popularity of the idea that scientific discoveries and major inventions typically provide the stimulus for inventions, the historical record of important inventions in petroleum refining, paper making, railroading, and farming revealed not a single, unambiguous instance in which either discoveries or inventions played the role hypothesized. Instead, in hundreds of cases, the stimulus was the recognition of a costly problem to be solved or a potentially profitable opportunity to be seized; in short, a technical problem or opportunity evaluated in economic terms. (p. 199)

Schmookler argued in great detail that it is the expected *profitability* of inventive activity, reflecting conditions in the relevant factor and product markets, that determines the pace and direction of industrial innovation. Schumpeter (1942) had expressed a similar view more than twenty years earlier.

> Was not the observed performance [of technological progress] due to that stream of inventions that revolutionized the technique of production rather than to the businessman's hunt for profits? The answer is in the negative. The carrying into effect of those technological novelties was of the essence of that hunt. And even the inventing itself, as will be more fully explained in a moment, was a function of the capitalist process which is responsible for the mental habits that will produce inventions. It is quite wrong ... to say, as so many economists do, that capitalist enterprise was one, and technological progress a second, distinct factor in the observed development of output; they were essentially one and the same thing or, as we may also put it, the former was the propelling force of the latter. (p. 110)

If Schumpeter and Schmookler are correct[2], then it would not be surprising to find productivity growth related to an economy's structure and policies, or to find variation in growth experiences in different parts of the world. It then becomes an important task of any theory of growth to explain the links between industrial innovation and economic growth, on the one hand, and between market conditions and innovation rates, on the other.

2. Mowery and Rosenberg (1989) see a greater role of scientific discovery in the process of technological innovation. Still, they cite many examples to show that "technological exploitation of new scientific understanding often requires considerable time because of the need for additional applied research before the economically useful knowledge can be extracted from a new but abstract formulation" (pp. 25–26). Similarly Dosi (1988) concludes, in his survey of sources and patterns of industrial innovation, that technical change reflects an interplay of technological opportunities created by scientific discoveries and inducements for applied research that emerge from market opportunities.

This is the starting point for our study. We focus on technological progress that results from *intentional* industrial innovation, that is, from the allocation of resources to research and other information-generating activities in response to perceived profit opportunities. Our goal is to understand how country characteristics and policy interventions affect this allocation, and also how global technological competition impinges upon the growth process in interdependent economies.

1.2 The Contribution of Industrial Innovation

It is difficult enough to measure the contribution of technological progress to improvements in standards of living, let alone to isolate the part of technological progress that is due to intentional industrial innovation. The most common method used by economists to decompose output growth into its various "sources" follows an approach developed by Abramovitz (1956) and Solow (1957) and later refined by Denison (1967) and others. "Growth accounting" begins with measurement of factor accumulation and then imputes output expansion to the inputs that have been accumulated by assuming that market factor prices reflect value marginal products. The part of output growth that cannot be attributed to the accumulation of any input—the famous "Solow residual"—is ascribed to technological progress.

Early growth accounting exercises left more than half of growth unaccounted for, and thus implicitly assigned a large role to technological progress (see Solow 1957; Kendrick 1961; Denison 1967). Some more recent efforts have substantially reduced the size of the residual by incorporating estimated changes in the quality of factor inputs (e.g., Jorgenson et al. 1987). Table 1.1, taken from Maddison (1987), gives the results from an especially careful, recent study. The table still shows a sizable contribution of total factor productivity gains to output growth in a number of countries, especially in the early postwar period.

There are several well-known problems that arise in interpreting results from growth-accounting exercises. First, GDP growth may not accurately measure growth in economic output because increases in the *quality* and *variety* of goods and services available to consumers are only imperfectly reflected in the national income accounts. The measurement of the contribution of new and improved varieties to real output growth requires the implementation of sophisticated index number procedures. It is generally believed that reported price indexes often underestimate the economic

Table 1.1
Solow residuals for six countries (annual average compound growth rates)

	1913–50			1950–73			1973–84		
	GDP	TFP	ATFP	GDP	TFP	ATFP	GDP	TFP	ATFP
France	1.06	1.42	0.61	5.13	4.02	3.11	2.18	1.84	0.93
Germany	1.30	0.81	0.19	5.92	4.32	3.61	1.68	1.55	1.13
Japan	2.24	1.10	0.04	9.37	5.79	4.69	3.78	1.21	0.43
Netherlands	2.43	1.25	0.53	4.70	3.35	2.38	1.58	0.81	0.14
United Kingdom	1.29	1.15	0.38	3.02	2.14	1.53	1.06	1.22	0.64
United States	2.78	1.99	1.19	3.72	1.85	1.05	2.32	0.52	−0.27

Source: Tables 11 and 20 from Maddison (1987). TFP (total factor productivity) equals GDP growth minus the imputed contributions of labor accumulation, residential capital accumulation and nonresidential capital accumulation. ATFP (augmented total factor productivity) equals TFP minus the imputed contributions of increases in labor quality and capital quality.

benefits from product innovation (e.g., see Griliches 1973; Bresnahan 1986; Trajtenberg 1990), in which case growth accounting will understate the extent of output growth attributable to advances in technology.

Second, the imputed figure for the contribution of factor accumulation to output growth will accurately measure the extra output that the accumulated factors actually can produce only if factors are paid their value marginal products. If product or factor markets are imperfectly competitive, manufacturing processes are subject to increasing returns to scale, or externalities are generated in factor use, then the Solow residuals will be biased measures of productivity growth (see Hall 1988, Caballero and Lyons 1989).

Third, and perhaps most critical, it may be simply inappropriate to use decomposition methods based on accounting identities to draw inferences about the underlying *causes* of economic growth. What does it mean, for example, that capital accumulation "accounted" for a certain proportion of output growth? Can we infer that investors would have chosen to install more machinery and equipment in the absence of any increases in the productivity of capital? The answer is no. It is certainly possible that managers' desires to further mechanize the production process provided the impetus for capital accumulation. But it is equally possible that the investments were made in response to improved technological conditions, either because extra equipment was needed to produce newly invented goods or because innovative manufacturing techniques made it profitable to install more (or different) machines. In these cases the accumulation of capital cannot be taken as the underlying source of output expansion. Lach and Shankerman (1989) provide evidence that industrial research may be the primitive force behind much of the output growth that accounting methods attribute to factor accumulation. These authors find, in panel data drawn from 191 firms in the U.S. manufacturing sector, that R&D "Granger-causes" capital investment, but capital investment does not Granger-cause R&D.[3]

Let us turn now to the data that bear on the intentional accumulation of knowledge by profit-seeking firms. Commercial research and development represents the main, though by no means the only, method by which business enterprises acquire technical information in modern, industrialized economies. Whereas in 1921 American industry employed only 2,275 scientists and engineers in research activities, the number increased to almost 46,000 in 1946 and 300,000 in 1962, and approached 600,000 by 1985 (Mowery and Rosenberg 1989, pp. 64, 71, 156). In Japan the number of scientific researchers working for private corporations has nearly doubled in ten years, from 157,279 in 1979 to 279,298 in 1988 (Agency of Industrial Science and Technology 1989). Table 1.2 shows that growth in industrial R&D has been widespread throughout the industrialized world. In the OECD nations as a group, real expenditures on R&D by business enterprises grew at a compound annual rate of 6 percent from 1975 to 1985, with the growth rate rising in many countries (and in the group as a whole) during the course of the decade. By 1985 annual spending on industrial research by OECD member countries had reached $155 billion, according to the organization's estimates.

Not only has spending on commercial research been growing in real terms, but its relative importance compared to other economic activities has been steadily increasing as well. Figure 1.2 depicts the trends in the ratio of industrial R&D to value added in industry in eight large and medium-sized economies. Industrial R&D intensities have risen in every one of the countries shown in the figure (and also in a larger sample including eleven additional OECD member countries; see OECD 1986, p. 35, and OECD 1989, p. 76), with dramatic increases having taken place in Japan, Germany, and Sweden. The story is similar when we compare the size of firms' investments in R&D to the magnitude of their spending on physical plant and equipment. The ratio of industrial research to gross fixed capital formation by business enterprises stood, in 1985, at 21 percent in the United States, 15 percent in the United Kingdom and Sweden,

3. Granger causality is a statistical test for temporal precedence. See Sargent (1979) for a textbook treatment.

Table 1.2
National trends in industrial R&D (all fields of science)

	1985		Compound real growth rates (%)			
	Billion $	Percentage of OECD Total	1975–85	1975–79	1979–85	1983–85
United States	78.2	50.4	5.9	4.5	6.7	7.4
Japan	26.8	17.2	9.8	6.6	12.0	12.6
Germany	14.3	9.2	5.6	8.2	3.9	6.5
United Kingdom[a]	9.1	5.8	3.3	5.0	2.1	5.8
France	8.6	5.5	4.6	3.8	5.1	6.7
Italy	4.0	2.6	6.3	2.6	8.9	12.0
Canada	2.7	1.8	9.0	7.6	10.0	9.9
Sweden[a]	2.1	1.3	na	3.9	na	12.3
Netherlands	1.9	1.2	2.7	0.2	4.4	7.5
Switzerland	1.4[b]	1.1	na	0.5	na	na
Belgium	1.2	0.8	5.0	6.0	4.2	4.8
Spain	0.9	0.6	6.1	0.1	10.3	16.9
Total OECD[c]	155.2	100	6	5	7	8.5

Source: Table 60 in OECD (1989).
a. Natural science and engineering only.
b. 1983
c. OECD estimates.

14 percent in France, 13 percent in Japan, and 12 percent in Germany (OECD 1989, p. 76). These figures too have been rising through time.

While industrial R&D now receives a substantial allocation of resources in nearly all industrial countries, the aggregate magnitudes mask large country-to-country variations. Expenditures on R&D by business enterprises in 1985 constituted 3.02 percent of industry value added in Sweden, 2.43 percent in Germany, and 2.26 percent in the United States, but only 0.93 percent in Canada, 0.92 percent in Italy, and 0.41 percent in Australia (OECD 1989, p.76).[4] Compared to the relatively large ratios of industrial R&D to gross fixed capital formation in the United States, the United Kingdom, and Sweden, the ratio was much more modest in Canada, where firms spent only 6.3 percent as much on R&D as on physical capital, and in Australia and Ireland, where the ratios were a mere 3.4 percent and 2.3

4. Countries also differ in the compositions of their industrial research. Business enterprises in the United States and the United Kingdom, for example, devote a significant portion of their research expenditures to defense and (in the case of the United States) space-related projects, whereas those in Japan, Switzerland, and Germany concentrate primarily on civil objectives (OECD 1989, pp. 21, 74–75).

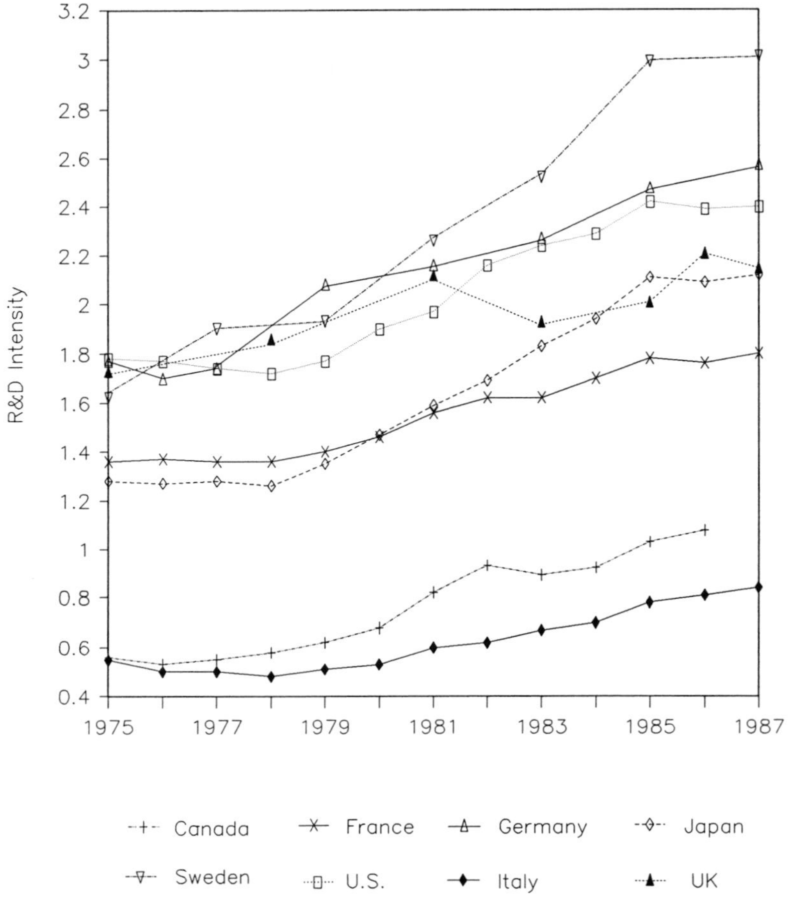

Figure 1.2
Industrial R&D as a percentage of value added in industry. Source: OECD data bank, January 1991.

Table 1.3
Industrial R&D as a percentage of sales in selected industries

	United States (1986)	Japan (1985)	Germany (1983)
Foods and beverage	0.4[a]	0.8	0.7
Textiles and apparel	0.4[a]	1.2	1.1
Chemical products,	5.1	3.8	4.4
drugs and medicines	8.3[b]	7.0	na
Rubber products	2.9	2.9	2.8
Ceramics	1.4[a]	2.6	1.9
Primary metals	1.3[c]	1.9	1.2
General machinery	7.4	2.7	3.3
Electrical machinery	9.1	5.1	7.6
Motor vehicles	3.6[d]	2.9	3.7
Precision instruments	10.5	4.5	4.8

Source: Table B-28 from National Science Foundation (1989); Table 7-4 from Agency of Industrial Science and Technology (1989); and Management and Coordination Agency (1988).
a. 1980.
b. 1985.
c. 1983.
d. 1984.

percent, respectively. It becomes a challenge for theory to explain these differences in research orientation.

Not only are commercial research expenditures spread unevenly across countries, but they also vary greatly across different industries in the world economy. The electrical machinery, electronics, office machinery and equipment, aerospace, and chemical (including pharmaceuticals) industries account for nearly three-quarters of all spending on industrial R&D in the OECD countries (OECD 1989, p. 78). Table 1.3 shows substantial differences in the research intensities of a selected group of industries, as measured by the ratio of R&D outlays by private corporations to sales revenue. Evidently technological opportunities vary greatly from sector to sector. We will want to remember this fact when it comes time to model industrial innovation in a multisector world economy.

Modern industrial firms acquire technical information in a variety of ways besides the formal research that they conduct in a laboratory setting. Many of the activities that firms undertake to generate productivity gains are not classified as R&D. For example, production engineers often improve operating efficiency by using trial-and-error methods to change the organization of the production line. The "just-in-time" inventory system represents one such (very important) technical improvement that was implemented on the factory floor (see Abegglen and Stalk 1985, ch. 5). The productivity gains often associated with learning by doing typically are achieved in a similar manner. Another example of a firm activity aimed at generating technological progress is the Quality Control Circle in Japanese corporations where workers meet to study production problems and suggest means of improving productivity. The scale of the information-gathering efforts that companies mount outside their research labs surely responds to market conditions, and so the productivity gains that are achieved in this way constitute "intentional industrial innovation."

It might seem that industrial innovation has little relevance to the growth processes in the less developed economies. The LDCs perform virtually no commercial R&D and make few significant discoveries that are original to the world economy. Yet the process of industrialization in these countries does involve substantial technical change, in the sense that producers gain mastery over products and processes that are new to the local economy. Pack and Westphal (1986) argue this point forcefully, noting that "the minor role of invention in industrialization simply means that much technological change consists of assimilating and adapting foreign technology." (p.105)

Case study research reveals the extent of indigenous effort required for technical change in the industrializing economies. Pack and Westphal (1986) summarize the findings of this research as follows:

> Important elements of the technology appropriate to particular circumstances can only be acquired through effort to apply existing knowledge to those circumstances. Effort is required in using technological information and accumulating technological knowledge to evaluate and choose technology; to acquire and operate processes and produce products; to manage changes in products, processes, procedures, and organizational arrangements; and to create new technology. This effort takes the form of investments in technological capability, which is the ability to make effective use of technological knowledge. (p. 105)

In other words, the process of assimilating existing technologies in the less developed countries is not unlike that of creating entirely new technologies in the developed world. In each case, learning requires an allocation of resources and investments respond to market incentives. Nor can we say a priori that the relative magnitudes of the learning efforts (compared to, say, the size of the industrial base) differ greatly in the two contexts. Understanding intentional industrial innovation may be every bit as important to a theory of economic development as it is to a theory of growth in the industrialized economies.

What then has been the contribution of industrial innovation to aggregate output growth? Few if any studies provide a reliable answer to this question for any country.[5] Typically, the issue has been approached with growth-accounting methods augmented to include a "stock of knowledge" (i.e., the cumulation of R&D investments less estimated depreciation). Knowledge is treated as an ordinary, accumulated input, along with tangible factors, such as capital and labor. Of course one cannot directly observe the reward paid to the knowledge stock as most of the returns are hidden in data on corporate profits. So an independent estimate of the rate of return to R&D must be found in order to impute output expansion to the accumulation of knowledge.[6] The rate of return on R&D has been estimated econometrically using cross-sectional data on firms or industries, by invoking the assumption that units in the sample (firms or industries, as the case may be) share a common rate of return. Only the "direct returns" to R&D (i.e., the returns that accrue to the firm or industry that conducts the R&D) are captured by these methods. While results from these studies vary, most investigators find private rates of return in excess of thirty percent (e.g., see Griliches 1973; Mansfield et al. 1977; Scherer 1982). Based on a return of 30 percent, Griliches (1973) estimates that R&D contributed perhaps 0.3 percent to measured productivity growth in 1966 and 0.2 percent in 1970. Using a similar 30 percent rate of return in its calculations, the U.S. Department of Labor (1989) found annual contributions of R&D to factor productivity growth in the nonfarm business sector ranging from 0.16 percent to 0.19 percent in the years between 1960 and 1987. They estimate that R&D contributed 0.49 percent per year to productivity growth in the manufacturing sector over the period from 1948 to 1987.

However, there are good reasons for being skeptical of these figures. Some have to do with the general problems that arise in interpreting the results from growth accounting exercises, as already discussed. Others reflect aspects of R&D investments that are unusual in degree, if not in kind, compared to other forms of accumulation. For example, we noted

5. Griliches (1979) reviews the approaches that have been used to measure the contribution of R&D to economic growth, and discusses the methodological and data problems associated with each one.

6. Problems also arise in estimating the lag between research outlays and impacts on productivity, in computing a proper price deflator for R&D expenditures, and in selecting a rate of depreciation for the knowledge base. These issues and the biases they introduce into growth accounting measures are discussed in U.S. Department of Labor (1989).

above that growth accounting relies on the assumption that product markets are perfectly competitive in order to equate market factor prices with value marginal products. In situations where much private R&D is being performed, product markets are quite unlikely to be competitive, since the returns to private R&D often come in the form of monopoly rents. Also most growth-accounting procedures assume that the technology for producing final output exhibits constant returns to scale. Yet this seems an untenable assumption about an aggregate production function that includes the knowledge stock as one of its arguments.[7]

A related point concerns the measurement of the rate of return to R&D. As we have noted above, most econometric studies seek to identify only the private return to research, or the productivity gains that accrue to the investing firm and others operating in the same industry. For reasons that we shall discuss in the next section, the social return to many forms of research may exceed the private return by a substantial margin. That is, research activities often generate sizable spillover benefits. These external benefits may not be concentrated in a single industry but rather may spread to many sectors in the economy. Mansfield et al. (1977) and Scherer (1982) report social returns to R&D that are more than double their estimates of the private returns, while Scherer (1982) and Bernstein and Nadiri (1988, 1989) provide evidence that technological spillovers extend across industry boundaries. Kendrick (1981) applies a substantially higher measure of the rate of return to R&D than the 30 percent figure used by Griliches (1973) and the U.S. Department of Labor (1989) in his growth accounting, and concludes that R&D contributed as much as 0.85 percent to annual productivity growth in the U.S. business sector during 1948–66, 0.75 percent during 1966–73, and 0.6 percent during 1973–78.

But even with a comprehensive measure of the return to R&D, the accounting method of attributing growth to various causes, including research, still would be subject to the (perhaps fatal) criticism that it cannot identify the primitive sources of output growth. In our view, the existing literature fails to provide an answer to the counterfactual question: What would the growth rate of output have been in the absence of any investments by firms in the creation of knowledge?

7. Romer (1990) suggests the following thought experiment. Suppose that all tangible inputs are doubled, holding constant the state of knowledge. Then, by a replication argument, it ought to be possible to produce double the output. Now if knowledge capital is doubled as well, output should increase still further. This argument relies on the public good attributes of knowledge, which we explain in the next section.

1.3 Technology as an Economic Commodity[8]

When firms invest in industrial R&D, the output that they produce is technology. Technology, a form of knowledge, has some peculiar properties as an economic commodity that bear on its role in the growth process. First, technology is a *nonrival* good. That is, when one agent uses technology to produce a good or a service, this action does not preclude others from also doing so, even simultaneously. This distinguishes technology from, say, a piece of capital equipment, which can only be used in one place at a time. Second, technology in many cases is a partially *nonexcludable* good. That is, the creators or owners of technical information often have difficulty in preventing others from making unauthorized use of it, at least in some applications. Again, this attribute of technology distinguishes it from capital equipment, which is readily excludable.

The excludability of a good reflects both legal and technological considerations. The legal authority of a country allocates property rights, which limit the freedom of agents to use certain goods without compensating the designated owners. Just as property rights are assigned to the owners of tangible goods, so intellectual property rights are assigned to the creators of new ideas, in order to allow them to appropriate (some of) the benefits from their inventive efforts. Countries differ in the breadth of the protection that they provide for intellectual property. Some grant exclusive rights to the originator of an idea for a long period of time, and in all potential uses, while others restrict both the duration and the scope of protection. Countries also differ in the resources they devote to enforcing intellectual property laws. Thus the degree of excludability of technology is partly a matter of policy choice. Technological considerations also come into play because it is easier for the owners of some types of property to prevent unauthorized uses than others. Moreover it is easier for the enforcement authorities to detect certain kinds of infringements than others. The theft of most physical commodities is comparatively easy to prevent, and when violations are alleged, it is relatively straightforward to establish culpability. Intangibles such as ideas are much harder to secure, and it is often more difficult for the state to ascertain whether an accused party actually has made illegal use of another's property. As Arrow (1962a) has put it:

8. Romer (1990) contains an excellent discussion of many of the issues that are touched upon in this section. Arrow (1962a) is the seminal contribution.

With suitable legal measures, information may become an appropriable commodity. Then the monopoly power can indeed be exerted. However, no amount of legal protection can make a thoroughly appropriable commodity of something so intangible as information. The very use of the information in any productive way is bound to reveal it, at least in part. (p. 615)

The partial nonexcludability of knowledge suggests that industrial R&D may generate "technological spillovers." By technological spillovers, we mean that (1) firms can acquire information created by others without paying for that information in a market transaction, and (2) the creators (or current owners) of the information have no effective recourse, under prevailing laws, if other firms utilize information so acquired. Many mechanisms exist for the propagation of technological spillovers. As the quote from Arrow suggests, some information may be conveyed simply by inspection of a product that has been produced with a new technology, or by observation of the actions that the creators take to exploit their knowledge. Other information may be publicly disclosed by inventors, either because they know it to be of a sort that is not covered by patent or other intellectual property protection, or because they believe that the applicable property rights could never be enforced. For example, researchers at Bell Laboratories published many of their findings in scholarly journals, presumably for one of these reasons. The mobility of highly skilled personnel between firms represents another vehicle for the spread of technical information among innovating firms.

It may be useful to distinguish two types of outputs that are (jointly) produced in the industrial research laboratory. Commercial research generates both *specific* technical information, which allows a firm to manufacture a particular product or to engage in a particular production process, and more *general* information with wider applicability.[9] Firms may be able to keep secret the detailed information concerning product attributes and production techniques. And even if they cannot, the applicable patent laws often can be relied upon to prevent others from copying specific product

9. Schmookler (1966) proposed exactly this distinction, claiming that "new technological knowledge can be subdivided into two broad categories: (a) knowledge, commonly denoted by the terms 'engineering' and 'applied science,' about whole classes of technical phenomena, and (b) knowledge about particular products and processes." (p. 196) He goes on to argue that "the distinction between an industry's production technology and its product technology is critical. The former relates to the knowledge used to produce its products—the machines, materials, and processes it uses to fabricate the goods it sells. The product technology relates to the knowledge used in creating or improving the products themselves." (p. 196)

designs or unique processes. So product specific information may be an excludable commodity in many cases. General information is much less likely to be so, both because it is harder to prevent the spread of universal principles and because it is more difficult to invoke the existing legal strictures to enforce proprietorship over such information.

Technological spillovers may be very important to the growth process. The general information that researchers generate and cannot prevent from entering the public domain often facilitates further innovation. Arrow (1962a) emphasized this point:

> Information is not only the product of inventive activity, it is also an input—in some sense, the major input apart from the talent of the inventor. The school of thought that emphasizes the determination of invention by social climate as demonstrated by the simultaneity of inventions in effect emphasizes strongly the productive role of previous information in the creation of new information... To appropriate information for use as a basis for further research is much more difficult than to appropriate it for use in producing commodities. (p. 618)

Thus innovation conceivably can be a self-perpetuating process. Resources and knowledge may be combined to produce new knowledge, some of which then spills over to the research community, and thereby facilitates the creation of still more knowledge. Of course it remains to be considered whether the private incentives are sufficient to sustain such a process.

There are reasons to believe that the process of industrial innovation may in fact be self-sustaining. The argument has two threads. First, the accumulation of an intangible such as knowledge is not subject to any physical bounds. Moreover there is nothing in the historical evidence to suggest that humans are exhausting the potential for advancing knowledge. One could never prove or disprove the claim that resources invested in R&D will continue to yield positive and nondiminishing contributions to the stock of knowledge into the indefinite future. But it seems at least possible that this will be the case, given the nature of the process of invention. Schumpeter (1942), for example, contrasted invention with the cultivation of new plots of land. He noted that the latter process must run into diminishing returns if the more productive plots are cultivated first, but that

> we cannot reason in this fashion about the future possibilities of technological advance. From the fact that some of them have been exploited before others, it cannot be inferred that the former were more productive than the latter. And those that are still in the lap of the gods may be more or less productive than any that have thus far come within the range of observation. (p. 118)

But even if man's potential for furthering technical understanding does not diminish over time, the process of industrial innovation may grind to a halt if the economic rate of return to invention falls too low. However, the economic properties of technology—in particular, the fact that it is non-rival and partially nonexcludable—suggest that this need not occur. Non-rivalry means that an aggregate production function relating the quantity of final output to the knowledge stock plus an exhaustive list of rival inputs, including capital, labor, natural resources, and so forth, ought to exhibit increasing returns to scale (see Romer 1990).[10] This property of the aggregate production function means that the marginal product of knowledge in generating output need not decline as more knowledge is accumulated. The partial nonexcludability of knowledge suggests a mechanism whereby investment incentives can be preserved. The technological spill-overs that result from commercial research may add to a pool of public knowledge, thereby lowering the cost to later generations of achieving a technological breakthrough of some given magnitude. Such cost reductions can offset any tendency for the private returns to invention to fall as a result of increases in the number of competing technologies.

1.4 Method and Organization of the Book

This book casts industrial innovation as the engine of long-run growth. We study the evolution of technology that results from investments made by forward-looking, profit-seeking agents. The first part of the book concentrates on a closed economy in order to develop an understanding of the relationship between market conditions and dynamic outcomes. The remainder considers growth in the context of an integrated world economy, reflecting our belief that the global nature of modern-day technological competition implies substantial interdependence in the growth processes of different nations.

We adopt a general-equilibrium approach to modeling industrial innovation. This framework imposes a desirable degree of discipline on the analysis, inasmuch as it forces us to account for the resources that are needed to generate growth. We assume throughout that agents have rational expectations (or, in situations where there is no uncertainty, perfect foresight). While we do not necessarily believe this to be a realistic assumption, it

10. This assertion is based on the argument that by replicating production processes, a doubling of output can be achieved by a doubling of only the *rival* inputs. See footnote 7 above.

seems preferable to alternatives that impose systematically biased beliefs. The latter specification may be fine for some descriptive purposes but can generate very misleading prescriptions for public policy.

The next chapter describes the treatment of technology in neoclassical growth theory. We begin with the Solow model with exogenous technological progress and proceed to extensions that allow technical change to be generated endogenously. In these extensions innovation is either the unintentional consequence of economic activities or the intentional result of research that takes place outside the profit sector. Much of the analysis in chapter 2 focuses on the conditions needed for sustained economic growth in the long run.

In chapters 3 and 4 we introduce alternative models of intentional industrial innovation. Chapter 3 deals with innovation that serves to expand the range of goods available on the market. Firms devote resources to R&D in order to invent new goods that substitute imperfectly for existing brands. Producers of unique products earn monopoly rents, which serve as the reward for their prior R&D investments. The model in chapter 4, which complements that in chapter 3, focuses on innovation that raises the qualities of a fixed set of goods. Again, commercial research is driven by profit opportunities, as producers of state-of-the-art products earn positive profits in their competition with manufacturers of lesser quality goods. In both chapters 3 and 4 the innovative products may be either consumer goods or intermediate products. If the latter, then innovation contributes to total factor productivity in the sector that manufactures final goods, and growth takes the standard form of an increase in the quantity of (final) output.

The initial presentations of the two models of endogenous innovation assume only a single primary factor of production. Chapter 5 extends these models to incorporate factor accumulation. In the first part of the chapter, we consider the accumulation of physical capital (i.e., plant and equipment). This provides a synthesis of the traditional growth theory and our approach based on knowledge accumulation. We find that growth is driven in the long run by the forces of innovation, which preserve the incentives for capital investment by raising the productivity of buildings and machines. The second part of the chapter deals with human capital. We allow individuals with finite lifetimes to choose between attending school to acquire skills and working immediately at unskilled jobs. The equilibrium determines an endogenous supply of human capital and a residual supply of unskilled workers. The chapter concludes with an investigation of how changes in the steady-state stocks of unskilled labor and human capital affect the long-run rates of innovation and growth.

The remainder of the book places the innovation process in an international context. In chapter 6 we begin the analysis of economic interdependence with the case of a small open economy. The small economy generates technologies for new or improved intermediate goods (or producer services), which it uses to manufacture two final traded products. We study the effects of commodity and asset trade on innovation and growth, and analyze the positive and normative implications of trade and technology policies.

Chapters 7 and 8 concentrate on the implications of international technological competition for long-run patterns of specialization and trade. In the models presented in each of these chapters, innovation in a country contributes to (endogenous) comparative advantage in a high-technology sector. The models feature intraindustry trade in high technology, and interindustry exchange of innovative goods for a more traditional manufactured product. We ask, What are the characteristics of a country that contribute to the development of a long-run comparative advantage in high technology? In chapter 7, where spillovers of technical knowledge are assumed to be international in reach, the answer is traditional: A country creates comparative advantage in high technology if it has a relative abundance of human capital that can be used in (skill-intensive) R&D activities. But if technological spillovers are geographically concentrated, as in chapter 8, then a country's size and prior research experience also have a role to play in determining its trade pattern. This chapter also shows how temporary policies can permanently alter the course of economic history.

The succeeding two chapters study the implications of international technological competition for realized rates of innovation and growth in an integrated world economy. Chapter 9 identifies a number of mechanisms by which international economic integration may affect a country's growth rate. We compare growth rates in autarky and free trade in models that are constructed to highlight some particular channel of international transmission. The chapter also touches upon the issue of gains from trade in dynamic economies. In chapter 10 our starting point is one of free trade, and we investigate the growth effects of various government policies. The analysis treats trade policies, technology policies, and industrial policies (i.e., targeted production subsidies) and emphasizes how policies in one country may influence the growth process in its trade partner.

Interdependencies between the learning processes in the industrialized North and the developing South are the subject of chapters 11 and 12. We assume that most learning in the South takes the form of imitation of technologies previously developed in the North, rather than of invention of entirely new products or processes. Imitation gives rise to product-cycle trade, as goods initially are invented and produced in the North, and then copied and exported by the South. The main issues that these chapters address concern the feedbacks between the two processes of industrial learning: Does faster imitation by the South (reflecting, perhaps, a lessened degree of protection of foreign intellectual property rights) impede innovation in the North, and does more rapid technological advance in the North spill over to the rate of growth in the South? The two chapters attempt to answer these questions in the context of our alternative models of endogenous innovation.

The concluding chapter attempts to draw together some of the broader lessons that emerge from the analysis.

2 Traditional Growth Theory

This chapter reviews traditional approaches to the theory of economic growth. The review is a selective one, focusing narrowly on two issues. First, we investigate the conditions under which the models predict sustained growth in per capita income. Second, we highlight the theory's treatment of the creation of knowledge and technological progress. The review is intended to place in context the novel approach that we adopt in this book.

At least since Harrod (1939) and Domar (1946), economists have looked to capital formation for their explanation of rising standards of living. It was Solow (1956) of course who formalized the idea that capital deepening could cause labor productivity to rise in a dynamic process of investment and growth. While many growth theorists have been less than clear on what they include in their concept of "capital," the formal treatments suggest a fairly narrow interpretation. The typical specification invokes a competitive manufacturing sector that employs the services of capital in a constant-returns-to-scale production technology. It also makes the technology for producing capital similar (and often identical) to that which applies to the production of consumer goods. These assumptions seem quite appropriate when "capital" refers to machinery and equipment. But intangibles such as human capital and knowledge capital have peculiar economic properties that may not be well represented by the standard formulations.

While the traditional approach casts capital formation as the major force behind economic growth, the supporting role played by knowledge accumulation certainly has not been overlooked. The accumulation of knowledge serves two distinct functions in the writings of Solow and many of his successors. First, technological progress may help to explain the ubiquitous "Solow residual" (see Solow 1957), the portion of measured growth in national product that cannot be attributed to the accumulation of inputs. Second, technological progress enables capital formation to continue even when the ratio of capital to primary resources begins to grow large.

Many of the early models treated technological progress as an exogenous process driven only by time. This would seem an appropriate assumption if advances in technical knowledge stemmed largely from activities that take place outside of the economic sector. The view that innovation is driven by basic research, which is implicit in the models with exogenous technology, was made explicit in a paper by Shell (1967). Shell introduced a public research sector that contributes technical knowledge to the profit-seeking entities in the Solow economy. This sector draws resources from the rest of the economy and is financed by taxes collected by the government. Still, the size of the sector is largely exogenous, reflecting the government's willingness to impose taxes to provide the funding for research.

Arrow (1962b) was the first to view technological progress as an outgrowth of activities in the economic realm. But whereas Shell treated knowledge creation as an intentional activity, Arrow modeled learning as an accidental occurrence. He made knowledge a by-product of capital formation, with benefits that spread throughout the economy. Romer (1986), who discussed the possibility that learning-by-doing might be a source of sustained growth, maintained this treatment of technological progress as wholly the outgrowth of an external economy. The assumption is convenient, as Arrow noted, because it makes investment in knowledge a possible outcome in a perfectly competitive market environment.

Our review outlines these various approaches to the creation of knowledge and the sources of growth. In section 2.1 we examine the Solow model, where savings are proportional to income, and labor productivity grows at an exogenous rate. Section 2.2 presents an extension of Solow that severs the fixed link between savings and income and makes savings behavior reflect intertemporal optimization on the part of households. While the extended formulation shares many of the properties of the original, the optimizing model seems better suited for tackling issues of efficiency and welfare, issues that will be of concern to us in the chapters to come. The final two sections develop models that reflect the insights of Arrow (1962b) and Romer (1986), and Shell (1967), respectively. Here we can see how economic incentives can affect the long-run rates of innovation and growth in situations where technological progress reflects the equilibrium allocation of an economy's resources.

2.1 Solow

We consider an economy that combines capital and labor to produce a single homogeneous commodity Z. This commodity can be consumed by households or installed by firms as fixed equipment. At every moment the technology for producing Z exhibits constant returns to scale. Over time the productivity of labor grows exogenously so that $1/A(t)$ units of labor are required at time t to complete the tasks that one unit performed at time 0. Then the quantity of output is related to the inputs by

$$Z(t) = F[K(t), A(t)L], \tag{2.1}$$

where $K(t)$ represents the economy's capital stock, L represents its fixed labor force, and where $F(\cdot)$ is concave and linearly homogeneous, and $A(t)$ increases monotonically through time. Using the properties of $F(\cdot)$, we can express the technology in "intensive form":

$$z = f(k) \equiv F(k, 1), \qquad \text{with } f'(k) > 0 \text{ and } f''(k) \leq 0, \tag{2.2}$$

where $z \equiv Z/AL$ denotes output per *effective* unit of labor and $k \equiv K/AL$ is capital per effective worker.[1] We also adopt the simplifying assumption that labor productivity grows at the constant rate g_A, so that

$$A(t) = e^{g_A t}. \tag{2.3}$$

Suppose now that each household saves a constant fraction s of its total income. Then aggregate savings at a point in time equals sZ. Savings are used to finance investment, which contributes to the economy's stock of capital. In the absence of depreciation (which we neglect for simplicity), capital formation matches aggregate savings, which with (2.1) and (2.2) implies that

$$\dot{K} = sALf(k). \tag{2.4}$$

Then (2.3) and (2.4) can be combined to yield

$$\dot{k} = sf(k) - g_A k, \tag{2.5}$$

a version of Solow's famous equation that guides the evolution of capital per effective worker.

Figure 2.1 depicts the movements in k. When $sf(k)$ exceeds $g_A k$, the capital-to-effective-labor ratio is rising. When the reverse is true, k is falling. The figure reflects two further assumptions. First, we have depicted

1. We henceforth omit the time arguments except where needed for clarity.

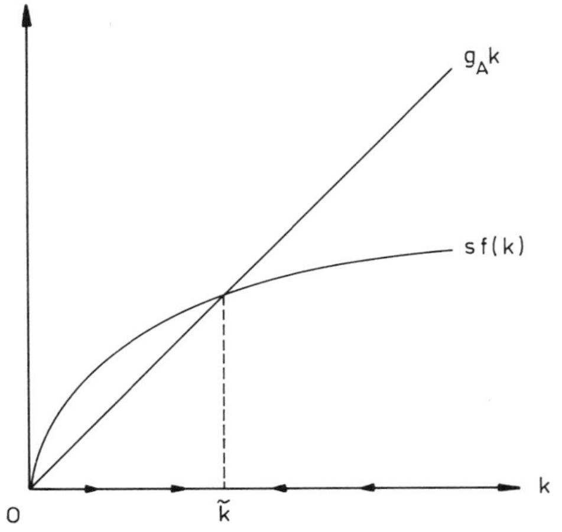

Figure 2.1

the curve $sf(k)$ as being steeper than the line g_Ak at points close to the origin. This requires an assumption that the marginal product of capital exceeds g_A/s when the capital-to-labor ratio is small. Second, we have shown the curve to be flatter than the line for sufficiently high values of k. This requires the marginal product of capital to fall below g_A/s when the capital-to-labor ratio grows large. When these restrictions are satisfied, as they surely will be if the economy obeys the "Inada conditions," the line and the curve must intersect somewhere in the positive orthant.[2] Capital per effective worker rises when k initially is less than $\tilde{k}$, and it falls when k initially exceeds $\tilde{k}$. The economy approaches a steady state at $\tilde{k}$, where the capital-to-effective-labor ratio is constant.

Along the equilibrium trajectory described by figure 2.1, the economy's growth rate approaches a constant. Since capital per effective worker tends to a constant, the capital stock must grow in the long run at the same rate as labor productivity. Then output too must grow at this rate (see [2.1]). The long-run rate of growth in per capita income is given by g_A, an exogenous constant reflecting the pace of technological progress. In this setting neither changes in household behavior nor the introduction of government policy can have any effect on the long-run growth rate. An increase in the savings rate, to take one example, causes capital to accumulate more rapidly for a while, until a new steady state is reached with greater capital per effective worker and a higher *level* of per capita income.

2. Inada (1964) proposed the technological restrictions that $f'(k) \to \infty$ as $k \to 0$ and $f'(k) \to 0$ as $k \to \infty$. These conditions are sufficient but not necessary for the existence of a steady state.

In the process the *rate* of accumulation settles down, once again, to the one that is dictated by the exogenous productivity growth.

In the absence of technological progress, growth cannot be sustained in the Solow economy when the Inada conditions are satisfied.[3] With diminishing returns to capital each new unit of capital generates less output than the one before it. A constant fraction of the income generated by the marginal unit of capital is saved. So less savings result from the marginal unit of capital than from the inframarginal units. Then the next addition to investment is smaller than the last, which generates still less additional output, and so on. In the limit, if the marginal product of capital approaches zero as the capital-to-labor ratio grows large, the rate of growth of output must approach zero as well.[4]

But, as Solow himself recognized (1956, pp. 64–66), sustained growth in per capita income will be possible, even without productivity growth, if the marginal product of capital is bounded from below by a positive number.[5] When $f'(k)$ tends to the constant $b > 0$ as k tends to infinity, the average product of capital tends also to the constant b. Then long-run returns to capital are not diminishing but rather are *constant*. In this case (2.5) implies proportional growth in capital per effective worker at the rate $\dot{k}/k = sb$ when $g_A = 0$. This gives as well the long-run rate of growth in the capital stock, since effective labor is constant in the absence of population growth and productivity growth. Output and income per capita grow also at this rate.[6] With constant returns to capital, increases in the savings rate do improve long-run growth performance.

---

3. Solow considered an economy with population growing at the exogenous rate g_L. For this economy, growth in per capita income ceases in the long run if technological progress is absent and the marginal product of capital eventually falls below g_L/s. Our result is a special case for $g_L = 0$. Similarly, if capital depreciates at the constant rate d, then if $g_A = g_L = 0$, the long-run growth rate is zero if $f'(k) < d/s$ for k large.

4. By differentiating the production function (2.1), we find that

$$\frac{\dot{Z}}{Z} = \frac{f'(k)k}{f(k)} \frac{\dot{K}}{K}$$

when $g_A = 0$. Substitution of the accumulation equation (2.3) into this expression gives $\dot{Z}/Z = sf'(k)$, which approaches zero along with $f'(k)$.

5. In the economy with positive population growth, sustained growth in the absence of technological progress requires that the marginal product of capital be bounded from below by a number that exceeds g_L/s, as k grows large.

6. A number of recent papers expand upon the idea that long-run growth in per capita income can be sustained if the returns to capital approach a constant when the capital-to-labor ratio grows large. See Rebelo (1991), King and Rebelo (1990), and Jones and Manuelli (1990). Note that constant long-run returns to capital obtain, for example, when the

2.2 Optimal Saving

We turn to an extension of the Solow model that incorporates endogenous determination of the savings rate. Whereas Solow imposed an exogenous link between savings and income, we will assume now that households allocate spending over time so as to maximize an intertemporal utility function. In all other respects (e.g., on the production side) we maintain the same specification as before.

The extended model will prove useful for examining the efficiency of the market allocation. Efficiency cannot be evaluated in the Solow framework because the model contains no metric for measuring consumer welfare. Even if a utility function were introduced into that framework, any finding of inefficiency in the market allocation would be at least partly attributable to the consumers' ad hoc savings behavior.

We suppose that consumers share identical preferences and that they maximize utility over an infinite horizon. As is well known, this representation of preferences applies when households can be viewed as infinitely lived dynasties and when each generation takes into account the well-being of its progeny (see Barro 1974). The utility that the representative household derives from an infinite stream of consumption beginning at time t takes the simple form

$$U_t = \int_t^{\infty} e^{-\rho(\tau - t)} \log C(\tau)\, d\tau, \tag{2.6}$$

where ρ represents the subjective discount rate and $C(\tau)$ is consumption at time τ. We have specified a logarithmic utility function, in place of a more general form, because we shall often find it convenient to impose this functional form in the chapters to come.[7]

Households can borrow or lend freely at the instantaneous interest rate $r(\tau)$. A household that is endowed with one unit of labor maximizes the utility indicator in (2.6) subject to an intertemporal budget constraint of the

---

production function $F(\cdot)$ has a constant elasticity of substitution between capital and labor that exceeds one; see Solow (1956, pp. 77–78).

7. For many of our applications, we could use the more general form,

$$U_t = \int_t^{\infty} e^{-\rho(\tau - t)} \frac{C(\tau)^{1-\sigma_c} - 1}{1 - \sigma_c}\, d\tau, \qquad \sigma_c > 0.$$

This alternative specification allows for a broad range of intertemporal elasticities of substitution (the logarithmic utility function being a special case with an elasticity $\sigma_c = 1$). However, the extra degree of generality adds little to our understanding, so we will sacrifice the generality in favor of simplicity.

form

$$\int_t^{\infty} e^{-[R(\tau)-R(t)]} p_Z(\tau) C(\tau)\, d\tau \leq \int_t^{\infty} e^{-[R(\tau)-R(t)]} w_L(\tau)\, d\tau + W(t), \tag{2.7}$$

where $R(\tau) \equiv \int_0^{\tau} r(s)\, ds$ represents the discount factor from time τ to time 0, p_Z denotes the price of the homogeneous good Z, w_L is the wage rate, and W is the value of the household's asset holdings. The constraint requires that the present value of spending not exceed the present value of labor income plus the value of initial wealth. In the aggregate the economy has labor income $w_L L$, and total assets worth $v_K K$, where v_K is the value of a unit of capital.[8]

The intertemporal optimization problem is readily solved. The first-order condition for maximizing U_t can be written as

$$\frac{e^{-\rho(\tau-t)}}{C(\tau)} = \zeta(t) e^{-[R(\tau)-R(t)]} p_Z(\tau) \qquad \text{for all } \tau \geq t, \tag{2.8}$$

where $\zeta(t)$ denotes the Lagrange multiplier on the budget constraint. This condition equates the marginal utility of consumption at time τ, as perceived from time t, with the product of the marginal utility of wealth and the discounted value of the cost of a unit of the consumer good at time τ. The condition implies that the value of spending, $E(\tau) = p_Z(\tau)C(\tau)$, must grow at an instantaneous rate equal to the difference between the interest rate and the subjective discount rate:

$$\frac{\dot{E}}{E} = \frac{\dot{C}}{C} + \frac{\dot{p}_Z}{p_Z} = r - \rho. \tag{2.9}$$

Note that (2.9) applies not only to the individual household but also to the aggregate economy, when E is taken to represent aggregate expenditure.

The economy lacks a monetary instrument. Therefore nothing pins down the price level at any time. We are free to set the time path for one nominal variable and to measure prices at every moment against the chosen numeraire. Of course the choice of numeraire has no effect on the evolution of *real* magnitudes such as the volume of output or relative prices. It proves convenient, if a bit unconventional, to normalize prices at every moment so that *nominal* spending remains constant. Accordingly we set

8. Note that consumption loans between households "net out" in the calculation of aggregate wealth. Only loans to firms that finance their acquisition of capital add to the aggregate wealth of the economy.

$$E(t) = 1 \qquad \text{for all } t, \tag{2.10}$$

which with (2.9) implies that

$$r(t) = \rho \qquad \text{for all } t; \tag{2.11}$$

that is, the *nominal* interest rate always equals the subjective discount rate.

On the production side, competition among manufacturers ensures that the rental rate for capital w_K matches the value marginal product of a machine $p_Z f'(k)$. Therefore the owner of a piece of capital equipment earns an infinite stream of "dividends" $w_K = p_Z f'(k)$. Besides these dividends a claim to a unit of capital yields an instantaneous capital gain (or loss) of $\dot{v}_K$. Households will be willing to hold the claims to the existing units of capital only if their total return matches the return to a perfectly substitutable asset, namely, a consumption loan of size v_K. Thus asset market equilibrium requires that the following "no-arbitrage" condition be satisfied:

$$p_Z f'(k) + \dot{v}_K = \rho v_K. \tag{2.12}$$

If there are no "bubbles" in asset prices, equation (2.12) implies that the value of a unit of capital at time t equals the present discounted value of the stream of rental income it yields subsequent to t, or

$$v_K(t) = \int_t^\infty e^{-\rho(\tau - t)} p_Z(\tau) f'[k(\tau)]\, d\tau, \tag{2.13}$$

where use has been made of (2.11) in the discounting. We will soon see that asset-price bubbles cannot arise in the dynamic equilibrium so that (2.13) indeed describes the market value of a unit of capital.

The claim to a unit of capital can be acquired in one of two ways. First, a household or firm can purchase such a claim in the asset market at a price of v_K. But here, as in the Solow economy, a new unit of capital can be produced by firms in the same manner as a unit of the consumer good. Thus it is possible for a household or firm to acquire capital equipment at a per unit cost p_Z. In a competitive economy, if $p_Z < v_K$, there would be unbounded demand for good Z for investment purposes. Such a situation cannot arise in a competitive equilibrium. On the other hand, if $p_Z > v_K$, all agents would prefer to acquire existing equipment rather than to install new units. It follows that, in equilibrium,

$$v_K \leq p_Z, \qquad \text{with equality whenever } \dot{K} > 0. \tag{2.14}$$

The market for the homogeneous good must clear at every moment in time. Aggregate consumption demand equals $C = 1/p_Z$, in the light of

(2.10) and the definition of E. Investment demand matches the additions to the capital stock in the absence of depreciation of the existing capital. Finally, (2.1) and (2.2) give total output. The market clears if and only if

$$\dot{K} = ALf(k) - \frac{1}{p_Z}. \tag{2.15}$$

Two more equations are needed to complete the system. First, the competitive wage rate must equal the value of the marginal product of labor:

$$w_L = p_Z A[f(k) - f'(k)k]. \tag{2.16}$$

Second, the budget constraint (2.7) must be satisfied with equality, as an additional requirement for the optimality of the consumer's spending program. This implies that

$$\frac{1}{\rho} = \int_t^\infty e^{-\rho(\tau-t)} w_L(\tau)\, L d\tau + v_K(t)K(t), \tag{2.17}$$

once (2.11) has been taken into account. Now equations (2.12) and (2.14)–(2.16) describe the equilibrium evolution of v_K, w_L, p_Z, and K, given the initial size of the capital stock $K_0(t)$. Equation (2.17) dictates what the initial value of capital must be if households embarking upon the path described by (2.12) and (2.14)–(2.16) are to obey their intertemporal budget constraints with equality.

Let us suppose, for the moment, that there is no technological progress; that is, $g_A = 0$. In this case $A(\tau)$ is a constant, and we can choose units for labor to make $AL = 1$. Then, combining the equation that expresses equilibrium in the product market, (2.15), with that which gives the incentive for investment, (2.14), we obtain an equation that relates capital formation to the value of a unit of capital and the size of the installed capital base:

$$\dot{K} = \begin{cases} f(K) - \dfrac{1}{v_K} & \text{for } v_K \geq \dfrac{1}{f(K)}, \\[2ex] 0 & \text{for } v_K \leq \dfrac{1}{f(K)}. \end{cases} \tag{2.18}$$

If, at a price of output equal to the value of a unit of capital, consumption demand does not exhaust the available output supply, then the capital stock expands. Otherwise, the price of output must exceed v_K, and all output will go to consumers. Figure 2.2 shows the direction of change in the capital stock implied by this equation, at different values of v_K and K.

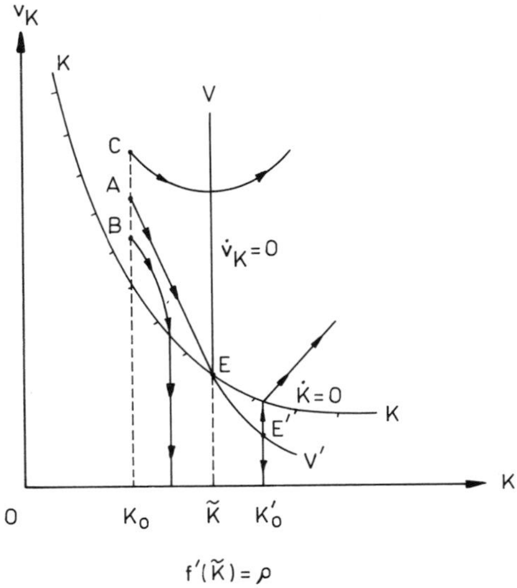

Figure 2.2

The capital stock is constant on or below the curve labeled *KK* and is rising above it.

The no-arbitrage condition (2.12) gives the evolution of the value of a unit of capital. Noting that $p_Z = v_K$ when $v_K > 1/f(K)$ and thus $\dot{K} > 0$, and that $p_Z = 1/f(K)$ when $v_K \leq 1/f(K)$ and thus $Z = C$, we have

$$\frac{\dot{v}_K}{v_K} = \begin{cases} \rho - f'(K) & \text{for } v_K > \dfrac{1}{f(K)}, \\ \rho - \dfrac{f'(K)}{v_K f(K)} & \text{for } v_K \leq \dfrac{1}{f(K)}. \end{cases} \tag{2.19}$$

The value of a machine falls when the yield (rental income divided by market value) exceeds the nominal interest rate, and it rises otherwise. This is necessary so that agents will be willing to hold the existing stock of capital. In figure 2.2 we have assumed the existence of a finite size of the capital stock $\tilde{K}$ at which the marginal product of capital is equal to the subjective discount rate. The value of a unit of capital is falling when $K < \tilde{K}$. For $K > \tilde{K}$, v_K rises above the curve labeled EV' (where $v_K = f'(K)/\rho f(K)$), and it falls below this curve. The value of a unit of capital is constant all along the locus labeled $VEE'V'$.

Suppose now that the economy inherits the capital stock K_0. The diagram depicts several trajectories beginning from this initial endowment along which the value of capital and the size of the capital stock obey the required laws of motion. These are the trajectories emanating from the points labeled A, B, and C. The trajectory emanating from B (and similarly all others emanating from points below point A) cannot be an equilibrium trajectory because along this path the value of capital eventually reaches zero, and then the no-arbitrage condition can only be satisfied if the value turns negative. A negative value for capital is impossible, however, because capital goods are freely disposable. Along the trajectory emanating from point C (and similarly all others emanating from points above point A) both the size of the capital stock and the value of a unit of capital grow without bound. This path, with a "bubble" in the asset-price of capital (i.e., a growing divergence between the value of a machine and the present discounted value of income stream that it generates), cannot be an equilibrium trajectory either because it implies that the household budget constraint (2.17) eventually cannot be satisfied with equality. In other words, the transversality condition for the household's optimization problem excludes the possibility of bubbles in the value of a unit of capital. Thus the equilibrium trajectory when the initial capital stock is K_0 is the one that emanates from the point A and leads to the stationary equilibrium at E.[9]

The economy depicted in the figure cannot sustain growth in the absence of technological progress. With constant returns to scale in capital and labor, and a constant stock of effective labor, investment causes the marginal product of capital to fall. Here we have assumed that it eventually falls to the level of the discount rate. Beyond this point consumers are unwilling to postpone consumption in order to receive a quantity of extra output in the future that is not so highly valued as the foregone consumption. The diminishing returns to capital lead the growth process to grind to a halt.

From this discussion it should be clear that, in the economy with optimal savings, just as in the Solow economy, sustained growth in per capita income will be possible even in the absence of technological progress if the marginal product of capital is bounded from below by a number $b > \rho$. In this case the value of a unit of capital falls in the long run at the rate $\dot{v}_K/v_K = \rho - b < 0$, and the capital stock grows in the long run at the rate

9. If the initial capital stock is larger than at $\tilde{K}$, such as at K_0', then the equilibrium is at E', and the size and value of the capital stock are forever constant. Any other trajectory that emanates from a point along the vertical line through K_0' ultimately implies either a violation of the transversality condition for consumer maximization or a negative value of the capital stock.

$b - \rho > 0$. Output and income per capita also grow asymptotically at this rate.[10]

The argument for sustained growth when the long-run returns to capital are constant (and sufficiently high) can be made more directly. From the household's intertemporal optimization problem, consumption grows at the rate $\dot{C}/C = r - \dot{p}_Z/p_Z - \rho$ (see [2.9]), that is, at a rate that is equal to the difference between the *real* interest rate in terms of output and the subjective discount rate. We have seen that the value of a unit of capital equals the price of output and that it falls at the rate $\rho - f'(K)$ when investment is taking place. Thus $\dot{p}_Z/p_Z = f'(K) - \rho$ when $\dot{K} > 0$. Since the nominal interest rate r equals the subjective discount rate ρ, the real interest rate equals the marginal product of capital when investment is positive. In the long run, when the marginal product of capital equals b, the real interest rate exceeds the subjective discount rate, and so households are happy to save part of their incomes in order to enjoy ever-increasing quantities of consumption.

Let us return now to an economy which has exogenous technological progress at the rate g_A. We describe only the long-run growth path, and concentrate on the case where $f'(k) < \rho$ for $k > \tilde{k}$ (where $k \equiv K/AL$, as before). From (2.14), (2.15), and the constant growth rate of A, we have

$$\frac{\dot{k}}{k} = \frac{f(k)}{k} - \frac{1}{v_K K} - g_A \tag{2.20}$$

in an equilibrium with ongoing capital accumulation. The no-arbitrage condition (2.12) and the investment-incentive equation (2.14) again imply that

$$\frac{\dot{v}_K}{v_K} = \rho - f'(k) \qquad \text{if } \dot{K} > 0. \tag{2.19'}$$

These two equations and the budget constraint (2.17) can be satisfied in the long run only if $\dot{K}/K = g_A$, $\dot{v}_K/v_K = \dot{p}_Z/p_Z = -g_A$, and $f'(k) = g_A + \rho$. In other words, the long-run rate of accumulation of capital matches the rate of exogenous labor productivity growth, and commodity prices and the value of installed equipment fall in the long run at this same rate. In the

10. The budget constraint (2.17) implies that the aggregate value of the capital stock $v_K K$ is bounded above by $1/\rho$ and below by zero. Therefore it must approach a constant in the long run. When this happens, $\dot{K}/K = -\dot{v}_K/v_K = b - \rho$. For example, in the case of a CES production function, which has $F(K, AL) = [K^{\alpha_Z} + (AL)^{\alpha_Z}]^{1/\alpha_Z}$ for $0 < \alpha_Z < 1$, we have $b = 1$. Then, if $\rho < 1$, the economy with optimal savings grows in the long-run at the rate $1 - \rho$.

long run the marginal product of capital equals the real interest rate, $g_A + \rho$. We see therefore that the exogenous technological progress keeps the marginal product of capital from falling to the level of the discount rate, and so the incentive to accumulate does not disappear even as the capital stock grows large.

Before leaving the neoclassical growth model, it will be useful as a benchmark for our later analysis to consider the efficiency of the market allocation. The welfare properties of the equilibrium trajectory are the same with and without exogenous technological progress, so to conserve on notation we return to the case of $g_A = 0$ and $AL = 1$. Let us solve now the social planner's problem, which was first discussed by Ramsey (1928), Cass (1965), and Koopmans (1965). Our objective is to maximize the utility indicator (2.6) subject to the resource constraint

$$\dot{K} = f(K) - C. \tag{2.21}$$

To this end, we form the current value Hamiltonian[11]

$$\mathscr{H} = \log C + \theta[f(K) - C] + \lambda[f(K) - C], \tag{2.22}$$

where $\theta(t)$ is the (current value) costate variable associated with the accumulation equation (2.21) and $\lambda(t)$ represents the Lagrange multiplier associated with the constraint that investment cannot be negative. The necessary and sufficient conditions for an optimal program comprise

$$\frac{\partial \mathscr{H}}{\partial C} = 0, \tag{2.23a}$$

$$\frac{\partial \mathscr{H}}{\partial \theta} = \dot{K}, \tag{2.23b}$$

$$\dot{\theta} = \rho\theta - \frac{\partial \mathscr{H}}{\partial K}, \tag{2.23c}$$

$$\dot{K} \geq 0, \quad \lambda \geq 0, \quad \text{and} \quad \lambda\dot{K} \geq 0, \tag{2.23d}$$

$$\lim_{t\to\infty} e^{-\rho t}\theta(t)K(t) = 0. \tag{2.23e}$$

Equation (2.23a) states that instantaneous consumption at every moment in time should maximize the current value Hamiltonian. Equation (2.23b) en-

11. The current value Hamiltonian is defined by $\mathscr{H}(\tau) \equiv \tilde{\mathscr{H}}(\tau)e^{\rho(\tau-t)}$, where $\tilde{\mathscr{H}}$ is the ordinary (i.e., present value) Hamiltonian. We use the current value formulation to simplify notation, as is common in optimal control problems with discounting. See, for example, Arrow and Kurz (1970, ch. 2) for further discussion.

sures that investment equals the difference between output and consumption. Equation (2.23c) requires that the gain in utility from the marginal unit of capital matches the utility gain that would derive from postponing the accumulation for a moment. The latter gain consists of the difference between the time cost of the forgone consumption $\rho\theta$ (since θ is the shadow price of capital) and the instantaneous rate of change in the (shadow) cost of capital $\dot{\theta}$. Finally, condition (2.23d) is the familiar complementary slackness condition that applies to the nonnegativity constraint on capital formation, and (2.23e) is the transversality condition.

If we combine (2.22) with (2.23a–c), we obtain two differential equations that guide the accumulation of capital and the shadow value of equipment along an optimal growth path. These are

$$\dot{K} = f(K) - \frac{1}{\theta + \lambda}, \tag{2.24}$$

$$(\theta + \lambda) f'(K) + \dot{\theta} = \rho\theta. \tag{2.25}$$

Notice that the market equilibrium equations (2.15) and (2.12) are identical to these optimality conditions, with v_K playing the role of θ and p_Z playing the role of $\theta + \lambda$. Moreover the investment-incentive condition (2.14) mimics the complementary slackness condition (2.23d) when v_K and p_Z play these roles. Finally, the equilibrium requirement that $v_K K$ be bounded from above by $1/\rho$ ensures the satisfaction of the transversality condition (2.23e) when v_K plays the role of θ. In short, the market prices provide the same incentives as the shadow prices, and thus the equilibrium allocation of resources coincides with the optimal allocation. The perfect-foresight, competitive equilibrium is efficient in the neoclassical economy because there are no market distortions to cause any misallocation of resources.

2.3 Learning by Doing

Arrow (1962b) proposed that knowledge might accumulate as firms engage in new activities. He linked the state of knowledge at date t to the cumulative amount of investment that had taken place somewhere in the economy before that time. One interpretation of this formulation is that firms generate additions to knowledge in the course of manufacturing capital goods (but not consumer goods) and that they cannot prevent this knowledge from flowing freely into the public domain. The knowledge then contributes to the productivity of resources in subsequent manufacturing activities.

To pursue the implications of Arrow's notion of "learning by doing," we develop a modified version of his model that is close in spirit to Sheshinski's (1967) formulation. We retain the assumptions concerning household behavior that were laid out in our discussion of the neoclassical economy. Moreover, we suppose, as before, that each firm's output of the good Z is a linearly homogeneous function of its inputs of capital and effective labor. But now we let the productivity of labor depend upon the economywide cumulative experience in the investment activity, that is, on the aggregate stock of capital. Then *aggregate* output of Z will be given by

$$Z = F[K, A(K)L]. \tag{2.26}$$

The first argument in $F(\cdot)$ represents the private input of capital by all firms in the economy. The second argument reflects their aggregate employment of *effective* labor, which depends in part upon the state of technology, as represented by the term $A(K)$.

Romer (1986) provides an alternative interpretation of this specification. He views K itself as knowledge, rather than as plant and equipment. Knowledge is created via an R&D process that uses the same inputs and in the same proportion as the production of tangible commodities. Firms invest in private knowledge, which they use together with labor to produce final output and additional knowledge. But at the same time they contribute inadvertently to a public pool of knowledge, which is represented here by $A(K)$. Finally, resource productivity varies positively with the stock of public knowledge. Thus in Romer (1986), as in Arrow (1962b) and Sheshinski (1967), technological progress is an accidental consequence of firms' private investment decisions.

Under both the Sheshinski and the Romer interpretations it continues to be the case that firms will invest in accumulating K only if the price of output does not exceed the value of a unit of (knowledge or physical) capital. That is, the investment-incentive condition (2.14) continues to apply. So the capital stock grows according to

$$\dot{K} = \begin{cases} F[K, A(K)L] - \dfrac{1}{v_K} & \text{for } v_K > \dfrac{1}{F[K, A(K)L]}, \\ 0 & \text{for } v_K \leq \dfrac{1}{F[K, A(K)L]}. \end{cases} \tag{2.27}$$

The no-arbitrage condition applies to the *private* return to capital. It equates the sum of the rental income and the capital gain on installed equipment (or ideas) to the interest cost of the funds that are invested. In place of (2.19) we have

$$\frac{\dot{v}_K}{v_K} = \begin{cases} \rho - F_K[K, A(K)L] & \text{for } v_K > \dfrac{1}{F[K, A(K)L]}, \\ \rho - \dfrac{F_K[K, A(K)L]}{v_K F[K, A(K)L]} & \text{for } v_K \leq \dfrac{1}{F[K, A(K)L]}, \end{cases} \tag{2.28}$$

where $F_K(\cdot)$ denotes the partial derivative of $F(\cdot)$ with respect to the first argument, that is, the portion of the return to a unit of capital that accrues to its owner.

Sheshinski assumed that there would be diminishing returns to cumulative investment in the creation of knowledge. His specification guaranteed that the ratio $A(K)/K$ would fall to zero as K grew large.[12] He also assumed that $f'(k) < \rho$ for k sufficiently large, where $k \equiv K/AL$ again is capital per effective worker and $f(\cdot)$ is the production function in intensive form. Under these assumptions the phase diagram for the Sheshinski economy looks exactly like the one depicted in figure 2.2 for the economy without endogenous learning. The Sheshinski assumptions ensure the existence of a capital stock $\tilde{K}$ such that $F_K[\tilde{K}, A(\tilde{K})L] = \rho$. Once the economy has accumulated this amount of capital, the private incentive for investment vanishes, and growth ceases to occur.

But Romer (1986) has pointed out that growth might be sustainable, even under the Inada conditions, if the accumulation of knowledge is not subject to long-run diminishing returns.[13] Suppose, for example, that $A(K)/K$ approaches the constant $1/a$ (that is not too small) as K tends to infinity. Then the only trajectory obeying (2.27) and (2.28) that also satisfies the budget constraint (2.17) with equality has a constant long-run rate of capital accumulation equal to $\dot{K}/K = f'(a/L) - \rho$, and long-run growth in labor productivity and final output that take place also at this rate. To see this, note that, by (2.28), v_K must fall at the rate $F_K[K, A(K)L] - \rho$, in a long-run equilibrium with sustained investment. But $F_K(\cdot)$ is homogeneous of degree zero, and so the marginal product is equal to $f'[K/A(K)L]$. This converges to $f'(a/L)$ by our assumption about the accumulation of knowl-

12. More precisely, he assumed that $A(K) = K^{\alpha}$, with $0 < \alpha < 1$.

13. Actually Romer assumed diminishing returns in the production of private knowledge from available resources, but increasing returns in the production of output from labor and total (public and private) knowledge. His condition for the sustainability of long-run growth amounts to an assumption that the diminishing returns in the former activity do not outweigh the increasing returns in the latter. Our simpler formulation captures the essence of his insights.

edge. Finally, the value of the capital stock must approach a constant so that the intertemporal budget constraint can be satisfied with equality. This implies that capital accumulates at the same rate that v_K falls.

Romer has described a competitive equilibrium where ongoing growth in per capita income is sustained by endogenous technological progress. Although the capital stock grows without bound along the equilibrium trajectory, the associated growth in labor productivity allows the effective labor force to keep pace. Thus, the capital-to-effective-labor ratio need not explode when there are constant returns in the creation of knowledge, and the marginal product of capital need not fall to the level of the subjective discount rate.

In the Romer economy government policies that affect the incentives for investment will alter the long-run growth rate. It should be apparent moreover that such policies can be justified on efficiency grounds. Investment activities create a social benefit that goes beyond the private return that accrues to the investor. This benefit comes in the form of an addition to the economy's knowledge base. Due to the existence of this positive externality from investment, the market allocation entails a suboptimal rate of capital formation.

2.4 Basic Research

Shell (1967) took a different approach from Arrow (1962b) to endogenizing the process of knowledge acquisition. In Arrow, knowledge is generated by activities performed by the private sector, although the creation of knowledge is not the specific purpose for which these activities are undertaken. Shell, on the other hand, makes knowledge the intended output of those who create it. But he places the innovators in a distinct research sector, and motivates them by curiosity (and government financing) rather than profit. This formulation would seem to fit best the activities of *basic* researchers, namely, individuals who generate ideas with far-reaching potential benefits that are difficult to appropriate.

Shell, like Sheshinski, developed a model in which all forms of accumulation ultimately cease. Rather than present his version of the model, we develop an alternative that yields sustained growth. We do so for two reasons. First, this allows us to show more clearly the relationship between his work and that of the others. Second, it allows us to highlight what we view to be the essential insight from Shell, namely that the creation of knowledge often requires the diversion of resources from other activities.

We continue with the basic specification discussed in the previous two sections. The production function $F(K_Z, AL_Z)$ describes again the relationship between inputs, the state of technology, and output of the homogeneous final good. The subscript Z indicates now that the factors are used in the manufacturing sector. The level of productivity increases with the cumulative output of the research sector because researchers make their findings freely available to all. For simplicity we assume that the same production function applies to the generation of knowledge as applies to the production of tangible commodities:

$$\dot{A} = F(K_A, AL_A), \tag{2.29}$$

where K_A and L_A are the inputs of capital and labor, respectively, into the research activity. Moreover we assume that the research sector employs these factors in the same proportion as the private sector, as it would, for example, if it were instructed by the government to achieve its results at minimum cost. An aggregate constraint on resource use limits K_A to $K - K_Z$ and L_A to $L - L_Z$, where K and L are the aggregate endowments.

Research expenses are financed by income taxes. The government taxes all income at the exogenous rate t_A, and uses all revenues to pay for basic research. Total tax receipts are given by $T = t_A F(K_A, AL_A) + t_A F(K_Z, AL_Z)$, and $T = t_A F(K, AL)$ under our assumption that factor proportions are similar in the two activities. Since factors in the research sector must be paid the same amount as they would earn in the private sector, the tax revenues allow for the hiring of research inputs that satisfy $T = w_L L_A + w_K K_A$. We note that $w_L L_A + w_K K_A = F(K_A, AL_A)$, by Euler's theorem. Therefore research output is related to the tax rate and the tax base by

$$\dot{A} = t_A F(K, AL). \tag{2.30}$$

In the private sector capital formation is the difference between manufactured output and consumption demand. Final output is given by $F(K_Z, AL_Z)$, which equals $(1 - t_A)F(K, AL)$ in the light of (2.29), (2.30), and the fact that factor proportions are the same in the two activities. Thus we have in place of (2.18) or (2.27) the following equation for capital accumulation:

$$\dot{K} = \begin{cases} (1 - t_A)F(K, AL) - \dfrac{1}{v_K} & \text{for } v_K \geq \dfrac{1}{(1 - t_A)F(K, AL)}, \\ 0 & \text{for } v_K \leq \dfrac{1}{(1 - t_A)F(K, AL)}. \end{cases} \tag{2.31}$$

Also owners of claims to capital equipment receive only the net-of-tax rental income $w_K = (1 - t_A)F_K(K, AL)$. Therefore the no-arbitrage condition implies that

$$\frac{\dot{v}_K}{v_K} = \begin{cases} \rho - (1 - t_A)F_K(K, AL) & \text{for } v_K \geq \dfrac{1}{(1 - t_A)F(K, AL)}, \\[2ex] \rho - \dfrac{F_K(K, AL)}{v_K F(K, AL)} & \text{for } v_K \leq \dfrac{1}{(1 - t_A)F(K, AL)}. \end{cases} \tag{2.32}$$

Equations (2.30)–(2.32) determine the evolution of K, v_K, and A.

Rather than describe again the entire trajectory, we turn immediately to the long-run outcome. It is easy to show (using as before the requirement that the intertemporal budget constraint be satisfied with equality) that the economy must converge to a balanced growth path. In the steady state the relative size of the two sectors is constant, and consumption, labor productivity, and the capital stock all grow at a common rate g_A. The value of a unit of capital falls in the long-run at the rate g_A, so the aggregate value of the capital stock approaches a constant. Then from (2.32) it follows that

$$g_A = (1 - t_A)f'(\tilde{k}) - \rho, \tag{2.33}$$

where $\tilde{k} \equiv \lim_{t\to\infty} K(t)/A(t)L$ is the steady-state ratio of capital to effective labor. Also from (2.30) we have

$$g_A = t_A Lf(\tilde{k}). \tag{2.34}$$

These two equations determine the steady-state capital-to-effective-labor ratio and the long-run growth rate.

In figure 2.3 we depict combinations of g_A and $\tilde{k}$ that satisfy equation (2.33) by the curve VV. This curve slopes downward because the marginal product of capital and hence the incentive to invest grow larger as capital per effective worker becomes smaller. The curve AA representing equation (2.34) slopes upward because greater levels of research and thus higher rates of growth can be financed when capital per worker and hence aggregate income are larger. The intersection point E gives the steady-state rate of growth in output and per capita income.

The modified Shell economy, like the Romer economy, realizes an endogenously determined rate of sustained growth. Variations in both economic structure and government policy affect the long-run growth rate. Consider, for example, the long-run implications of an increase in the subjective discount rate. This shifts the VV curve down, and the equilibrium from E to E'. The growth rate falls because consumers are less

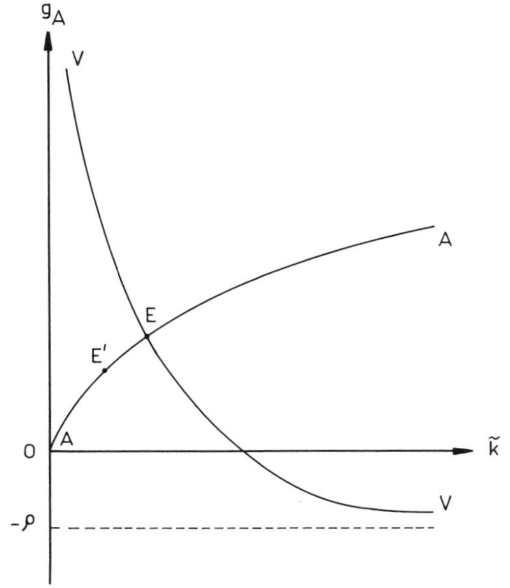

Figure 2.3

patient, thus less willing to finance capital accumulation. With the smaller capital-to-effective-labor ratio that results, there is less income at every moment and thus less tax revenue to finance research.

The rate of growth is most directly affected by changes in the income tax rate. When the government increases t_A, the AA curve shifts up because there is more tax revenue for given k to finance basic research. At the same time the VV curve shifts down because there is less incentive to invest in capital when aftertax returns are lower. On net, the growth rate may increase or decrease. It increases if the higher rate of taxation on the smaller income base (at a given level of technology) leads to greater government tax receipts. This must be the case if the tax rate is initially small. It decreases, on the other hand, if tax receipts decline, as they must when the tax rate is close to one. An optimal tax rate can readily be calculated that weighs the benefits of faster technological progress against the costs associated with the tax distortion. In general, the optimal rate will be smaller than the one that maximizes the steady-state growth rate.

The explanation for sustained growth in the Shell economy is the same as what we have described before. Technological progress, resulting here from basic research, keeps the marginal product of capital from falling to the level of the discount rate. But the example demonstrates a further proposition, one that we will encounter many times in the remainder of this book. That is, advances in technology often come at a resource cost and so reduce the inputs that are available for manufacturing.

In this chapter, we have reviewed a number of competitive models of capital accumulation and equilibrium growth. We have shown that sustained investment in capital equipment requires the existence of a mechanism that prevents the marginal product of capital from becoming too low. In other words, a reduced-form production function relating national output to capital and primary inputs must exhibit nondiminishing returns to the former as the capital stock grows large. Constant returns can result from any of several sources. First, it may be a property of the technology that primary inputs are inessential to production and so become of negligible importance once sufficient capital has been accumulated. Second, exogenous advances in productivity may keep the marginal product of capital from falling too far, even as the accumulation of machines tends to lower the value of each one. Finally, there may be endogenous advances in productivity that perform exactly the same role. Endogenous acquisition of technical knowledge can result from the intentional allocation of resources to research, or it may be a by-product of other industrial activities.

The remainder of this book is devoted to the development of a theory of growth based on endogenous innovation. In this theory productivity gains stem from intentional investment in R&D by profit-seeking firms. Our approach proceeds along Schumpeterian lines. That is, we assume that firms devote resources to R&D in order to capture a stream of monopoly profits. This forces us to leave the familiar setting of the competitive model, which has of course been the workhorse of traditional growth theory. Nonetheless, our approach can be readily combined with the traditional theory (as we show in chapter 5) and should be viewed as a complement for it, rather than as a substitute.

3 Expanding Product Variety

In this chapter we present the first of our models of endogenous growth based on intentional industrial innovation. Here, and in the remainder of the book, we treat commercial research as an ordinary economic activity that requires the input of resources and responds to profit opportunities. Returns to R&D come in the form of monopoly rents in imperfectly competitive product markets. To begin with, we abstract from factor accumulation so that all savings are channeled to the creation of new technology. Alternative vehicles for investment (such as physical capital and human capital) will be reintroduced in chapter 5.

Industrial research may be aimed at reducing the cost of producing known commodities (process innovation) or at inventing entirely new commodities (product innovation). We may further distinguish product innovation according to whether the newly invented goods bear a vertical or horizontal relation to existing products. That is, innovative products may perform similar functions to those performed by existing goods, but provide greater *quality*, or they may serve new functions, thereby expanding *variety* in consumption or specialization in production. In this chapter we develop a simple model of increasing product diversity. Chapter 4 is devoted to endogenous quality upgrading.

We begin in the next section with a specification that treats technology as an entirely private product. Entrepreneurs invest resources in order to develop unique goods. An ordinary production function relates inputs (primary factors of production) to outputs (blueprints for new goods). Product designs are assumed to be proprietary information, either because their details can be kept secret or because patents effectively deter unauthorized uses. Each new product substitutes imperfectly for existing brands, and innovators exploit limited monopoly power in the product market.

We assume that the potential for developing new products is unlimited and that the resource requirements for invention remain fixed. Thus ideas do not become exhausted, and there are no diminishing returns in the creation of knowledge. Nonetheless, growth ultimately ceases in this simplest model of endogenous innovation. The reasons are similar to those that were discussed in chapter 2 in the context of the neoclassical model of capital accumulation. Even if the resource cost of creating new goods does not rise, the economic return to invention may decline as the number of available products increases. When the rate of return to R&D falls to the level of the discount rate, private agents cease to be willing to defer consumption in order to invest in product development.

However, as we noted in chapter 1, there are features of technology as an economic commodity that distinguish it from ordinary capital. These features are absent from the model of section 3.1. In particular, technology is a nonrival good, and it may be a nonexcludable one in at least some uses. We argued in chapter 1, citing Arrow (1962a) and Schmookler (1966), that it might be especially difficult for innovators to prevent others from usurping their ideas that can serve as the basis for further research. Thus industrial R&D often generates technological spillovers that facilitate subsequent innovation.

In section 3.2 we modify our specification of the innovation process to capture these distinctive characteristics of knowledge capital. The extended model distinguishes between two types of output of industrial research. We assume that innovators can appropriate the returns to *product-specific information* which enables them to manufacture new products, but not the returns to *general information* (or applied science) which serves as an input in the inventive activity. With this modification, we find that the process of endogenous innovation can be self-sustaining. The section explores the conditions needed for sustained growth and examines the links between parameters describing tastes and technology and the economy's long-run growth rate.

Section 3.3 introduces government policy. We consider both technology policies that directly augment the incentives for research and industrial policies that do so indirectly by encouraging production of technology-intensive goods. Surprisingly, perhaps, the two types of policies have very different effects on the growth rate in our one-sector economy. In the last section of the chapter, we turn from positive to normative issues, and discuss the welfare properties of the equilibrium trajectory and the nature of the policy interventions that are needed to achieve an efficient growth path.

3.1 Brand Proliferation[1]

Consumer Behavior

We begin with a description of consumer behavior. As in chapter 2 the representative household maximizes utility over an infinite horizon. Intertemporal preferences take the same form as before, namely,

$$U_t = \int_t^\infty e^{-\rho(\tau - t)} \log D(\tau)\, d\tau. \tag{3.1}$$

Here $D(\tau)$ represents an index of consumption at time τ, and ρ is the subjective discount rate. The natural logarithm of the consumption index measures instantaneous utility at a moment in time.

We want the index D to reflect households' tastes for diversity in consumption. Then these tastes will generate demands for differentiated products, and we can study innovation that serves to expand the set of available varieties. We take the product space to be continuous and ignore integer constraints on the number of goods. Consumers' preferences extend over an infinite set of products, which we index by $j \in [0, \infty)$. At any moment only a subset of these varieties is available in the marketplace. Households can purchase at time t all brands that have been developed in the research lab prior to t. Without further loss of generality we may represent the set of brands available on the market by the interval $[0, n(t)]$. With this convention $n(t)$ is the measure of products invented before time t. We shall refer to n as the "number" of available varieties.

We adopt for D a specification that imposes a constant (and equal) elasticity of substitution between every pair of goods. Specifically,

$$D = \left[\int_0^n x(j)^\alpha\, dj \right]^{1/\alpha}, \qquad 0 < \alpha < 1, \tag{3.2}$$

where $x(j)$ denotes consumption of brand j. This specification, due to Dixit and Stiglitz (1977), has proved quite tractable in many contexts in which product differentiation is of central concern. It is straightforward to show that, with these preferences, the elasticity of substitution between any two products is $\varepsilon = 1/(1 - \alpha) > 1$, and a household spending an amount E maximizes instantaneous utility by purchasing

1. The model presented here is a special case of one developed by Judd (1985). However, our method of analysis is quite different from his.

$$x(j) = \frac{Ep(j)^{-\varepsilon}}{\int_0^n p(j')^{1-\varepsilon} dj'}, \tag{3.3}$$

units of brand $j \in [0, n]$, where $p(j)$ is the price of that brand.[2] The demands in (3.3) feature a constant price elasticity of ε and a unitary expenditure elasticity for each product. They can be aggregated across consumers to yield aggregate demands with exactly the same form, but with E then representing aggregate spending.

The Dixit-Stiglitz preferences have several attractive properties for our purposes. First, since new goods substitute imperfectly for old, the specification accommodates increasing diversity in consumption. Second, the CES formulation gives rise to aggregate demand functions that have a particularly simple form. A single parameter α characterizes different tastes for variety. This attribute facilitates analysis of the relationship between the extent of market power enjoyed by successful innovators and the equilibrium growth rate. However, one implication of the preferences may be less appealing in the present context. The specification implies that innovative products are in no way superior to older varieties, despite the fact that they have been invented later in time, and perhaps after great strides have been taken in applied science. This complete symmetry between new and old commodities eliminates any possibility of product obsolescence. Fortunately the model of quality improvements that we will develop in chapter 4 can address this shortcoming of the present formulation, and so the two models together can account for both the vertical and horizontal aspects of product innovation.

Before proceeding, it is useful to develop an alternative interpretation of the consumption index D. This interpretation, due to Ethier (1982a), will prove useful in later chapters. In place of the above, we may think of households as consuming a single homogeneous consumption good in quantity D. But now we suppose that the final good is assembled from differentiated intermediate inputs or "producer services." Competitive firms manufacture the consumer good according to a technology given by (3.2), where $x(j)$ represents the input of intermediate good or service j into final production.[3]

---

2. Note that the first-order condition for maximizing (3.2) subject to the budget constraint $E = \int_0^n p(j)x(j)\,dj$ implies that $x(j)p(j)^{\varepsilon} = \zeta^{-\varepsilon}D$, where ζ is the Lagrange multiplier associated with the constraint. The demand function in (3.3) follows from the definition of E and the fact that $x(j)p(j)^{\varepsilon}$ is independent of j and so can be pulled outside the integral.

3. In later chapters we will introduce additional primary inputs that combine with differentiated intermediates in the production of final goods. For now we suppose that manufacturing of final output requires only the various intermediate processes and components.

When we interpret (3.2) as a production function, the technology exhibits constant returns to scale at any moment in time. That is, if a firm producing final goods were to increase its use of every *available* input proportionately, then output would increase by the same factor of proportionality. Competition in the supply of consumer goods ensures an equilibrium price p_D equal to the minimum attainable unit manufacturing cost, or

$$p_D = \left[\int_0^n p(j)^{1-\varepsilon}\,dj\right]^{1/(1-\varepsilon)}. \tag{3.4}$$

The derived demand for input j by a firm that manufactures D units of the final good can be found using Shephard's lemma, and is given by

$$x(j) = Dp(j)^{-\varepsilon}\left[\int_0^n p(j')^{1-\varepsilon}\,dj'\right]^{-1/\alpha}, \qquad j \in [0, n]. \tag{3.5}$$

Clearly aggregate derived demand also can be represented by (3.5), with D reflecting aggregate output of the consumption good. Finally, we have $D = E/p_D$ as a condition for equilibrium in the market for final output. The formal equivalence of the alternative interpretations is seen now by replacing D in (3.5) by E/p_D, and noting (3.4).

The production function (3.2) has one property that is especially significant for the analysis of growth. With this technology total factor productivity rises with the number of available varieties. To see this most clearly, suppose that all intermediate inputs were produced according to the same constant-returns-to-scale production function. In a symmetric equilibrium all produced inputs would bear the same price and manufacturers of consumer goods would employ equal quantities $x(j) = x$ of each. Then (3.2) implies that $D = n^{1/\alpha}x$. The same quantity of resources is needed to produce a bundle of differentiated inputs of a given size, regardless of its composition, so we can use $X = nx$ to measure the resources embodied in final goods. Then final output per unit of primary input (i.e., total factor productivity) is given by $D/X = n^{(1-\alpha)/\alpha}$. With $0 < \alpha < 1$, we see that the productivity of a given stock of resources rises with the number of available varieties. Ethier (1982a) ascribes this property of the technology to the gains from increasing degrees of *specialization* in production. That is, when n grows, manufacturing involves an ever larger number of finer production processes.

Returning to the consumers' allocation problem, we consider now its intertemporal component. The representative household maximizes (3.1) subject to an intertemporal budget constraint. Using $D = E/p_D$, we can rewrite the maximand as

$$U_t = \int_t^{\infty} e^{-\rho(\tau - t)}[\log E(\tau) - \log p_D(\tau)]\, d\tau. \tag{3.6}$$

This substitution of indirect for direct utility applies not only when the final good is homogeneous (whence $E = p_D D$ by definition) but also when the consumer goods are differentiated. In the latter case (3.4) provides the ideal price index p_D associated with the consumption index D.

Note that indirect utility in (3.6) is weakly separable in the level of spending and the price index. This property of the specified preferences simplifies the intertemporal maximization problem greatly. In effect, the household can solve its optimization problem in two stages. First, it can choose the composition of given levels of spending to maximize instantaneous utility. Then it can optimize separately the time path of spending. The latter problem is in fact identical to the one that we solved in chapter 2. Thus the maximization of (3.6) subject to an intertemporal budget constraint requires that spending evolve according to (compare [2.9])

$$\frac{\dot{E}}{E} = r - \rho. \tag{3.7}$$

This condition holds for every household and also for aggregate spending.

As we did in chapter 2, we impose a normalization of prices that makes nominal spending constant through time. With

$$E(t) = 1 \qquad \text{for all } t, \tag{3.8}$$

equation (3.7) implies, once again, that

$$r(t) = \rho \qquad \text{for all } t. \tag{3.9}$$

The final decision facing households concerns the allocation of their wealth across available assets. We have already implicitly assumed the existence of a market for consumption loans. We will also allow firms to issue equity in order to finance their R&D investments. Then households can acquire ownership shares in profit-making firms. Successful innovators will face no uncertainty in the perfect-foresight equilibrium of our model. This assumption renders stocks and bonds as perfect substitutes, and so in equilibrium these assets yield equal rates of return. Although households become indifferent as to the composition of their portfolios when returns are equalized, the requirement that there be no profitable arbitrage opportunities plays a critical role in the determination of the dynamic equilibrium.

Producer Behavior and Static Equilibrium

We turn now to the production side of the economy. Producers undertake two distinct activities. They create blueprints for new varieties of differentiated products, and they manufacture the products that have been developed previously. The up-front R&D expense can be regarded as a fixed cost in the production cycle of a given commodity. This cost need only be borne once, and its size is independent of the number of units that are subsequently produced. Since we shall take the fixed costs to be "large," in a sense that will be made precise, not all of the infinitely many producible goods will be introduced at a given point in time.

We assume that each known variety of the differentiated product is manufactured by a single, atomistic firm. This assumption can be justified in one of two ways. First, the government may grant infinitely lived patents to the original inventors of innovative products. Alternatively, we may suppose that imitation is costly and that firms engage in ex post price competition. In this case, no entrepreneur would ever invest resources to copy a brand that is already available on the market. A copier would earn zero profits in Bertrand competition with the original innovator, and so would be unable to recoup a positive cost of imitation.[4]

We assume that all known differentiated products are manufactured subject to a common constant-returns-to-scale technology. In this chapter attention is confined to an economy that is endowed with a single primary factor of production, which we call "labor." So production of any variety requires a certain amount of labor per unit of output. By an appropriate choice of units, we may set the input-output coefficient to one.

The specified technology makes marginal manufacturing costs at time t equal to the wage rate $w(t)$. Facing the demand function in (3.3), the unique supplier of variety j maximizes operating profits

$$\pi(j) = p(j)x(j) - wx(j)$$

by charging a price $p(j) = w/\alpha$ (where here and henceforth we suppress the

4. Imitation might occur if producers of clones enjoyed a cost advantage over the original developers of innovative products. This possibility naturally arises, for example, when innovators produce in high-wage countries while imitators reside in low-wage countries. We study the relationship between imitation of this sort and trade between high-wage and low-wage countries in chapters 11 and 12.

time arguments when no confusion arises from doing so). In the momentary equilibrium all varieties are priced equally at p, where

$$p = \frac{w}{\alpha}. \tag{3.10}$$

With symmetric demands and $E = 1$, this pricing strategy yields per brand operating profits of

$$\pi = \frac{1 - \alpha}{n}. \tag{3.11}$$

The profits recorded in (3.11) are one component of the return to the owners of a firm. We may think of these profits as being paid out continuously to shareholders as dividends. Equity holders may expect also to enjoy capital gains (or suffer capital losses) on their ownership shares. In a perfect-foresight equilibrium these expected gains or losses must match the change in the value of the firm that actually transpires. We let $v(t)$ denote the value of a claim to the infinite stream of profits that accrues to a typical firm operating at time t. In the brief time interval between t and $t + dt$, the total return to the owners of this firm amounts to $\pi dt + \dot{v}dt$. We have already argued that arbitrage in capital markets ensures equality between this yield and that on a riskless loan. The latter return for an investment of size v is $rvdt$. Thus equilibrium in the capital market requires

$$\pi + \dot{v} = rv. \tag{3.12}$$

Equation (3.12) is closely analogous to the no-arbitrage condition (2.12) in chapter 2, which related the nominal interest rate to the total return to a unit of capital.

We assume henceforth that the stock market value at time t of a firm that operates in a deterministic environment equals the present discounted value of its profit stream subsequent to t.[5] That is,

5. To simplify the exposition, we treat (3.13) as an assumption rather than deriving it as a condition of equilibrium. Strictly speaking, equilibrium in the capital market ensures only that there are no unexploited profit opportunities, but not that assets should have any particular value. Share prices might diverge from the value given in (3.13) if they contain "speculative bubbles" (e.g., see the discussion in chapter 5 of Blanchard and Fischer 1989). However, equity bubbles cannot emerge in a dynamic equilibrium when infinitely lived households maximize "lifetime" utility subject to an intertemporal budget constraint. We have already seen that bubbles on capital values are excluded in the neoclassical model of chapter 2. Some later footnotes will show how similar arguments apply here. Thus the absence of bubbles need not be *assumed*. Nonetheless, we will speak in the main text as if (3.13) were a condition of equilibrium and violations imply an inconsistency in expectations about future profits.

$$v(t) = \int_t^\infty e^{-[R(\tau)-R(t)]}\pi(\tau)\,d\tau, \tag{3.13}$$

where $R(t)$ again represents the cumulative discount factor applicable to profits earned at time t. Notice that differentiation of (3.13) with respect to t yields (3.12). Thus, when firms are valued according to "fundamentals," the no-arbitrage condition automatically is satisfied.

We turn next to the technology for product development. We suppose that an entrepreneur can add *incrementally* to the set of available products by devoting a given *finite* amount of labor to R&D for a brief interval of time. This specification implies that the resource costs of product development are "large" in two senses of the word. First, it makes the cost of acquiring a blueprint similar in order of magnitude to the value of the stream of profits that the entrepreneur can subsequently earn, even though development takes negligible time while the profit stream lasts indefinitely. Second, it implies that even if the entirety of the economy's resources were to be applied to developing new products, the economy could achieve only a high rate of change in the measure of available varieties, and not a discrete jump in the number of brands. For this reason product innovation must be spread over time.

Firms may enter freely into R&D. They finance the up-front product development costs by issuing equity.[6] An entrepreneur who devotes l units of labor to R&D for a time interval of length dt acquires the ability to produce $dn = (l/a)dt$ new products. The total cost of such a research venture is $wldt$. The effort creates value for the entrepreneur of $v(l/a)dt$, since each blueprint has a market value of v. Value maximization by entrepreneurs implies that l will be chosen as large as possible whenever $v/a > w$ and that it will be set to zero when $v/a < w$. The former case cannot arise in general equilibrium, since it implies an unbounded demand for labor by research enterprises. The latter case corresponds to a momentary equilibrium with no investment in R&D. We conclude that

$$wa \geq v, \qquad \text{with equality whenever } \dot{n} > 0. \tag{3.14}$$

The combination of free entry and constant returns to scale in the research lab prevents entrepreneurs from earning excess returns.

6. Equity and debt are perfect substitutes in this setting of complete information and no uncertainty. Therefore we may also think of the development costs as being financed by debt issue or by some combination of debt and equity.

The final requirement for a static equilibrium is that the labor market clears. The population supplies L units of labor services at every moment in time. These services are applied to R&D and to the production of differentiated goods. If the flow of new products is $\dot{n}$, then total employment in R&D equals $a\dot{n}$. The representative variety of differentiated product bears a price p. Aggregate spending is $E = 1$. So each firm sells $1/np$ units. In the aggregate, the measure n of manufacturers demand $1/p$ units of labor. Thus labor market equilibrium requires

$$a\dot{n} + \frac{1}{p} = L. \tag{3.15}$$

Since employment in every activity must be nonnegative, the equilibrium price must satisfy

$$p \geq \frac{1}{L}. \tag{3.16}$$

This completes the specification of the model. Let us recap briefly. At every moment in time history dictates the existing number of products $n(t)$. Expectations about future profitability (which ultimately are fulfilled) determine the value of the representative firm, and market participants take this value as exogenous. Given $n(t)$ and $v(t)$, we can solve for the prices and the allocation of resources that satisfy the requirements for a static equilibrium. The free-entry condition (3.14) gives the wage as a function of firm value. The pricing equation (3.10) gives prices as a function of the wage rate. Capital market equilibrium and our normalization (3.8) imply a constant nominal interest in (3.9). Then the absence of arbitrage opportunities requires a certain rate of change in firm value given by (3.12), while labor market equilibrium implies a certain allocation of labor to R&D. From these outcomes we can calculate the "next" period's n and v, and so the economy moves forward through time. In the next subsection we examine the qualitative properties of the equilibrium trajectory.

Equilibrium Dynamics

The inverse relationship between the number of available varieties and profits per brand (see [3.11]) suggests that product development may never get underway if an economy inherits a sufficiently diverse set of differentiated commodities. This intuitive proposition can be verified as follows. Let the number of varieties in existence at time t be $n(t)$ and suppose provisionally that no R&D takes place after t. Then labor market equilibrium (3.15) requires that the entire labor force be employed in manufacturing, or that $1/p = L$. Thus $w = \alpha/L$ by the pricing equation (3.10). Next (3.9), (3.11), and (3.13) imply that $v(t) = (1 - \alpha)/\rho n(t)$. With this value of the firm and wage level, the hypothesis that $\dot{n} = 0$ is consistent with the free-entry condition (3.14) if (and only if) $n(t) \geq \bar{n}$, where

$$\bar{n} = \frac{(1 - \alpha)L}{\alpha \rho a}. \tag{3.17}$$

In other words, when the initial number of brands exceeds $\bar{n}$, there always exists a perfect-foresight equilibrium with no product development. We will soon see that with these initial conditions, the dynamic equilibrium without any R&D is unique.

Suppose, on the other hand, that the economy inherits relatively few products. Then, at least initially, the perfect-foresight trajectory features an active R&D sector. During the initial phase of the dynamic equilibrium, the introduction of new varieties causes more manufacturing firms to compete for a fixed supply of labor. Equilibrium markups do not vary with n (see [3.10]), but sales per brand decline. Thus the profit rate falls over time. Eventually new inventions drive the profit rate down to the level of the discount rate. At that point the private incentive for commercial R&D disappears.

To establish these claims, let us consider a time interval over which new brands are being developed. During this period $v = wa$, by (3.14). Combining this free-entry condition with the pricing equation (3.10) and the constraint (3.16) that employment in R&D be nonnegative, we find that R&D is profitable only when the reward for successful research is sufficiently high; that is $\dot{n} > 0$ implies that $v > \bar{v}$, where

$$\bar{v} = \frac{\alpha a}{L}. \tag{3.18}$$

Also, when R&D is taking place, the number of new brands introduced per unit time equals employment in research (i.e., the total labor supply less the number of workers engaged in manufacturing) divided by the parameter reflecting the productivity of labor in product development. From the free-entry condition (3.14), the pricing equation (3.10), and the resource constraint (3.15) we have $\dot{n} = L/a - \alpha/v$. Therefore the number of varieties evolves according to

$$\dot{n} = \begin{cases} \dfrac{L}{a} - \dfrac{\alpha}{v} & \text{for } v > \bar{v}, \\[2ex] 0 & \text{for } v \leq \bar{v}. \end{cases} \tag{3.19}$$

Next we substitute the formulas for the interest rate (3.9) and the profit rate (3.11) into the no-arbitrage condition (3.12) to derive an equation for the change in firm value as a function of the current value of a blueprint and the number of available brands. The result is

$$\dot{v} = \rho v - \frac{1-\alpha}{n}. \tag{3.20}$$

We have thus reduced the requirements for a dynamic equilibrium to two differential equations in the variables n and v. These equations can be analyzed using the phase diagram in figure 3.1.

The hyperbola vv shows combinations of n and v for which the value of the typical firm remains momentarily unchanged. The negative slope of this curve can be understood as follows. An increase in v raises the opportunity cost of holding shares in the representative firm. Then capital markets will expect zero capital gains only if the dividend rate is correspondingly higher. A higher dividend rate requires higher profits, and so a smaller set of competing brands.

The number of differentiated products remains constant at points on or below the horizontal line through $v = \bar{v}$. This is because product innovation requires a sufficiently high firm value to justify the large costs of R&D. We see that the system is stationary at point E and at all points along vv below this point. To complete the phase diagram, we note that all trajectories are vertically oriented below the horizontal line through $\bar{v}$. In this region no product development takes place. Above the horizontal line active innovation leads to an expanding range of products ($\dot{n} > 0$), with the value of a blueprint declining below vv and rising above it. The diagram illustrates some representative trajectories.[7]

Now we can use the figure to describe the equilibrium dynamics. Suppose that the economy inherits $n_0 < \bar{n}$ brands. The figure shows four (of the infinitely many) trajectories that emanate from points with this initial condition. Along each of these trajectories, the requirements for a static

7. The reader should note the similarities between this phase diagram and figure 2.2, which showed the movements in the value of a unit of capital and the size of the capital stock in the neoclassical growth model. We will develop the analogy between the formal structure of the two models further below.

equilibrium are met at every moment in time, and the differential equations that link time periods also are satisfied. The paths differ, however, in the initial value $v(t)$ that they assign to the representative brand. Two of them—those that assign the lowest values to $v(t)$—imply a sequence of capital losses leading ultimately to a nonpositive value of the typical firm. Since firms always set positive markups and earn positive profits, investors cannot rationally expect negative equity values. Therefore we can rule out these trajectories as candidates for equilibrium.

A similar argument applies to the trajectory that assigns the highest initial value to $v(t)$ among those that are drawn. If the economy follows this growth path, then in the long run both the number of available varieties and the value of the representative firm will increase without bound. But an infinite measure of brands implies zero profits for each producer (see [3.11]). The stock market places a value of zero on a firm that earns no profits.[8] It follows that expectations cannot be fulfilled along this trajectory, or along any other with similar properties. The initial valuation is too high to be consistent with perfect foresight.

Only the saddle path leading to point E reflects expectations that can be fulfilled everywhere. It follows that this path describes the unique dynamic equilibrium. The equilibrium has the property that the value of any firm at time t exactly matches the present value of the profits that accrue to that firm after t. In all cases where the initial number of brands is less than $\bar{n}$, new products are introduced for a while, but at an ever decreasing rate. In the long run the growth process grinds to a halt, and the economy attains a stationary equilibrium with $\bar{n}$ products.

Consider now the case in which the economy inherits $n_0' > \bar{n}$ products. We refer once again to figure 3.1. All trajectories that assign an initial value to the firm in excess of that at point E' imply an unbounded number

8. Here is where we use the assumption that the value of a firm equals the present discounted value of its future profits; that is, that there are no bubbles in asset prices. The divergent trajectories can be ruled out without resort to (3.13) based on the transversality condition for the household's optimal spending program. Optimality of the consumption profile from time t onward requires that the present value of consumption subsequent to t equal the present value of wage income plus the value of net asset holdings at t. Since $E(\tau) = 1$ for all τ, the present value of consumption from any t onward equals $1/\rho$. If the total value of equities $n(\tau)v(\tau)$ were to grow without bound (as it does along the divergent trajectories), ultimately households would not satisfy their intertemporal budget constraints with equality. This argument implies that the aggregate value of the stock market must remain finite. It excludes bubble paths along which the value of a representative equity rises steadily while ongoing growth in variety implies ever-declining profits per firm. Recall that a similar argument was invoked in chapter 2 to rule out divergent paths for the value of capital.

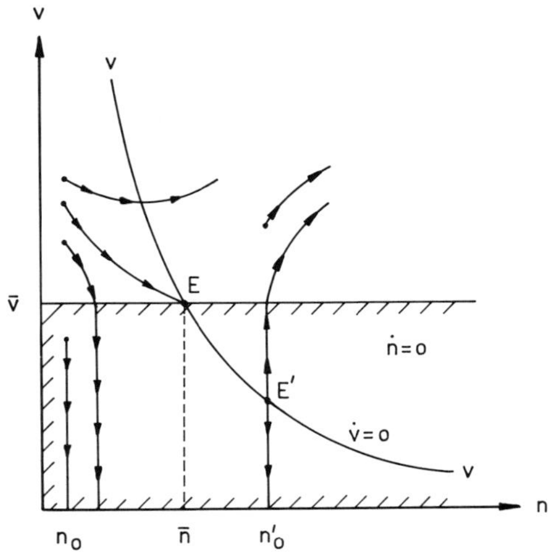

Figure 3.1

of varieties and an infinite value of the typical firm in the long run. As before, these trajectories can be ruled out. Similarly those that assign a value $v(t)$ less than that at point E' undervalue the firm. Evidently the perfect-foresight trajectory must begin at point E'. But point E' is a rest point of the dynamic system. It follows that the economy immediately enters a stationary state. This establishes the uniqueness of the aforementioned equilibrium without innovation for the economy that inherits a large number of differentiated products.

To understand why growth must peter out (if ever it begins) in our model of expanding product variety, let us calculate the long-run profit rate $\pi/\bar{v}$ (i.e., the inverse of the price-to-earnings ratio). Using (3.11), (3.17), and (3.18), we find that $\pi/\bar{v} = \rho$ at point E. Thus product development ultimately drives the profit rate down to the level of the discount rate. When that occurs, there is no further incentive to invest in R&D. There is a clear analogy between the outcome here and that in the neoclassical model of capital accumulation and growth in the first two sections of chapter 2. In that setting, we recall, investment in capital equipment under conditions of constant returns to scale causes the marginal product of capital to fall through time. If labor is an essential input, then the marginal product of capital ultimately declines to the level of the discount rate. At that point the incentive to accumulate additional capital vanishes. In both the neoclassical growth model and the model of product development described in this section, the processes of investment run into diminishing returns.

There is another similarity between the two models. In both cases investment leads to the accumulation of an entirely private good. But whereas this treatment may be quite natural in the case of capital equipment (unless investment generates externalities of the sort described by Arrow 1962b, as discussed in section 2.3), our arguments in chapter 1 suggest that the current specification of the R&D process may miss an important feature of knowledge as an economic commodity. In the next section we shall modify the model to address this shortcoming.

3.2 Public Knowledge Capital

In the previous section we treated knowledge capital as a private good, much like our treatment of physical capital through most of chapter 2. Investment in R&D gave rise to a design for a new product, the returns to which were fully appropriated by the inventor. As we have seen, this specification implies the cessation of growth in the long run. But, arguably, it neglects an important characteristic of many types of knowledge. As we discussed in chapter 1, the originators of many new ideas often cannot appropriate all of the potential benefits from their creations. Some uses of the information may not be recognized by the original inventors, or their pursuit may require more expertise than the innovators have or can readily acquire in the market. In other cases property rights may be difficult to define and enforce, so the inventors will be unable to exclude others from making free use of their innovative ideas. In this section we modify our formulation of knowledge creation to allow for the existence of such non-appropriable benefits from industrial research.

We follow Romer (1990) in distinguishing between two products of R&D. First, each research project gives rise, as before, to a design for a new commodity. This blueprint yields appropriable returns to the inventor in the form of a stream of monopoly profits. Second, each research project contributes to a stock of general knowledge capital $K_n(t)$. This capital stock represents a collection of ideas and methods that will be useful to later generations of innovators. It may include components such as the scientific properties of particular materials, the chemical formulas for certain compounds, or the structure of new computer algorithms. We assume that the contributors to K_n cannot monitor the use of this body of knowledge, nor can they enforce any property rights. Accordingly, we treat knowledge capital as a public input into R&D.

In place of our previous technology for product innovation, we assume now that

$$\dot{n} = \frac{L_n K_n}{a}, \tag{3.21}$$

where L_n represents aggregate employment in R&D. This means that advancements in the fields of applied science and engineering reduce the labor requirements for designing new products. Of course our previous formulation is a special case of (3.21) with $K_n(t) \equiv 1$.

Equation (3.21) represents a production function for blueprints. We also need to specify the link between research activity and the accumulation of general knowledge capital (i.e., a production function for K_n). In principle, we might want this specification to incorporate lags in the dissemination of knowledge (e.g., see Mansfield 1985; Adams 1990). We might also want to allow for a general nonlinear relationship between total investment in research and the knowledge stock that accumulates as a consequence. Such a nonlinear specification would be appropriate if the marginal contribution of a particular project to general knowledge were a function of the prevailing state of knowledge. The process of knowledge accumulation might be characterized by increasing returns, for example, if there existed important complementarities between different ideas. On the other hand, the relationship between research and knowledge might be one of decreasing returns, if science were characterized by a limited "store of ideas," and if earlier contributions were more significant than later ones.

We choose, however, to concentrate our attention in the main text on a formulation that ignores these potential complications. Our specification posits an immediate contribution by each R&D project to the stock of knowledge capital, and makes this contribution independent of the aggregate amount of R&D that has been undertaken in the past. We take the knowledge capital stock to be proportional, at every moment, to the economy's cumulative experience at R&D. By an appropriate choice of units for measuring knowledge capital, the factor of proportionality may be set to one, so that

$$K_n = n. \tag{3.22}$$

After deriving our results for this simplest of specifications, we shall discuss how they would be modified in more general cases. The formal analysis of these alternative cases has been relegated to two appendixes.[9]

9. The reader should note the formal similarity between our formulation, borrowed from Romer (1990), and the earlier specification of learning spillovers from investment in physical capital, due to Arrow (1962b). As we described in section 2.3, Arrow supposed that the productivity of any given firm would increase with cumulative aggregate investment due to

With this new treatment of knowledge as a (partially) public good, we must modify two of the equations in section 3.1 that characterized the dynamic equilibrium. First, the R&D activity now requires $a\dot{n}/K_n = a\dot{n}/n$ units of labor per unit time to develop $\dot{n}$ new products per unit time, so the labor-market-clearing condition (3.15) becomes

$$\frac{a\dot{n}}{n} + \frac{1}{p} = L. \tag{3.23}$$

Second, the cost of a blueprint now is $wa/K_n = wa/n$. So the free-entry condition (3.14) should read

$$\frac{wa}{n} \geq v, \qquad \text{with equality whenever } \dot{n} > 0. \tag{3.24}$$

These changes do not affect the differential equation for the value of the firm (3.20), but they do alter the form of the equation that prescribes the evolution of the number of varieties. In place of (3.19), we have

$$\frac{\dot{n}}{n} = \begin{cases} \dfrac{L}{a} - \dfrac{\alpha}{vn} & \text{for } v > \dfrac{\alpha a}{nL}, \\[2ex] 0 & \text{for } v \leq \dfrac{\alpha a}{nL}. \end{cases} \tag{3.25}$$

Equations (3.20) and (3.25) together determine the equilibrium dynamics.

Before beginning the analysis of the new equilibrium growth path, we can simplify matters by defining two new variables. We use $V \equiv 1/nv$ to represent the *inverse* of the economy's aggregate equity value and $g \equiv \dot{n}/n$ to denote the instantaneous rate of "innovation" in the economy (i.e., the rate at which new products are being introduced). Using these new variables, we can rewrite (3.25) as

$$g = \begin{cases} \dfrac{L}{a} - \alpha V & \text{for } V < \dfrac{L}{\alpha a}, \\[2ex] 0 & \text{for } V \geq \dfrac{L}{\alpha a}. \end{cases} \tag{3.26}$$

Also the definitions of V and g imply that $\dot{V}/V = -g - \dot{v}/v$. Combining this with (3.20), we have

---

externalities generated in the course of producing capital. Similarly we suppose here that productivity in a given research lab increases with cumulative aggregate investment in R&D.

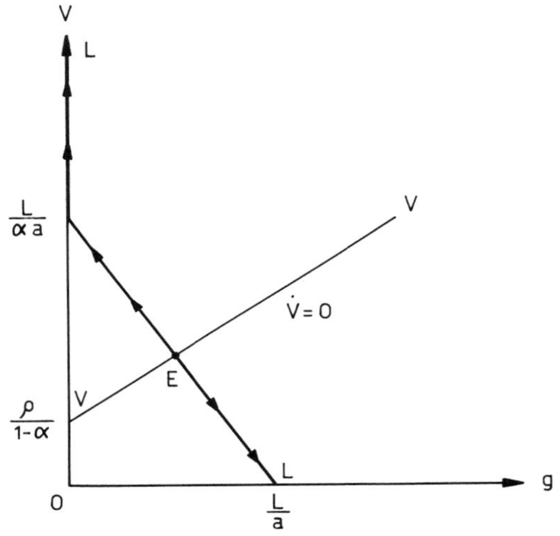

Figure 3.2

$$\frac{\dot{V}}{V} = (1 - \alpha)V - g - \rho. \tag{3.27}$$

We have thus reduced the system of equilibrium relationships to a single differential equation, (3.27), plus one side condition, (3.26). We proceed now with a diagrammatic analysis of the equilibrium dynamics.

In figure 3.2 the kinked curve *LL* depicts (3.26). This equation, which must be satisfied at every moment in time, expresses a constraint on resource use. The higher is the rate of innovation, the greater is employment in R&D. Therefore a smaller amount of labor remains for manufacturing, and so the supply of goods must be lower. Lower output implies higher prices, higher wages, a greater value of the typical firm, and thus a smaller inverse value of the stock market. The line labeled *VV* shows combinations of V and g that imply that $\dot{V} = 0$ (i.e., a rate of decline in the share price of the representative firm that exactly matches the rate of new product development). From the no-arbitrage condition (3.20) we see that a smaller aggregate value of the stock market (or larger inverse value) is associated with a faster rate of decline in firm value. Everywhere above *VV*, the number of varieties grows less rapidly than the value of the typical firm falls (so V rises), while below the line the opposite is true. The arrows show the implied directions of movement along *LL*.

Figure 3.2 has been drawn to depict the case in which $L/a > \alpha\rho/(1 - \alpha)$. For parameter values that obey this restriction, the intersection point of the

VV line with the horizontal axis falls below the lowermost point where the LL curve coincides with this same axis. Then, the two curves must intersect in the positive orthant, as shown. The intersection point is one where the dynamic forces in the economy effect no change in V and g over time. In other words, if the economy were to reach this point, then innovation would continue at a fixed rate, the division of resources between R&D and manufacturing would remain constant through time, and the aggregate value of the stock market would not change. But in fact expectations can be fulfilled only if the economy jumps *immediately* to this steady state. Suppose, on the contrary, that the initial expectations of subsequent profits implied an inverse valuation of stocks at time t greater than that associated with point E. Then in the long run the dynamics of the system would drive g to zero, while V would grow without bound. Since $V = 1/nv$, if the number of varieties stopped growing, V could tend to infinity only if the value of the representative firm were to approach zero. But with a finite measure of varieties, profits per brand remain strictly positive. Since equities maintain a strictly positive value, this path entails unfulfilled expectations. Suppose, on the other hand, that $V(t)$ were smaller than that at E. Then the dynamics would drive V arbitrarily close to zero, while the rate of innovation would approach its maximal value of L/a. But the fact that the number of products would be growing continuously would imply via (3.9), (3.11), and (3.13) that

$$v(t) < \int_t^\infty e^{-\rho(\tau - t)} \frac{1-\alpha}{n(t)} d\tau = \frac{1-\alpha}{\rho n(t)}.$$

Then $V(t) > \rho/(1-\alpha) > 0$. Evidently expectations must be contradicted along such a trajectory as well.[10] The only remaining possibility is for the economy to begin at point E and remain there forever.

In the steady-state equilibrium represented by point E, product development continues indefinitely, always at a constant rate. Using the equation for $\dot{V} = 0$ and (3.26), we may calculate the steady-state rate of innovation,

$$g = (1-\alpha)\frac{L}{a} - \alpha\rho. \tag{3.28}$$

Sustained innovation is possible in this case because the cost of product development falls with the accumulation of knowledge capital, even as the

10. Once again, the argument relies on the assumption that assets are priced at their fundamental values. A stronger argument that does not rely on this assumption can be made along the lines of footnote 8 above.

return to the marginal innovation declines. The nonappropriable benefits from R&D keep the state of knowledge moving forward, and so the private incentives for further research are maintained.

In appendix A3.1 we treat the case of a nonlinear relationship between cumulative research and the stock of knowledge capital, while maintaining the assumption that research spillovers involve no transmission lags. We find that endogenous technological progress can be sustained in the long run not only for the linear example analyzed here but also for more general production functions for knowledge capital. The key assumption that we require for the sustainability of innovation is that $K_n/n \geq \bar{k} > \alpha a p/(1-\alpha)L$ as n grows large. That is, the average product of cumulative research in the production of knowledge capital must be bounded from below by a constant that depends on parameter values.[11] If this condition is not satisfied, then the contribution of research to general knowledge capital eventually becomes too small to preserve the private incentive for product development. Then the long-run trajectory looks much like the one described in the preceding section.[12]

Let us return to the case of a linear relationship between cumulative research and public knowledge capital, and ask what the equilibrium implies about the rate of growth of final output and the rate of growth of GDP. Concerning the former, there is a simple answer when the differentiated products are interpreted to be intermediate goods. Since the allocation of labor is constant in the steady state, so too is $X = nx$. Final output, which by (3.2) equals $Xn^{(1-\alpha)/\alpha}$, grows at the constant rate $g_D = g(1-\alpha)/\alpha$. Clearly faster innovation implies faster output growth in this case.

Our original interpretation of the differentiated products as consumer goods demands a somewhat more subtle calculation of the growth rate of output. In that setting each invention lowers the price of some final product from (as it were) infinity to a finite level. Thus innovation causes steady deflation in an *ideal* price index of final goods.[13] Since the quantity of

11. This condition is analogous to the one that we encountered in chapter 2, where sustained output growth required that the average product of capital be bounded suitably from below.

12. The argument is similar to the one we gave in section 2.3 to explain why growth peters out in the Sheshinski (1967) economy but not in the Romer (1986) economy. Sheshinski assumed diminishing returns to investment in the accumulation of knowledge, whereas Romer explored the possibility that the ratio of knowledge to capital might approach a positive constant.

13. Feenstra (1990b) shows how the introduction of new goods should be reflected in the calculation of a price index when preferences take the CES form.

output remains constant, a measure of *real* output rises through time. It is not difficult to show in fact that real output grows at the rate $g(1-\alpha)/\alpha$ in this case as well. This finding supports our contention that the two interpretations for D can be used interchangeably.

As for GDP, we define this in the usual way as the sum of value added in manufacturing and R&D; $G \equiv p_D D + v\dot{n}$. Then real GDP grows at a rate equal to a weighted average of the growth rates of the index of manufactured output D and of research output $\dot{n}$ with the sectors' value shares serving as weights. In the equilibrium that we have described, research output grows at rate g (i.e., $\ddot{n}/\dot{n} = \dot{n}/n = g$), while manufactured output grows at rate g_D. Thus real GDP grows at rate $g_G = [\theta_D(1-\alpha)/\alpha + (1-\theta_D)]g$, where $\theta_D \equiv p_D D/(p_D D + v\dot{n})$. In the steady-state equilibrium, θ_D remains constant through time (because the value of output in each sector is constant), and so real GDP grows at a rate that is proportional to the rate of innovation.[14]

From (3.28) it is apparent that the economy innovates faster the larger is its resource base (large L), the more productive are its resources in the industrial research lab (small a), the more patient are its households (small ρ), and the greater is the perceived differentiation of products (small α). A larger resource base means, in this simple specification, more employment in every activity. Among the activities that expand is that which generates new knowledge.[15] A smaller discount rate means more savings, a lower cost of capital, and so more innovation and faster growth. Finally, a smaller value of α implies a greater taste for variety, thus a less elastic demand for each product, a larger opportunity for monopoly profits, and a higher return to R&D.

Appendix A3.2 examines the implications of a prolonged period of knowledge dissemination. We use the specification

$$K_n(t) = \kappa \int_{-\infty}^{t} e^{-\kappa(t-\tau)} n(\tau)\, d\tau, \qquad \kappa > 0.$$

With this distributed lag formulation, research results begin to percolate through the research community immediately after a project terminates, but the initial impact on the stock of knowledge capital is small. As the

14. In the OECD member countries R&D comprises 2.3 percent of GDP (OECD 1989, p. 20). Therefore the distinction between the rates of growth of GDP and of manufactured output can be ignored for most practical purposes.

15. We will have more to say about the relationship between the size of an economy and its equilibrium growth rate in chapter 5 below.

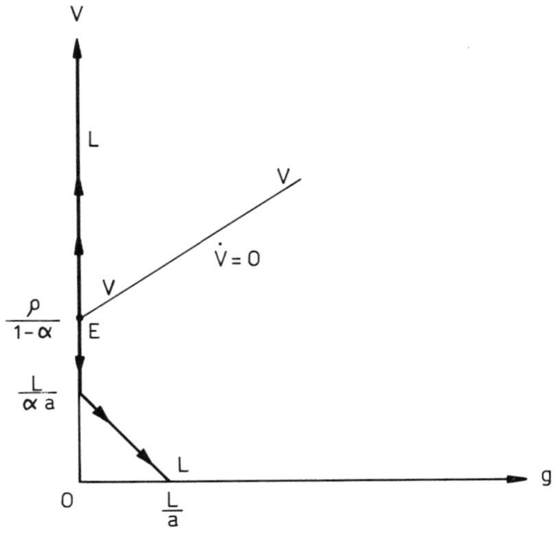

Figure 3.3

findings become better known and appreciated, the spillover benefits cumulate. The parameter κ measures the speed of dissemination, with $\kappa \rightarrow \infty$ representing the limiting case of instantaneous diffusion.

We find that dissemination lags affect not only the speed of convergence to the steady state but also the dynamics of the long-run equilibrium. This is true despite the fact that all of the potential spillovers from any research project eventually enter the public domain, no matter what the size of κ. The calculations in the appendix show, in particular, that the more quickly an economy assimilates general scientific knowledge (i.e., the larger is κ), the greater will be the steady-state ratio of the stock of knowledge to the number of varieties. And a higher value of K_n/n contributes to faster innovation and more rapid growth in the long run.

Before leaving this section, we return briefly to the specification without dissemination lags to investigate the nature of the dynamic equilibrium when the parameter restriction that we used in drawing figure 3.2 is violated. Figure 3.3 depicts the dynamic forces at work when $L/a \leq \alpha\rho/(1-\alpha)$. Here the intersection of the VV line with the kinked LL curve occurs at a point E along the vertical axis. The economy jumps immediately to this point, which represents a stationary state without innovation.[16] Evidently R&D will not be privately profitable in an economy that is too

16. All other trajectories can be ruled out by familiar arguments concerning the absence of bubbles in asset prices.

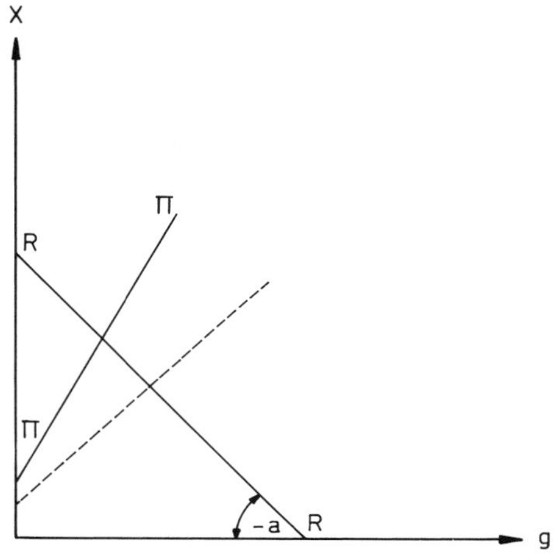

Figure 3.4

small, too impatient, or too inefficient in the research lab, or in one where households do not sufficiently value variety in consumption.[17]

3.3 Industrial Policies

In the last section we developed a model that predicts sustained growth in real per capita income. We also examined how various parameters describing tastes and technology interact to determine the endogenous growth rate. In this section we continue our investigation of the factors that influence long-run growth performance by introducing two sorts of government policies. We focus here on the positive effects of government intervention, deferring normative analysis until the next section.

Before proceeding, it will be useful to introduce a new diagram that portrays the long-run equilibrium. In figure 3.4 we have plotted as RR the resource constraint linking the steady-state aggregate output of manufactured goods X and the rate of innovation g. Since each unit of output requires one unit of labor, while product development at rate g uses ag units of labor, the resource constraint takes the form

$$ag + X = L. \tag{3.29}$$

The transformation curve RR is a straight line with slope $-a$. Next we

17. Romer (1990) noted that stagnation may occur in an economy that has an insufficient endowment of the resources needed for industrial research.

recast the no-arbitrage condition in terms of g and X. In an equilibrium with an active R&D sector, the value of the representative firm is $v = wa/n$ (see [3.24]). Wages are constant in a steady state ($w = nv/a = 1/aV$, and $\dot{V} = 0$). Aggregate sales are equal to $X = 1/p = \alpha/w$. So the no-arbitrage condition (3.20) can be written as

$$\frac{(1-\alpha)X}{\alpha a} = g + \rho. \tag{3.30}$$

We have depicted this relationship, which equates the profit rate (expressed in terms of the aggregate output of manufactures) and the real interest rate in terms of R&D, by the line **ΠΠ** in the figure. The steady state is found at the intersection of RR and **ΠΠ**.

We consider first a policy whereby the government pays a fraction ϕ of all research expenses. Such a subsidy to R&D lowers the private cost of invention to $(1-\phi)wa/n$. This changes the incentives facing entrepreneurs in exactly the same way as would a decline in the unit labor requirement for R&D from a/n to $(1-\phi)a/n$. With the policy in effect, the free-entry condition implies that $v = (1-\phi)wa/n$ in an equilibrium with $g > 0$. The resource constraint is not affected by the government intervention, but the no-arbitrage condition becomes

$$\frac{(1-\alpha)X}{\alpha a(1-\phi)} = g + \rho. \tag{3.30'}$$

From (3.30′) we see that any increase in the subsidy rate causes the **ΠΠ** line to rotate in a clockwise direction about its intersection with the horizontal axis. The dotted line in the figure represents such a change. The figure shows that a subsidy to R&D spurs product development (for a similar result, see Romer 1990). Faster innovation and growth come at the expense of the quantity of manufactured output.

Next we consider a subsidy to manufacturers of differentiated products. This might seem a similar policy to subsidization of R&D, inasmuch as it too augments the profitability of developing new goods. However, we shall find presently that there is an important difference. Let ϕ_x denote the ad valorem rate of subsidy, so that manufacturers receive $p(1+\phi_x)$ for every unit of output that they sell. This policy clearly does not affect the resource constraint RR. And what about **ΠΠ**? With the policy in place, firms maximize profits by charging a net-of-subsidy price of $p = w/\alpha(1+\phi_x)$, thereby selling $1/np = \alpha(1+\phi_x)/wn$ units. Subsidy-inclusive profits per brand become $\pi = (1+\phi_x)(1-\alpha)/n$, and the dividend rate, $\pi/v = (1+\phi_x)(1-\alpha)/wa$. But aggregate sales now vary with the wage rate according to $X = \alpha(1 + \phi_x)/w$. Substituting for w in the expression for π/v, we find that (3.30) continues to express the no-arbitrage condition. In short, the policy instrument has no bearing on the location of the $\Pi\Pi$ line. It follows that an output subsidy effects no change in the intersectoral allocation of resources, and thus no change in the equilibrium growth rate.

What accounts for this difference between the alternative subsidy policies? Clearly they must introduce different incentives for private agents. A subsidy to R&D increases an entrepreneur's return from inventing a new product. But at the initial wage rate it leaves unchanged the incentive that a firm has to produce from an existing blueprint. Resources move therefore from manufacturing to research. A subsidy to output, on the other hand, augments both the profitability of research and the profitability of manufacturing at the initial wage rate. In our one-sector model these two activities (and only these two) compete for a common resource pool. By promoting both activities, the government effectively promotes neither. The output subsidy serves only to bid up the equilibrium wage rate.[18]

3.4 Welfare

We are concerned not only with the determinants of the equilibrium growth rate but also with the welfare properties of the dynamic equilibrium. We investigate next whether market forces provide adequate incentives for innovation and growth. In circumstances where they do not, we inquire into the nature and scope of the government interventions that might be used to decentralize an efficient growth path.

Our primary interest lies in the economy with sustainable growth that was described in section 3.2. But it proves useful to begin our normative analysis with the no-spillovers model of section 3.1. In that setting, we recall, entrepreneurs may introduce new products for a while, but innovation ultimately comes to an end when the available variety becomes sufficiently great. After we have derived the welfare properties of the equilibrium trajectory for this case, it will be relatively easy for us to understand the source of any divergence between the equilibrium and optimal growth paths in the economy with knowledge spillovers.

18. In later chapters we will extend our model to include a second manufacturing sector and a second primary factor of production. Such a formulation yields an even more striking conclusion about the growth effects of a production subsidy. If differentiated products are intermediate in their relative use of skilled labor between R&D, on the one hand, and traditional manufacturing (or agriculture), on the other, a government policy to promote *production* of innovative goods tends to slow innovation and growth.

Economy without Knowledge Spillovers

We aim to derive the optimal growth path for the economy described in section 3.1 where the returns to research are fully appropriable. We take the utility of the representative household as our measure of social welfare. The social planner's problem can be usefully decomposed into two component parts. These are (1) a static problem, which determines the optimal allocation of labor to the various brands j, for a given division of resources between manufacturing and R&D, and (2) a dynamic problem, which determines the optimal course of product development. We treat the two subproblems in turn.

The Static Allocation Problem

In the static problem aggregate employment in manufacturing X is taken as given. We seek the allocation of labor among the various brands that maximizes the indicator of instantaneous utility in (3.2). Each unit of output of every brand requires one unit of labor. So our problem is to maximize D subject to the constraint

$$\int_0^n x(j)\,dj \le X. \tag{3.31}$$

The index D treats all goods symmetrically. Moreover the input requirements for each one are the same. Since the specified preferences reflect a taste for diversity, it is clear that the optimal allocation must involve equal production of all known varieties; that is, $x(j) = X/n$ for $j \in [0, n]$. Of course the market equilibrium described in section 3.1 achieves just such a division of employment in manufacturing.

The Dynamic Allocation Problem

We consider next the allocation of labor to R&D and manufacturing that maximizes (3.1). To achieve the dynamic optimum, the static allocation must be efficient at all times. For this to be so, we need $x(j) = X/n$, as we have just seen. Then $D = n^{(1-\alpha)/\alpha}X$, by (3.2). Substituting for D in (3.1), we can reformulate the dynamic allocation problem as the maximization of

$$U_t = \int_t^\infty e^{-\rho(\tau - t)}\left[\left(\frac{1}{\alpha} - 1\right)\log n(\tau) + \log X(\tau)\right]d\tau \tag{3.32}$$

subject to the resource constraint

$$a\dot{n} + X = L. \tag{3.33}$$

This is a standard problem of optimal control, similar to the one that we faced in chapter 2. To solve it, we again form the current value Hamiltonian,

$$\mathscr{H} = \left(\frac{1}{\alpha} - 1\right)\log n + \log X + \theta\left(\frac{L - X}{a}\right), \tag{3.34}$$

where θ is a costate variable representing the (current) shadow value of variety.[19] From (3.34) we obtain the necessary and sufficient conditions for a maximum that apply along an optimal trajectory with ongoing innovation. These are

$$\frac{1}{X} = \frac{\theta}{a}, \tag{3.35}$$

$$\dot{\theta} = \rho\theta - \frac{1 - \alpha}{\alpha n}, \tag{3.36}$$

$$\lim_{\tau \to \infty} e^{-\rho\tau}\theta(\tau)n(\tau) = 0, \tag{3.37}$$

and the resource constraint (3.33).

Let us define $v \equiv \alpha\theta$ so that $\dot{v} = \alpha\dot{\theta}$. Then (3.33), (3.35), and (3.36) imply that

$$\dot{n} = \frac{L}{a} - \frac{\alpha}{v} \tag{3.38}$$

and

$$\dot{v} = \rho v - \frac{1 - \alpha}{n}. \tag{3.39}$$

But we recognize these requirements for the optimal evolution of the number of varieties and the value of a blueprint as ones that are fulfilled along the *equilibrium* growth path of the market economy (see [3.19] and [3.20]). The equilibrium trajectory also satisfies the transversality condition (3.37) because both the measure of products and the value of the typical firm remain bounded in the long run. We have thus established the Pareto efficiency of the market allocation for an economy that inherits less than $\bar{n} = [(1 - \alpha)/\alpha\rho]L/a$ products.[20]

19. The use of the current value Hamiltonian was discussed in chapter 2. See also Arrow and Kurz (1970, ch. 2).

20. When $n(t) \geq \bar{n}$, no innovation takes place in the market equilibrium. It is easy to show that this too represents a Pareto efficient outcome.

What accounts for the Pareto optimality of the laissez-faire outcome? To answer this question, we must identify and measure several potential market failures that may cause private and social incentives to diverge. First, a static distortion may arise in this economy due to the noncompetitive pricing of differentiated products. Such a distortion would certainly be present if there existed a second manufacturing sector offering goods priced at marginal cost. However, in the absence of any competitive sector, markup pricing distorts household decisions only to the extent that the degree of monopoly power varies across goods.[21] In our economy with constant and equal elasticities of demand for every product, all markups over marginal cost are equal. It follows that relative prices reflect relative marginal costs, and so no static distortion emerges here.

Two other market failures are present in this economy. The first arises because entrepreneurs do not take into account the surplus that accrues to households when a new good contributes to product diversity. We refer to this as the *consumer-surplus effect*. The second can be traced to the fact that entrepreneurs base their innovation decisions on considerations of private profitability, without paying heed to the adverse effect on the profits of others. We call this the *profit-destruction effect*, in view of the close relationship to Schumpeter's (1942) notion of creative destruction. The fact that innovation generates these two external effects suggests that the market equilibrium might be dynamically inefficient. However, it is a special property of the CES preferences that these opposing distortions just happen to be of equal magnitude.[22] The market provides entrepreneurs with the socially correct incentive to innovate because the tendency to neglect consumers and thus underinvest exactly offsets the tendency to ignore competing producers, and so to overinvest.

Economy with Knowledge Spillovers

We turn finally to the economy with knowledge spillovers. Recall that these spillovers cause the input requirements for product development to fall with the accumulation of general knowledge capital. The presence of knowledge spillovers does not, however, alter in any way the social planner's static allocation problem. Static optimization again achieves $D =$

21. This argument was first made by Lerner (1934) in his classic article on measurement of the degree of monopoly power. An especially clear statement of it may be found in Samuelson (1965, pp. 239–240).

22. See appendix A3.3 for a formal demonstration of this. Related issues are discussed in Dixit and Stiglitz (1977) and Judd (1985).

$n^{(1-\alpha)/\alpha}X$. We face once more the problem of maximizing (3.32), but this time subject to the resource constraint given in (3.29). The current value Hamiltonian for this problem takes the form

$$\mathscr{H} = \left(\frac{1}{\alpha} - 1\right)\log n + \log X + \theta\left[\frac{(L - X)n}{a}\right]. \tag{3.40}$$

From this Hamiltonian we derive the necessary and sufficient conditions for a maximum, which comprise (3.29), (3.37),

$$\frac{1}{X} = \frac{\theta n}{a} \tag{3.41}$$

and

$$\dot{\theta} = \rho\theta - \frac{1 - \alpha}{\alpha n} - \frac{\theta(L - X)}{a}. \tag{3.42}$$

To aid us in interpreting these conditions, let us define $M \equiv \theta n$, the shadow value of the total amount of available variety. The definition implies that $\dot{M}/M = \dot{\theta}/\theta + \dot{n}/n$. Then we can substitute this expression, (3.29), and (3.41) into (3.42) to reduce the necessary and sufficient conditions for an optimum to

$$\dot{M} = \rho M - \left(\frac{1}{\alpha} - 1\right) \tag{3.43}$$

and the transversality condition

$$\lim_{\tau \to \infty} e^{-\rho\tau} M(\tau) = 0. \tag{3.44}$$

The only solution to (3.43) that satisfies (3.44) has $M(\tau) = (1 - \alpha)/\alpha\rho$ for all $\tau \geq t$. The social planner must choose the level of R&D employment at every moment in time to maintain a constant aggregate value of variety. This optimal program implies, via (3.29) and (3.41), a constant rate of innovation g^*, given by

$$g^* = \frac{1}{1 - \alpha}\left[(1 - \alpha)\frac{L}{a} - \alpha\rho\right]. \tag{3.45}$$

Of course the expression in (3.45) applies only when it yields a nonnegative value for g^*; otherwise, it is best to allocate all available resources to manufacturing.

We are ready now to compare the equilibrium and optimal growth paths. Recall that the market trajectory also is characterized by a constant

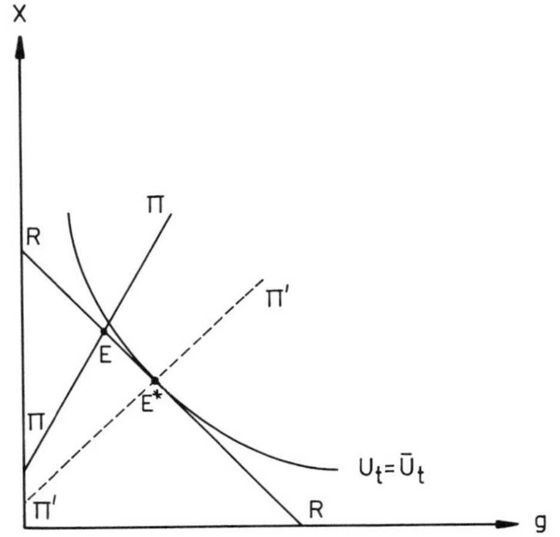

Figure 3.5

rate of innovation. Using the formula for the free-market rate of product development given in (3.28), we see that $g^* = g/(1-\alpha) \geq g$; that is, the efficient trajectory entails more rapid innovation than the equilibrium trajectory whenever the latter involves an active R&D sector. In the light of our finding that the market outcome is Pareto efficient in the absence of knowledge spillovers, this new result should not be surprising. As before, the consumer-surplus and profit-destruction effects offset one another. But, now, there exists an additional source of market failure. With a nonappropriable component to research output, each innovator contributes unwittingly to the stock of general knowledge capital. This helps later generations of entrepreneurs in their innovation efforts. The *intertemporal-spillover effect* is in addition to the two effects previously identified, and so the marginal innovation generates on net an external benefit to society.

The fact that the optimal growth path features a constant rate of innovation allows us to represent this allocation graphically in a diagram akin to figure 3.4. In figure 3.5 we have reproduced the resource constraint *RR* that limits total employment in the two activities. This constraint applies to the social planner just as it does to the market economy. We have also drawn one of a family of indifference curves that represents the social planner's (and therefore the representative household's) intertemporal preferences. To derive these curves, we start with the utility function given in (3.32), impose the assumption that the number of varieties grows at a constant rate g (and thus, by implication, manufacturing employment is constant), and integrate the right-hand side. This gives

$$\rho U_t = \left(\frac{1}{\alpha} - 1\right)\log n_t + \left(\frac{1}{\alpha} - 1\right)\frac{g}{\rho} + \log X. \tag{3.46}$$

At time t the economy inherits the number of existing brands n_t from history. Therefore (3.46) expresses a preference trade-off between the rate of growth in varieties and current consumption of existing brands. Since utility in (3.46) is a quasi-concave function of g and X, the indifference curves have the usual shape.

The optimal allocation maximizes U_t subject to the resource constraint in (3.29). Clearly the efficient allocation is found at the point of tangency between an indifference curve and RR. This point is labeled E^* in the figure. Our previous arguments establish that the point E^* is located to the right of point E, the free-market allocation. The latter point is found, as before, at the intersection of RR and the no-arbitrage line $\Pi\Pi$.

How then might the government intervene in the market to attain an efficient outcome? It stands to reason that a Pigouvian subsidy to R&D could be used to encourage entrepreneurs to internalize the net positive externality associated with product development. In the absence of other distortions that cause the equilibrium and optimal allocations to diverge, this single policy tool should be sufficient to sustain the first best. Our analysis of the effects of such a subsidy to R&D establishes that these conjectures are correct. We have seen that an R&D subsidy rotates the $\Pi\Pi$ curve in a clockwise direction about its intersection with the horizontal axis. The first-best subsidy is the one that gives rise to the no-arbitrage line labeled $\Pi'\Pi'$. It is a simple matter to calculate the size of the requisite intervention. Let ϕ^* be the subsidy to R&D that achieves the innovation rate g^* as a market allocation. Then from (3.29), (3.30′), and (3.45), we have

$$\phi^* = \frac{g^*}{g^* + \rho}. \tag{3.47}$$

The optimal subsidy rate is larger, the larger is the resource base, the more productive are resources in R&D, the lower is the subjective discount rate, and the smaller is the elasticity of substitution between differentiated products. We note that the government could use the instrument of an R&D subsidy to spur innovation to an even faster rate than g^*. But such an acceleration of innovation and growth would come at the expense of household welfare. As with other investment opportunities, the long-term benefits from more rapid innovation must be weighed against the immediate cost in terms of foregone consumption.

This chapter has introduced endogenous innovation that reflects intentional investments of resources by forward-looking entrepreneurs. The entrepreneurs seek technological gains in response to profit opportunities. Inventions serve to expand the range of available products. We find that when individual investors can appropriate all of the benefits from their research efforts, the process of investment in technology runs into diminishing returns. In this case product development may occur for a while, but ultimately the innovation process grinds to a halt. On the other hand, if the creation of knowledge generates nonappropriable benefits that allow later generations of researchers to proceed at lower resource cost than their predecessors, then the process of endogenous innovation and growth may be sustained.

We have studied the economic conditions that give rise to ongoing technological progress. The spillover benefits from research must not decline too rapidly over time, and the economy must be sufficiently large, sufficiently productive in the research lab, sufficiently desirous of new products and sufficiently patient, for R&D to remain a viable activity through time. We have also explored in the context of our simple, one-sector, one-factor model how parameters reflecting tastes, technology, and government policy influence the equilibrium growth rate. Finally, we have examined the normative properties of the free-market growth trajectory. We found the equilibrium growth path to be efficient, when R&D generates only private knowledge capital. But when R&D contributes to a stock of public knowledge capital, the market provides insufficient incentives for industrial research.

In later chapters we will extend the model to incorporate further manufacturing activities, additional primary resources, and opportunities for international transactions of various sorts. These elaborations will broaden substantially the scope for the economic and policy environment to influence the equilibrium growth process. However, before we turn to the new issues that arise in these richer contexts, we devote the next chapter to a second form of endogenous innovation, one that serves to raise the quality of an existing set of manufactured goods.

APPENDIX

A3.1 Nonlinear Accumulation of Knowledge Capital

In the main text we assumed that the contribution of each new R&D project to the stock of general knowledge capital is the same, no matter how much research has taken place beforehand. Arguably, the production function for scientific knowledge need not exhibit constant returns to scale in this sense. A plausible case can be made for regions of either increasing or decreasing returns. Increasing returns arise when complementarities are important, so that the usefulness of some bit of knowledge expands when further information becomes available. Decreasing returns set in when there is "crowding" of ideas; that is, when later intellectual contributions are less significant than earlier, more fundamental discoveries.

In this appendix we introduce a general functional relationship between aggregate cumulative R&D (as measured by n) and the current stock of knowledge capital. In particular, we let

$$K_n = f(n),$$

with $f' > 0$. This formulation encompasses our models in sections 3.1 and 3.2 as special cases, with $f(n) \equiv 1$ in the former and $f(n) = n$ in the latter.

We replace the resource constraint (3.23) and the free-entry condition (3.24) with the following, more general, forms:

$$\frac{a\dot{n}}{K_n} + \frac{1}{p} = L; \tag{A3.1}$$

$$\frac{wa}{K_n} \geq v, \qquad \text{with equality whenever } \dot{n} > 0. \tag{A3.2}$$

Then the equation that describes the course of product development becomes

$$\frac{\dot{n}}{n} = \begin{cases} k(n)\dfrac{L}{a} - \alpha V & \text{for } V < k(n)\dfrac{L}{\alpha a}, \\[2ex] 0 & \text{for } V \geq k(n)\dfrac{L}{\alpha a}, \end{cases} \tag{A3.3}$$

where $k(n) \equiv K_n/n = f(n)/n$ is the ratio of the stock of knowledge capital to cumulative experience in R&D, and $V \equiv 1/nv$ as before. The value of the typical blueprint evolves according to (3.20), which, with (A3.3) and the definition of V, implies that

$$\frac{\dot{V}}{V} = \begin{cases} V - k(n)\dfrac{L}{a} - \rho & \text{for } V < k(n)\dfrac{L}{\alpha a}, \\[2ex] (1-\alpha)V - \rho & \text{for } V \geq k(n)\dfrac{L}{\alpha a}. \end{cases} \tag{A3.4}$$

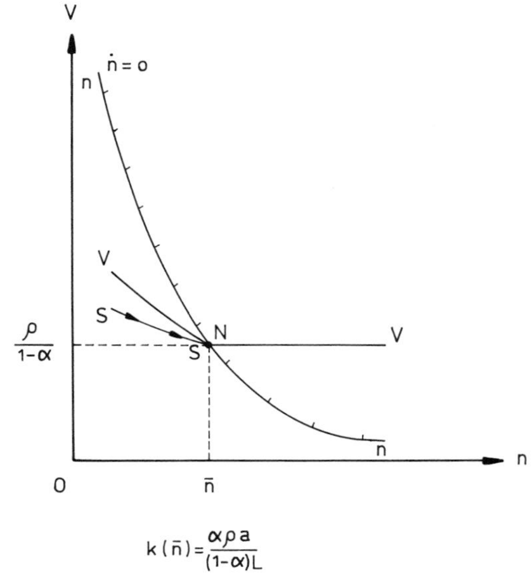

Figure A3.1

Consider figure A3.1, which depicts the case in which $k'(n) < 0$ for all n. The existence of decreasing returns in the accumulation of knowledge is sufficient for this situation to arise.[23] In the figure the region above and including the curve nn represents combinations of n and V for which the number of brands is constant ($\dot{n} = 0$). The curve VV shows combinations of these variables for which the aggregate value of the stock market does not change. This curve slopes downward in the region where $\dot{n} > 0$ and is horizontal in the region where $\dot{n} = 0$. The figure has been drawn under the further assumption that for sufficiently large n, the ratio of knowledge capital to cumulative R&D drops below the critical value of $[\alpha\rho/(1 - \alpha)]a/L$. In this case the two curves intersect in the positive orthant.

Point N represents a stationary equilibrium for this economy. If the economy inherits less than $\bar{n}$ brands, then point N is approached along the (saddle path) trajectory labeled SS. If the initial number of brands exceeds $\bar{n}$, then the economy enters a stationary state immediately. In either event no innovation takes place in the long run. We see that if returns to R&D in the production of knowledge are decreasing and the contribution of new R&D to the stock of knowledge becomes sufficiently small, then long-run stagnation is inevitable, just as it is in the absence of knowledge spillovers.

Figure A3.2 depicts another case with $k'(n) < 0$, but one where $k(n)$ is bounded from below by a number greater than $[\alpha\rho/(1 - \alpha)]a/L$. This requires the elasticity

23. To see this, note that $f'' > 0$ and $f(0) \geq 0$ imply that $nf' < f$, which in turn implies that $k' < 0$.

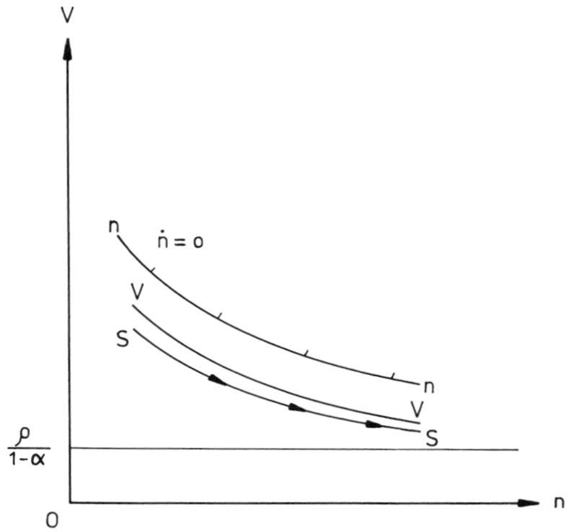

Figure A3.2

of $f(\cdot)$ to approach 1 as n grows large. The nn and VV curves do not intersect in this case. The economy proceeds along the perfect-foresight trajectory SS, which converges asymptotically to VV from below. The value of the stock market and the number of available brands both increase continually along this path, and the economy tends toward a constant growth rate. Evidently innovation can be sustained even with decreasing returns in the accumulation of general knowledge, provided that the ratio of knowledge capital to cumulative research remains sufficiently high.

Next we consider the possibility that $k(n)$ is everywhere an increasing function of n. Increasing returns in the production of knowledge ($f'' > 0$) is necessary but not sufficient for this to be so.[24] We suppose also that (1) $k(n_t)L/\alpha a < \rho/(1-\alpha)$, (2) $k(n)L/\alpha a > \rho/(1-\alpha)$ for n sufficiently large, and (3) $k(n)$ is bounded from above. Figure A3.3 depicts this case. Conditions (1) and (2) ensure the existence of an intersection of nn and the horizontal line at $V = \rho/(1-\alpha)$ in the positive orthant, at a point such as N. Let $\bar{n}$ be the number of varieties at this point. If the economy inherits less than $\bar{n}$ brands, then no innovation occurs and the value of the stock market is forever constant at $\rho/(1-\alpha)$. If the initial number of products exceeds $\bar{n}$, R&D continues forever. The economy travels along the perfect-foresight trajectory labeled SS and converges on the VV curve from above. In the long run the rate of innovation approaches a constant, finite value.

If condition (1) fails so that $k(n_t)L/\alpha a \geq \rho/(1-\alpha)$, then the nn curve emanates from a point on the horizontal axis above $V = \rho/(1-\alpha)$. Under these conditions sustained growth obtains for any initial number of brands. Provided that $k(n)$ is bounded, the growth rate approaches a finite constant in the long run. If, on the

24. If $f(0) = 0$, then $f'' > 0$ is necessary and sufficient for $k'(n)$ positive.

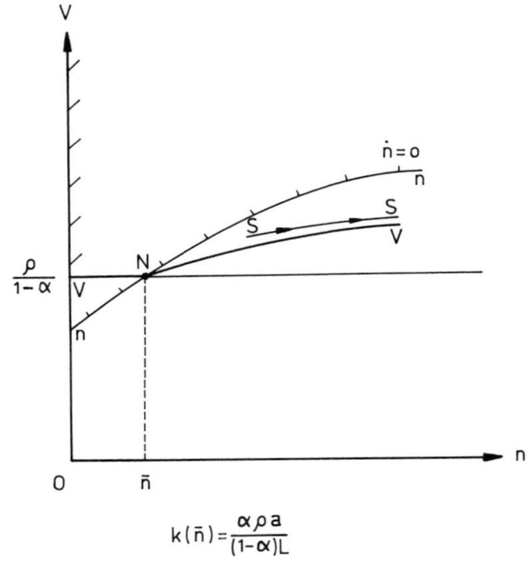

Figure A3.3

other hand, condition (3) is violated so that the ratio of knowledge to R&D grows without bound, then the economy grows in the long run at an ever increasing rate.

A3.2 Lags in the Dissemination of Knowledge

Now we modify the basic model to incorporate lags in the dissemination of general knowledge. We suppose that the contribution of each completed research project to the knowledge capital stock is spread over time. As noted in the main text, we adopt a distributed lag formulation whereby

$$K_n(t) = \kappa \int_{-\infty}^{t} e^{-\kappa(t-\tau)} n(\tau)\, dt, \qquad \kappa > 0. \tag{A3.5}$$

Notice that (A3.5) implies a linear long-run relationship between cumulative research experience and the stock of knowledge capital.

Differentiating (A3.5) with respect to t gives

$$\frac{\dot{K}_n}{K_n} = \kappa\left(\frac{n}{K_n} - 1\right). \tag{A3.6}$$

Since the number of known varieties cannot decline, (A3.5) implies that $K_n \leq n$.[25]

25. Since $n(t) \geq n(\tau)$ for all $t \geq \tau$, (A3.5) implies that

$$K_n(t) \leq \kappa \int_{-\infty}^{t} e^{-\kappa(t-\tau)} n(t)\, d\tau = n(t).$$

Therefore the term in parenthesis in (A3.6) cannot be negative, and so $\dot{K}_n \geq 0$. In our formulation knowledge can accumulate but never disappear.

The resource constraint (A3.1) and the free-entry condition (A3.2) that we derived for the economy with nonlinear knowledge accumulation also apply in the current setting. They give rise to differential equations for the number of brands and the inverse of the aggregate stock-market value that are the same as in appendix A3.1, except that the level of $k \equiv K_n/n$ depends now not only on cumulative experience in R&D but also on the timing of those research activities. For a given n, k will be larger the greater is the time that has passed since the bulk of the research was completed. In place of (A3.3) and (A3.4), we have

$$\frac{\dot{n}}{n} = \begin{cases} k\frac{L}{a} - \alpha V & \text{for } V < k\frac{L}{\alpha a}, \\ 0 & \text{for } V \geq k\frac{L}{\alpha a}, \end{cases} \tag{A3.7}$$

and

$$\frac{\dot{V}}{V} = \begin{cases} V - \frac{kL}{a} - \rho & \text{for } V < k\frac{L}{\alpha a}, \\ (1-\alpha)V - \rho & \text{for } V \geq k\frac{L}{\alpha a}, \end{cases} \tag{A3.8}$$

where k depends now on the entire sequence of product developments.

How does k change through time? From (A3.6) and (A3.7) we can derive

$$\frac{\dot{k}}{k} = \begin{cases} \kappa\left(\frac{1}{k} - 1\right) - k\frac{L}{a} + \alpha V & \text{for } V < k\frac{L}{\alpha a}, \\ \kappa\left(\frac{1}{k} - 1\right) & \text{for } V \geq k\frac{L}{\alpha a}. \end{cases} \tag{A3.9}$$

Now the dynamic equilibrium can be analyzed using the two differential equations (A3.8) and (A3.9).

In figure A3.4 we have drawn the phase diagram for the case of $L/\alpha a > \rho/(1-\alpha)$. This parameter restriction, as before, is needed to make R&D a viable activity. In the figure the ray through the origin with slope $L/\alpha a$ defines the lower boundary of the (shaded) region in which no new products are being introduced (see [A3.7]). In this region the $\dot{V} = 0$ locus, labeled VV, is horizontal and the $\dot{k} = 0$ locus, labeled kk, is vertical. Below the ray both of these curves slope upward, the former being linear and the latter concave. The kk curve has a slope that is everywhere greater than $L/\alpha a$, whereas the VV line is less steep than this ray. So there is a unique point of intersection of the two curves, which represents the steady-state equilibrium for the economy with dissemination lags.

We can use familiar arguments to establish that the saddle path, labeled SS in the figure, represents the only trajectory consistent with fulfilled expectations.

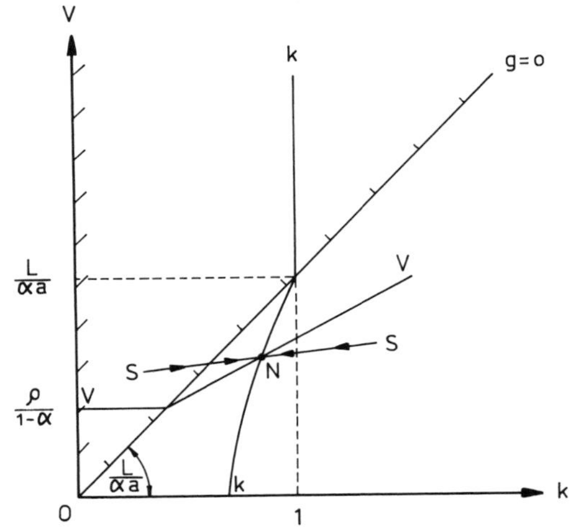

Figure A3.4

Thus the economy converges to the steady state at point N. Evidently, if the inherited ratio of the knowledge stock to experience in R&D falls short of the long-run ratio $\bar{k}$, knowledge accumulates more rapidly than blueprints (so k grows) and the stock market declines in aggregate value over time.[26] Indeed, if k_0 is sufficiently small, there is an initial phase of the dynamic equilibrium during which R&D is unprofitable, and no product development takes place until science "catches up." When the initial knowledge stock happens to be large in comparison to the number of differentiated varieties, the rate of innovation exceeds the rate of growth of knowledge, and the ratio of knowledge capital to blueprints falls along the path to the steady state.

The figure also reveals the behavior of the innovation rate along the equilibrium trajectory. From (A3.7) we see that the rate of innovation is constant (and positive) along lines parallel to and below the ray labeled $g = 0$. In the vicinity of point N, these lines are steeper than the saddle path SS. Therefore the rate of innovation grows over time if point N is approached from below, and falls over time if it is approached from above.

Figure A3.5 can be used to determine the steady-state rate of innovation. In this figure the line VV represents combinations of k and g that imply $\dot{V} = 0$. Using (A3.7) and (A3.8), we derive the equation for this line,

$$g = k(1 - \alpha)\frac{L}{a} - \alpha\rho. \tag{A3.10}$$

26. We must take the initial value of k, namely, k_0, as given, as well as the history of $n(\tau)$ for $\tau < 0$. Our model cannot deal with the "beginning of time," when the stock of knowledge is zero and so R&D is prohibitively costly.

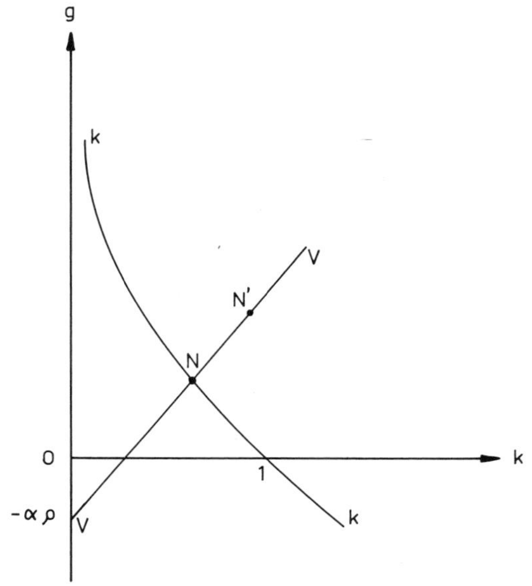

Figure A3.5

We have noted (see footnote 25) that the distributed lag formulation in (A3.5) implies that $K_n < n$, or $k < 1$. By comparing (A3.10) and (3.28) in the main text, we see immediately that, other things equal, an economy with dissemination lags grows less rapidly in the long run than one in which knowledge diffuses instantaneously (in which case $k = 1$). Lags in dissemination affect not only the speed of convergence to the steady state but also the dynamics of the long-run equilibrium.

Next we derive the combinations of k and g that imply a constant ratio of the stock of knowledge capital to the number of differentiated varieties. Using (A3.6), we find

$$g = \kappa\left(\frac{1}{k} - 1\right). \tag{A3.11}$$

This curve, labeled kk in figure A3.5, intersects the VV curve at the steady-state point N. We can verify now that faster assimilation of knowledge means more rapid innovation in the long run. An increase in κ causes the kk curve to rotate in a clockwise direction about its point of intersection with the horizontal axis. The steady-state point shifts up along VV, to a point such as N'. In the limit, as κ approaches infinity, the kk curve becomes vertical, and we are back to the case that was discussed in the main text.

A3.3 Consumer-Surplus and Profit-Destruction Effect

In this appendix we calculate the external benefits and costs created by the introduction of marginally greater variety at time t. We imagine that an external agent (e.g., a Martian) provides an additional product at all times after time t and repatriates all profits that accrue to the extra product. We consider the effects of this perturbation of the equilibrium on the welfare of domestic agents.[27] Our setting is the economy without knowledge spillovers that was described in section 3.1.

For the purpose of these calculations it proves useful to depart from our usual normalization and to use a unit of labor as numéraire instead. Then $w = 1$ and $p = 1/\alpha$ at every moment in time. The effect of the extra variety provided at all moments after t on the welfare of agents other than the external one is found by differentiating (3.6) and using (3.4) and $p(j) = 1/\alpha$. This gives

$$\frac{dU_t}{dn} = \int_t^\infty e^{-\rho(\tau-t)} \frac{1-\alpha}{\alpha} \frac{1}{n(\tau)} d\tau + \int_t^\infty e^{-\rho(\tau-t)} \frac{1}{E(\tau)} \frac{dE(\tau)}{dn(\tau)} d\tau. \qquad \text{(A3.12)}$$

The first term on the right-hand side of (A3.12) is the marginal benefit to consumers at initial prices from the extra diversity in consumption. This term represents the consumer-surplus effect. The second term reflects the effect of the new product on the level of aggregate spending. We will see that spending falls due to a loss in profit income that results from the extra competition of the new brand. Therefore this term represents the profit-destruction effect.

By definition, spending is equal to income minus savings. In a closed economy savings equals investment, so aggregate savings at time τ amounts to $a\dot{n}(\tau)$. Therefore $E(\tau) = L + \Pi(\tau) - a\dot{n}(\tau)$, where L here represents labor income (recall that labor is numéraire) and Π is aggregate profit income. If we imagine that the new, externally provided product does not affect the path of product development, then its effect on aggregate spending matches its effect on the aggregate profits of all (internal) producers. Each producer earns profits of $\pi = E(1-\alpha)/n$ (this is the analog of [3.11] when $E \neq 1$). Thus the loss in profits suffered by the representative producer as a result of the marginal addition to variety is given by

$$\frac{d\pi}{dn} = -\frac{E(1-\alpha)}{n^2} + \frac{1-\alpha}{n}\frac{dE}{dn}.$$

In total, the change in the profits of the n producers other than the external one is given by

$$\frac{d\Pi}{dn} = -\frac{E(1-\alpha)}{n} + (1-\alpha)\frac{dE}{dn}.$$

27. We ignore the profits that accrue to the "extra" product in our calculations because in equilibrium the present discounted value of the returns to the marginal innovation just matches the product development cost. In other words, the *private* return to the marginal innovator contributes nothing to social surplus.

Notice that there is a multiplier effect: Each firm loses profits not only because it must compete with the extra brand but also because other firms lose profits, hence income and spending decline. Now since $dE = d\Pi$, we have

$$\frac{dE}{dn} = -\frac{1-\alpha}{\alpha}\frac{E}{n}. \qquad \text{(A3.13)}$$

Substituting for dE/dn in the second term of (A3.12), it is clear that the profit-destruction effect is equal in magnitude, but opposite in sign, to the consumer-surplus effect.

4 Rising Product Quality

Innovative products often displace earlier vintage goods from the marketplace. Our model of ongoing commercial research in chapter 3 did not capture this characteristic of the innovation process because, for simplicity, we chose to treat new goods and old goods as symmetric there. In this chapter we develop an alternative model of intentional industrial innovation that features endogenous product obsolescence as an outgrowth of continuing technological advancement. Whereas the earlier model associated economic growth with an expansion in the range of industrial products, the new one equates growth with an increase in the average quality of a fixed set of commodities. Clearly the two models describe different aspects of reality, and so should be viewed as complements rather than as substitutes.

As before, we shall assume that technological progress stems from costly investments undertaken by profit-seeking agents. Now entrepreneurs will target their research efforts at particular goods that they see on the market, and attempt to develop superior versions of these goods. When successful in the research lab, an innovator creates a new "state of the art" that captures market share at the expense of a previous generation product. Growth will be sustained if commercial R&D remains an economically viable activity so that the average quality of industrial products continues to rise.[1]

1. This chapter builds on work by Aghion and Howitt (1990) and Segerstrom et al. (1990). These authors have developed models of quality innovation that are similar in spirit to ours. There are some important differences, however. Aghion and Howitt assume that an R&D race plays out at an economywide level and that each successful innovation improves all industrial products. By contrast, Segerstrom et al., like we, envision patent races that take place at the industry level. But they assume that the races occur sequentially so that research labs are active in only one industry at a time. After every innovation, research in an industry ceases for a long period. In the model that we present here, research labs operate continuously, and R&D races occur in many industries simultaneously.

In what follows, we treat quality as unidimensional. Innovative goods are better than older products simply because they provide more "product services" in relation to their cost of production. In this simplified view of product quality, a compact disc player would be regarded as a superior version of the phonograph. The two goods surely perform similar functions of audio reproduction, and the CD player generates less background noise and fewer distortions. Yet our treatment abstracts from the obvious reality that these, like most, sophisticated products are distinguished by more than a single characteristic, and thus consumers may disagree about which is better.

Our model is based on the notion of a *quality ladder*. We suppose that every product potentially can be improved an unlimited number of times, and that each improvement engenders a discrete jump in the level of services that the good provides. Firms that manufacture state-of-the-art products earn positive profits in imperfectly competitive markets. Potential investors foresee these profit opportunities and compare them to the cost of research. In all this the model is similar to that of chapter 3, but with one difference. In the current setting innovators must look ahead to their own eventual demise, since later technical improvements will render their own innovative products obsolete. So, when calculating the expected return to an investment, entrepreneurs must recognize the finite duration of every profit stream.

Technological spillovers play an important role in this model, just as they did before. But the spillovers take a slightly different form here. When an innovator brings a new product to the market, researchers are able to study its attributes. Rivals can then begin their efforts to improve upon the new state of the art, even though they have not succeeded in producing the good themselves. In other words, we assume as before that inventions contribute to a pool of public knowledge and that such knowledge facilitates subsequent innovation. But now we attach bits of public information to particular product lines, rather than make all such information valuable in every research endeavor.

Section 4.1 presents the simplest growth model with quality ladders, where the sizes of the quality increments are taken to be exogenous. We derive the economy's dynamic trajectory and investigate the determinants of the equilibrium growth rate. In the process we discover a striking resemblance between the properties of the dynamic equilibrium and those that characterized the equilibrium in the preceding chapter. Specifically, the two models share identical reduced forms, suggesting that the same forces drive the different forms of innovation. In section 4.2 we extend the model to allow the size of the quality jumps to be determined endogenously. Firms are assumed to weigh the greater cost of more ambitious research projects against the extra profits that they could earn with a greater quality advantage. Finally, in section 4.3 we investigate the normative properties of the dynamic equilibrium, for the cases of both exogenous and endogenous quality increments.

4.1 The Basic Model

We begin with a schematic representation of the model. In figure 4.1 the horizontal axis represents a number of industries indexed by j. Each j corresponds to a different product line, and all such products substitute imperfectly for one another. Expansion of variety will not concern us here, so we take the set of commodities to be fixed through time. In the formal analysis we let j vary continuously in the unit interval; that is, $j \in [0, 1]$.

Each product j potentially can be produced in an unlimited number of vertically differentiated varieties, or "qualities." The figure shows (the log of) quality along the vertical axis. We denote by $q_m(j)$ the quality of the mth generation of product in industry j, and assume that each new generation of product provides exactly λ times as many services as the product of the generation before it. That is, $q_m(j) = \lambda q_{m-1}(j)$ for all m and j, $\lambda > 1$. For now we take λ to be exogenous, constant, and common to all in-

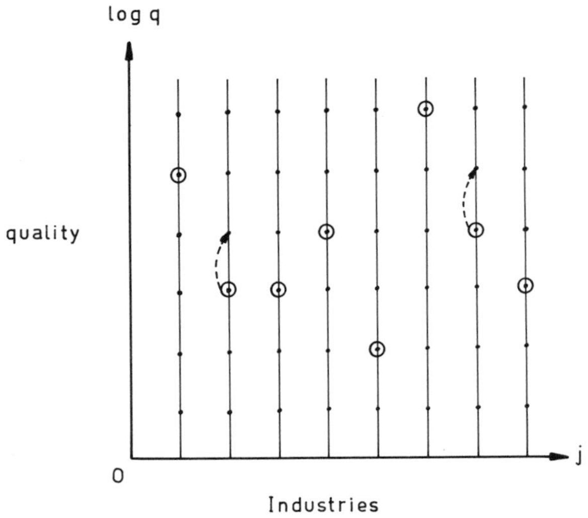

Figure 4.1

dustries. The different generations of products are denoted by heavy dots along the vertical rays in figure 4.1. These dots appear equidistantly along the (logarithmic) quality "ladders."

At a moment in time the most recently invented (and highest quality) product available in every industry defines the state of the art. These top-of-the-line products are marked by circles in the figure. The producers in every industry that have the ability to manufacture the state of the art or some previous generation of product compete as oligopolists. From this competition there emerges a flow of profits to the various producers. These profits reward the firms that have previously enjoyed success in the research lab. At the same time researchers race to bring out the next generation of product in every industry. When some laboratory achieves a technological breakthrough in the line j, the state of the art for that industry jumps by one generation. The breakthroughs are indicated by dotted lines with arrows in the figure. Over time the distribution of state-of-the-art products evolves upward, and with it the well-being of agents in the economy.[2]

Let us turn now to the formal specification, starting with the household sector. Intertemporal preferences take the same form as before (see [2.6] and [3.1]), namely,

$$U_t = \int_t^{\infty} e^{-\rho(\tau - t)} \log D(\tau)\, d\tau. \tag{4.1}$$

A household's instantaneous utility is given by

$$\log D(t) = \int_0^1 \log\left[\sum_m q_m(j) x_{mt}(j)\right] dj, \tag{4.2}$$

where $x_{mt}(j)$ denotes consumption of quality m in product line j at time t. The summation in (4.2) extends over the set of qualities of product j that is available at time t. The highest available quality in each case is the state of the art. We choose units so that the lowest quality of each product (the one available at time $\tau = 0$) offers one unit of service; that is, $q_0(j) = 1$. This implies that $q_m(j) = \lambda^m$.

2. We note that our model could alternatively be interpreted as describing a series of process innovations. With this interpretation, each technological breakthrough causes costs in some product line to fall by a factor of $1/\lambda$. Then the producer with the state-of-the-art technology captures the market by underpricing its rivals in the Bertrand competition. Process and product innovations are similar here because each represents a means by which producers can provide greater "services" at a given cost.

The consumption index in (4.2) has the property that vertically differentiated products in a given industry substitute perfectly for one another, once the appropriate adjustment is made for quality differences. Products of different industries enter utility symmetrically, and the elasticity of substitution between every pair of product lines is equal to one. So households maximize static utility by spreading their expenditure evenly across the (unit measure of) product lines, and by purchasing the single brand $\tilde{m}_t(j)$ in each line that carries the lowest price per unit of quality. This budget allocation yields the static demand functions

$$x_{mt}(j) = \begin{cases} \dfrac{E(t)}{p_{mt}(j)} & \text{for } m = \tilde{m}_t(j), \\ 0 & \text{otherwise,} \end{cases} \tag{4.3}$$

where $E(t)$ again denotes spending at time t and $p_{mt}(j)$ represents the price of quality m of product j at time t. The demands in (4.3) feature unitary price and expenditure elasticities. Aggregate demands take exactly the same form, but with $E(t)$ then representing economywide expenditure.

As before, we can lend an alternative interpretation to (4.2), one that treats this as a production function for a homogeneous good. Under this interpretation final output D is assembled from an assortment of intermediate inputs, each of which can be purchased in a variety of different qualities. Naturally better-quality inputs are more productive in manufacturing the final good. Competition among suppliers of the consumer good leads as before to a price p_D equal to the minimum unit production cost, or

$$p_D = \exp\left\{\int_0^1 \log\left[\frac{\tilde{p}(j)}{\tilde{q}(j)}\right] dj\right\}, \tag{4.4}$$

where $\tilde{p}(j)$ and $\tilde{q}(j)$ are the price and quality, respectively, of the brand $\tilde{m}(j)$ of intermediate input j that bears the lowest quality-adjusted price. With the unit cost function in (4.4), firms that produce D units of the final good use, in the aggregate, $x(j) = Dp_D/\tilde{p}(j)$ units of variety $\tilde{m}(j)$, and no units of any other brand of product j. The aggregate demands in (4.3) follow from the condition for equilibrium in the final goods market, namely $E = p_D D$.

Households face the same intertemporal maximization problem as before. In particular, indirect lifetime (or dynastic) utility again is additively separable in the log of spending and the log of the ideal price index associated with the consumption index D (see [3.6]). We recall from chapter 3 that the optimal spending profile obeys

$$\frac{\dot{E}}{E} = r - \rho, \tag{4.5}$$

and satisfies the intertemporal budget constraint with equality. We again choose aggregate spending to serve as numéraire. Then

$$E(t) = 1 \qquad \text{for all } t, \tag{4.6}$$

and (4.5) implies that

$$r(t) = \rho \qquad \text{for all } t. \tag{4.7}$$

Once a good has been invented in the research lab, producers with the requisite know-how and any applicable patent rights can manufacture it with constant returns to scale. In principle, production costs might vary with the type of product or with its technological generation. Production costs may rise with each new generation, if better-quality products require more sophisticated components. Alternatively, they may fall with each innovation, if new products are manufactured with more streamlined production techniques. For simplicity, however, we shall ascribe identical production technologies to all goods j and to all qualities q. Then with labor as the only primary factor, we can choose units so that one unit of any (producible) good requires one unit of labor input. This makes the marginal cost of every good equal to the wage rate w.

What is the outcome of the oligopolistic competition in industry j? This depends upon market conduct and market structure in the industry. Concerning conduct, we assume that all firms engage in price competition. There are several different market structures for us to consider. First, suppose that two or more firms are able to manufacture the same state-of-the-art product. Then Bertrand competition among equal-cost producers of perfect substitutes implies marginal-cost pricing and zero operating profits. This situation never arises when imitation is costly, and when (as we shall assume here) the ability to produce the current generation of products confers no advantage in developing later generation varieties. No firm would ever devote resources to imitation without prospect of profit or some other benefit from doing so. Alternatively, we could rule out the occurrence of situations with multiple producers of the same good by assuming that the patent laws protect indefinitely a firm's exclusive right to sell the goods that it invents.

Next suppose that one firm has access to the technology for a state-of-the-art product, while another is able to manufacture the product that is one step behind on the quality ladder. We will refer to the former firm as

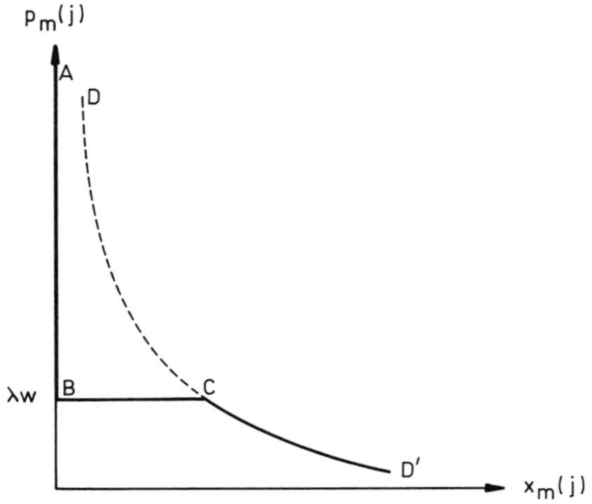

Figure 4.2

the industry "leader" and the latter as the "follower." Suppose, for the moment, that the follower sets a price of w, which is of course the lowest price consistent with nonnegative profits. Then the leader perceives a demand curve such as the one labeled $ABCD'$ in figure 4.2. Consumers, who are willing to pay a premium for the superior, state-of-the-art product, nonetheless prefer the earlier vintage good when the leader's price exceeds λw. Thus demand is zero along the segment AB. On the other hand, when the leader sets a price below λw, its product offers better value than the follower's, and the leader garners all of industry demand. Thus the segment CD' of the industry demand curve DD' represents demand for the leader's product. Finally, when the prices set by the leader and follower correspond exactly after allowing for the quality difference, the leader can sell any amount along the elastic segment BC.

Clearly the leader would not wish to charge any price greater than λw, for sales and profits would be zero in that case. Nor would it wish to charge a price discretely below λw because the unit elasticity of industry demands implies that the firm receives no marginal revenue for its sales beyond C. So the leader responds optimally to its rival's price of w by setting its own price a shade below λw. By doing so, it captures all of industry demand and comes as close to the monopoly price as industry competition allows. Note that the follower's price of w also represents an optimal response to the leader's choice of λw. The follower earns zero profits when charging this amount or higher, while it incurs operating losses when it charges any price below unit cost. We conclude that the technological leader practices "limit pricing" in the Bertrand-Nash equilibrium, thereby driving the follower from the market.

Similar reasoning suggests that if a leader were to hold a k-step quality lead over its nearest rival, it would set a price just below $\lambda^k w$, and the follower would respond optimally with a price of w. We see that the state-of-the-art product carries the lowest quality-adjusted price, regardless of the size of its technological lead. We are justified therefore in using $\tilde{p}(j)$ to denote the price of the leading brand in industry j and $\tilde{q}(j)$ to denote its quality.

We argue below that industry leaders undertake no research in the general equilibrium. In equilibrium the reward from gaining a second (or third, etc.) step on the nearest follower does not justify the research cost. So all innovations are carried out by followers (or outsiders), who then find themselves *exactly* one step ahead of the former leaders that they have displaced. Accepting these assertions as true for the moment, it follows that all products bear the same price $\tilde{p}(j) = p$, where[3]

$$p = \lambda w. \tag{4.8}$$

The price in (4.8) yields the leader sales of $1/\lambda w$ per unit time (see [4.3] and recall that $E = 1$ by choice of numéraire), and a flow of profits given by

$$\pi = 1 - \delta, \tag{4.9}$$

where $\delta \equiv 1/\lambda$.

We specify now the technology for product improvement. We assume that R&D entails uncertain prospects. Any firm that invests resources in this activity at intensity ι for a time interval of length dt will succeed in its attempt to develop the next generation product with probability ιdt. With probability $(1 - \iota dt)$, its efforts will fail and the firm will find itself no better off in terms of its prospects for subsequent success than it would have been had it undertaken no research whatsoever. To achieve an R&D intensity of ι, a firm must invest $a\iota$ units of labor per unit of time.

3. An issue arises here concerning the starting point of the analysis. We assume that every industry has a unique leading firm, which implicitly requires that there has been at least one innovation in each industry prior to time 0. We will show below that with this assumption the economy jumps immediately to a steady state with a constant rate of innovation. Alternatively, we might assume that the economy begins at time 0 with a universally known backstop technology for each good, and with perfect competition in each industry until the first quality improvement takes place. With this alternative assumption, the requirements for sustained innovation are somewhat more stringent than here, but if R&D does continue in the long run, the economy converges to the same steady state.

There are several notable features of this formulation. First, it imposes constant returns to scale in research effort. A research firm's probability of success is strictly proportional to its resource input. Second, as in Lee and Wilde (1980), it implies that R&D is a memoryless process. That is, firms derive no benefit from the cumulation of their unsuccessful research efforts. Finally, our specification implies that newcomers can attempt to develop innovative products without having themselves taken all of the steps in creating the technologies for previous generation products. Implicitly, we assume that researchers gain valuable information by inspecting and analyzing the current state-of-the-art product. In particular, they learn all the properties of the product that must be mastered before the development of the next generation can be pursued. In this sense our specification incorporates a spillover benefit from innovation that is not unlike the one introduced in chapter 3.

Consider now the problem facing a firm that is not a leader in any industry. This firm can target any product for potential improvement. If the ensuing research effort happens to succeed, the firm takes over industry leadership for the chosen product and begins to earn a flow of profits π as given by (4.9). These profits continue until the next research success is achieved (by another firm) in the same product line. The profits in (4.9) do not vary with j. Thus research firms will be indifferent as to the target of their innovation efforts, provided that the expected duration of leadership in all industries is the same. We study here only symmetric equilibria in which all products are targeted to the same aggregate extent. In these equilibria researchers expect future innovations to be as likely in one industry as the next, and so have no reason to prefer entry into any particular product line.

We let v denote the stock market value of an industry-leading firm that is one quality step ahead of its nearest rival. At a cost of $wa\iota dt$, an entrepreneur can purchase a lottery ticket that attains the value v with probability ιdt. The entrepreneur can finance this venture by issuing equity claims that pay nothing in the event that the research effort fails but entitle the claimants to the income stream associated with industry leadership if the effort succeeds. Since the risks associated with individual research efforts are idiosyncratic, well-diversified equity holders will be unanimous in their demands that the entrepreneur maximize the expected net gain from research; that is, a newcomer firm should choose its research intensity to maximize $(v\iota dt - wa\iota dt)$. This requires that $\iota = 0$ whenever $v < wa$ and calls for unbounded research whenever $v > wa$. Positive but finite R&D investments can take place only when $v = wa$. Then individual research firms become indifferent as to the scale of their research efforts. We conclude that

$$wa \geq v, \qquad \text{with equality whenever } \imath > 0. \tag{4.10}$$

This free-entry condition, like (3.14) in chapter 3, relates the value of a firm to the (expected) cost of market entry. It applies when $\imath$ represents the R&D activity of any particular research firm, and also when it denotes the scale of aggregate research effort.

We can show now that extant industry leaders undertake no research. These firms might contemplate investing in R&D in order to attain a two-step quality advantage over their nearest competitors. If successful in such an endeavor, a leader would be able to charge a price of $\lambda^2 w$, as we have seen, and make sales of $1/\lambda^2 w$. This strategy would yield a stream of maximal profits equal to $1 - \delta^2$, which would then continue until the next research success was achieved. But the leader earns profits $\pi = 1 - \delta$ even if it refrains from conducting research. So the *incremental* gain per unit time that rewards a research success by an extant leader amounts to $(1 - \delta^2) - (1 - \delta) = \delta(1 - \delta)$. This reward is strictly smaller than the incremental gain of $1 - \delta$ that accrues to a nonleader who achieves a research success. The supply of nonleaders willing to invest in R&D at the equilibrium rate of interest is perfectly elastic. It follows that the cost of capital in equilibrium will be such that industry leaders find R&D projects to have negative expected present value.[4]

We turn now to the stock-market valuation of profit-making enterprises. As in chapter 3, a no-arbitrage condition relates expected equity returns to the interest rate on a riskless bond. Equity claims pay dividends πdt in a time interval of length dt. The owners of a firm also enjoy capital gains of $\dot{v}dt$ in the event that all of the R&D efforts targeted at the firm's product fail. We use $\imath$ henceforth to denote the *aggregate* intensity of research targeted at a state-of-the-art product, namely, the total amount of labor devoted to improving the typical product divided by the parameter a

4. An extant leader might engage in research for another reason. It might seek thereby to deter rival entrepreneurs from targeting its particular product line for their research efforts. Suppose that a firm's R&D spending were observable but that its success or failure in the laboratory could be kept secret. Then an entrepreneur who has witnessed a leader engage in research knows that with some positive probability the firm has already succeeded in developing the next generation product. The entrepreneur stands to gain nothing from bettering a product that has already been (secretly) improved by the extant leader. So the entrepreneur might elect to target instead a different product for which the perceived probability of preemption were zero. To avoid the issues raised by deterrent research, we assume that the scale of a firm's R&D operations cannot be observed by its rivals. This assumption makes it infeasible for a leader to use research to deter rivals' entry.

reflecting the productivity of labor in research. Then equity owners attain the capital gain $\dot{v}dt$ with probability $(1 - \iota dt)$, since the individual research efforts are statistically independent. On the other hand, with probability ιdt, one of the targeted research efforts will succeed, in which case the extant leader will forfeit all of its income potential and its owners will suffer a capital loss of size v. Summing these various components of the equity return, and neglecting terms of order $(dt)^2$, the (expected) yield on ownership shares in an industry-leading firm totals $(\pi + \dot{v} - \iota v)dt$. Since research outcomes in different industries are (by assumption) uncorrelated, the risks faced by any particular industry leader are idiosyncratic. Therefore shareholders can earn a safe return by holding a well-diversified portfolio of shares of firms in different industries. It follows that the expected return on any stock must equal the return on an equal size investment in a riskless bond, or

$$\pi + \dot{v} - \iota v = rv. \tag{4.11}$$

We close the model by equating labor demand to labor supply. With a research intensity of ι in every industry and a unit measure of industries, total employment in R&D equals $a\iota$. Each industry produces $1/p = \delta/w$ units of output. Each unit of output requires one unit of labor. So δ/w is the aggregate demand for labor by manufacturers. The labor market clears when

$$a\iota + \frac{\delta}{w} = L. \tag{4.12}$$

Of course employment in R&D must be nonnegative. Therefore the equilibrium wage must satisfy

$$w \geq \frac{\delta}{L}. \tag{4.13}$$

We are ready to describe the rational-expectations equilibrium. Equations (4.7), (4.9), and (4.11) imply the following differential equation that guides the value of the typical firm:

$$\frac{\dot{v}}{v} = \iota + \rho - \frac{1 - \delta}{v}. \tag{4.14}$$

Using $V \equiv 1/v$ to represent the inverse of the aggregate value of the stock market (recall that the total measure of profit-making firms equals one in this case), we can rewrite (4.14) as

$$\frac{\dot{V}}{V} = (1 - \delta)V - \iota - \rho. \tag{4.15}$$

When $\iota = 0$, $v \leq wa$ by the free-entry condition (4.10), while $w = \delta/L$ by the full-employment condition (4.12). Therefore we must have $v \leq a\delta/L$ whenever $\iota = 0$. Conversely, whenever $\iota > 0$, $v = wa$ by (4.10). This and (4.13) imply that $v \geq a\delta/L$. Finally, these considerations and (4.12) imply the following equation for the intensity of R&D:

$$\iota = \begin{cases} \dfrac{L}{a} - \dfrac{\delta}{v} & \text{for } v > \dfrac{a\delta}{L}, \\[2ex] 0 & \text{for } v \leq \dfrac{a\delta}{L}. \end{cases} \tag{4.16}$$

Using our change of variables, we can rewrite this equation as

$$\iota = \begin{cases} \dfrac{L}{a} - \delta V & \text{for } V < \dfrac{L}{a\delta}, \\[2ex] 0 & \text{for } V \geq \dfrac{L}{a\delta}. \end{cases} \tag{4.17}$$

We now have a system of one differential equation (4.15) and a side condition (4.17) that together determine the rate of innovation and the (inverse) value of the stock market.

It should be apparent that the system comprising (4.15) and (4.17) is identical to one that we analyzed before. In our model of product innovation with knowledge spillovers, the linear differential equation (3.27) and the side condition (3.26) determined the same two variables (i.e., the rate of innovation and the inverse value of the stock market) as here. The only differences between the corresponding equations involve the replacement of α in our model of product differentiation by δ here, and the replacement of g (the rate of introduction of new products) by ι. We will soon discuss the reasons why these alternative models of innovation happen to yield identical reduced forms. But first let us derive the implications of this finding for the dynamic equilibrium with endogenous quality upgrading.

The same diagrammatic analysis that we presented in figures 3.2 and 3.3 can be applied to the current situation. In figure 4.3 we have replicated figure 3.2, except that ι now replaces g on the horizontal axis and δ replaces α in the expressions for labeled points. In the new figure LL depicts equation (4.17) while VV represents combinations of ι and V for which

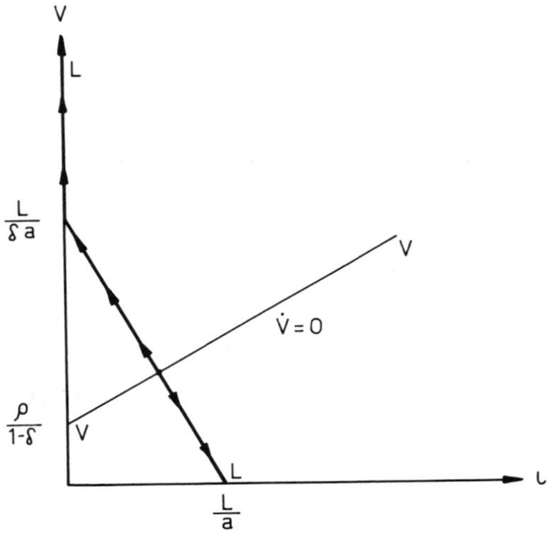

Figure 4.3

$\dot{V} = 0$. The figure applies whenever $L/a > \delta\rho/(1-\delta)$, so the two curves intersect in the positive orthant.

In the case under consideration, the economy jumps immediately to a steady state with $V = L/a + \rho$ and

$$\iota = (1-\delta)\frac{L}{a} - \delta\rho. \tag{4.18}$$

Any other trajectory implies an eventual inconsistency in the stock-market valuation of firms. A trajectory along which ι tends to zero while V grows without bound violates rational expectations, because investors expect the value of the typical firm to approach zero; yet in the absence of any risk of losing its place in the market, each leading firm must have a value of $\pi/\rho = (1-\delta)/\rho > 0$. Similarly a trajectory along which V approaches zero while ι remains positive cannot be self-fulfilling because investors expect claims to industry-leading firms eventually to attain unlimited value; yet with $\iota > 0$ their value can never exceed $(1-\delta)/\rho$.[5]

In the dynamic equilibrium described by equation (4.18), each industry experiences sporadic technological breakthroughs, with the arrival of these

5. In the absence of bubbles in asset prices, the no-arbitrage condition (4.11) implies a value of the firm equal to the expected discounted value of profits. Bubbles cannot arise when infinitely lived households maximize lifetime utility, as we have noted before. With $\pi = 1 - \delta$, $r = \rho$, and $\iota = 0$, the present value of profits is $(1-\delta)/\rho$. The expected present value of profits must be less than this amount when $\iota > 0$.

research successes guided by independent Poisson processes. The model predicts an evolving distribution of product qualities, with individual products continuously swapping relative positions within the distribution. Whereas the time path for technological progress in any particular industry is both lumpy and stochastic, the process of technological advance at the aggregate level is smooth and nonrandom. By the law of large numbers, a constant fraction ι of all products is upgraded at every moment in time. This implies, as we shall see, a constant growth rate g_D of the consumption index D.

To calculate g_D, we substitute (4.3), (4.6), and (4.8) into (4.2) to derive

$$\log D(t) = \int_0^1 \log \tilde{q}_t(j)\,dj - \log w - \log \lambda. \tag{4.19}$$

The wage rate w is constant along the equilibrium trajectory ($w = 1/aV$). So growth in the consumption index stems solely from quality upgrading. These innovations cause the integral on the right-hand side (i.e., the average across industries of the log of the state-of-the-art quality) to grow. We compute the integral as follows. Let $f(m, t)$ denote the probability that a given product will take exactly m steps up the quality ladder in a time interval of length t. Then, because we have a continuum of industries, each following the same Poisson process of technological innovation, the law of large number implies that $f(m, t)$ represents as well the fraction of industries that experiences exactly m quality improvements. Summing over the possible values of m, we have

$$\int_0^1 \log \tilde{q}_t(j)\,dj = \sum_{m=0}^{\infty} f(m, t) \log \lambda^m.$$

We recognize the right-hand side as being equal to the product of $\log \lambda$ and the expected number of improvements in a time interval of length t. But now we can invoke the properties of the Poisson distribution to argue that the expected number of improvements is ιt (Feller 1968, p. 159). Therefore

$$\log D(t) = \iota t \log \lambda - \log w - \log \lambda \tag{4.20}$$

and

$$g_D = \iota \log \lambda. \tag{4.21}$$

From (4.18) and (4.21) we see that the pace of innovation and the rate of growth are faster the larger is the labor force L, the greater is the productivity of labor in R&D (i.e., the smaller is a), and the more patient are households. These results mimic those for the model of expanding product variety in chapter 3, which is not surprising in the light of the similarity in the expressions for the rates of innovation in each case (compare [3.28] and [4.18]). Also output growth is faster in our model of rising product quality, the larger are the steps of the quality ladder. This is true for two reasons. First, an increase in λ augments the incentive for R&D and therefore causes ι to rise. Second, such an increase raises the contribution that each successful research effort makes to aggregate output growth.

The analysis of the case in which $L/a \leq \delta\rho/(1-\delta)$ is the same as for the analogous case in the model of expanding product variety. We need not repeat all of the arguments. Suffice it to say that the economy is forever stagnant under these conditions. No innovation takes place when an economy is too small, too impatient, too unproductive in research, or when circumstances afford too little monopoly profit for a successful research venture.

Why do the alternative models of the innovation process share the same reduced form? Clearly some common features must underlie the two approaches. We have noted already the central role that knowledge spillovers play in making growth sustainable in each case. In both models we have posited constant returns to scale in the research laboratory. This, together with the assumption of free entry into research, implies a cost-based determination of the value of the firm. Also free entry in each case implies a profit rate equal to the real "effective" interest rate. In the model of expanding product variety we saw that the real interest rate was the sum of the nominal interest rate ρ and the rate of innovation g, since prices fell at rate g in the dynamic equilibrium. In the model of this chapter the nominal and real interest rates coincide. But industry leaders face now a constant risk of losing their earnings potential. This raises the *effective* discount rate above the real interest rate by an amount equal to the flow probability of economic demise. The rate of innovation ι reflects the appropriate risk adjustment. Finally, the particular functional forms that we have chosen in each case to represent preferences give rise to similar pricing rules. In the model of product variety, firms practice markup pricing because the elasticity of demand facing each monopolist has been assumed to be a constant. And in the model of quality upgrading, prices also are a fixed multiple of production costs, this time because the proportional quality advantage of each innovator over its nearest price-setting rival has been assumed to be constant.

The similarity in the structures of the two models of innovation and growth will prove useful in several upcoming chapters. This feature will facilitate a unified treatment of a number of topics, including, for example, the effects of resource accumulation on growth (chapter 5), the effects of trade policy on welfare and growth in a small open economy (chapter 6), and the determination of the long-run pattern of trade in a world of dynamic comparative advantage (chapter 7).

4.2 Endogenous Quality Increments

The basic model of the last section can readily be extended to allow firms to choose the size of their quality increments. We follow broadly the approach taken by Aghion and Howitt (1990, sec. 6). Suppose, as before, that an entrepreneur who undertakes R&D at intensity ι for a time interval of length dt achieves success in the research lab with probability ιdt. Now, however, suppose that the resource cost of the research effort depends upon the size of the innovation that the entrepreneur pursues. In particular, research at intensity ι requires $a(\lambda)\iota$ units of labor per unit time when the entrepreneur attempts to develop a product that provides λ times as many services as the state of the art. We assume that $a' > 0$ and $a'' > 0$.

Entrepreneurs now must choose both the scale of their operations and the size of their quality increments. To find the optimal choices, we consider the maximization of the expected net benefit from R&D. Let $v(\lambda)$ represent the stock market value of a firm whose product provides λ times as many services as the brand of its nearest competitor. Then an entrepreneur chooses ι and λ at every moment to maximize $\iota v(\lambda)dt - wa(\lambda)\iota dt$. The optimal choice of quality increment satisfies the first-order condition

$$v'(\lambda) = wa'(\lambda), \tag{4.22}$$

which equates the marginal benefit from a larger innovation to the marginal cost of achieving it. Larger innovations yield greater benefits because the stock market values more highly firms that enjoy wider quality leads over their nearest rivals.

As before, the maximization of net benefits from R&D with respect to the choice of research intensity yields either a corner solution or a condition of indifference. In the event that the R&D sector operates at a positive but finite scale, we must have equality between the value of a firm and the (expected) cost of developing the associated technological lead in the research lab:

$$v(\lambda) = wa(\lambda) \qquad \text{if } \iota > 0. \tag{4.23}$$

With the value given in (4.23), each individual entrepreneur becomes indifferent as to its research intensity, since net benefits are zero in any event. But, as in the previous formulation, the general equilibrium does determine the *aggregate* rate of innovation.

To calculate the optimal choice of λ for each entrepreneur, it proves convenient to assume provisionally that the economy jumps immediately to a steady state. We can check subsequently that this assumption is warranted. In the steady state the no-arbitrage condition (4.11) can be used to calculate the relationship between the value of the firm and the magnitude of its quality lead over its nearest industry rival. If v, π, $\imath$, and ρ do not vary over time, then (4.11), (4.7), and (4.9) imply that

$$v(\lambda) = \left(1 - \frac{1}{\lambda}\right)\left(\frac{1}{\imath + \rho}\right). \tag{4.24}$$

That is, each firm has a value equal to the *expected* discounted value of its constant stream of profits $\pi = 1 - 1/\lambda$. In computing this present value, the market uses the "effective" (or risk-adjusted) discount rate $\imath + \rho$, which accounts for the constant flow probability that the profit stream will come to an end at any moment.

We can use (4.24) now to calculate $v'(\lambda)$. Substituting the result into the first-order condition (4.22) and using (4.23) and (4.24), we find

$$\frac{1}{\lambda - 1} = \frac{\lambda a'(\lambda)}{a(\lambda)}. \tag{4.25}$$

This equation determines the optimal quality increment from properties of the research technology alone. The right-hand side is the elasticity of the resource requirement with respect to the size of the attempted innovation. The condition states that the larger is this elasticity, the smaller will be each step up the quality ladder.

Having determined the size of λ under the assumption that the economy jumps immediately to a steady state, it is easy to verify that this assumption indeed is valid. No further algebra is necessary. Since the equilibrium conditions derived in section 4.1 were shown to hold for an arbitrary, constant value of λ, they must apply for the particular value of λ that satisfies (4.25). We have seen already that these conditions require an instantaneous transition to the steady state. Therefore the transition to the steady state is immediate here as well.[6]

6. It is possible, as before, that the equilibrium will involve zero growth. If the cost of quality improvements is such that the profit-maximizing step size is small, we may have $\imath = 0$ in the steady state. Ongoing innovation requires $\lambda > 1 + a(\lambda)\rho/L$ for the value of λ that satisfies (4.25).

4.3 Welfare

We examine now the welfare properties of the equilibrium growth path. We begin with the basic model of section 4.1, where the size of each increment to product quality is given exogenously. Our interest lies in the optimal frequency of quality improvements. Afterward we return to the extended model of section 4.2, in order to compare the size of innovations that are determined by market forces to the socially optimal innovation size.

Exogenous λ

We seek the dynamic allocation of resources that maximizes the utility of the representative household given in (4.1). As in the welfare analysis of chapter 3, the social planner's problem can be decomposed into separate static and dynamic resource allocation problems.

The Static Allocation Problem

In the static problem we take the allocation of the work force to the research and manufacturing activities as given, and ask what is the optimal division of labor among the various industries. Let X denote once again the aggregate employment in manufacturing. Then the static problem is to maximize the instantaneous utility indicator (4.2) subject to the constraint that

$$\int_0^1 \left[\sum_m x_m(j) \right] dj \leq X. \tag{4.26}$$

Of course at any moment the choice of $x_m(j)$ extends over only those varieties that can feasibly be produced at that time.

Since all varieties of any product require the same input of labor, it is obvious that the planner produces only state-of-the-art varieties. Then (4.2) reduces to

$$\log D(t) = \int_0^1 \log \tilde{q}_t(j)\, dj + \int_0^1 \log \tilde{x}_t(j)\, dj, \tag{4.27}$$

where $\tilde{q}_t(j)$ and $\tilde{x}_t(j)$ are the quality (as before) and quantity of the state-of-the-art variety in industry j. Clearly the maximization of $D(t)$ subject to (4.26) requires an equal allocation of employment to all industries; $x_t(j) = X(t)$ for $j \in [0, 1]$. This allocation is the same as obtains in the market equilibrium.

The Dynamic Allocation Problem

Next we derive the optimal dynamic allocation of labor to research and manufacturing. Our objective is to maximize the utility indicator (4.1). To this end, we require an expression for $\log D(\tau)$ that applies when the allocation of resources to each industry has been optimal at every moment of time up to τ. From (4.27) the maximal value of $\log D(\tau)$ has two components. The first depends on the entire past history of allocations to R&D. The second depends only upon the static allocation. We have seen earlier in this chapter that $\int_j \log \tilde{q}_\tau(j)dj$ is equal to the product of $\log \lambda$ and the expected number of quality improvements that take place in an industry in a time interval of length τ. Improvements occur in each industry according to a time-varying Poisson process with instantaneous arrival rate $\imath(s)$. Then the expected number of successes before time τ equals $I(\tau) \equiv \int_0^\tau \imath(s)ds$. This fact, together with what we know to be the optimal allocation of resources across industries, allows us to write the maximand as

$$U_t = \int_t^\infty e^{-\rho(\tau-t)}[\log X(\tau) + (\log \lambda)I(\tau)]\,d\tau. \tag{4.28}$$

We maximize (4.28) subject to the dynamic equation

$$\dot{I}(\tau) = \imath(\tau), \tag{4.29}$$

the nonnegativity constraint $\imath(\tau) \geq 0$, and the resource constraint

$$a\imath(\tau) + X(\tau) = L \qquad \text{for all } \tau. \tag{4.30}$$

We can treat this as a problem of optimal control, analogous to the ones that we solved in section 3.4. We use (4.28)–(4.30) to form the current value Hamiltonian,

$$\mathscr{H} = \log X + (\log \lambda)I + \theta\left(\frac{L - X}{a}\right), \tag{4.31}$$

where θ again is a costate variable, this time representing the shadow value of a quality improvement. From (4.31) we derive the necessary and sufficient conditions for a maximum that apply whenever the nonnegativity constraint $\imath(\tau) \geq 0$ does not bind. These conditions comprise (4.30),

$$\frac{1}{X} = \frac{\theta}{a}, \tag{4.32}$$

$$\dot{\theta} = \rho\theta - \log \lambda, \tag{4.33}$$

and the transversality condition

$$\lim_{t\to\infty} e^{-\rho t}\theta(t)I(t) = 0. \tag{4.34}$$

The solution to (4.33) and (4.34) requires that $\theta(\tau) = (\log \lambda)/\rho$ for all τ, that is, a constant shadow value of quality improvements. Substituting this value of θ into (4.32), and using (4.30) we find the optimal rate of innovation

$$\iota^* = \frac{L}{a} - \frac{\rho}{\log \lambda}. \tag{4.35}$$

When the right-hand side of (4.35) is negative, the nonnegativity constraint binds and all labor should be devoted to manufacturing. In any event the optimal dynamic allocation of labor to manufacturing and R&D does not vary over time. The optimal rate of innovation is larger (if positive), the larger is the labor force, the smaller is the subjective discount rate, the larger are the steps of the quality ladder, and the more productive is labor in the industrial research laboratory.

We can depict the optimal allocation graphically using a diagram similar to the one that we developed in section 3.4. When the rate of innovation and the employment of labor in manufacturing are constant, lifetime utility in (4.28) can be expressed as

$$\rho U_t = \log X + \frac{\iota}{\rho}\log \lambda + I(t)\log \lambda. \tag{4.36}$$

In figure 4.4 we show a representative level curve for U_t. This curve, representing a preference trade-off between current consumption and the rate of improvement of average product quality, has the usual shape for an indifference curve. The resource constraint (4.30) implies a linear relationship between feasible levels of current consumption and rates of innovation. We show this constraint as RR in the figure. The optimum is found at E^*, the point of tangency between RR and the indifference curve.

We wish to compare the optimal and equilibrium allocations. As we have noted already, the market provides an efficient division of resources to the various industries j at any point in time. This particular finding relies, as it did in section 3.4, on the assumed absence of any competitive sectors of the economy. If such sectors existed, then the market equilibrium would entail too little output of the innovative products because these goods are priced above their marginal cost of production. Concerning the division of resources between manufacturing and R&D, we refer again to figure 4.4.

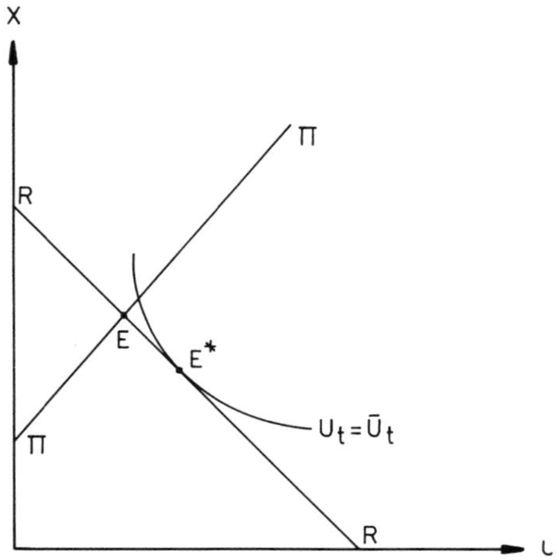

Figure 4.4

The resource constraint RR applies also to the market equilibrium. The equilibrium allocation is found at the intersection of this line and another, labeled ΠΠ, representing the no-arbitrage condition. The equation for ΠΠ is derived by substituting $V = 1/wa = X/\delta a$ into (4.15) and noting that $\dot{V} = 0$ in the steady state. This gives

$$\frac{(1-\delta)X}{\delta a} = \iota + \rho, \tag{4.37}$$

which equates once again the rate of profit to the effective interest rate. The market equilibrium is found at point E.

We show now that point E may lie above or below point E^* along RR. In other words, the market rate of innovation may be too high or too low.[7] Our demonstration of this makes use of figure 4.5. In this figure we have plotted the curve for $\lambda/(\lambda - 1)$. This curve must fall below the horizontal line at height $L/\rho a + 1$ if innovation is to take place in the market equilibrium.[8] Therefore $\iota = 0$ for $\lambda \leq \lambda_0$ in the figure, and $\iota > 0$ for $\lambda > \lambda_0$. Next we use (4.18) and (4.35) to compute

$$\iota^* - \iota = \frac{\rho}{\lambda}\left(\frac{L}{\rho a} + 1 - \frac{\lambda}{\log \lambda}\right), \tag{4.38}$$

7. Aghion and Howitt (1990) have shown that the equilibrium growth rate also can exceed the optimal rate in their (related) model of product innovation.

8. Recall that $\iota > 0$ if and only if $L/a\delta > \rho/(1-\delta)$. This condition is equivalent to the one described in the text.

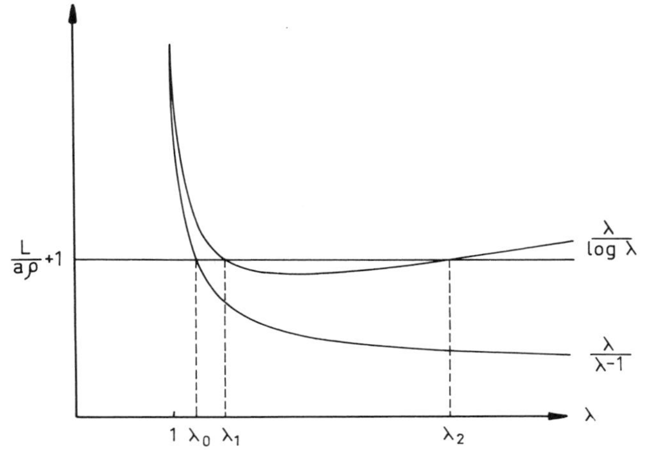

Figure 4.5

which holds whenever both ι and ι^* are positive. Figure 4.5 depicts the curve for $\lambda/\log\lambda$. When this curve lies below the line through $L/\rho a + 1$, the term in parenthesis in (4.38) is positive. This occurs for $\lambda \in (\lambda_1, \lambda_2)$ in the figure. Then $\iota^* > \iota$. For $\lambda \in (\lambda_0, \lambda_1)$ and $\lambda > \lambda_2$, on the other hand, the term in parenthesis is negative. Then $\iota > \iota^*$. We conclude that the market incentives for R&D are insufficient in this economy when the steps of the quality ladder are of intermediate size, but they are excessive when the steps are either quite small or quite large.

This finding stands in contrast to our results in section 3.4. There we found that the market incentives for product development always are insufficient when industrial research generates technological spillovers. The different conclusion can be understood with reference to the prevailing market distortions that we have identified before. A successful innovator generates three external effects that cause the private and social incentives for R&D to diverge. These are (1) a positive spillover for consumers of the innovative product (the consumer-surplus effect); (2) a negative spillover for existing producers (the profit-destruction effect); and (3) a further external benefit that arises due to the knowledge spillover to later innovators (the intertemporal-spillover effect). The two positive spillovers generated by any innovation accrue directly to households. The consumer-surplus benefit is reflected in the fact that consumers pay the same price for a product in a particular line after an innovation occurs as before, but they obtain greater consumer services afterward. The intertemporal benefit is realized after the new product becomes obsolete, when future generations of innovations build upon the higher-quality product. The combined discounted value of these two benefits is equal to $(\log \lambda)/\rho$. The negative spillover from an innovation arises because the displaced leader forfeits a stream of monopoly profits. This causes a windfall loss for owners of the displaced firm, who at every moment expect to receive their profits with probability $1 - \iota dt$. Also, the loss of profit income means less demand for other state-of-the-art products, hence reduced profits for the owners of these other firms. In the appendix we show that the present value of the pecuniary externality imposed upon shareholders of other firms equals $(\lambda - 1)/(\iota + \rho)$. If this adverse effect happens to outweigh the beneficial spillover to consumers, as it certainly will when λ is near one or very large, then the private incentives for R&D are too great in the market equilibrium.

As before, the optimal growth path can be achieved as a market outcome if the government introduces a policy that causes entrepreneurs to face the appropriate incentives to innovate. In this case the optimal policy may be either a tax or subsidy to R&D. Suppose the government pays a fraction ϕ of research expenses, where $\phi < 0$ represents a tax on R&D. With such a policy in place, each entrepreneur faces private R&D costs per unit of research intensity equal to $(1 - \phi)wa$. From the entrepreneur's point of view, this is exactly like a change in the unit input requirement from a to $(1 - \phi)a$. The no-arbitrage condition becomes, instead of (4.37),

$$\frac{(1-\delta)X}{\delta a(1-\phi)} = \iota + \rho. \tag{4.37'}$$

The effect of the policy then is to rotate the $\Pi\Pi$ curve in figure 4.4. Clearly the government can achieve any point along RR, including the optimum at E^*, by an appropriate choice of ϕ. When $\iota^* < \iota$, a tax on R&D will be required.

Optimal λ

Suppose now that the social planner can choose the size of each step on the quality ladder. Recognizing that the optimal choices of innovation frequency and size will not vary over time, we can state the problem as one of maximizing the right-hand side of (4.36), subject to the resource constraint

$$a(\lambda)\iota + X = L. \tag{4.39}$$

Again we can substitute for X from the resource constraint and solve a problem that has $\iota \geq 0$ and $\lambda \geq 0$ as the only constraints. The first-order conditions for this problem imply that (at an interior optimum)

$$\frac{\log \lambda^*}{\rho} = \frac{a(\lambda^*)}{L - a(\lambda^*)\iota^*}, \tag{4.40}$$

$$\frac{a'(\lambda^*)\iota^*}{L - a(\lambda^*)\iota^*} = \frac{\iota^*}{\rho\lambda^*}, \tag{4.41}$$

where ι^* and λ^* are the optimal rate and size of innovation, respectively.

The first of these conditions can be rearranged to yield the following expression for the optimal rate of innovation:

$$\iota^* = \frac{L}{a(\lambda^*)} - \frac{\rho}{\log \lambda^*}. \tag{4.42}$$

This equation is the same as (4.35), except that now the expression on the right-hand side must be evaluated at the optimal λ^*. The second condition can be rewritten, using (4.40), as

$$\frac{\lambda^* a'(\lambda^*)}{a(\lambda^*)} = \frac{1}{\log \lambda^*}. \tag{4.43}$$

This equation determines the optimal size of innovation as a function of properties of the technology for product improvement alone.

We compare the equilibrium and optimal sizes of innovation with the aid of figure 4.6. The equilibrium value of λ is found where the elasticity of $a(\lambda)$

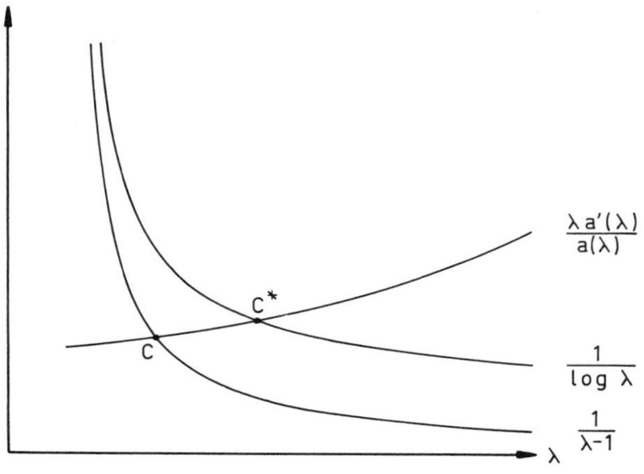

Figure 4.6

is equal to $1/(\lambda - 1)$, at a point such as C in the figure (see [4.25]). The optimum occurs where this same elasticity is equal to $1/\log \lambda$, at C^*. Note that $1/(\lambda - 1) < 1/\log \lambda$ for all $\lambda > 1$. The elasticity of $a(\lambda)$ may be an increasing or a decreasing function of λ, but if decreasing, it must intersect the $1/(\lambda - 1)$ schedule from below. It follows that point C^* must lie to the right of point C. In other words, market forces give rise to quality steps that are *smaller* than is optimal.

It should be noted that the optimal size of innovation cannot be decentralized by means of a simple tax or subsidy policy. Consider, for example, the effects of an ad valorem subsidy to output at rate ϕ_x on the entrepreneur's choice of λ. The subsidy causes a firm with a quality lead of λ over its nearest rival to charge a price $p(\lambda) = \lambda w/(1 + \phi_x)$ because the rival can profitably undercut any price above this level. With this price the leader makes sales of $x(\lambda) = (1 + \phi_x)/\lambda w$, and earns subsidy-inclusive profits of $\pi(\lambda) = (1 + \phi_x)(1 - \delta)$. Its stock-market value becomes $v(\lambda) = (1 + \phi_x)(1 - \delta)/(\iota + \rho)$. Then the first-order condition (4.25) for the entrepreneur's optimal choice of λ requires

$$\frac{1 + \phi_x}{\lambda^2(\iota + \rho)} = wa'(\lambda).$$

When we substitute for $w = v(\lambda)/a(\lambda)$ using (4.23), we find that this first-order condition requires the same choice of λ as in (4.25), irrespective of the subsidy rate ϕ_x.

Consider, instead, a policy whereby the government bears a fraction ϕ of the R&D costs. This policy has no effect on the relationship between the value of the firm and the size of its technological lead. However, the subsidy reduces the private cost of R&D that enters the net-benefit calculation, and so alters the entrepreneur's first-order condition to

$$v'(\lambda) = w(1 - \phi)a'(\lambda).$$

The relationship between R&D costs and the value of the firm also changes. In place of (4.23), free entry now implies that

$$v(\lambda) = w(1 - \phi)a(\lambda).$$

Combining these two and using (4.24), we find that (4.25) continues to hold; the choice of step size also is not affected by a subsidy to R&D.

In order to influence the entrepreneur's choice of quality increment, the government would need a policy instrument that directly rewarded larger innovations. Such policies might be difficult to design. The government could, perhaps, use patent policy for this purpose. Governments often set novelty requirements whereby patents are granted only to products that are sufficiently different from existing varieties.[9] In our context, if novelty were defined in terms of the size of the quality improvement over the existing generation of product, and if imitation were costless in the absence of patent protection, then a policy of minimum novelty requirements could be used to regulate higher values of λ.

If the government lacks the ability to alter the size of innovations because it cannot differentially reward larger advances, then its optimal choice of innovation frequency will be affected as well. In place of the first-best problem whose solution is given by the joint satisfaction of (4.40) and (4.41), the government faces under these circumstances a second-best problem with λ given. The second-best optimal rate of innovation satisfies a first-order condition such as (4.40), but with the equilibrium value of λ in place of the first-best λ. In general, the second-best rate of innovation may be higher or lower than the first-best rate.

This chapter has developed a model of endogenous innovation that complements the one presented in chapter 3. Here, entrepreneurs race to bring out the next generation of a continuum of products. Each research success brings a step up the "quality ladder" in the targeted industry. Entrepreneurs invest in research in order to capture the quasi-rents from having a (temporary) technological lead in their industry. In making their investment decisions, the entrepreneurs recognize that, eventually, they too will be displaced by (further) innovations.

There are many similarities between the models in the two chapters. Each predicts faster growth when the resource base is larger, when inputs are more productive in the research lab, when agents are more patient, and when society values innovative products more highly. In fact in the one-sector variants that we have described so far, the alternative specifications yield identical reduced forms. The two models do diverge, however, when it comes to normative issues. We established in section 4.3 that quality upgrading may take place either too quickly or too slowly. By contrast, we saw that the economy with knowledge spillovers in chapter 3 always introduces new products less rapidly than is optimal.

9. Green and Scotchmer (1989) study the role of such policies in a partial-equilibrium model of endogenous R&D.

APPENDIX

A4.1 Externalities from Product Upgrading

In this appendix we calculate the external benefits and costs associated with the marginal innovation in the model of quality upgrading. As in appendix A3.3 we imagine that an external agent has achieved a single technological breakthrough, this time representing an improvement in quality in some product line j at time t. We perturb the market equilibrium by dI at every moment in time after t (thereby preserving the initial path of innovation) and compute the impact on the welfare of actors other than the one who collects the profits from the marginal innovation.

Once again, it proves useful for the purpose of these calculations to use a unit of labor as numéraire. Then $w = 1$ and $p = \lambda$. The effect of the extra product improvement on the welfare of agents other than the external one is found by differentiating (4.28) with respect to I. Noting that $pX = E$ so that $X = E/\lambda$, we have

$$\frac{dU_t}{dI} = \int_t^{\infty} e^{-\rho(\tau-t)} \log \lambda \, d\tau + \int_t^{\infty} e^{-\rho(\tau-t)} \frac{1}{E(\tau)} \frac{dE(\tau)}{dI(\tau)} d\tau. \tag{A4.1}$$

This equation is analogous to (A3.12). The first term on the right-hand side of (A4.1) is the marginal benefit to households at initial prices from consuming indefinitely a product of higher quality.[10] This combines the consumer-surplus effect and the intertemporal-spillover effect. The discounted value of these two positive externalities is $(\log \lambda)/\rho$. The second term reflects the effect of the new product on aggregate spending by agents other than the external one. Since these agents suffer a loss of profit income, their spending falls in response to the extra innovation.

Spending equals total income minus savings, and savings equals investment in a closed economy. So $E(\tau) = L + \Pi(\tau) - a\iota$, where $\Pi(\tau)$ is aggregate profit income accruing to all innovative products other than the single, externally provided one. Since we take the (constant) rate of quality upgrading to be unaffected by the introduction of the marginal product at time t, the change in spending at all times $\tau > t$ matches again the change in profit income (see appendix A3.3).

Consider now the loss in profits in the industry j where the "extra" innovation has taken place. In the event that there has been no further quality upgrade in that industry before time τ, the economy forfeits profits equal to $(1 - 1/\lambda)E$ at time τ. There will also be a multiplier effect since the profit shortfall in industry j induces a cut in aggregate spending and so a reduction in sales and income in other industries. The aggregate change in profit income, including the multiplier effect, is $d\Pi/dI = -(1 - 1/\lambda)E + (1 - 1/\lambda)dE/dI$. Nothing that $d\Pi = dE$, aggregate spending is reduced by $(\lambda - 1)E$ at time τ if no research success has occurred

10. Consumers enjoy a higher-quality good during the tenure of the new product as industry leader and also after it has been replaced by later generation products. The latter products are one quality increment better than they would have been had their inventors not had the technology of the "extra" innovation to build upon.

in industry j subsequent to the externally generated innovation. The probability of there occurring no research success between t and τ is given by $e^{-\iota(\tau-t)}$, in view of the Poisson process for research breakthroughs in every industry. Thus the expected decline in aggregate spending at time $\tau \geq t$, which results from the marginal innovation at time t, equals

$$\frac{dE(\tau)}{dI(\tau)} = -E(\tau)(\lambda - 1)e^{-\iota(\tau-t)}. \tag{A4.2}$$

Now we can susbstitute (A4.2) into the second term in (A4.1) and compute the integral. We find that the utility loss associated with the profit-destruction effect measures $(\lambda - 1)/(\iota + \rho)$. The equilibrium rate of innovation is $\iota = (1 - 1/\lambda)L/a - \rho/\lambda$ (see [4.18]). So (A4.1) becomes

$$\frac{dU_t}{dI} = \frac{\log \lambda}{\rho} - \frac{\lambda}{L/a + \rho}.$$

Clearly this expression has the same sign as the expression for the difference between the optimal and market rates of innovation in (4.38). The market rate of innovation is less than the optimal rate if and only if the combined consumer-surplus and intertemporal-spillover effect outweighs the profit-destruction effect.

5 Factor Accumulation

In chapters 3 and 4 we departed from traditional growth theory in our treatment of the factors of production. Whereas the traditional theories give pride of place to the processes of physical and human capital formation, we emphasized instead the accumulation of disembodied knowledge. As we discussed at length in chapter 1, knowledge differs from other forms of capital in one important respect. Whereas the application of the services of skilled workers and capital equipment in one use necessarily precludes the simultaneous application of these services in additional uses, there exist no such constraints on the widespread use of knowledge. This unique characteristic of knowledge (in degree, if not in kind) has important implications for the sustainability of growth. The diminishing returns that undoubtedly apply to the accumulation of "ordinary" capital in an environment with fixed stocks of primary resources need not apply to the accumulation of knowledge. In principle, at least, a doubling of knowledge can double output even if primary inputs are held constant because the same bits of knowledge may be used to make each and every input more productive.

In developing our theory of growth based on innovation, we chose to push the more familiar vehicles for accumulation into the background. In fact we made R&D the sole form of investment, and a primary input that we called "labor" the sole factor of production. It is time now to see how the different accumulation processes relate to one another and to show how the new theory can be integrated with the old. Our inquiry in this chapter has three distinct components. First, we introduce opportunities for investment in plant and equipment, and study the interaction between endogenous innovation and capital formation. Second, we allow for the possibility that individual agents will choose to acquire specialized skills and technical training, and examine the special role that human capital can play in the generation of new technologies. Finally, we investigate the relationship between the size and composition of an economy's steady-state factor supply and its long-run rates of innovation and growth.

The modern growth experiences of many different countries share the common characteristic that accumulation of physical capital goods is a strong concomitant to growth in per capita income. Empirical researchers regularly find in cross-country and panel data sets a statistically significant partial correlation between the share of investment in GDP, or the rate of growth in the capital stock, and the rate of growth in per capita income.[1] These regularities have been so persistent in the data, and so pronounced, that a whole generation of growth theorists was led to study capital accumulation as the driving force behind income growth. But correlations reveal little about causation. Capital accumulation might occur mostly in *response* to knowledge accumulation, as technological innovations raise the marginal productivity of capital and so make investment in machinery and equipment more profitable. Indeed, this is the conclusion we draw from our analysis in section 5.1, where we introduce opportunities for investment in machinery into the two canonical models of endogenous innovation from chapters 3 and 4. Our finding that innovation drives investment is at least consistent with another bit of cross-country evidence, namely, the high positive correlation between the growth rate of the capital stock (or the ratio of investment to GDP) and the realized gain in total factor productivity, which has been noted by Baumol et al. (1989). Moreover it is supported by evidence reported in Lach and Schankerman (1989) that, at the firm level, R&D Granger-causes investment, but investment does not Granger-cause R&D.

Growth in per capita income has also been found to correlate positively with a country's stock of human capital (e.g., as proxied by the literacy rate or school enrollment rate; see Romer 1989b; Barro 1989b). While this evidence is consistent with our results in chapters 3 and 4, that greater resources imply faster growth, our one-factor model with an exogenous supply of primary inputs hardly does justice to a reality in which advances in technology are most often engineered by highly trained individuals who have invested heavily in the development of their technical skills. Since unskilled workers generally substitute quite imperfectly for skilled labor in generating new knowledge and ideas, a model that distinguishes at least these two inputs will be necessary before we can draw any conclusions

1. See Dowrick and Nguyen (1989), Romer (1989a), and Barro (1989a, b) for recent evidence of this sort.

about the special role that education and training may play in the growth process.

In section 5.2 we endogenize the stock of human capital in a two-factor model of innovation and growth. We depart from some authors (e.g., Lucas 1988; Ohyama 1989) in taking the view that a finite population of individuals can accumulate only a bounded quantity of human capital. The finite duration of an individual's lifetime limits the number of specialized skills that he or she can acquire. Disembodied knowledge, on the other hand, conceivably could grow without bound.[2] To some extent the distinction between our approach and the others is semantic, reflecting a difference in what is termed "human capital," and what "knowledge." Even in our model the *value* of human capital can grow indefinitely as the acquired cognitive skills (e.g., the ability to perform and interpret calculations or the ability to construct flow charts) are combined with ever more sophisticated technologies. But the distinction becomes important when it comes to modeling the incentives that exist for private investments in schooling and training, on the one hand, and in applied science and product development, on the other. In any event our model of education and innovation in section 5.2 features a steady-state equilibrium with a constant (but endogenous) *level* of human capital and a constant *rate* of technological progress.

Section 5.3 addresses the relationship between the size and composition of a country's factor endowment and its long-run rate of growth. A literal interpretation of this comparative statics exercise might regard countries as differing in their stocks of such natural resources as arable land, petroleum reserves, and mineral deposits, or in their populations of unskilled labor. But the model of section 5.2 enables a broader interpretation. Countries may differ in their literacy rates, their average years of schooling, or in their numbers of scientists and engineers. These differences may arise due to different societal attitudes (tastes) toward education, different technologies of schooling or training, or because governments have followed idiosyncratic policies regarding human capital development. Section 5.2 shows how these long-run differences in educational and skills attainment may emerge endogenously. Then the comparative statics exercises carried out in section 5.3 allow us to predict how differences in stocks of human capital impinge upon countries' relative growth performances.

2. Romer (1989b, 1990) emphasizes the distinction between the human capital embodied in an individual and the disembodied knowledge that outlives the individual. He argues that the former component of knowledge is subject to rivalry (because the individual can be in only one place at a time), while the latter is not.

In the preceding chapters we found that, ceteris paribus, larger economies devote more resources to R&D than smaller ones, and as a result they innovate more and grow faster. When we generalize to economic environments with more than one factor of production, we find that the same results apply to economies that differ uniformly in their supplies of all inputs. But the composition of a country's factor bundle also matters for its long-run rate of expansion. A country that has more human capital, for example, will innovate faster than another with less of this input because human capital is used intensively in the industrial research lab. But an abundance of the factors used intensively in sectors that generate little or no innovation may in fact be detrimental to long-run growth.

5.1 Physical Capital

Physical capital could be introduced into the models of chapters 3 and 4 in several different ways. Capital goods might be homogeneous or differentiated, and they might be used in the production of intermediate goods, or final goods, or both. For simplicity, we pursue only one possible variant here. We assume that innovative products are intermediate inputs into the production of a single, final good. The final good Y can be consumed by households or purchased by firms as capital equipment. The technology for producing final output requires, besides intermediates, the input of "labor" and of "machinery." Intermediates are produced by labor alone, and labor also is the sole input into R&D.[3]

The intermediate goods here may be horizontally differentiated, as in the model of chapter 3, or they may be vertically differentiated, as in the model of chapter 4. In the former case an expansion of the available variety of intermediates augments total factor productivity in the final goods industry. These productivity gains stem from increased specialization in production. In the latter case improvements in the quality of the inputs also raise productivity in the sector that manufactures final goods. We find that our conclusions regarding the role of physical capital in the growth process are common to these alternative specifications of technological progress. For this reason we choose not to limit ourselves to a single interpretation of the nature of innovation.

---

3. Romer (1990) adopts an alternative specification. He interprets the innovative products as horizontally differentiated capital goods, all of which are produced from the homogeneous final output. These capital goods and labor combine to produce the final product. Both specifications yield similar predictions about the long-run behavior of the aggregate capital stock.

Many small firms manufacture final goods subject to constant returns to scale. We aggregate these firms to the industry level, and express the technology as

$$Y = A_Y K^{\beta} D^{\eta} L_Y^{1-\beta-\eta}, \qquad 0 < \beta, \eta, \beta + \eta < 1, \tag{5.1}$$

where A_Y is a constant reflecting the choice of units, K denotes the aggregate capital stock, D represents an index of intermediate goods, and L_Y represents the total employment of labor in the final goods industry. For the index of intermediate inputs, we use either

$$D = \left[\int_0^n x(j)^{\alpha}\, dj\right]^{1/\alpha}, \qquad 0 < \alpha < 1, \tag{5.2a}$$

if inputs are horizontally differentiated (see [3.2]), or

$$\log D = \int_0^1 \log\left[\sum_m \lambda^m x_m(j)\right] dj, \qquad \lambda > 1, \tag{5.2b}$$

if a fixed set of inputs can be produced in various qualities (see [4.2]). In (5.2a), $x(j)$ represents the input of component j in the production of final goods, while in (5.2b), $x_m(j)$ denotes the input of the variety of component j whose quality is λ^m.[4]

The market for the final good Y is assumed to be perfectly competitive. Therefore the price of this good p_Y equals its marginal production cost. By a suitable choice of units (and thus the constant A_Y), we have

$$p_Y = p_D^{\eta} w_K^{\beta} w_L^{(1-\beta-\eta)}, \tag{5.3}$$

where w_L is the wage rate of labor, w_K is the rental rate on capital, and p_D is the minimum cost to manufactures of obtaining one unit of the quantity index D. Note that p_D represents a price index, reflecting both the prices of the underlying intermediates and the state of technology. Using Shephard's lemma, we can derive from (5.3) the following aggregate demands for labor, capital, and intermediates, respectively, by producers of final goods:

$$L_Y = (1 - \beta - \eta)\frac{p_Y Y}{w_L}, \tag{5.4}$$

$$K = \frac{\beta p_Y Y}{w_K}, \tag{5.5}$$

4. As before, we can make the quality at time 0 of the state-of-the-art variety of each component equal to 1, by an appropriate adjustment to the constant term A_Y. Then λ^m is the quality of a component that has undergone exactly m improvements since time 0.

$$D = \frac{\eta p_Y Y}{p_D}. \tag{5.6}$$

Any intermediate good can be produced using one unit of labor. Then the marginal cost of each intermediate is w_L. Our previous analysis has established that the prices of these goods are proportional to unit costs in both models of product innovation. We have seen that

$$p_x = \frac{w_L}{\delta}, \tag{5.7}$$

where p_x is the price of the typical intermediate input, and $\delta = \alpha$ if the economy is one with expanding input variety or $\delta = 1/\lambda$ if the economy is one with rising input quality.

Recall that producers use all available intermediates in the model of chapter 3, while they buy only state-of-the-art varieties in the equilibrium of chapter 4. But, in either case, all components facing positive demand are employed in equal quantities. Therefore the index of intermediate inputs can be expressed as

$$D = A_D X, \tag{5.8}$$

where X denotes the aggregate volume of intermediate output (the number of products times the quantity employed of each one), and A_D represents an index of the productivity of intermediates. The productivity measure reflects either the available variety of components or the average quality of each component. In either case, $p_D D = p_x X$, so (5.8) implies that

$$p_D = \frac{p_x}{A_D}. \tag{5.9}$$

Let us derive now the exact form of $A_D(t)$ under the two alternative specifications. With horizontally differentiated intermediate goods, each demanded to the same extent, (5.2a) and $X = nx$ imply that

$$A_D(t) = n(t)^{(1-\alpha)/\alpha}. \tag{5.10a}$$

When intermediates are vertically differentiated, (5.2b) and the fact that only state-of-the-art varieties are demanded in positive quantities imply that

$$\log D = \int_0^1 \log \tilde{q}(j)\, dj + \log X,$$

where $X = x$ in this case (because the measure of different product lines is one) and $\tilde{q}(j)$ represents the quality of the state-of-the-art brand of product j. As we explained in chapter 4, the first term in this expression equals $I(t)\log\lambda$, where $I(t) \equiv \int_0^t \iota(\tau)\,d\tau$ reflects the total "number" of research successes in all industries from time $\tau = 0$ to $\tau = t$. Substituting for D in (5.8), we find that the productivity measure in this case takes the form

$$A_D(t) = \lambda^{I(t)}. \tag{5.10b}$$

We adopt the same specification for the research activities as before. In the case of horizontal product differentiation, a/n units of labor are needed to develop a new variety. Here, as in section 3.2, n reflects the available stock of general knowledge capital. With quality upgrading, $a\iota$ units of labor are required to achieve a flow probability of research success of ι. We have seen that, in both models, $nv = w_L a$ gives the aggregate value of the stock market in an equilibrium with ongoing innovation. Then the inverse of the aggregate stock-market value V is given by

$$V = \frac{1}{w_L a}. \tag{5.11}$$

We maintain also the previous specification of intertemporal preferences. Households maximize

$$U_t = \int_t^\infty e^{-\rho(\tau - t)} \log C(\tau)\,d\tau, \tag{5.12}$$

where $C(\tau)$ denotes their consumption at time τ of the homogeneous final good. From these preferences we have derived the optimal allocation of spending over time,

$$\frac{\dot{E}}{E} = r - \rho. \tag{5.13}$$

We again impose the normalization

$$E(t) = 1 \qquad \text{for all } t, \tag{5.14}$$

which implies, as before, that

$$r(t) = \rho \qquad \text{for all } t. \tag{5.15}$$

Now we consider the conditions for market clearing. Capital goods and intermediate inputs each have only a single use, so equilibrium in these markets is subsumed in our writing the same magnitudes for supply and for derived demand by final good producers. The remaining market-clearing conditions apply to the labor market and to the market for final output. Labor is used in R&D and in the production of intermediate and final goods. Employment in R&D equals $a\gamma$, where γ is the rate of innovation; that is, $\gamma = g$ in the model of expanding input variety, or $\gamma = \iota$ in the model of rising input quality. The quantity of labor used in manufacturing intermediates is X, and $X = \delta\eta p_Y YVa$ by (5.6), (5.7), (5.11), and the fact that $p_D D = p_x X$. Derived demand for labor by final good producers equals $(1 - \beta - \eta)p_Y YVa$, in view of (5.4) and (5.11). The sum of these demands exhausts the fixed labor supply L or (after dividing through by a),

$$\gamma + [1 - \beta - (1 - \delta)\eta]p_Y YV = \frac{L}{a}. \tag{5.16}$$

Final output is either consumed or invested. We ignore depreciation for simplicity, so investment demand equals $\dot{K}$, the rate of increase in the capital stock. Households consume the quantity $C = E/p_Y$. Taking account of our normalization, (5.14), market clearing requires

$$\dot{K} + \frac{1}{p_Y} = Y. \tag{5.17}$$

Finally, we have two no-arbitrage conditions. The one that applies to the return on equity claims equates the sum of the firm's dividend rate and the expected rate of capital gain to the risk-free interest rate. In either model of innovation, it can be expressed by

$$\frac{\dot{V}}{V} + \gamma = (1 - \delta)\eta p_Y YV - \rho. \tag{5.18}$$

In the model of expanding product variety, the left-hand side equals $-\dot{v}/v$, the rate of capital loss on the representative firm. The right-hand side represents the difference between the profit rate and the interest rate.[5] In the case of rising product quality, the left-hand side equals $-\dot{v}/v - \iota$, which similarly reflects the expected capital loss on shares because each profit-making firm faces a flow probability of ι of a total capital loss in the event of a research success by a follower. Again in this case, the right-hand side equals the difference between the profit rate and the interest rate.[6]

5. Profits per firm constitute a fraction $(1 - \alpha)$ of spending on each intermediate, which, by (5.6), are given by $\eta p_Y Y/n$. Thus $\pi/v = (1 - \alpha)\eta p_Y YV$.

6. In this case profits per firm are $\pi = (1 - 1/\lambda)\eta p_Y Y$ and $v = 1/V$.

A second no-arbitrage condition applies to the return to physical capital (see chapter 2). Each capital good costs p_Y to purchase. The machine earns an instantaneous rental charge of w_K. Its value rises (or falls) at the rate of increase (or decrease) in the price of new capital goods. Therefore the total yield on installed capital equals $w_K/p_Y + \dot{p}_Y/p_Y$. Equating this riskless return to the interest rate, we have

$$\frac{w_K}{p_Y} + \frac{\dot{p}_Y}{p_Y} = \rho. \tag{5.19}$$

The dynamic evolution of the economy is described now by three differential equations, (5.17)–(5.19), along with two side conditions (one given by [5.16], the other derived from the pricing relationships). But the analysis of this system of equations proves complex and yields few interesting insights. For this reason we choose to concentrate on the steady-state properties of the model.[7] In the steady state the aggregate value of the stock market remains constant. With $\dot{V} = 0$, equation (5.18) gives a relationship between the steady-state rate of innovation and the long-run value of $p_Y YV$ (the ratio of the value of final output to stock market value). The labor market-clearing condition (5.16) gives another relationship between these same two variables. Combining these two equations, we can solve for the long-run rate of innovation. We find

$$\gamma = (1 - \nu)\frac{L}{a} - \nu\rho, \qquad 0 < \nu \equiv 1 - \frac{(1 - \delta)\eta}{1 - \beta} < 1. \tag{5.20}$$

Naturally this equation applies only when $L/a \geq \nu\rho/(1 - \nu)$; otherwise, innovation ceases in the long run.

Equation (5.20) bears a striking resemblance to the expressions for the rate of innovation that apply in the absence of capital accumulation (compare [3.28] and [4.18]). As before, the pace of innovation is faster in the long run the larger is the fixed resource base, the greater is the productivity of labor in R&D, the more patient are households, and the greater is the degree of monopoly power enjoyed by successful innovators. We find now that innovation is spurred by a large share of intermediates and a large share of capital in the cost of manufacturing final goods. When these shares are large, the labor share in final production is small, and more of the

7. We can show that the economy always converges to a steady state, provided that the initial stock market value is chosen to preclude bubble paths. The absence of bubble paths is ensured by the transversality condition for the household's dynamic optimization problem, as before.

fixed labor force is available for employment in the knowledge-generating activity.

In the long run the forces that drive innovation fully determine the pace of economic expansion. Just as in the neoclassical growth models of chapter 2, private investment in capital equipment continues to take place only because the productivity gains that derive from the innovation keep the marginal product of capital from falling. For this reason the rate of capital formation eventually falls into line with the rate of technological progress.[8]

The steady-state rates of expansion of output and the aggregate capital stock are readily computed. Equations (5.16) and (5.18) imply a constant long-run value of final output, $p_Y Y$, since the long-run value of the stock market is constant. Then (5.17) requires a constant rate of investment $\dot{K}/Y$ which in turn implies that capital and output must grow at the same proportional rates in the steady state. Let $g_Y = \dot{Y}/Y = \dot{K}/K$ denote this common rate of growth. The production function (5.1) yields, upon differentiation, the familiar growth-accounting relationship,

$$g_Y = \eta \frac{\dot{A}_D}{A_D} + \beta \frac{\dot{K}}{K},$$

where the first term here represents the rate of increase of total factor productivity.[9] Using now the expressions for the rate of increase in the productivity of intermediates, which we calculate for the two different underlying models of innovation from (5.10a) and (5.10b), we find

$$g_Y = \frac{\eta}{1-\beta} \mu \gamma, \tag{5.21}$$

where $\mu = (1 - \alpha)/\alpha$ in the model of expanding input variety and $\mu = \log \lambda$ in the the model of rising input quality. We see that the capital stock and final output grow in the long run at a rate that is proportional to the rate of innovation. Output grows faster when the shares of capital and intermediates in final production are large, both because these parameters imply a faster rate of innovation and because they imply faster output growth for any given rate of innovation.

---

8. Note that our conclusion reflects the assumed differences in the economic properties of private capital and (quasi-public) knowledge. To the extent that some public capital goods such as transportation and communications networks resemble knowledge capital in generating widespread benefits that are subject to limited rivalry, government investment in these forms of infrastructure might serve as a further engine to growth (see Barro 1990).

9. In this calculation the allocation of labor to the production of intermediates and final goods is taken as constant, as indeed it is in the steady state.

What about the rate of investment $\dot{K}/Y$, a variable that has featured prominently in the cross-country regressions of growth performance? In the steady state with $\dot{K}/K = \dot{Y}/Y$, $\dot{K}/Y = g_Y K/Y$. From (5.5) the capital-to-output ratio equals $\beta p_Y/w_K$, while (5.19) implies that $p_Y/w_K = 1/(\rho + g_Y)$ in the long run (when the price of final output falls at the rate of real output growth). Combining these expressions, we have

$$\frac{\dot{K}}{Y} = \frac{\beta g_Y}{\rho + g_Y}. \tag{5.22}$$

The investment ratio moves monotonically with the rate of growth of final output, and thus also with the rate of innovation. In terms of the primitive parameters of the model, the long-run rate of investment increases with the size of the fixed labor supply, with productivity in R&D, with the cost shares of capital and intermediates in final output, and with the degree of monopoly power enjoyed by innovators, while it decreases with the subjective discount rate. All of these parameters have of course qualitatively the same effects on the long-run rate of innovation.

Our analysis suggests that physical capital may play only a supporting role in the story of long-run growth. For this reason, and to keep our analysis of endogenous innovation as simple as possible, we will abstract from capital equipment and (ordinary) investment in the remainder of this book.

5.2 Human Capital

Next we extend our model of endogenous growth to allow for accumulation of human capital. By "human capital" we mean a set of specialized skills that agents can acquire by devoting time to an activity called "schooling." The more time that an individual spends in school, the greater is the measure of human capital that the individual acquires. Since in reality unskilled workers and skilled labor generally perform very different tasks in both the industrial research lab and in the manufacturing enterprise, we will treat these two types of labor as distinct, and imperfectly substitutable, inputs. We assume, in accordance with reality, that specialized skills are employed relatively more intensively in the industrial research lab than elsewhere in the economy.

A variety of approaches to the training and education process could be combined with the underlying models of technological change that we have developed so far in this book. The literature on human capital has achieved a high degree of sophistication, and many of the available models include much richness of institutional detail. But our goal here is rather modest. We wish to establish only that factor supplies can readily be made endogenous together with the rate of technological change. This demonstration will serve to justify our frequent assumption later on that countries differ in the composition of their long-run resource endowments. For our purposes a simple approach that builds on Findlay and Kierzkowski (1983) will suffice.

We assume now that the economy is populated with a continuum of agents. Each agent lives for a time interval of finite length T. The age distribution is uniform at every moment, with a density of N/T individuals of every age between 0 and T. At each instant the individuals who die (those who reach age T) are replaced in the population by an equal number of newborns. Therefore the total population has constant measure N.

We make the rather strong assumption that all individuals are alike in their capacity for learning. The agents also share a common set of preferences. Lifetime utility of an individual born at time t is given by

$$U_t = \int_t^{t+T} e^{-\rho(\tau-t)} \log D(\tau)\, d\tau, \tag{5.23}$$

where $D(\tau)$ represents now an index of consumption at time τ, and D can take either the form given in (5.2a) or that given in (5.2b). In other words, we allow once again for either horizontal or vertical product differentiation, and for innovation that involves either an expansion in product variety or a rise in average product quality.[10] The intertemporal utility function in (5.23) is the natural analog to (5.12), which we applied to the infinitely lived household, and it too implies that spending increases at a rate equal to the difference between the interest rate and the subjective discount rate. By normalizing aggregate spending again so that $E = 1$ at every moment, we have $r(t) = \rho$ for all t, as before.

At every instant, each agent must allocate his or her time to one of three activities. The individual may choose to take employment as an unskilled worker, to take employment as a skilled worker, or to spend the time accumulating human capital. For simplicity, we neglect all inputs into training other than the time devoted by the individual pupil. We assume that an individual who devotes a period of length S to learning activities

10. In contrast to section 5.1, we will interpret the innovative products here as being differentiated consumer goods. Of course, as we have noted before, an exactly equivalent interpretation allows them to be intermediate goods that are combined (with no further resource input) into a single, consumable product.

acquires in that time the measure $h(S)$ of specialized skills, where $h(\cdot)$ is an increasing and concave function and $h(0) = 0$.[11] Skilled workers are paid in proportion to the measure of skills they possess. Therefore a worker who has spent S years in school earns a flow salary of $h(S)w_H$ when employed as a skilled worker, where w_H is the reward paid to a unit of human capital. All unskilled workers receive the wage w_L, regardless of their ages or levels of training.

Differentiated products are manufactured with both skilled and unskilled labor as inputs. We let $c_x(w_L, w_H)$ denote the unit manufacturing cost of any one of these goods. As before, producers of innovative goods set prices at a multiple of unit cost so that

$$p_x = \frac{1}{\delta} c_x(w_L, w_H), \tag{5.24}$$

where p_x is the price of a typical state-of-the-art product and $\delta = \alpha$ or $\delta = 1/\lambda$, depending upon the underlying interpretation of the technological progress. Equilibrium in the product markets requires that the value of output be equal to aggregate spending, or

$$p_x X = 1, \tag{5.25}$$

where X represents the aggregate quantity of manufactured output.

Specialized skills and unskilled labor are also required in the industrial research lab. We specify a research technology that exhibits constant returns to scale, and denote by $c_\gamma(w_L, w_H)\gamma$ the total cost of achieving a rate of innovation of γ. Recall that γ may represent either the rate of new product introduction $\dot{n}/n$ or the arrival rate of quality improvements ι in an economy with product upgrading. In either case Shephard's lemma implies that the demands for unskilled labor and human capital in the R&D activity are $a_{L\gamma}(w_L, w_H)\gamma$ and $a_{H\gamma}(w_L, w_H)\gamma$, respectively, where $a_{j\gamma}(\cdot)$ is the partial derivative of $c_\gamma(\cdot)$ with respect to w_j. Similarly the quantities of unskilled labor and human capital employed in the manufacturing sector are $a_{Lx}(w_L, w_H)X$ and $a_{Hx}(w_L, w_H)X$, where $a_{jx}(\cdot)$ is the partial derivative of $c_x(\cdot)$ with respect to w_j. Factor market clearing requires

$$a_{L\gamma}(w_L, w_H)\gamma + a_{Lx}(w_L, w_H)X = L, \tag{5.26}$$

11. A more complete specification would include education capital as a separate input into the creation of human capital. Presumably the function relating skills acquisition to time spent in school would depend also on the per student availability of education capital. Then economies that differed in their stocks of this input would differ as well in the quantities of human capital accumulated by their populations.

$$a_{H\gamma}(w_L, w_H)\gamma + a_{Hx}(w_L, w_H)X = H, \tag{5.27}$$

where L and H are the aggregate supplies of unskilled labor and human capital, respectively. These factor supplies will of course be determined now by the equilibrium schooling decisions of individuals in the economy.

For ease of exposition we again describe only the steady-state equilibrium. In the steady state, factor rewards and commodity prices are constant through time. By familiar arguments, a no-arbitrage condition equates the long-run profit rate for the representative producer of a state-of-the-art product to the sum of the interest rate and the expected rate of capital loss in the steady state. This gives

$$\frac{(1-\delta)p_x X}{c_\gamma(w_L, w_H)} = \rho + \gamma \tag{5.28}$$

for both underlying models of the innovation process.

We turn finally to the decision problem facing each individual as regards the allocation of time. Two aspects of the optimal education program are apparent. First, an individual will devote time to training only if he or she intends to take employment subsequently as a skilled worker. Second, since wages are constant in the steady state, any individual who plans to acquire a positive level of skills will devote the first part of life to this endeavor. By doing so, he or she achieves the maximum return to a given investment in training. It follows from these considerations that an individual contemplating education must compare the present value of lifetime earnings as an unskilled worker,

$$\int_t^{t+T} e^{-\rho(\tau-t)} w_L \, d\tau = \frac{1}{\rho}(1 - e^{-\rho T}) w_L, \tag{5.29}$$

with the present value of the income that the individual could obtain by spending the first S years in school, and then receiving a flow salary of $w_H h(S)$ for the remaining years of life. The present value of this latter income stream equals

$$\int_{t+S}^{t+T} e^{-\rho(\tau-t)} w_H h(S) \, d\tau = \frac{1}{\rho}(e^{-\rho S} - e^{-\rho T}) w_H h(S), \qquad S \leq T. \tag{5.30}$$

In order to make the comparison, the individual must first ascertain what would be the optimal duration of training given that he or she opts for any education at all. The optimum period of time in school is such that the marginal benefit from extending the stay by dS just equals the marginal opportunity cost of the extra time spent outside the labor force. The marginal benefit takes the form of a stream of returns to $h'(S)dS$ additional units of human capital, which the skilled worker born at time t reaps from time $t + S$ to time $t + T$. These potential earnings have a present value (discounted to time t) of $(e^{-\rho S} - e^{-\rho T})w_H h'(S)dS/\rho$. The marginal cost is $e^{-\rho S} w_H h(S)dS$, the present value of the forgone earnings from time $t + S$ to time $t + S + dS$. The first-order condition for an interior optimum (which we assume to obtain) implies that

$$1 - e^{-\rho(T-S)} = \frac{\rho h(S)}{h'(S)}. \tag{5.31}$$

Since the left-hand side of (5.31) is declining in S, while the right-hand side is increasing, any interior solution to this equation in the range $S \in (0, T)$ must be unique. An immediate implication of (5.31) is that the optimal investment in education for those who opt to become skilled is independent of the prevailing wage rates. On the margin both the cost and benefit of extra schooling are proportional to the reward to human capital, and so this variable cancels in the comparison of the two.

An individual evaluates the potential present value of earnings as a skilled worker by substituting into (5.30) the value of S that solves (5.31). The individual compares this sum to the present value of unskilled wages in (5.29). Since we have assumed that all individuals are identical in their capacity to acquire skills, all will make the same choice unless the two options happen to offer the same discounted lifetime income. To ensure that some agents will choose each vocation, it is sufficient for us to suppose that each type of labor is an essential input into manufacturing. With this assumption, individuals must be indifferent in equilibrium between educating themselves optimally and receiving no training at all. Using (5.29) and (5.30), this equilibrium condition can be expressed as

$$\frac{w_H}{w_L} = \frac{1 - e^{-\rho T}}{(e^{-\rho S} - e^{-\rho T})h(S)}. \tag{5.32}$$

Equations (5.31) and (5.32) together determine the equilibrium relative rewards of the two primary inputs. Long-run relative factor prices depend only on the discount rate and on the technology for human-capital accumulation. Note that in equilibrium the salary of a skilled worker $w_H h(S)$ must exceed the wage of an unskilled worker w_L to ensure that the former workers receive compensation for their time spent in school.

To close the model, we relate the factor supplies in (5.26) and (5.27) to the optimal schooling choices of the individuals. Let ψ_S denote the fraction of the population that opts to acquire special skills. Then, at any moment in time, a measure of $\psi_S SN/T$ individuals is out of the labor force, attending school.[12] Of the remaining individuals,

$$L = (1 - \psi_S)N \tag{5.33}$$

work as unskilled laborers, and $(T - S)\psi_S N/T$ take jobs requiring skills. Each skilled worker has acquired the measure $h(S)$ of human capital, so

$$H = \frac{T - S}{T}\psi_S Nh(S). \tag{5.34}$$

Equations (5.24)–(5.28) and (5.31)–(5.34) constitute nine equations that determine the steady-state values of the endogenous variables. Equations (5.24)–(5.28) are familiar ones that relate product prices, factor rewards, the aggregate output of manufactures, and the rate of innovation to the supplies of the primary factors. Equations (5.31)–(5.34) are new. They relate the fraction of the population that chooses to acquire specialized skills, the level of educational attainment of the representative trained worker, and the supplies of the two primary inputs, to the relative factor rewards.

Our expanded model allows us to address some new issues. Consider, for example, the long-run effects of a change in the productiveness of time spent in school, as might result from additional public investment in education capital. For the purpose of this exercise, let $h(S) = A_S\bar{h}(S)$, where $\bar{h}(S)$ represents the initial technology for investment in human capital and A_S is a parameter reflecting productivity in the education sector (initially $A_S = 1$). We investigate the effect of an increase in A_S on the long-run rate of growth.

It is evident from (5.31) that a change in A_S has no bearing on the optimal length of time spent in school. This reflects the fact that an equiproportionate improvement in the productivity of training at all levels of education raises both the cost and the benefit of further education, and both to the same extent. It follows that the effects of A_S on γ come only through the induced change in relative factor prices. When schooling becomes more productive, individuals will remain indifferent between seeking an education and working as unskilled laborers only if the relative reward to unskilled labor compared to skilled labor increases. The inverse relationship between A_S and $\omega \equiv w_H/w_L$ can be seen in (5.32).

12. The measure of individuals of age S or less is SN/T in view of the uniform age distribution. Of these a fraction ψ_S attends school.

Using (5.33) and (5.34), we can write the total population N as the sum of the number of unskilled workers and the number of individuals who are employed as skilled workers or are in training for such positions:

$$L + \frac{T}{T - S}\frac{H}{h(S)} = N. \tag{5.35}$$

The factor-market-clearing conditions (5.26) and (5.27) relate the aggregate quantities of the two factors to the levels of activity in the two sectors. Combining these with the product-market-clearing condition (5.25) and the pricing equation (5.24) allows us to express the factor quantities as

$$L = \frac{\theta_{L\gamma} c_\gamma \gamma + \theta_{Lx}\delta}{w_L}, \tag{5.36a}$$

$$H = \frac{\theta_{H\gamma} c_\gamma \gamma + \theta_{Hx}\delta}{w_H}, \tag{5.36b}$$

where θ_{ij} is the share of factor i in the total cost of activity j, for $i = L, H$, and $j = \gamma, x$. These factor shares depend only upon the relative factor price ω.

Next we use the product-market-equilibrium condition (5.25), together with the fact that R&D costs $c_\gamma(w_L, w_H)$ are linearly homogeneous in the factor prices, to rewrite the no-arbitrage condition (5.28) as

$$w_L c_\gamma(1, \omega) = \frac{1 - \delta}{\rho + \gamma}. \tag{5.37}$$

In figure 5.1 this equation is represented by the ray ΠΠ. The ray slopes upward because, for a given relative factor price ω, an increase in the reward to unskilled implies a greater cost of innovation, hence a smaller rate of innovation that is consistent with a total rate of return on equities equal to ρ. The figure also shows the line NN, which represents the resource constraint (5.35) in light of the factor demands (5.36a, b), the expression for $c_\gamma(w_L, w_H)$ that derives from (5.37), and the relationship between w_H and w_L that is implied by (5.32). The equation for this line takes the form

$$\left[\theta_{L\gamma}(1 - \delta)\left(1 - \frac{\rho}{\rho + \gamma}\right) + \theta_{Lx}\delta\right] + B(S)\left[\theta_{H\gamma}(1 - \delta)\left(1 - \frac{\rho}{\rho + \gamma}\right) + \theta_{Hx}\delta\right] = w_L N, \tag{5.38}$$

where $B(S)$, representing the ratio of the lifetime earnings of unskilled and

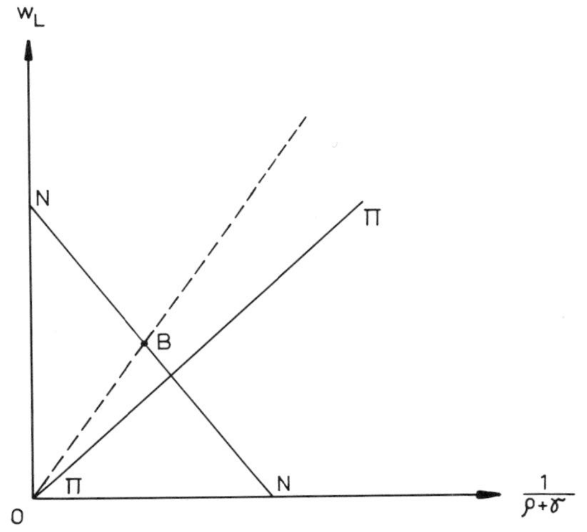

Figure 5.1

skilled workers, is given by

$$B(S) \equiv \frac{T}{T-S} \frac{e^{-\rho S} - e^{-\rho T}}{1 - e^{-\rho T}}.$$

The line *NN* slopes downward because a decline in w_L for given ω means an increase in the derived demand for both factors, and so must be accompanied by a fall in the rate of innovation which alleviates the resource constraint.

The lines in figure 5.1 have been drawn for the time of training S that derives from the optimal schooling decision and the relative wage ω that makes individuals indifferent between attending and not attending school. Now we can use the figure to find the long-run effects of an increase in schooling productivity on the economy's rate of industrial innovation. As we have already noted, the increase in A_S leaves S unchanged but lowers ω. The fall in ω rotates $\Pi\Pi$ in a counterclockwise direction, as depicted by the dotted line in the figure. That is, for given w_L, more R&D will be conducted when the relative (and hence absolute) wage of skilled workers is lower. The shift in *NN* depends upon the relationship between the relative wage and the factor shares. If, for example, the elasticity of substitution between skilled and unskilled labor is equal to one in both activities (i.e., there are Cobb-Douglas production functions), then the factor shares will be independent of ω. In this case the *NN* curve remains in place, and so the new steady-state equilibrium is given by point *B*. For more general production functions the *NN* curve may shift in either direction. But even when it shifts up, the magnitude of the vertical shift at the initial γ never exceeds that of the ΠΠ curve.[13] It follows that an increase in the productivity of schools always speeds the pace of technological progress in the long run.

Before leaving this section, we review briefly the mechanism that links the quality of education with the rate of innovation. When A_S rises, all entrants into the labor force who formerly were indifferent between the two occupations, suddenly prefer to become skilled. Then the relative wage of skilled workers must fall sufficiently to restore their indifference. Although in the long run the fraction of the population that seeks training may rise or fall,[14] the aggregate stock of human capital in the economy must expand. In other words, even if ψ_S falls, the adverse effect of this on H will be more than offset by the beneficial effect on the level of skills $h(S)$ attained by the representative trainee.[15] The extra human capital makes possible an expansion in research activities, which entrepreneurs are willing to undertake due to the accompanied reduction in research costs. Thus R&D operations expand and the rate of innovation rises.

5.3 Country Size and Resource Composition

Our final task in this chapter is to examine more closely the relationship between the size of an economy, the composition of its resource base, and

13. The ΠΠ curve shifts up proportionately by $\hat{w}_L = -\theta_{H\gamma}\hat{\omega}$ (recall that $\hat{\omega} < 0$), where a "hat" denotes a proportional rate of change ($\hat{w}_L = dw_L/w_L$, etc.). We find the proportional shift in the *NN* curve by logarithmically differentiating (5.38), noting the relationship $\hat{\theta}_{Li} = -\theta_{Hi}(1 - \sigma_i)\hat{\omega}$ that is derived, for example, by Jones (1965). Here σ_i represents the elasticity of substitution between skilled and unskilled labor in sector i. The vertical shift is given by

$$\hat{w}_L = -[\lambda_{\gamma N}\theta_{H\gamma}(1 - \sigma_\gamma) + \lambda_{xN}\theta_{Hx}(1 - \sigma_x)]\hat{\omega},$$

where the λ_{iN} are positive fractions that sum to one, and $\theta_{H\gamma} > \theta_{Hx}$ in light of the relative skill intensiveness of R&D compared to manufacturing. When the *NN* line shifts up, it cannot do so by more than ΠΠ because

$$\lambda_{\gamma N}\theta_{H\gamma}(1 - \sigma_\gamma) + \lambda_{xN}\theta_{Hx}(1 - \sigma_x) = \theta_{H\gamma}\left[\lambda_{\gamma N}(1 - \sigma_\gamma) + \frac{\lambda_{xN}(1 - \sigma_x)\theta_{Hx}}{\theta_{H\gamma}}\right] < \theta_{H\gamma}.$$

14. The reader may verify, using (5.24)–(5.28) and (5.32)–(5.34), that if the elasticity of substitution between unskilled labor and human capital in both activities is zero (i.e., there are fixed-coefficient technologies), then the fraction seeking education increases with A_S if $a_{Hx} = a_{L\gamma} = 0$ but decreases with A_S if $a_{Hx}/a_{Lx} = a_{H\gamma}/a_{L\gamma}$.

15. This claim can be established by total differentiation of the system of equations that includes (5.26), (5.27), (5.28), and (5.32), after substituting for X, L, and H in the first two of these using (5.24)–(5.25) and (5.33)–(5.34), and for p_xX in (5.28) using (5.25).

the long-run rate of growth. It would certainly be possible to base this inquiry on an extended version of the model of the previous section. But a model with exogenous factor supplies permits a simpler exposition without, at this point, any significant loss of generality. We know now that differences in resource supplies could readily be derived from differences in population size and education productivity, using the specification and methods of section 5.2.

Resource composition matters most in a growth context when various manufacturing activities differ both in the intensity with which they employ various primary inputs and in their potential for contributing to innovation and productivity growth. In reality opportunities for technological progress are not uniform across sectors of the economy (see chapter 1), and different sectors do employ the factors of production in different combinations. For our purposes it will be enough to consider an economy with two consumer goods Y and Z. The sector that produces good Z represents those activities in the economy that offer relatively little prospect for technological advance. We refer to this sector as the "traditional" manufacturing sector and assume that the technology there does not change over time. The other manufacturing sector, which produces good Y, represents that part of the economy where the scope for innovation is greatest. We call this the "high-technology" sector.

Good Z is produced by unskilled labor and human capital in competitive firms that operate according to a constant-returns-to-scale technology. We assume that this technology, which can be represented by the unit cost function $c_Z(w_L, w_H)$, requires the most intensive use of unskilled labor among the three productive activities. Perfect competition implies marginal cost pricing, or

$$p_Z = c_Z(w_L, w_H). \tag{5.39}$$

The high-technology sector manufactures the final good Y from intermediate inputs. The production function is simply $Y = D$, where D represents one or the other of the indexes of differentiated intermediate inputs given in (5.2a) and (5.2b).[16] Then the equilibrium price of good Y equals the price index for intermediates p_D given in (5.9). The index reflects the state of technology and the prices of the component inputs. As before, we assign to each component the same unit cost function $c_x(w_L, w_H)$, and add now the assumption that the production of components requires more

16. Of course this is equivalent to assuming that households directly consume a bundle of differentiated products and that Y represents a subutility index.

intensive use of human capital than the production of traditional goods but less intensive use of this factor than research activities. Equation (5.24) continues to describe the pricing of (state-of-the-art) components.

We now suppose that the utility function of the representative households takes the form

$$U_t = \int_t^{\infty} e^{-\rho(\tau-t)}[\sigma \log C_Y(\tau) + (1-\sigma)\log C_Z(\tau)]\,d\tau, \quad 0 < \sigma < 1, \tag{5.40}$$

where C_i is consumption of good i. With these preferences consumers devote a fraction σ of their spending to good Y and the remaining fraction $1-\sigma$ to good Z. Also these preferences imply the spending pattern described in (5.13). We normalize again so that $E = 1$.

With our normalization of aggregate spending, demand for good Y equals σ/p_Y, and that for good Z equals $(1-\sigma)/p_Z$. The equilibrium condition in the market for product Z is simply

$$Z = \frac{1-\sigma}{p_Z}. \tag{5.41}$$

Household purchases of good Y have value σ. In equilibrium this must match the value of output, which in turn is equal to the total cost of production $p_D D$ and the aggregate cost of the component intermediates $p_x X$. Therefore market clearing for the high-technology good implies that

$$p_x X = \sigma. \tag{5.42}$$

The no-arbitrage condition (5.28) continues to apply to the steady-state returns to R&D.[17] The left-hand side of (5.28) gives the instantaneous profit rate for a successful innovator, while the right-hand side gives the sum of the interest rate and the rate of expected capital loss. Finally, we have the factor-market clearing conditions. These are analogous to (5.26) and (5.27) and take the form

$$a_{L\gamma}(w_L, w_H)\gamma + a_{Lx}(w_L, w_H)X + a_{LZ}(w_L, w_H)Z = L, \tag{5.43}$$

$$a_{H\gamma}(w_L, w_H)\gamma + a_{Hx}(w_L, w_H)X + a_{HZ}(w_L, w_H)Z = H, \tag{5.44}$$

where a_{iZ} is the input of factor i per unit of output of the traditional goods and all of the other variables have the same definitions as before.

17. With exogenous factor supplies, the steady state is achieved instantaneously here. Transition dynamics would arise, however, if we allowed a process of resource accumulation such as that described in section 5.2.

Equations (5.24), (5.28), (5.39), and (5.41)–(5.44), which determine the steady-state product prices, factor rewards, and output levels, and the steady-state rate of innovation, are reminiscent of the equilibrium conditions that apply in a static, two-sector model with product differentiation in one of the sectors (see, e.g., Helpman and Krugman 1985, ch. 7). There is one difference, however. Whereas the static models based on Chamberlin's notion of monopolistic competition assume zero profits at every moment in time, we require the absence of excess profits only in the present-value sense. Our no-arbitrage condition, which ensures that innovation yields only a "normal" return, replaces the average-cost pricing equation of the static models.

We investigate the effects of variations in the stocks of one or both of the primary factors of production. Rather than deriving results for the general production structure that we have described, we analyze two special cases that allow us to bring out most clearly the economic forces at work.

Example 5.1

The first special case is designed to highlight the role that factor intensities play in linking factor supplies to long-run rates of innovation and growth. In this example, we assume that all technologies have fixed input coefficients. Then, substituting from (5.24), (5.39) and (5.41)–(5.42) into (5.43) and (5.44), the factor-market-clearing conditions can be expressed as

$$a_{L\gamma}\gamma + \frac{a_{Lx}\sigma\delta}{c_x} + \frac{a_{LZ}(1-\sigma)}{c_Z} = L, \tag{5.45}$$

$$a_{H\gamma}\gamma + \frac{a_{Hx}\sigma\delta}{c_x} + \frac{a_{HZ}(1-\sigma)}{c_Z} = H, \tag{5.46}$$

where the a_{ij}'s now are constants. These conditions are depicted by the lines *LL* and *HH* in figure 5.2. The line *LL* (associated with [5.45]) is steeper than the line *HH* (associated with [5.46]) because high technology is relatively more human-capital intensive than the traditional manufacturing sector; that is, $a_{Hx}/a_{Lx} > a_{HZ}/a_{LZ}$. The lines are drawn for a particular rate of innovation γ, which in a moment we will take to be the equilibrium rate.

When input coefficients are fixed, the cost of innovation can be written as a linear function of the unit cost of manufacturing intermediates and the unit cost of the traditional consumer good. To do so, we solve the pair of equations, $c_i = w_H a_{Hi} + w_L a_{Li}$, $i = x, Z$ for the factor prices, and then

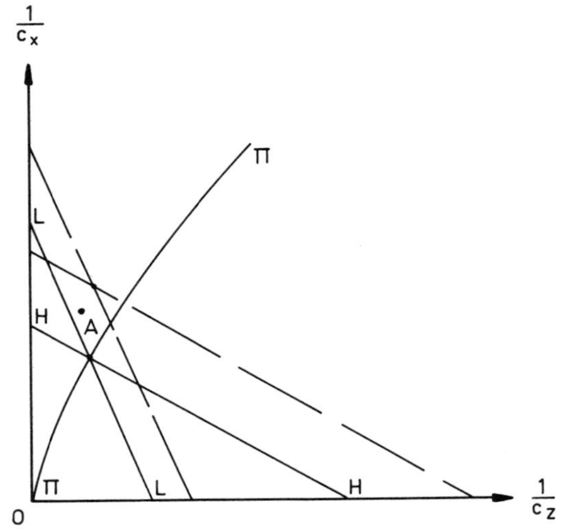

Figure 5.2

substitute these solutions into $c_Y = w_H a_{HY} + w_L a_{LY}$. This gives a relation of the form $c_Y = B_x c_x - B_Z c_Z$, where B_x and B_Z are positive constants. An increase in c_x for given c_Z raises the cost of innovation because, by the Stolper-Samuelson theorem, it raises the reward to human capital while reducing the reward to unskilled labor. An increase in c_Z has the opposite effects on factor prices and hence on the cost of R&D.

With this cost relationship and (5.42), we can rewrite the no-arbitrage condition (5.28) as

$$B_x c_x - B_Z c_Z = \frac{(1-\delta)\sigma}{\rho + \gamma}. \tag{5.47}$$

This equation appears in figure 5.2 as the curve ΠΠ. It is drawn for the particular (equilibrium) value of γ that makes the three curves intersect at a common point.

We consider first a pure expansion in the size of the economy, that is, an equiproportionate increase in the supplies of both factors. This expansion shifts both the *LL* and the *HH* lines up and to the right, as depicted by the dotted lines. It is easy to show that the new intersection between these two lines must lie above the ΠΠ curve. Therefore the two factor-market-clearing conditions and the no-arbitrage condition cannot all be satisfied at the initial rate of innovation. To restore equilibrium, the rate of innovation must rise.[18] Such an increase in γ shifts the $\Pi\Pi$ curve upward and the *HH* and *LL* lines back downward, enabling a common intersection again at a point such as *A*. We conclude that a *proportionally* larger economy experiences faster innovation in the long run.[19]

We now compare two economies that differ only in their stocks of human capital. An increase in *H* shifts the *HH* line out, as shown in figure 5.3. Again, the new point of intersection with the (original) *LL* line lies above the $\Pi\Pi$ curve. So the rate of innovation must rise. The new equilibrium is at a point such as A'. An economy with a larger stock of human capital devotes more of this resource to R&D, the most human capital intensive of the three activities. With fixed input coefficients it must devote more labor to R&D as well. As a consequence its rate of innovation is higher.

Finally, we consider two economies that differ in their labor supplies. An expansion in *L* shifts the *LL* line to the right, as illustrated in figure 5.4. Now the new intersection with the (original) *HH* line occurs below the $\Pi\Pi$ curve. As a result the rate of innovation must fall to restore equilibrium at a point such as A''. An economy with a larger endowment of unskilled labor engages in more labor-intensive manufacturing, but in *less* human-capital-intensive R&D, than an otherwise identical country with a smaller unskilled labor force. As a result its knowledge stock and its real GDP grow more slowly.

We find then that a larger economy need not grow faster than a smaller one, if the composition of their factor endowments differs. In an economy with fixed input coefficients, an expansion in the factor used most intensively in the R&D sector necessarily speeds innovation and growth, but an expansion of the factor used least intensively in this activity slows down growth. These results reflect the well-known Rybczynski theorem that applies to two-factor trade models. When one resource endowment grows, the activity that uses this resource most intensively must expand to absorb the increased supply. But this draws the remaining factor into the expanding sector as well. So the remaining sector, which uses the second (non-expanding) factor most intensively, must contract.

18. With our factor intensity rankings, a decline in the rate of innovation causes the intersection of the *LL* and the *HH* curves to move up and to the left. At the same time it causes the $\Pi\Pi$ curve to shift down and to the right. Hence no fall in γ could possibly effect a common intersection of the three curves if the intersection of *LL* and *HH* begins above the $\Pi\Pi$ curve.

19. In appendix A5.1 we show that this result holds more generally, that is, for production functions that allow any degree of substitution between human capital and unskilled labor.

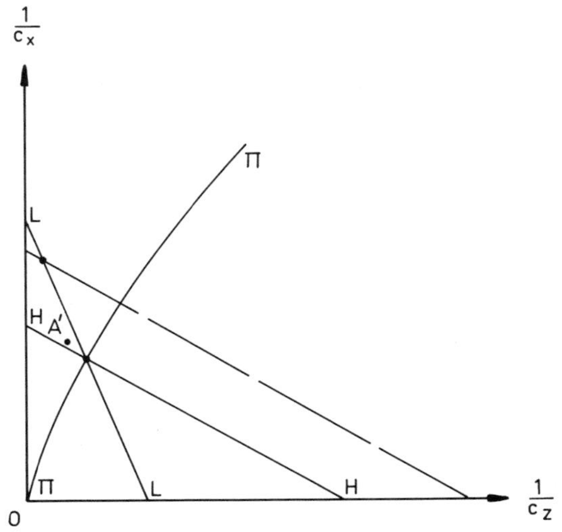

Figure 5.3

Example 5.2

The second example is constructed to illustrate the role that factor substitutability can play in linking resource endowments to rates of innovation and growth. We assume that R&D and the sector that produces high-technology goods employ only human capital; that is, $a_{Ly} = a_{Lx} = 0$. The traditional manufacturing sector can have any arbitrary (constant-returns-to-scale) production technology.

After substituting for Z using (5.39) and (5.41), and some rearranging, the labor-market-equilibrium condition takes the form

$$\omega(1 - \sigma)\theta_{LZ}(\omega) = w_H L, \tag{5.48}$$

where θ_{LZ} represents the share of labor in the cost of manufacturing good Z and $\omega \equiv w_H/w_L$ is the relative reward to human capital, as before. The share of unskilled labor in the cost of traditional manufactures varies according to $\hat{\theta}_{LZ} = -\theta_{HZ}(1 - \sigma_Z)\hat{\omega}$, where θ_{HZ} is the share of human capital in the cost of producing good Z and σ_Z is the elasticity of substitution between human capital and unskilled labor in this sector. From this we see that the share of unskilled labor in the unit cost rises with the relative reward to human capital if and only if the elasticity of substitution between labor and human capital in the production of good Z exceeds one. And even when θ_{LZ} falls with ω, it does so less quickly than ω itself (i.e., the elasticity is greater than minus one). This implies that the left-hand side of

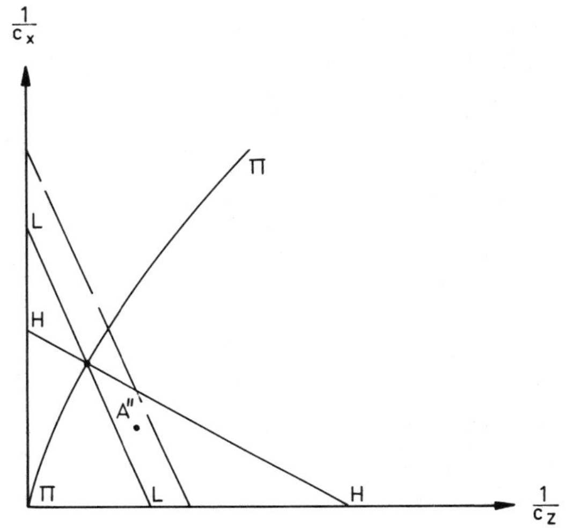

Figure 5.4

(5.48) increases with ω. The equation can be depicted therefore by an upward sloping curve such as that labeled LL in figures 5.5 and 5.6.

Next observe that when R&D requires only human capital, the cost of innovation takes the simple form $c_\gamma = w_H a_{H\gamma}$. Using (5.42), we rewrite the no-arbitrage condition (5.28) as

$$\frac{(1-\delta)\sigma}{w_H a_{H\gamma}} = \gamma + \rho. \tag{5.49}$$

Clearly the rate of innovation rises here in response to any change in factor supplies if and only if the reward to human capital (and so the cost of R&D) falls.

Finally, with high-technology products manufactured from human capital alone, (5.24) and (5.42) imply that $X = \delta\sigma / w_H a_{Hx}$. This expression and (5.39), (5.41), and (5.49) allow us to rewrite the condition for equilibrium in the market for human capital as

$$\sigma + (1-\sigma)\theta_{HZ}(\omega) = w_H(H + \rho a_{H\gamma}). \tag{5.50}$$

Note that the share of human capital in the cost of producing good Z falls with ω if and only if the elasticity of substitution between labor and human capital in the production of good Z exceeds one.

Figure 5.5 applies when the elasticity of substitution is less than one. In this case (5.50) can be depicted by an upward-sloping curve, such as the

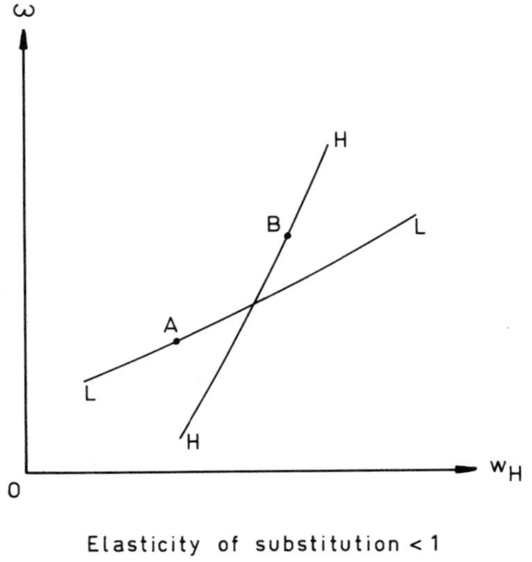

Figure 5.5

one labeled *HH* which must be steeper than the *LL* curve at their point of intersection.[20] Then an increase in the stock of human capital shifts the *HH* curve to the left and the equilibrium to a point such as *A*. The reward to human capital falls and with it the cost of R&D. The rates of innovation and growth both rise as a result. An increase in the supply of unskilled labor, on the other hand, shifts the *LL* curve to the left and the equilibrium to a point such as *B*. This means a higher reward to human capital and slower rates of innovation and growth. These results correspond exactly to those for example 5.1 (in which the elasticity of substitution was zero).

But now consider figure 5.6, which is relevant when the elasticity of substitution between labor and human capital exceeds one. In this case the *HH* curve slopes downward. An increase in the stock of human capital again shifts *HH* to the left and again depresses the reward to human capital (the new equilibrium is at a point such as *A*′). Again, the rate of growth rises. But now an increase in the supply of labor also causes the reward to human capital to fall, as the *LL* curve shifts to the left and the intersection of the two curves moves to a point such as *B*′. In this case factor accumulation accelerates innovation, no matter which of the factor supplies is the

20. Along the *LL* curve we have $\hat{\omega}/\hat{w}_H = [1 - \theta_{HZ}(1 - \sigma_Z)]^{-1}$, whereas along the *HH* curve $\hat{\omega}/\hat{w}_H = [\sigma + (1 - \sigma)\theta_{HZ}]/(1 - \sigma)\theta_{LZ}\theta_{HZ}(1 - \sigma_Z)$. When $0 < \sigma_Z < 1$, the latter expression is larger.

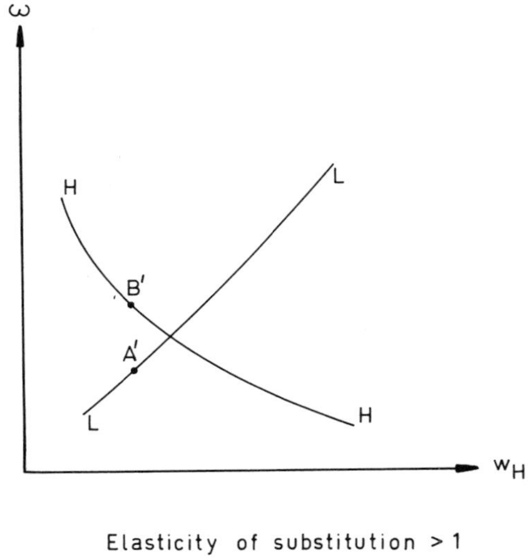

Figure 5.6

one to expand. With enough substitutability between the factors of production, larger economies necessarily grow faster than smaller ones.

This chapter has attempted to integrate factor accumulation into our theory of growth based on endogenous innovation. First, we allowed for investment in physical capital. We followed the traditional approach that treats capital as a homogeneous commodity produced by the same means as consumption goods. The capital is then used to produce final output in combination with labor and innovative components. In this setting the innovation that occurs in the intermediate goods sector drives both long-run growth and long-run capital formation. The productivity advances that stem from industrial research preserve the incentives for investments in machinery.

Next we introduced opportunities for technical training and endogenized the stocks of human capital and unskilled labor. We studied an economy of overlapping generations, each one populated by a continuum of identical agents. Individuals elect whether to devote time to acquiring skills and, if so, how long to spend outside the labor force. The steady state is characterized by constant stocks of each factor and by a fixed division of resources between manufacturing and research.

Having shown that factor composition can be related to primitive causes, we proceeded to study the relationship between input supplies and long-run growth. A country that has a greater steady-state supply of the factor most essential for industrial research will allocate more resources to R&D in equilibrium and will experience faster innovation and growth as a consequence. But a country that has an abundance of the factor used least intensively in R&D will find itself specializing relatively in other activities. Assuming that R&D makes greatest use of skilled labor, we find that accumulation of human capital always leads to faster long-run growth. But an increase in an economy's endowment of unskilled labor may lead to a contraction of its research activities. Then a larger economy with a paucity of human capital may grow slower than a smaller one where this factor is relatively more abundant. Still, the growth rate must increase with the size of an economy if all factor supplies are expanded equiproportionately or if elasticities of factor substitution in all manufacturing activities exceed one.

APPENDIX

A5.1 When Does Larger Size Mean Faster Growth?

In this appendix we use the model of section 5.2 to derive two results concerning the relationship between country size and the long-run rate of innovation. First, we show that the accumulation of any factor must lead to a higher rate of innovation when the elasticities of substitution in both manufacturing sectors exceed one. Then we establish that an equiproportionate expansion of all factor endowments must spur innovation, irrespective of the production technology.

To begin, we substitute the pricing equations (5.24) and (5.39) and the product-market-clearing conditions (5.41) and (5.42) into the factor-market-clearing conditions (5.43) and (5.44) to obtain

$$\theta_{L\gamma}(w_L, w_H)c_\gamma(w_L, w_H)\gamma + \theta_{Lx}(w_L, w_H)\delta\sigma + \theta_{LZ}(w_L, w_H)(1-\sigma) = w_L L, \tag{A5.1}$$

$$\theta_{H\gamma}(w_L, w_H)c_\gamma(w_L, w_H)\gamma + \theta_{Hx}(w_L, w_H)\delta\sigma + \theta_{HZ}(w_L, w_H)(1-\sigma) = w_H H, \tag{A5.2}$$

where the θ_{ij}'s are factor shares, as in the main text. Next we use the no-arbitrage condition (5.28) and the market-clearing condition for high-technology goods (5.42) to derive

$$c_\gamma(w_L, w_H)(\rho + \gamma) = (1-\delta)\sigma. \tag{A5.3}$$

Together, these three equations determine equilibrium values of the factor rewards and the rate of innovation. Logarithmic differentiation of this system yields

$$\begin{bmatrix} b_{11} & b_{12} & \lambda_{L\gamma} \\ b_{21} & b_{22} & \lambda_{H\gamma} \\ \theta_{L\gamma} & \theta_{H\gamma} & \gamma/(\rho+\gamma) \end{bmatrix} \begin{bmatrix} \hat{w}_L \\ \hat{w}_H \\ \hat{\gamma} \end{bmatrix} = \begin{bmatrix} \hat{L} \\ \hat{H} \\ 0 \end{bmatrix}, \tag{A5.4}$$

where λ_{ij} represents the fraction of the total supply of factor i allocated to activity j. The b_{ij} coefficients are defined as follows:

$$b_{11} = -\sum_i \sigma_i\theta_{Hi}\lambda_{Li} - \sum_{i\neq\gamma} \theta_{Li}\lambda_{Li},$$

$$b_{12} = \sum_i \sigma_i\theta_{Hi}\lambda_{Li} - \sum_{i\neq\gamma} \theta_{Hi}\lambda_{Li},$$

$$b_{21} = \sum_i \sigma_i\theta_{Li}\lambda_{Hi} - \sum_{i\neq\gamma} \theta_{Li}\lambda_{Hi}$$

$$b_{22} = -\sum_i \sigma_i\theta_{Li}\lambda_{Hi} - \sum_{i\neq\gamma} \theta_{Hi}\lambda_{Hi},$$

where σ_i again represents the elasticity of substitution in activity i, Σ_i means summation over $i = \gamma, x, Z$ and $\Sigma_{i\neq\gamma}$ means summation over $i = x, Z$. In the derivation of these expressions we have used $\hat{\theta}_{Li} = \theta_{Hi}(1-\sigma_i)(\hat{w}_L - \hat{w}_H)$ and $\hat{\theta}_{Hi} = \theta_{Li}(1-\sigma_i)(\hat{w}_H - \hat{w}_L)$.

The determinant of the matrix on the left-hand side of (A5.4) is given by

$$\Delta = \frac{\gamma}{\rho + \gamma}(b_{11}b_{22} - b_{12}b_{21}) + \theta_{H\gamma}(\lambda_{L\gamma}b_{21} - \lambda_{H\gamma}b_{11}) + \theta_{L\gamma}(\lambda_{H\gamma}b_{12} - \lambda_{L\gamma}b_{22}).$$

From the definition of the b_{ij}'s, the right-hand side obtains its minimum value when the elasticities of substitution are all equal to zero. In this case the first term equals

$$\frac{\gamma}{\rho + \gamma}\left[\left(\sum_{i \neq \gamma} \theta_{Li}\lambda_{Li}\right)\left(\sum_{i \neq \gamma} \theta_{Hi}\lambda_{Hi}\right) - \left(\sum_{i \neq \gamma} \theta_{Hi}\lambda_{Li}\right)\left(\sum_{i \neq \gamma} \theta_{Li}\lambda_{Hi}\right)\right]$$

$$= \frac{\gamma}{\rho + \gamma}(\lambda_{Hx}\lambda_{LZ} - \lambda_{Lx}\lambda_{HZ})(\theta_{Hx}\theta_{LZ} - \theta_{HZ}\theta_{Lx}),$$

which is positive, because our relative intensity ranking implies $\lambda_{Hx}/\lambda_{Lx} > \lambda_{HZ}/\lambda_{LZ}$, $\theta_{Hx} > \theta_{HZ}$, and $\theta_{Lx} < \theta_{LZ}$. When $\sigma_i = 0$, the sum of the remaining two terms equals

$$\sum_{i \neq \gamma} (\theta_{H\gamma}\theta_{Li} - \theta_{L\gamma}\theta_{Hi})(\lambda_{H\gamma}\lambda_{Li} - \lambda_{L\gamma}\lambda_{Hi}),$$

which also is positive under our assumed factor intensity ranking. We conclude that $\Delta > 0$.

From (A5.4) we now compute

$$\hat{\gamma} = \frac{1}{\Delta}\left[\sum_i \sigma_i\theta_{Li}\lambda_{Hi} - \sum_{i \neq \gamma} (\theta_{H\gamma} - \theta_{Hi})\lambda_{Hi}\right]\hat{L}, \tag{A5.5}$$

$$\hat{\gamma} = \frac{1}{\Delta}\left[\sum_i \sigma_i\theta_{Hi}\lambda_{Li} + \sum_{i \neq \gamma} (\theta_{H\gamma} - \theta_{Hi})\lambda_{Li}\right]\hat{H}. \tag{A5.6}$$

From our relative intensity rankings, it is evident that $d\gamma/dH > 0$, irrespective of the sizes of the elasticities of substitution, and that $d\gamma/dL < 0$ when $\sigma_i = 0$ for all i. Next observe that $d\gamma/dL > 0$ when $\sigma_i = 1$ for $i = x$, Z. Since the right-hand side of (A5.5) increases with the σ_i, it follows that the rate of innovation responds positively to an increase in the stock of unskilled labor whenever the elasticities of substitution in both manufacturing sectors equal or exceed one.

We consider now the effects of an equiproportionate expansion of both factor endowments; that is $\hat{L} = \hat{H} = \hat{F}$. Using (A5.5) and (A5.6), we calculate

$$\hat{\gamma} = \frac{1}{\Delta}\left[\sum_i \sigma_i(\theta_{Li}\lambda_{Hi} + \theta_{Hi}\lambda_{Li}) + \sum_{i \neq \gamma} (\theta_{H\gamma} - \theta_{Hi})(\lambda_{Li} - \lambda_{Hi})\right]\hat{F}. \tag{A5.7}$$

Since production of good Z is the most labor intensive of the three activities, full employment of all factors requires $\lambda_{LZ} > \lambda_{HZ}$ (i.e., the ratio of human capital to unskilled labor in the production of good Z falls short of the ratio of aggregate endowments H/L). If in addition $\lambda_{Lx} > \lambda_{Hx}$, then the right-hand side of (A5.7) is clearly positive, which implies that the rate of innovation increases when both inputs expand equiproportionately. If, on the other hand, $\lambda_{Lx} < \lambda_{HX}$, the fact that $\theta_{Hx} > \theta_{HZ}$ implies that

$$\sum_{i \neq y} (\theta_{Hy} - \theta_{Hi})(\lambda_{Li} - \lambda_{Hi}) > (\theta_{Hy} - \theta_{HZ}) \sum_{i \neq y} (\lambda_{Li} - \lambda_{Hi})$$

$$= (\theta_{Hy} - \theta_{HZ})(\lambda_{Hy} - \lambda_{Ly}) > 0.$$

The last inequality follows from the fact that R&D is the most human-capital-intensive activity, which implies that with full employment of both factors the ratio of human capital to unskilled labor in that activity must exceed *H/L*. Thus the term in square brackets in (A5.7) is positive even when $\lambda_{Lx} < \lambda_{Hx}$. We conclude that an equiproportionate expansion in all factor endowments leads to a faster pace of technological progress in the long run.

6 Small Open Economy

The preceding chapters have developed a framework for the analysis of long-run growth. There, in order to highlight the processes underlying innovation and growth, our attention was confined to a single economy operating in isolation. Now it is time to introduce international trade in goods, capital, and ideas. We begin in this chapter with the simplest case of a small country.

We adopt the usual trade theorist's interpretation of a small economy as being one that does not affect the larger economic environment in which it operates. In the present context this definition has several implications. First, the small country faces perfectly elastic demand in world markets and trades at exogenously given prices. Second, if the small economy trades on world capital markets, it does so at an exogenously given rate of interest. Finally, the R&D activities of the small country do not influence the rate of accumulation of knowledge capital in the world at large, either because its investments in knowledge generate no cross-border knowledge spillovers or because the spillovers that it does generate are negligible in magnitude. Of course no real country fits this description of smallness. Nonetheless, the construct of the small open economy remains a useful one, inasmuch as it allows us to study the channels through which world markets influence domestic behavior without our needing to worry initially about the reverse feedback relationships.

In this chapter, we implement the theoretical notion of smallness by confining innovation to a sector that produces nontradable goods. The small economy that we consider trades two final goods at an exogenously given relative price. The pattern of trade reflects the country's factor endowments. That is, each of the two sectors manufacturing tradable goods makes intensive use of a different primary factor of production. At any moment in time the economy specializes relatively in producing the good that makes intensive use of its abundant factor. Over time productivity gains expand production possibilities in both tradables sectors. The productivity gains stem from endogenous innovation in the sector that produces nontradable components.

In modeling innovation, we incorporate one or the other of the mechanisms introduced in chapters 3 and 4. Under one possible interpretation of the model in this chapter, entrepreneurs develop new varieties of differentiated intermediate goods. Under the alternative interpretation entrepreneurs seek improvements in the quality of a fixed set of components. The two interpretations yield similar predictions about the impact of trade on innovation and growth, but they differ as before in their normative implications.

We begin with an economy that trades only the two consumer goods, and later introduce the potential for international trade in financial assets. Finally, in the last section, we allow for international flows of knowledge capital. In each case we derive the dynamic allocation of resources and study the role that the trading environment plays in determining the equilibrium growth rate. We also examine the welfare properties of the equilibrium trajectory in each setting.

6.1 A Model with Nontraded Intermediates

We study a small country that trades two final goods at exogenously given world prices. Local producers manufacture these goods using primary and intermediate inputs. The primary factors, (unskilled) labor and human capital, are available in fixed and inelastic supply. We distinguish the sectors that produce final goods by the intensity of their use of the two primary factors. In fact, to highlight the role played by cross-sectoral differences in factor intensitites, we make the differences as extreme as possible. We assume that each sector makes direct use of only one primary input. The sector that produces good Y employs human capital in amount H_Y and the sector that produces good Z employs unskilled labor in amount L_Z.

Each final good is manufactured according to a time-invariant, Cobb-Douglas technology with constant returns to scale. Letting Y and Z denote the aggregate outputs of the two final goods, we have

$$Y = A_Y D_Y^{\beta} H_Y^{1-\beta}, \tag{6.1}$$

$$Z = A_Z D_Z^{\beta} L_Z^{1-\beta}. \tag{6.2}$$

In (6.1) and (6.2), D_i represents an index of the intermediate inputs used in sector i, $i = Y, Z$, and A_i is an arbitrary constant reflecting the choice of units. We have made the sectors equally intensive in their use of intermediate inputs in order to ensure the existence of a balanced growth path. Without this assumption the importance of one of the sectors would decline over time until that sector eventually vanished from the long-run equilibrium.

If both final goods are manufactured in positive quantities, then each must have a unit cost equal to its world price. The applicable unit cost functions are dual to the Cobb-Douglas production functions in (6.1) and (6.2). With appropriate choices of the constants A_i, $i = Y, Z$, in (6.1) and (6.2), incomplete specialization in the production of final goods implies that

$$p_Y = w_H^{1-\beta} p_D^{\beta} \tag{6.3}$$

and

$$p_Z = w_L^{1-\beta} p_D^{\beta}, \tag{6.4}$$

where p_i is the world price of good i, $i = Y, Z$, w_j is the reward to factor j, $j = H, L$, and p_D is an index of the prices of intermediates. Production of a good ceases if its unit cost rises above the world price.

Intermediates are not traded. As we mentioned before, this is an assumption of convenience here, one that allows us to introduce innovation in this sector without forcing us to abandon the small country paradigm. Of course in later chapters we will want to allow innovation in sectors that compete internationally. But at this point our goal is simply to introduce some of the ways that world trade might influence the incentives for industrial innovation and growth.

We have seen before (e.g., in chapter 5) that many details of the equilibrium growth path do not depend on the form of the innovation that drives growth. That is true here as well. The mechanisms by which trade and trade policy affect innovation and growth are the same when entrepreneurs aim to expand the range of horizontally differentiated products as when they attempt to raise the quality of a fixed set of products. Once again, we will not commit ourselves to one or the other of the underlying models of product innovation, but rather we will pursue the alternative specifications in parallel. In the formulation with endogenous product variety, we recall that

$$D_i = \left[\int_0^n x_i(\omega)^{\alpha} \, d\omega \right]^{1/\alpha}, \qquad 0 < \alpha < 1, \tag{6.5a}$$

where $x_i(j)$ denotes the input of intermediate j in the production of final good i. In the formulation with endogenous product quality,

$$\log D_i = \int_0^1 \log\left[\sum_m q_m(j)x_{mi}(j)\right]dj, \tag{6.5b}$$

where $x_{mi}(j)$ represents the input of quality m of intermediate product j in the production of final good i. In either event, when technological developments allow D_i to be manufactured with fewer resources, this raises total (direct plus indirect) factor productivity in the production of final goods.

Suppose, as before, that the various components are produced with similar constant-returns-to-scale technologies. Let $c_x(w_L, w_H)$ denote the marginal and average cost of producing any known intermediate. Then our previous analysis indicates an equilibrium price for every component of

$$p_x = \frac{1}{\delta}c_x(w_L, w_H), \tag{6.6}$$

where $\delta = \alpha$ in the case of horizontally differentiated intermediates and $\delta = 1/\lambda$ in the case of quality differentiated inputs.

Since all intermediates bear the same price, all are demanded to the same extent by final good producers. As in chapter 5, we can express the indexes of intermediate inputs in (6.5a) and (6.5b) as

$$D_i = A_D X_i, \tag{6.7}$$

where X_i denotes the aggregate quantity of intermediate inputs used in the production of final good i (the number of intermediates times the quantity employed of each one) and A_D represents the productivity of intermediates. The productivity parameter reflects either the available variety of differentiated intermediates (and thus the possibilities for specialization in the production of final goods) or the average quality of components. By familiar arguments,

$$A_D(t) = n(t)^{(1-\alpha)/\alpha} \tag{6.8a}$$

under the former interpretation, and

$$A_D(t) = \lambda^{I(t)} \tag{6.8b}$$

under the latter.[1] In either case (6.7) implies that

$$p_D = \frac{p_x}{A_D}. \tag{6.9}$$

1. Recall that $I(t) \equiv \int_0^t \imath(\tau)d\tau$.

For an economy that is incompletely specialized in its production of final goods, equations (6.3), (6.4), (6.6), and (6.9) allow us to solve for the prices of the primary and produced inputs as functions of the state of technology A_D and the prices of the final goods. If world prices remain constant, as we shall assume, then the price of the typical intermediate good and the rewards to the two primary inputs all grow at a common rate. This rate equals the product of the cost share of intermediates β and the rate of productivity growth $\dot{A}_D/A_D$ (see appendix A6.1).[2]

We assume now that R&D requires the input of human capital, but not unskilled labor. As before, we let a denote the input coefficient in this activity. This means that either a/n units of human capital are needed to invent one new product per unit time (n here reflecting the local stock of knowledge capital), or that $a\iota$ units of human capital are needed to achieve a flow probability of ι of quality improvement in every industry producing intermediates. The usual free-entry condition $v = w_H a/n$ equates the value of a firm in the nontradables sector to the cost of market entry. Of course $n = 1$ in the model with a fixed (unit) measure of intermediate products. Using $V \equiv 1/nv$ to represent once again the inverse of the aggregate value of the stock market, we have

$$V = \frac{1}{w_H a}. \tag{6.10}$$

We adopt the by now familiar specification of the demand side. Households maximize an intertemporal utility function of the form

$$U_t = \int_t^{\infty} e^{-\rho(\tau - t)} \log u[C_Y(\tau), C_Z(\tau)]\, d\tau, \tag{6.11}$$

where $C_i(\tau)$ is the consumption of final good i at time τ. Here $u(\cdot)$ represents instantaneous utility, which we take to be nondecreasing, strictly quasi-concave, and homogeneous of degree one in its arguments. For the time being, we do not allow international trade in financial assets. Households use their savings to accumulate claims on domestic profit-making enterprises or to acquire riskless domestic bonds. If r represents the instantaneous interest rate in the local capital market, the optimal path for spending satisfies[3]

2. The term $\beta\dot{A}_D/A_D$ represents the rate of total factor productivity gain in the transformation of primary factors and components into final output.

3. The linear homogeneity of $u(\cdot)$ implies the homotheticity of preferences, so indirect utility can be expressed as $v(p_Y, p_Z, E) = E/\Phi(p_Y, p_Z)$, where $\Phi(\cdot)$ is a price index. The

$$\frac{\dot{E}}{E} = r - \rho \tag{6.12}$$

as usual. Of course we are no longer free to choose spending as numéraire, because nominal magnitudes are pegged by the exogenously given world prices.

The absence of international capital flows implies that the small country's trade must be balanced at every moment in time. Trade balance requires that the value of spending be equal to national income:

$$E = p_Y Y + p_Z Z. \tag{6.13}$$

We turn next to the no-arbitrage condition. Starting from the equality between the expected return on equities and the sure return on a riskless bond, we can derive an expression analogous to (5.18):

$$\frac{\dot{V}}{V} + \gamma = (1 - \delta)\beta(p_Y Y + p_Z Z)V - r, \tag{6.14}$$

where γ is the rate of innovation, either g in the model of expanding product variety or ι in the model of rising product quality. The first term on the right-hand side of (6.14) represents the profit rate (flow of profits divided by the equity value) for a typical producer of intermediates. The equation thus equates the excess of the dividend rate over the interest rate to the expected rate of capital loss on shares in the representative firm.

The remaining equilibrium conditions reflect the clearing of factor markets. Each primary factor is used to manufacture components and one of the final goods. In addition human capital is employed in research labs. Market clearing implies that

$$a\gamma + (a_{HY} + a_{Hx}a_{XY})Y + (a_{Hx}a_{XZ})Z = H, \tag{6.15}$$

$$a_{Lx}a_{XY}Y + (a_{LZ} + a_{Lx}a_{XZ})Z = L, \tag{6.16}$$

where a_{HY} and a_{XY} are the per unit inputs of human capital and (aggregate) intermediates, respectively, in the production of good Y, a_{LZ} and a_{XZ} are the per unit inputs of labor and (aggregate) intermediates in the production of good Z, and a_{jx}, $j = H, L$, is the input of factor j in the production of a unit of the aggregate intermediate good X. The left-hand sides of (6.15) and (6.16) give the derived (direct-plus-indirect) factor demands by the two final goods sectors and the derived demand by the research sector, if any.

optimality of (6.12) follows by familiar arguments once we replace $\log u(\cdot)$ in (6.11) by $\log v(\cdot) = \log E - \log \Phi(p_Y, p_Z)$.

In all cases the unit input coefficients minimize the respective unit costs. Each input coefficient varies with the relative rewards to the inputs used in the particular production process and the state of technology. In appendix A6.1 we show that given constant world prices of the traded goods, a typical unit input coefficient applicable to the production of either final good declines at the rate $\beta \dot{A}_D / A_D$, which is just equal to the rate at which the input prices are rising.

This completes the specification of the model. Let us derive now the equilibrium dynamics. Appendix A6.1 shows that (6.15) and (6.16) can be rewritten as

$$a\gamma + b_{HY}\overline{Y} + b_{HZ}\overline{Z} = H, \tag{6.17}$$

$$b_{LY}\overline{Y} + b_{LZ}\overline{Z} = L, \tag{6.18}$$

where $\overline{Y} \equiv YA_D^{-\beta}$, $\overline{Z} \equiv ZA_D^{-\beta}$, and the coefficients b_{ji}, $j = H, L$, $i = Y, Z$, depend only on relative factor prices, and not on the state of technology. Recall that relative factor prices do not vary along an equilibrium trajectory. It follows that the input coefficients b_{ji} remain constant as well.

The terms $\overline{Y}$ and $\overline{Z}$ represent output levels adjusted for changes in total factor productivity. With constant relative factor prices and rising productivity, the derived (direct-plus-indirect) factor demands are proportional to these magnitudes. Equations (6.17) and (6.18) imply that the productivity-adjusted final ouptut measures are constant whenever the rate of innovation is constant. If γ is small, the country may actively produce both final goods ($Y > 0$ and $Z > 0$), in which case $\overline{Y}$ and $\overline{Z}$ will vary linearly with γ. For larger values of γ (those in excess of some critical value γ_c), the R&D activity absorbs so much of the country's stock of human capital that production of the human-capital-intensive good Y falls to zero. Then the relationship between $\overline{Z}$ and the rate of innovation becomes nonlinear (because b_{HZ} varies with γ in this case).[4]

Let us define now the productivity-adjusted value of the national product $\overline{Q} \equiv p_Y\overline{Y} + p_Z\overline{Z}$, and the productivity-adjusted primary input prices $\overline{w}_i \equiv w_i A_D^{-\beta}$, $i = H, L$. If we multiply (6.17) by $\overline{w}_H$, (6.18) by $\overline{w}_L$, and sum the resulting equations, we obtain (see appendix A6.1 for the details)

$$\overline{w}_H a\gamma + [1 - (1 - \delta)\beta]\overline{Q} = \overline{w}_H H + \overline{w}_L L. \tag{6.19}$$

Equation (6.19) expresses an aggregate constraint on resource use, equating

4. These points are discussed in detail in appendix A6.1, which shows also how γ_c is determined.

the total value of primary resources to the sum of the values of the resources employed in R&D and in manufacturing.

Next we turn our attention back to the no-arbitrage condition (6.14). From (6.10) $\dot{V}/V = -\dot{w}_H/w_H = -\beta\dot{A}_D/A_D$. Then (6.8) implies that $\dot{V}/V = -\beta\mu\gamma$, where $\mu = (1-\alpha)/\alpha$ in the model of expanding product variety and $\mu = \log\lambda$ in the model of rising product quality. Also trade balance (6.13) implies that $E = A_D(t)^\beta(p_Y\bar{Y} + p_Z\bar{Z})$. Let us suppose, provisionally, that γ is constant. Then so too are $\bar{Y}$ and $\bar{Z}$, and $\dot{E}/E = \beta\mu\gamma$. Substituting for $\dot{V}/V = -\beta\mu\gamma$ in (6.14) and for $\dot{E}/E = \beta\mu\gamma$ in (6.12), and combining, we find

$$(1-\delta)\beta(p_Y Y + p_Z Z)V = \gamma + \rho.$$

Finally, we substitute for V from (6.10), and use the definitions of productivity-adjusted input prices and output levels, to derive

$$\frac{(1-\delta)\beta\bar{Q}}{a\bar{w}_H} = \gamma + \rho. \tag{6.20}$$

Equations (6.19)–(6.20) comprise two equations in the two variables $\bar{Q}$ and γ that describe the economy's allocation of resources to the manufacturing and research activities. These equations implicitly involve the productivity-adjusted factor prices, which are fully determined by world output prices for values of γ below γ_c, and are functions of these prices and γ for rates of innovation in excess of γ_c. Provided that the solution to this system yields nonnegative values for $\bar{Q}$ and γ, our assumption of a constant rate of innovation is justified. The economy jumps immediately to a steady state, with a constant rate of growth of factor productivity and a constant rate of output growth in the sectors that produce final goods.

The equilibrium allocation can be depicted in a diagram akin to figures 3.4 and 4.4. In figure 6.1 the curve *RR* represents the resource constraint (6.19). It slopes downward because, when more resources are devoted to manufacturing, fewer remain for employment in the research lab. When the rate of innovation is less than γ_c, *RR* is linear because $\bar{Y}$, $\bar{Z}$, and therefore $\bar{Q}$, vary linearly with γ in this range. When the innovation rate exceeds γ_c, and thus the economy produces only one final good (i.e., good Z), the relationship between γ and $\bar{Q}$ is nonlinear. We have also depicted the no-arbitrage condition (6.20) by the curve $\Pi\Pi$. This curve slopes upward, as usual, because more manufacturing activity means a higher profit rate, hence a faster pace of innovation. The relationship also is linear for $\gamma < \gamma_c$, because $\bar{w}_H$ is independent of γ in this range. For $\gamma > \gamma_c$, on the other hand,

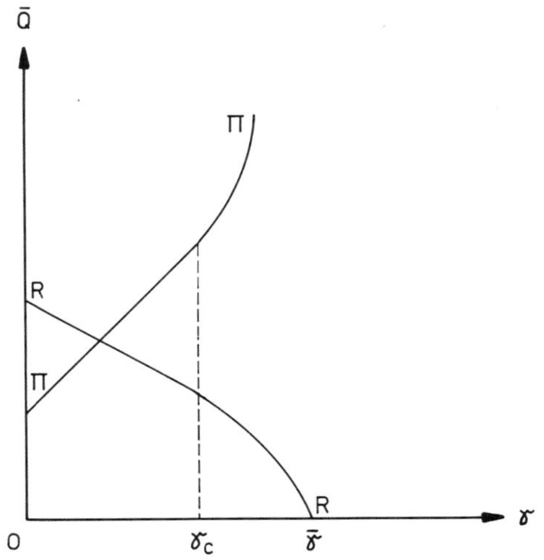

Figure 6.1

$\bar{w}_H$ varies positively with γ, and $\Pi\Pi$ becomes nonlinear, as shown. We find the equilibrium division of resources between manufacturing and R&D at the point of intersection of the two curves.

Equations (6.19) and (6.20) can be solved for the steady-state growth rate

$$\gamma = (1 - v)\frac{h}{a} - v\rho, \qquad 0 < v = 1 - (1 - \delta)\beta < 1, \tag{6.21}$$

where $h \equiv H + \bar{w}_L L/\bar{w}_H$ measures the market value of the resource endowment in units of human capital. The structure of this expression should be quite familiar (e.g., compare [3.30], [4.18], and [5.20]). But the interpretation will be somewhat different now because the measure of resources h is not exogenous here but rather depends upon the equilibrium relative factor prices.

6.2 Trade and Growth

Does trade promote innovation in our model of the small economy? The answer is, "It depends." When trade causes resources to be released from the manufacturing sectors, which then find their way into research labs, the rate of innovation rises. But when the sectors that expand in response to trading opportunities compete with the research labs for factor inputs, international integration may retard growth. The model of the small economy provides a convenient launching pad for our investigation of the relationship between trade and growth, because in this setting the induced factor movements are relatively easy to comprehend.

Formally, the effects of trade on growth are found by comparing the equilibrium that has been described above with one that would arise in the absence of trade (i.e., in a situation of "autarky"). The production side of the autarkic economy mimics that of the trading economy, except that the autarky product prices differ from those in world markets. The autarky relative price of the good imported by the small country exceeds its relative price under free trade. We can therefore derive the qualitative effects of trade by examining the implications of an exogenous decline in the relative price of the importable good.

To keep matters simple, let us suppose that the small country is incompletely specialized in its production of final goods both in autarky and in the trading equilibrium (this assumption is made for expositional convenience but does not affect the conclusions). Then both of the equilibrium points lie along the linear portion of *RR* in figure 6.1. When the country produces both final goods, the productivity-adjusted input prices are fully determined by the prices of the final goods, as we have seen. Equations (A6.1) and (A6.2) in the appendix, which have been derived from (6.3), (6.4), (6.6), and (6.9), link $\bar{w}_H$ and $\bar{w}_L$ to p_Y and p_Z. Differentiating these equations, and letting a "hat" over a variable denote a proportional rate of change, we find

$$\hat{\bar{w}}_H = \frac{1 - \beta\theta_{Hx}}{1 - \beta}\hat{p}_Y - \frac{\beta\theta_{Lx}}{1 - \beta}\hat{p}_Z, \tag{6.22}$$

$$\hat{\bar{w}}_L = \frac{-\beta\theta_{Hx}}{1 - \beta}\hat{p}_Y + \frac{1 - \beta\theta_{Lx}}{1 - \beta}\hat{p}_Z, \tag{6.23}$$

where θ_{jx}, $j = H, L$ denotes the value share of factor j in the cost of producing intermediate inputs. Equations (6.22) and (6.23) imply that an increase in the relative price of the human capital-intensive final good raises the relative reward to human capital. This is of course the familiar Stolper-Samuelson result of international trade theory.

Consider then a country that imports the human capital-intensive final good in the trade equilibrium. For such a country participation in world trade brings about a decline in the relative price of this good, thus a reduction in the relative reward to human capital. The resource base measured in units of human capital expands as a consequence of economic integration. It follows from (6.21) that the country's growth rate increases.

The intuitive explanation for this result is straightforward. International competition forces the sector that produces the importable good Y to contract. Then an incipient excess supply of human capital develops, which causes the salary of skilled workers to fall. The R&D sector expands in response to the decline in the cost of innovation.

Exactly the opposite is true in an economy that exports the human capital-intensive good. This economy experiences, as a consequence of its trade, an increase in the relative price of human capital, a contraction of its available resource stock h, and thus a decline in its growth rate. The exportable sector expands in this economy at the expense of the sector that generates technological progress.

Our findings are special but informative. They are special because innovation has been confined to a sector producing nontradable goods and because we have assumed that the two tradables sectors make equally intensive use of the innovative products. These assumptions eliminate any *direct* effect that trade might have on the *profitability* of R&D. But the results are informative, for they highlight the general-equilibrium interactions between the R&D sector and others in the economy. In virtually any economy the *cost* of R&D will be affected in one way or the other by the changes in relative factor price that attend a country's integration into world markets.[5]

The results extend immediately to include the impact of trade *policy* on innovation and growth. An import tariff or export subsidy that raises the relative domestic price of the labor-intensive good spurs innovation and growth in the small economy, whereas trade policy that promotes the human-capital-intensive final good has the opposite effects. We note, however, that these statements say little about the social desirability of such policies. For that we need a complete welfare analysis of the trade equilibrium, a task to which we now turn.

6.3 Trade and Welfare

In chapters 3 and 4 we identified several reasons why the equilibrium allocation of resources might deviate from the socially optimal allocation in economies with endogenous innovation. The potential market distortions

5. For example, in chapter 9, we will find that trade may impede innovation in a *large*, human-capital-rich economy even if that country enjoys international spillovers of knowledge capital as a result of its foreign commerce. There, as here, it is the intersectoral reallocation of resources effected by trade, and the attendant adjustment in factor prices, that accounts for the possibly adverse impact of trade on the incentives for R&D.

fell into two categories: static and dynamic. We argued that a static distortion would arise whenever market power was exploited to varying degrees in different manufacturing sectors. Here two competitive sectors producing final outputs coexist with a sector that sells innovative goods at noncompetitive prices. So we will need to consider the allocative inefficiency caused by the monopoly pricing of components. We also argued that dynamic distortions result from the failure of innovators to take into account their spillover contributions to consumer surplus and to knowledge capital, and their adverse impact on profits earned by extant producers. These considerations continue to be relevant in the present context.

We begin our analysis by addressing the social planner's problem. Then we discuss how the optimal allocation might be decentralized. In general, attainment of the first-best allocation requires two policy instruments, one to correct the static distortion and another to offset the net effect of the dynamic externalities. We also examine the second-best policy problem that arises when the government has a limited set of policy instruments at its disposal. In particular, we investigate whether R&D policies might be used alone to improve welfare and whether trade policies can play such a second-best role.

Our objective again is to maximize the welfare of the representative household. Using the expression for indirect utility (given in footnote 3), and noting the trade balance condition (6.13), we can express the maximand for the first-best allocation problem as[6]

$$U_t = \int_t^{\infty} e^{-\rho(\tau-t)}[\log \bar{Q} + \log A_D(\tau)^{\beta} - \log \Phi(p_Y, p_Z)]\, d\tau.$$

We will not prove again that the optimal dynamic allocation requires a constant rate of innovation.[7] Rather, we take this as given, and simply solve for the optimal γ. To this end we replace $A_D(\tau)^{\beta}$ by $A_D(t)^{\beta} e^{\beta\mu\gamma(\tau-t)}$, making use of the fact that when the rate of innovation is constant, productivity grows at the constant rate $\mu\gamma$. Now we can integrate the expression for U_t to derive

6. In writing the maximand in this way, we impose the condition that consumers face world prices of the final goods. It is a well-known fact that marginal rates of substitution in consumption should match world prices in a first-best allocation and also in a second-best allocation in which the government uses only R&D taxes and subsidies to improve welfare.

7. The proof follows along similar lines to those presented in chapters 3 and 4. In particular, we treat the maximization as a problem in optimal control and derive the necessary and sufficient conditions for an optimum from the Hamiltonian.

$$\rho U_t = \beta \log A_D(t) - \log \Phi(p_Y, p_Z) + \log \bar{Q} + \frac{\beta\mu\gamma}{\rho}. \tag{6.24}$$

Since the first two terms on the right-hand side of (6.24) are exogenous or predetermined at time t, we have here a preference ordering over steady-state allocations to research and manufacturing.

The social planner maximizes utility in (6.24) by choosing $\bar{Q}$ and γ subject to a resource constraint. One way to express the constraint is to equate the shadow value of available resources to the sum of the shadow values of the resources allocated to the various activities. Standard tenets of cost-benefit analysis (e.g., see Little and Mirrlees 1969) dictate that the shadow value of the resources embodied in final output should match the value of that output at international prices. So if we let w_j^* denote the shadow price of factor j, $j = H, L$ and define $\bar{w}_j^* \equiv w_j^* A_D^{-\beta}$, we can write the resource constraint as

$$\bar{w}_H^* a\gamma + \bar{Q} = \bar{w}_H^* H + \bar{w}_L^* L. \tag{6.25}$$

The solution to the maximization problem is depicted in figure 6.2. We have drawn the resource constraint (6.25) as R^1R^1. The social planner faces a better trade-off than the market between $\bar{Q}$ and γ, since the planner uses inputs efficiently in manufacturing but the market does not. Therefore R^1R^1 lies beyond the constraint RR of figure 6.1, which depicts the feasible combinations of manufactured output and innovation rates for the market

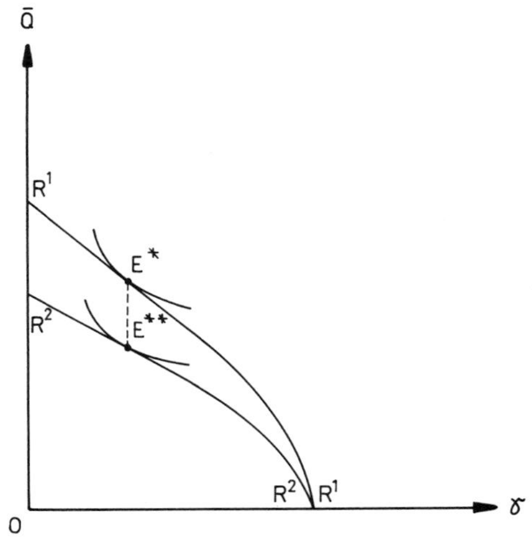

Figure 6.2

economy. The figure also shows some representative indifference curves associated with the preferences in (6.24). We find the first-best allocation at point E^*, where an indifference curve is tangent to R^1R^1. Direct calculation using (6.24) and (6.25) gives the optimal rate of innovation as $\gamma^* = h^*/a - \rho/\beta\mu$, where $h^* \equiv H + \bar{w}_L^* L/\bar{w}_H^*$.

Now let us suppose that the market equilibrium is characterized by incomplete specialization in the production of final goods (as in figure 6.1). We will argue that in this case $h^* = h$, hence

$$\gamma^* = \frac{h}{a} - \frac{\rho}{\beta\mu}. \tag{6.26}$$

The reason is as follows: The market prices of the primary factors differ from their shadow prices only because the intermediate inputs are not competitively priced. But from (A6.1) and (A6.2) we see that $\bar{w}_H$ and $\bar{w}_L$ respond equiproportionately to changes in the markup on components. It follows that the ratio of shadow to market input prices is the same for both factors. Therefore $\bar{w}_H^*/\bar{w}_L^* = \bar{w}_H/\bar{w}_L$, and so $h^* = h$.

We can now compare the equilibrium and optimal rates of innovation. From (6.21) and (6.26) we have

$$\gamma^* - \gamma = \nu\gamma^* + \rho\left(\nu - \frac{1-\nu}{\beta\mu}\right), \qquad \nu = 1 - (1-\delta)\beta. \tag{6.27}$$

In order to evaluate (6.27), we must distinguish between the alternative interpretations of innovation in the intermediate goods sector. When innovation takes the form of an expanding range of inputs, the term in parenthesis on the right-hand side of (6.27) equals $(1-\alpha)(1-\beta)$. In this case, the right-hand side is positive, and the optimal rate of innovation exceeds the market rate. But when innovation entails improvements in the quality of inputs, the term in parentheses equals $1 - \beta + \beta/\lambda - (\lambda - 1)/\lambda \log \lambda$, which may be positive or negative. In this case the rate of innovation in the market equilibrium can be too high or too low. These results mimic of course our findings in chapters 3 and 4 where we studied the respective closed economies. Here, as there, the marginal innovation generates spillover benefits to both consumers and to later generations of innovators, while imposing a negative externality on extant producers. Only in the case of expanding product variety can we be sure that the positive spillover effects dominate.

The government requires two policy instruments in order to achieve the first-best allocation in a decentralized equilibrium. An appropriate subsidy to final good producers in proportion to the cost of their components could be used to eliminate the static distortion associated with monopoly pricing. The optimal subsidy equates the user cost of intermediates with the marginal cost of producing them. It moves the economy from the distorted resource constraint RR to the true constraint R^1R^1. Then a policy directed at R&D can be used in combination with the input subsidy to ensure an efficient rate of innovation. This policy would move the economy along R^1R^1 to the optimal point E^*. In the case of horizontally differentiated inputs, the first-best policy package always includes a subsidy to R&D. Appendix A6.2 establishes that the optimal subsidy rate equals $\gamma^*/(\gamma^* + \rho)$ in this case. With quality differentiated inputs, on the other hand, a tax on R&D may be indicated. The optimal tax rate (derived in the appendix) is $(\lambda - 1)\rho/(\gamma^* + \rho)\log\lambda - 1$, which surely is positive whenever $\gamma > \gamma^*$ and also is positive for some parameter values such that $\gamma < \gamma^*$.

6.3.1 Second-Best R&D Subsidies

An interesting question arises as to whether the same prescriptions for R&D policy apply when the government cannot or does not implement the first-best subsidy on the use of intermediate inputs. To address this question, we consider the welfare implications of a policy whereby the government bears a fraction ϕ of the private cost of R&D but allows market forces to govern the determination of input prices and thus the choice of techniques in production.

With the R&D policy in place, and assuming incomplete specialization in the production of final goods, input prices are determined by (6.3), (6.4), (6.6), and (6.9). Thus the factor-market clearing conditions (6.15) and (6.16) of the laissez-faire equilibrium apply. From these we can derive the resource constraint (6.19). In other words, the equilibrium with a tax or subsidy applied to R&D occurs somewhere along the curve RR in figure 6.1. To find the equilibrium associated with any particular value of ϕ, we need only to modify the no-arbitrage condition to reflect the actual incentives facing entrepreneurs. In place of $a\bar{w}_H$ in the denominator of (6.20), we have $a\bar{w}_H(1 - \phi)$, since entrepreneurs pay a fraction (or multiple) of private R&D costs. The new expression for the $\Pi\Pi$ curve becomes

$$\frac{(1 - \delta)\beta\bar{Q}}{a\bar{w}_H(1 - \phi)} = \gamma + \rho.$$

Changes in ϕ cause the $\Pi\Pi$ curve to rotate about its intersection with the horizontal axis. It follows that, by varying ϕ, the government can achieve any point along RR as a decentralized equilibrium.

In figure 6.2 we have reproduced the equilibrium resource constraint (i.e., the curve RR from figure 6.1) as R^2R^2. As we have just seen, the second-best allocation falls somewhere along this curve, when the government has only R&D policies at its disposal. We find the constrained optimum at the point of tangency between R^2R^2 and an indifference curve at E^{**} in the figure. Algebraically we maximize (6.24) subject to (6.19). The solution gives the second-best rate of innovation,

$$\gamma^{**} = \frac{h}{a} - \frac{\rho}{\beta\mu}, \tag{6.28}$$

whenever the point of tangency lies along the flat segment of R^2R^2.

Notice that $\gamma^{**} = \gamma^{*}$ (i.e., the first and second-best rates of innovation coincide).[8] It follows that the second-best R&D policy ought to encourage research whenever the market rate of innovation is lower than the first-best rate, and discourage research when the market rate is higher than the first-best rate. This prescription makes the second-best optimal policy qualitatively the same as the first-best R&D policy in the model with expanding input variety (i.e., a subsidy) but not necessarily so in the model with rising input quality.

6.3.2 Second-Best Trade Policies

What are the welfare implications of trade policy? To answer this question, we introduce T_i, $i = Y, Z$ to represent one plus the rate of trade protection provided to sector i, where protection takes the form of an import tariff if good i is imported or an export subsidy if that good is exported. We continue to use p_i to denote the domestic price of good i, and let $\tilde{p}_i$ stand for the (exogenous) international price. Then $p_i = T_i\tilde{p}_i$. For the remainder of this section we assume the economy to be incompletely specialized in its production of final goods. In the event, equations (6.3), (6.4), (6.6), and (6.9) apply with the trade policies in place, and (6.19) again expresses the resource constraint. Of course $\bar{Q}$ now represents the value of the national product at productivity-adjusted *domestic* prices, which differs from its value at international prices.

Our economy exhibits the Ricardo-Barro neutrality property (Barro 1974). That is, the equilibrium allocation is not affected by the inter-

8. This result and the following discussion do not apply when the second-best rate of innovation happens to fall along the curved portion of R^2R^2, that is, when complete specialization in the production of the labor-intensive final good is indicated.

temporal structure of budget deficits, provided that the government's budget balances in present-value terms. Without loss of generality, we can assume that the government maintains a balanced budget at all times. It redistributes tariff revenues by instantaneous lump-sum rebates and finances trade subsidies by lump-sum levies. Trade balance now implies that aggregate spending is equal to the value of ouput at domestic prices plus net government transfers, or

$$E = Q + \sum_i (T_i - 1)\tilde{p}_i M_i, \tag{6.29}$$

where M_i denotes the volume of imports of good i (negative for exports). Using (6.29) and the homotheticity of preferences, we can show that $\dot{E}/E = \beta \dot{A}_D/A_D$ holds along a balanced-growth trajectory. Then it is possible to derive (6.20) again from (6.14) as the relevant form of the no-arbitrage condition.

Our welfare criterion is given once more by (6.24). We have already seen that trade policies affect the division of resources between R&D and manufacturing. This is one channel through which these policies influence social welfare. Trade policies also drive a wedge between domestic consumer prices and world prices, and so distort household purchase decisions. Finally, trade policies influence the efficiency of resource allocation within the manufacturing sector. We need to assess these various components of the effect on welfare in order to ascertain the desirability of one type of policy or another. For convenience we restrict our attention to small departures from free trade.

To find the total effect of trade policy on welfare, we differentiate (6.24) with respect to T_Y and T_Z, and evaluate at $T_i = 1$. Noting the trade balance condition (6.29), Roy's identity, and $p_i = T_i \tilde{p}_i$, we find

$$\rho dU = \hat{\bar{Q}} + \frac{\beta\mu}{\rho} d\gamma - \theta_Y \hat{T}_Y - \theta_Z \hat{T}_Z,$$

where θ_i, $i = Y, Z$, is the share of sector i in the value of final output. Then we differentiate (6.19) and (6.20), and use (6.22) and (6.23), to obtain[9]

9. Our calculations also make use of the following relationships derived from (6.15) and (6.16):

$$\frac{\bar{w}_H H}{\bar{Q}} = (1 - \beta)\theta_Y + \delta\beta\theta_{Hx} + \frac{\bar{w}_H a\gamma}{\bar{Q}},$$

$$\frac{\bar{w}_L L}{\bar{Q}} = (1 - \beta)\theta_Z + \delta\beta\theta_{Lx}.$$

$$d\gamma = \frac{\beta(1-\delta)w_L L}{(1-\beta)w_H a}(\hat{T}_Z - \hat{T}_Y)$$

and

$$\hat{\bar{Q}} = \theta_Y \hat{T}_Y + \theta_Z \hat{T}_Z + \frac{\beta(1-\delta)\theta_{Lx}}{1-\beta}(\hat{T}_Y - \hat{T}_Z).$$

Finally, we substitute these terms into the expression for the change in welfare, which yields

$$(1-\beta)\rho\, dU$$

$$= \left\{(1-\delta)\beta\theta_{Lx} - \frac{\beta\mu(\gamma+\rho)}{\rho}[\delta\beta\theta_{Lx} + (1-\beta)\theta_Z]\right\}(\hat{T}_Y - \hat{T}_Z). \tag{6.30}$$

We need to evaluate the sign of the term in the curly brackets in (6.30) in order to identify the nature of the trade intervention that improves welfare. Let us concentrate, for the moment, on the economy with an expanding range of intermediate products. We know that under free trade this economy grows more slowly than is optimal. Nonetheless, a trade policy that promotes growth ($\hat{T}_Z > 0$) may reduce its aggregate welfare, and one that impedes growth ($\hat{T}_Y > 0$) may raise its welfare. The ambiguity, which may seem surprising at first, is entirely consistent with the theory of the second best. We recall that the economy suffers not only from a dynamic distortion that causes suboptimal innovation and growth but also from a distortion in the static allocation of resources. This latter distortion implies an inefficiently small output of components for any given scale of R&D activity. Trade policy operates on both of the distorted margins. Thus a policy that alleviates the dynamic distortion need not raise welfare if it happens to exacerbate the static inefficiency. Similarly a policy that promotes static efficiency at the expense of dynamic efficiency may sometimes increase welfare.

Consider, for example, an economy that is poorly endowed with unskilled labor and relatively unproductive in the research lab. In this economy both θ_Z and γ will be close to zero. Then the expression in curly brackets equals $\beta(1-\beta)(1-\alpha)\theta_{Lx} > 0$.[10] In this case a trade policy that retards growth ($\hat{T}_Y > 0$) raises welfare, whereas one that promotes growth ($\hat{T}_Z > 0$) reduces welfare. When research productivity is low, R&D is not

10. Note that θ_{Lx} is a function of productivity-adjusted factor prices, which depend in turn only on the domestic prices of final output. Thus θ_{Lx} can take on any value between zero and one, even when a is large and L is small.

very sensitive to changes in factor prices. And when unskilled labor is scarce, there is little scope for one final goods industry to expand at the expense of the other. This in turn implies that relatively little human capital will move between the R&D labs and the plants that produce good Y in response to trade initiatives. In these circumstances, the effects of trade policy on growth, though present, are relatively muted and are dominated in the welfare calculus by the induced changes in the output of intermediates.

Now consider a case where the production of intermediates requires only the input of human capital. Such an economy has $\theta_{Lx} = 0$, and so the term in curly brackets in (6.30) is negative. This economy always gains from a trade policy that promotes growth. When the government of this economy supports the labor-intensive industry, the reward to human capital falls. This encourages both innovation and the production of intermediate goods. With both γ and X rising in response to trade policy, aggregate welfare must rise as well.[11]

Needless to say, the ambiguity concerning the nature of the second-best trade policy remains for an economy that innovates by improving the quality of its products. In such an economy even the desired direction of change in the size of the research sector is, a priori, unclear.

6.4 International Capital Flows

We introduce now the potential for the small country to engage in international asset trade. We let agents (firms and households) in the country borrow and lend at an exogenous and constant interest rate $\tilde{r}$. With perfect capital mobility, the international interest rate must prevail domestically:

$$r = \tilde{r}. \tag{6.31}$$

This relationship replaces the trade balance equation (6.13), which no longer needs to be satisfied at every moment in time.[12]

11. We can calculate the effect of trade policy on the output of intermediates using $p_x X A_D^{-\beta} = \beta \bar{Q}$, the formula for $\hat{Q}$ from above, and the expression for $\hat{p}_x$ that comes from differentiating (6.3), (6.4), (6.6), and (6.9). This gives

$$\hat{X} = \left[\frac{1-(1-\delta)\beta}{1-\beta}\theta_{Lx} - \theta_Z\right](\hat{T}_Y - \hat{T}_Z).$$

Using this expression and (6.30), it is straightforward to show that in an economy with horizontal differentiation of intermediates, a contraction in the output of components is necessary but not sufficient for a growth-promoting trade policy to reduce welfare.

12. Instead, we have only the requirement that trade be balanced in present value. This condition is automatically satisfied if each household obeys its intertemporal budget constraint.

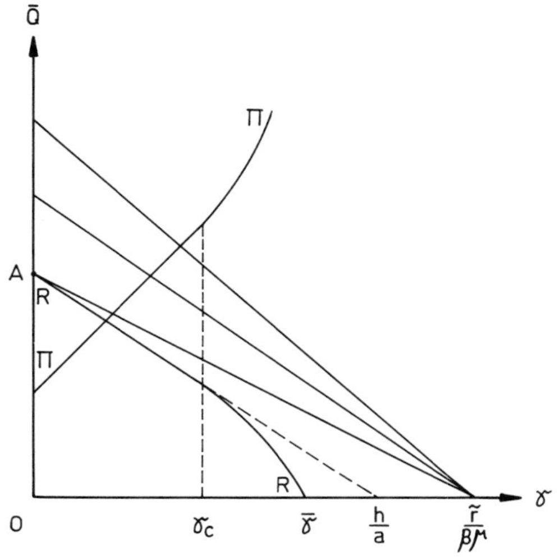

Figure 6.3

Substituting for r in (6.14) using (6.31), and noting (6.10) and $\dot{V}/V = -\beta\mu\gamma$ as before, we can derive the new no-arbitrage condition

$$\frac{(1-\delta)\beta\bar{Q}}{a\bar{w}_H} = \tilde{r} + \gamma(1-\beta\mu). \qquad (6.32)$$

This equation, together with (6.19), determines the equilibrium rate of innovation and the productivity-adjusted level of manufactured output in the small economy that trades goods and assets.

The equilibrium is depicted in figure 6.3. The resource constraint RR is the same as for the economy without capital flows. The linear portion of the no-arbitrage curve ΠΠ (which applies for $\gamma < \gamma_c$) is flatter than before. But the curve emanates from a point on the vertical axis that may be above or below that for the economy without asset trade. It is easy to see that, the lower is the international interest rate, the faster is output growth. Also the advent of asset trade speeds output growth if and only if the international interest rate falls below the equilibrium interest rate that prevails in the absence of such trade. In the event that capital flows retard growth, they do so because households choose to reallocate some of their savings from local research ventures to (initially) higher-yielding foreign bonds.

We derive now the optimal allocation of resources for a small economy that borrows and lends on international capital markets. Expenditure grows optimally at the rate $\dot{E}/E = \tilde{r} - \rho$. So utility of the representative household can be expressed as

$$\rho U_t = \log E(t) + \frac{\tilde{r} - \rho}{\rho} - \log \Phi(p_Y, p_Z). \tag{6.33}$$

From (6.33) we see that maximization of U_t is equivalent to maximization of the initial level of spending $E(t)$.

Initial spending is limited by the intertemporal budget constraint

$$\int_t^\infty e^{-\tilde{r}(\tau-t)} E(t) e^{(\tilde{r}-\rho)(\tau-t)}\, d\tau = \int_t^\infty e^{-\tilde{r}(\tau-t)} \bar{Q} A_D(t)^\beta e^{\beta\mu\gamma(\tau-t)}\, d\tau + F(t),$$

where $F(t)$ represents the value of net domestic holdings of foreign bonds (possibly negative) at time t.[13] In writing the constraint in this way, we have made use of the fact that spending and output grow at the constant rates of $\tilde{r} - \rho$ and $\beta\mu\gamma$, respectively.[14] Integrating on both sides of the constraint, we find

$$E(t) = \frac{\rho \bar{Q} A_D(t)^\beta}{\tilde{r} - \beta\mu\gamma} + \rho F(t). \tag{6.34}$$

Equation (6.34) shows again a trade-off between the initial output of manufactures $\bar{Q}$ and the rate of innovation γ. The indifference curves associated with this equation (i.e., the combinations of $\bar{Q}$ and γ that yield a given value of $E[t]$) are represented by straight lines that emanate from the point $\gamma = \tilde{r}/\beta\mu$ on the horizontal axis of figure 6.3. The first-best allocation achieves the uppermost indifference curve consistent with the first-best resource constraint R^1R^1 (not drawn). The second-best allocation (for a government that cannot subsidize the production of components) achieves the highest indifference curve that touches RR.

Figure 6.3 depicts the case in which $\tilde{r} > \beta\mu h/a$, where h is computed using the factor rewards that prevail if the economy does not specialize in its production of final goods. In this case the pivotal point of the indifference curves lies to the right of the point where an extension of the linear portion of RR (and also the linear portion of the undrawn R^1R^1) intersects the horizontal axis. The figure shows that the optimal allocation (both first best and second best), which is represented by the point labeled

13. For simplicity, we limit asset trade to the exchange of indexed bonds. If, instead, foreign residents held claims to domestic profit-making firms, the government of the small economy would have an additional consideration in its choice of an optimal allocation. That is, the government could in some cases use the intersectoral allocation of resources to affect local factor prices and thus the value of foreign equity holdings.

14. Here again we simply assume that the optimal growth path involves a constant rate of innovation and hence a constant rate of growth in output. As before, we could formally prove that the optimal growth path has this property.

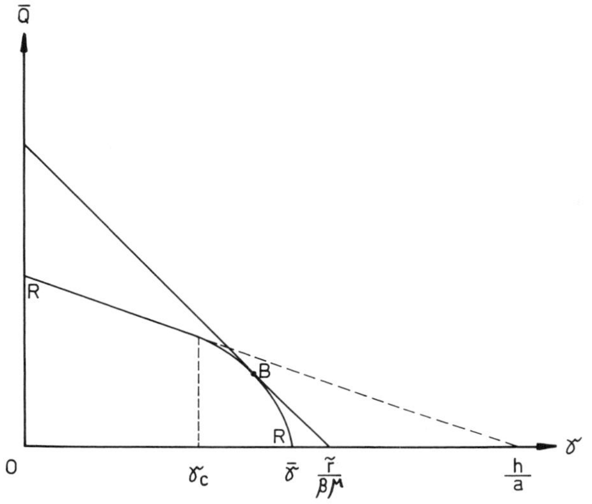

Figure 6.4

A, calls for the small economy to specialize in manufacturing and to refrain from any research. Intuitively, if the world interest rate is high, the rewards to local research will not be sufficiently great to cover the opportunity cost of capital. Foreign bonds will dominate domestic R&D as a vehicle for investment.

Figure 6.4 illustrates the solution to the welfare maximization problem for intermediate values of the world interest rate that satisfy $\bar{\gamma} < \tilde{r}/\beta\mu < h/a$, where $\bar{\gamma} \equiv H/a$ is the maximum feasible rate of innovation. In the figure the curve labeled *RR* may be taken to represent either the first-best resource constraint R^1R^1, or the second-best resource constraint R^2R^2. The optimal allocation (first best or second best, depending upon the interpretation of *RR*) is found at point *B*. Here the economy maximizes welfare by devoting resources to the production of one final good (the labor-intensive good) and to research. When the world interest rate is still lower than that represented by figure 6.4, so that $\tilde{r}/\beta\mu < \bar{\gamma}$, it is feasible for the small economy to achieve unbounded utility by innovating at a rate equal to or greater than $\tilde{r}/\beta\mu$. In this case the small country may cease to be "small" in the long run, and in any event its social maximization problem is not well defined.

6.5 International Knowledge Flows

We have assumed thus far that the small country generates all of its technical know-how by its own research efforts. In making this assumption, we have neglected perhaps the most important mechanism by which integration into the world economy can promote innovation and growth. That is, a country that interacts with the outside world may gain access to the large body of knowledge that has already been accumulated in the international research community, as well as to some of the new discoveries that are being made there. Our treatment of innovation has stressed the public-good characteristics of knowledge: the fact that ideas can be used in many applications in various geographic locations at the same time (nonrivalry), and the fact that it may be difficult for the originators of many ideas to prevent others from using them without monetary compensation (nonexcludability). These same considerations remain relevant in an international context. If the residents of a country meet and interact with foreign counterparts, they may find occasions to learn technical information that contributes to their country's stock of general knowledge. These opportunities might never arise if the country opts for economic isolation.

We begin in this section to explore the effects of international knowledge spillovers by examining the innovation process of a small economy that learns from its trade partners. We return to the setting used at the start of this chapter, where the country trades two final goods but not financial assets. Henceforth we focus exclusively on the version of our model that treats innovative intermediate goods as horizontally differentiated products. This specification has the desirable property for the purposes at hand that the stock of knowledge appears explicitly as a distinct variable. We can then ask how the country's international relations affect the process by which this knowledge is accumulated.

It is plausible to suppose that the foreign contribution to the local knowledge stock increases with the number of commercial interactions between domestic and foreign agents. That is, we may assume that international trade in tangible commodities facilitates the exchange of intangible ideas. This assumption can be justified in several ways. First, the larger the volume of international trade, the greater presumably will be the number of personal contacts between domestic and foreign individuals. These contacts may give rise to an exchange of information and may cause the agents from the small country to acquire novel (for them) perspectives on technical problems. Second, imports may embody differentiated intermediates that are not available in the local economy. The greater the quantity of such imports, the greater perhaps will be the number of insights that local researchers gain from inspecting and using these goods. Third, when local goods are exported, the foreign purchasing agents may suggest ways to improve the manufacturing process. In the context of our model, the recommendations might take the form of ideas for new intermediate inputs. The number of such suggestions is likely to increase with the quantity of goods exported. It seems reasonable to assume therefore that the extent of the spillovers between any two countries increases with the volume of their bilateral trade.[15]

To pursue the implications of this hypothesis, we let $K_n(t)$ denote the stock of knowledge capital in the small country, and suppose that the growth of K_n depends not only on spillovers from local research but also on those from international contacts. In particular, we specify

$$K_n(t) = G[n(t), T(t)],$$

where T represents the cumulative volume of trade (exports plus imports) up to time t.[16] We take $G(\cdot)$ to be increasing in both arguments and homogeneous of degree one. The latter assumption allows us to define the "intensive" function $\Psi(\cdot) \equiv G[1, T(t)/n(t)]$ such that

$$K_n = n\Psi\left(\frac{T}{n}\right). \tag{6.35}$$

Equation (6.35) generalizes our earlier treatment, which had $\Psi(T/n) \equiv 1$ (or any positive constant). Whereas formerly an entrepreneur required a/n units of human capital to invent a new variety of differentiated input, now $a/n\Psi(T/n)$ units are needed. This change necessitates two modifications in our equilibrium relationships. The market-clearing condition for human capital now becomes

$$\frac{a}{\Psi(T/n)}g + (a_{HY} + a_{HX}a_{XY})Y + (a_{HX}a_{XZ})Z = H, \tag{6.15$'$}$$

while free entry into R&D implies that

15. This view finds support from a recent study of Korea's industrialization process. Rhee, Ross-Larson, and Pursell (1984) surveyed 113 Korean exporters, who identified foreign buyers and foreign suppliers as important sources for technical information in 29 percent of the cases. According to this study, "foreign buyers and suppliers provide access to information about what product styles are wanted and about how to make products of a desired style. They come in, too, with models and patterns for Korean engineers to follow, and they even go out to the production line to teach workers how to do things." (p. 41)

16. It might be preferable to enter exports and imports as separate arguments into $G(\cdot)$. In order to aggregate the two, we must convert their different magnitudes into a common unit using some relative price. Then, if the relative price changes, the measure of trade volume also changes even if the quantities of exports and imports do not. However, for present purposes we may perform the aggregation using international relative prices. These are given to the small economy and are taken to be fixed over time.

$$V = \frac{\Psi(T/n)}{w_H a}. \tag{6.10'}$$

We have seen above that when the rate of innovation is g, final outputs expand in the long run at the rate $g\beta(1-\alpha)/\alpha$, where (we recall) $1-\alpha$ is the inverse of the elasticity of demand for every component and β is the aggregate share of components in the cost of producing final goods. Spending also grows in the long run at this rate, and with constant terms of trade, so does consumption of each final good. Therefore the volume of trade grows at the rate $g\beta(1-\alpha)/\alpha$ as well. It follows that T/n will either shrink to zero, grow without bound or tend to a finite constant in the long run, depending upon whether α is larger than, smaller than, or equal to $\beta(1-\alpha)$. We treat each of these possibilities in turn.

Suppose that $\alpha > \beta(1-\alpha)$. Then the relative importance of the international spillovers as a source of the accumulation of domestic knowledge declines with time. In the long run cumulative trade makes a negligible contribution to K_n in comparison with the contribution made by cumulative local research. Thus the economy tends to a steady state with $K_n = n\bar{\psi}$, where $\bar{\psi} \equiv \Psi(0)$ is just a positive constant. The long-run growth path of the economy in this case is the same as for an economy that does not acquire information from abroad. The steady-state innovation rate is given by

$$\gamma = (1-\nu)\bar{\psi}\frac{h}{a} - \nu\rho, \qquad 0 < \nu = 1-(1-\alpha)\beta < 1, \tag{6.21'}$$

and the long-run effects of government policies are the same as before. In particular, trade policies that alter domestic relative prices influence the long-run rate of growth by the mechanism described in section 6.2, but there is no new effect introduced by the presence of international knowledge spillovers related to trade. Trade policies do, however, have an additional impact on growth in the transition to the steady state. Before the cumulative volume of trade becomes trivial in comparison to the number of available varieties, a policy that expands trade (e.g., an export subsidy or an import subsidy) encourages knowledge acquisition from abroad, while policies that contract trade reduce international knowledge spillovers. The former type of policy accelerates growth along the transition path, while the latter type slows transitional growth.

Now suppose that $\alpha < \beta(1-\alpha)$. Then the ratio of the cumulative trade volume to the number of varieties tends to infinity, giving rise to one of two possible scenarios. First, the value of $\Psi(\cdot)$ may tend to a finite constant. This would occur, for example, if $G(\cdot)$ had a CES form, with an elasticity of substitution between information from domestic and foreign sources in excess of one. Then the long-run behavior of the economy again mimics that of an economy without international spillovers. In contrast to the case where T/n tends to zero, however, the knowledge gained from trade contacts continues to drive growth in the long run. But a marginal increase in the amount of trade (e.g., as might be effected by a policy intervention) has no impact on the steady-state rates of innovation and growth because the full contribution of trade to the innovation process eventually is realized with or without the encouragement of policy.

A different type of long-run dynamics obtains when $\alpha < \beta(1 - \alpha)$ and $\Psi(\cdot)$ has no upper bound. Then productivity in the research lab increases indefinitely, which causes the rates of innovation and utility growth to become unbounded.[17]

The final case to consider is an interesting one, even though it represents a razor-edge in the present formulation. This case applies in an economy with $\alpha = \beta(1 - \alpha)$. In such an economy both the volume of trade and number of varieties grow at the common rate g in the long run, and the ratio of the two approaches an endogenously determined finite value. Let us define $\tau \equiv \lim_{t \to \infty} T(t)/n(t)$. Using this definition, the formula for the long-run rate of innovation becomes

$$\gamma = (1 - v)\Psi(\tau)\frac{h}{a} - v\rho, \qquad v = 1 - (1 - \alpha)\beta = 1 - \alpha. \qquad (6.21'')$$

The equilibrium value of τ is found in the solution to the steady-state system.[18] Here a policy that alters the extent of trade affects the long-run growth rate by two mechanisms. Let us consider, for example, the effects of an import tariff. We have seen already that a tariff raises $h \equiv H + \bar{w}_L L/\bar{w}_H$ if the import good uses unskilled labor relatively intensively

17. In this case a technical problem arises in the calculation of the equilibrium in that the household's maximization problem is not well defined. Since there is not much to say about the equilibrium with an unbounded rate of growth, we will not pursue any solution to the technical problem.

18. If the small country exports good Z, for example, the ratio of current exports to the number of varieties tends to $(\bar{Z} - \sigma_Z \bar{E}/p_Z)$, when $\alpha = \beta(1 - \alpha)$, where $\bar{Z}$ and $\bar{E}$ are defined as before and $\sigma_Z(p_Y/p_Z)$ is the share of spending devoted to good Z. The value of imports must equal the value of exports at world prices. So the ratio of imports to the number of varieties tends to $(\tilde{p}_Z/\tilde{p}_Y)(\bar{Z} - \sigma_Z \bar{E}/p_Z)$. Finally, the cumulative volume of trade is approximately equal to $1/g$ times the current volume of trade in the long run. Therefore $\tau = (1 + \tilde{p}_Z/\tilde{p}_Y)(\bar{Z} - \sigma_Z \bar{E}/p_Z)/g$.

and reduces h otherwise. The tariff also depresses imports and exports at every moment in time and so reduces the long-run value of τ. This reduces research productivity and works to slow long-run growth. We conclude that a tariff must retard growth under these circumstances if the import-competing sector is intensive in its use of human capital, but that the net effect is ambiguous if the import good is unskilled labor intensive.

The welfare analysis must be similarly modified to reflect the spillover benefits from trade. If trade policy had no effect on relative factor prices (as, for example, when the country specializes completely in the production of a single final good), then a small intervention to promote trade would necessarily increase welfare (see Grossman and Helpman 1991c). In the more general case the analysis is more complicated. We can conclude, however, that the introduction of international knowledge spillovers that are related to the volume of commodity trade introduces a pro-trade bias into our welfare results. An export subsidy will be beneficial in all cases where it previously was identified to be so, and in additional cases as well. An import tariff, on the other hand, may reduce social welfare even if it both encourages local R&D and stimulates production of intermediate goods.

Our initial examination of the implications of economic integration for growth performance has focused on the small country. We have studied an economy that invents nontraded intermediate goods, which it uses along with primary factors to manufacture two final products. The final goods are traded on international markets at exogenously given world prices. In this setting international trade can have direct and indirect effects on the innovation process. Trade may facilitate the transmission of technical information from foreign sources. Then an integrated economy will enjoy productivity gains in the research lab that spur its technological progress. International trade also affects conditions in local factor markets. A country that imports human-capital-intensive goods finds that international integration reduces derived demand for human capital and thereby lowers the cost of innovation. In such a country the indirect effect of trade also is to encourage growth. But trade may impede growth in a country that exports human capital-intensive goods because the exportables sector draws human capital away from research activities.

The small-country paradigm proves especially useful for welfare analysis. We have found that growth may be too fast or too slow in a small country that generates endogenous productivity gains. In any event a technology policy (R&D tax or subsidy) can always be used to raise social welfare, and an appropriate intervention of this sort, coupled with a subsidy to input production, achieves the first best. Complications arise, however, in the use of second-best instruments, of which trade policy represents a notable example. Trade policies that boost the growth rate, even in situations where equilibrium growth is slower than optimal, may reduce social welfare if they exacerbate a static inefficiency. The static allocation generally is distorted because innovative components are priced above their marginal cost of production. Thus trade policies that cause a reduction in the output of intermediates may be harmful even when they promote faster growth, while policies that encourage production of intermediates may be beneficial even when they cause a slowdown of growth.

APPENDIX

A6.1 Derivation of Figure 6.1

In this appendix we provide the detailed analytical arguments that support the qualitative features of figure 6.1. Our starting point is the system of pricing equations (6.3), (6.4), (6.6), and (6.9). These equations imply that

$$p_Y = \left[\frac{c_x(\bar{w}_L, \bar{w}_H)}{\delta}\right]^{\beta} \bar{w}_H^{1-\beta} \equiv \bar{c}_Y(\bar{w}_L, \bar{w}_H), \tag{A6.1}$$

$$p_Z = \left[\frac{c_x(\bar{w}_L, \bar{w}_H)}{\delta}\right]^{\beta} \bar{w}_L^{1-\beta} \equiv \bar{c}_Z(\bar{w}_L, \bar{w}_H), \tag{A6.2}$$

$$p_x = \frac{c_x(\bar{w}_L, \bar{w}_H)}{\delta} A_D^{\beta}, \tag{A6.3}$$

where $\bar{w}_i \equiv w_i A_D^{-\beta}$, $i = H, L$. Naturally (A6.1) and (A6.2) apply only if both final goods sectors are active in the equilibrium. Otherwise, one of these equations becomes an inequality. The functions $\bar{c}_Y(\cdot)$ and $\bar{c}_Z(\cdot)$ represent reduced-form cost functions that account for the direct and indirect use of primary inputs in the production of consumer goods, as well as the markup charged by the manufacturers of intermediate products. Given final commodity prices, we can use (A6.1) and (A6.2) to calculate equilibrium productivity-adjusted primary input prices, provided that there is no specialization in the production of final goods. These factor prices can then be used in (A6.3) to calculate the price of the representative intermediate good.

Unit input coefficients in the production of components are given by the gradient to the unit cost function $c_x(w_L, w_H)$. Since these coefficients are homogeneous of degree zero in the factor prices, we can express them as $a_{ix}(\bar{w}_L, \bar{w}_H)$, $i = H, L$. The input coefficients in the production of the final goods minimize the respective unit costs given on the right-hand sides of (A6.2) and (A6.3). The Cobb-Douglas specification implies that $a_{HY} = (1 - \beta)p_Y/w_H$, $a_{XY} = \beta p_Y/p_x$, $a_{LZ} = (1 - \beta)p_Z/w_L$, and $a_{XZ} = \beta p_Z/p_x$. It follows immediately that when the prices of the final goods are constant, the unit input coefficients decline at the rate of growth of the respective input prices. Thus, for example, the input of human capital per unit output of good Y falls at the rate of increase in the reward to human capital, and the aggregate input of intermediate goods per unit output of good Z falls at the rate of increase of component prices.

Substituting these values for the unit input coefficients in (6.15) and (6.16), and making use of (A6.1)–(A6.3), we derive (6.17) and (6.18), where the coefficients that describe the direct-plus-indirect input of the primary factors per unit of productivity-adjusted final output are given by

$$b_{HY}(\bar{w}_L, \bar{w}_H) = \bar{c}_Y(\bar{w}_L, \bar{w}_H)\left[\frac{(1 - \beta)}{\bar{w}_H} + \frac{\beta\delta a_{Hx}(\bar{w}_L, \bar{w}_H)}{c_x(\bar{w}_L, \bar{w}_H)}\right], \tag{A6.4}$$

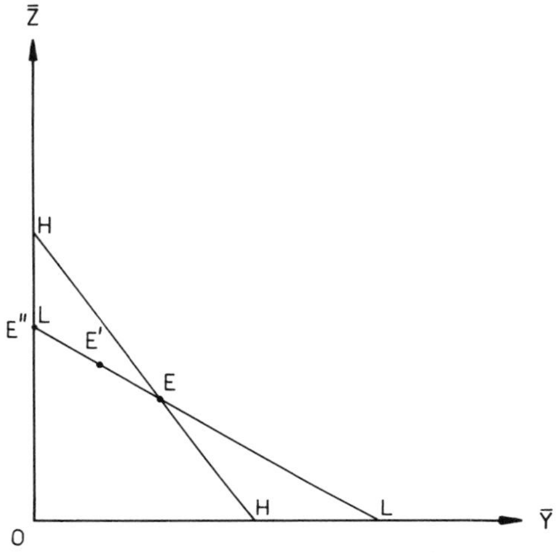

Figure A6.1

$$b_{LY}(\overline{w}_L, \overline{w}_H) = \overline{c}_Y(\overline{w}_L, \overline{w}_H)\frac{\beta\delta a_{Lx}(\overline{w}_L, \overline{w}_H)}{c_x(\overline{w}_L, \overline{w}_H)}, \tag{A6.5}$$

$$b_{HZ}(\overline{w}_L, \overline{w}_H) = \overline{c}_Z(\overline{w}_L, \overline{w}_H)\frac{\beta\delta a_{Hx}(\overline{w}_L, \overline{w}_H)}{c_x(\overline{w}_L, \overline{w}_H)}, \tag{A6.6}$$

$$b_{LZ}(\overline{w}_L, \overline{w}_H) = \overline{c}_Z(\overline{w}_L, \overline{w}_H)\left[\frac{(1-\beta)}{\overline{w}_H} + \frac{\beta\delta a_{LX}(\overline{w}_L, \overline{w}_H)}{c_x(\overline{w}_L, \overline{w}_H)}\right]. \tag{A6.7}$$

The input coefficients in (A6.4)–(A6.7) apply only when both final goods are produced. In the event $b_{HY}/b_{LY} > b_{HZ}/b_{LZ}$; that is, the final good Y is relatively more human capital intensive in its total (direct plus indirect) factor usage than is the final good Z.

We can use (6.17) and (6.18), or figure A6.1, to derive the relationship between the productivity-adjusted output levels, $\overline{Y}$ and $\overline{Z}$, and the rate of innovation γ for values of γ that imply incomplete specialization in the production of final goods. In the figure the line LL depicts the labor-market clearing condition,

$$b_{LY}\overline{Y} + b_{LZ}\overline{Z} = L,$$

while the line *HH* depicts the human-capital market-clearing condition,

$$b_{HY}\overline{Y} + b_{HZ}\overline{Z} = H - a\gamma.$$

All the coefficients b_{ji} in these equations are evaluated at the productivity-adjusted factor prices that satisfy (A6.1) and (A6.2). Now consider an increase in γ. This shifts the *HH* line inward, and the equilibrium point from *E* to *E'*. The result is a standard Rybczynski effect: Output of the human-capital-intensive industry contracts while that of the labor-intensive industry expands.

As long as both consumer good industries remain in operation, the productivity-adjusted output levels respond linearly to the innovation rate. Then the productivity-adjusted value of manufactured output, $\bar{Q} \equiv p_Y \bar{Y} + p_Z \bar{Z}$, is a linear function of γ, as described by (6.19). To obtain (6.19), we multiply (6.17) by $\bar{w}_H$, (6.18) by $\bar{w}_L$, and sum the resulting equations using (A6.1), (A6.2), and (A6.4)–(A6.7).

It is evident from figure A6.1 that when the rate of innovation reaches a critical value γ_c, the vertical intercept of the HH line coincides with the vertical intercept of the LL line at point E'' (we assume that both final goods are produced when $\gamma = 0$). At this point the economy specializes in the production of the labor-intensive final good, and it does similarly for values of γ that are even higher.

For values of γ in excess of γ_c, the factor-market-clearing conditions become

$$b_{HZ}\bar{Z} = H - a\gamma, \tag{A6.8}$$

$$b_{LZ}\bar{Z} = L, \tag{A6.9}$$

in view of the specialization in final production. Taking the ratio of these two equations, and making use of (A6.6) and (A6.7), we obtain

$$(1-\beta)\frac{\bar{w}_H}{\bar{w}_L} + [1-\beta(1-\delta)]l_X\left(\frac{\bar{w}_H}{\bar{w}_L}\right) = \delta\beta\frac{L}{H-\alpha\gamma}, \tag{A6.10}$$

where $l_X = a_{LX}/a_{HX}$ is the ratio of labor to human capital in the production of intermediates. Naturally $l_X(\cdot)$ increases with the relative reward to human capital. Consequently the left-hand side of (A6.10) also increases with $\bar{w}_H/\bar{w}_L$. The implication is that larger values of γ in the range $\gamma > \gamma_c$ are associated with relatively higher rewards to human capital.

The ray LH in figure A6.2 depicts the combinations of the productivity-adjusted rewards to labor and human capital that satisfy (A6.10) for a given value of $\gamma > \gamma_c$. The downward-sloping curve ZZ in this figure shows combinations of these factor rewards that satisfy (A6.2), the pricing equation for good Z. Equilibrium factor rewards for an economy that produces only the single final good Z are given by the coordinates of the intersection point E. When γ increases, the ray LH rotates in a clockwise direction, thereby shifting the equilibrium to a point such as E'. We conclude that for $\gamma > \gamma_c$, higher values of γ are associated in equilibrium with higher values of $\bar{w}_H$ and lower values of $\bar{w}_L$.

An economy specialized in the production of the labor-intensive final good has $\bar{Q} = p_Z\bar{Z}$. This fact and (A6.2), (A6.7), and (A6.9) imply that

$$\bar{Q}[(1-\beta) + \beta\delta\theta_{Lx}] = \bar{w}_L L,$$

where θ_{Lx} is the labor share in the cost of manufacturing intermediates. The share of labor depends of course on relative factor rewards. From this equation we calculate

$$\hat{\bar{Q}} = \hat{\bar{w}}_L - \frac{\beta\delta\theta_{Lx}}{(1-\beta)+\beta\delta\theta_{Lx}}\hat{\theta}_{Lx}. \tag{A6.11}$$

As usual (e.g., see Jones 1965)

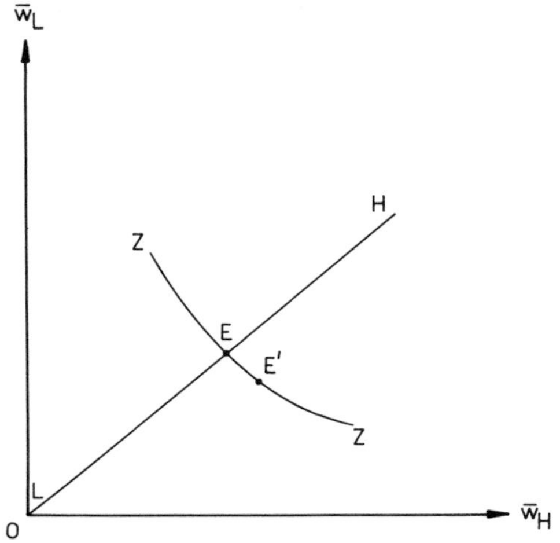

Figure A6.2

$$\hat{\theta}_{Lx} = \theta_{Hx}(1 - \sigma_x)(\hat{\bar{w}}_L - \hat{\bar{w}}_H), \tag{A6.12}$$

where σ_x denotes the elasticity of substitution between labor and human capital in the production of components. Also from (A6.2) we have

$$\theta_{Hx}\hat{\bar{w}}_H + \theta_{Lx}\hat{\bar{w}}_L = 0. \tag{A6.13}$$

Substituting for $\hat{\theta}_{Lx}$ in (A6.11) using (A6.12) and (A6.13), we derive

$$\hat{\bar{Q}} = \left[\frac{(1-\beta)(1-\delta\theta_{Lx}) + \delta\theta_{Lx}\sigma_x}{(1-\beta) + \delta\beta\theta_{Lx}}\right]\hat{\bar{w}}_L. \tag{A6.15}$$

It follows from this equation that higher values of γ in the range $\gamma > \gamma_c$ are associated with lower values of $\bar{Q}$ (because $\bar{w}_L$ is lower, and the expression in brackets in (A6.15) is positive).

We are now prepared to draw figure 6.1. We have seen that for $\gamma < \gamma_c$, γ and $\bar{Q}$ are linearly related by the resource constraint. For $\gamma > \gamma_c$ there is still an inverse relationship between the two variables, but it no longer is a linear one. This gives us the *RR* curve. Similarly, when $\gamma < \gamma_c$, the ΠΠ curve depicting equation (6.20) is linear because $\bar{w}_H$ is independent of γ in this range. When $\gamma > \gamma_c$, $\bar{w}_H$ increases with γ, and the ΠΠ curve becomes nonlinear. Thus figure 6.1 has the qualitative features that we described in the text.

A6.2 First-Best Subsidy to R&D

In order to decentralize the first-best allocation, the government of the small economy requires two policy instruments. A subsidy to users of intermediate goods can be used to correct for the exercise of market power by the producers of these inputs. The optimal subsidy equates the user price of inputs to the marginal cost of their production. This policy must be combined with a subsidy or tax on R&D, which faces entrepreneurs with the appropriate incentives to innovate. In this appendix we calculate the size of the optimal ad valorem tax or subsidy to R&D.

When final good producers pay the marginal cost $c_x(\cdot)$ for their inputs, total sales of each input equals $\beta\bar{Q}/nc_x$. Producers of these inputs receive c_x/δ per unit, so their flow of profits is $\pi = (1/\delta - 1)\beta\bar{Q}/n$. Therefore the no-arbitrage condition that applies under the optimal policy regime can be written as

$$\frac{(1-\delta)\beta\bar{Q}^*}{(1-\phi^*)\delta a\bar{w}_H^*} = \gamma^* + \rho, \tag{A6.15}$$

where ϕ is the fraction of R&D costs borne by the government; the asterisk indicates that a variable is evaluated at the social optimum. From the resource constraint (6.25) that applies to the social planner, we have $\bar{Q}^*/\bar{w}_H^* = h - a\gamma^*$. Substituting this expression into (A6.15) and rearranging, we derive

$$1 - \phi^* = \frac{(1-\delta)\beta[(h/a) - \gamma^*]}{\delta(\gamma^* + \rho)}. \tag{A6.16}$$

In the model of expanding product variety, $h/a - \gamma^* = \rho\alpha/\beta(1-\alpha)$ from (6.26) and the fact that $\mu = (1-\alpha)/\alpha$ in this case. Then, since $\delta = \alpha$ for this model, (A6.16) implies that $1 - \phi^* = \rho/(\gamma^* + \rho)$, or $\phi^* = \gamma^*/(\gamma^* + \rho)$.

In the model of rising product quality, $h/a - \gamma^* = \rho/\beta(\log\lambda)$, from (6.26) and $\mu = \log\lambda$. Substituting this expression into (A6.16), and noting that $\delta = 1/\lambda$, we find $1 - \phi^* = (\lambda - 1)\rho/(\gamma^* + \rho)(\log\lambda)$, or

$$\phi^* = 1 - \frac{(\lambda - 1)\rho}{(\gamma^* + \rho)(\log\lambda)}.$$

This expression may be positive or negative, indicating the need for either an subsidy or an R&D tax, as the case may be.

From (6.27) we can calculate the relationship between the optimal and equilibrium rates of innovation in the model of quality upgrading. After some rearranging, we find

$$\gamma^* - \gamma = \nu(\gamma^* + \rho)\left\{1 - \frac{(\lambda - 1)\rho}{[\lambda - (\lambda - 1)\beta](\gamma^* + \rho)(\log\lambda)}\right\}.$$

Comparing this expression to the expression for ϕ^*, and noting that $\lambda - (\lambda - 1)\beta = (\lambda - 1)(1 - \beta) + 1 > 1$, we see that $\phi^* > 0$ implies that $\gamma^* > \gamma$, but $\gamma^* > \gamma$ does not necessarily imply that $\phi^* > 0$.

7 Dynamic Comparative Advantage

Trade economists typically explain the pattern of trade using static notions of comparative advantage in which the state of technology in every country is taken as a given. In some familiar models comparative advantage stems from differences in production capabilities across countries. Such models can provide only limited insight into the causes of the observed pattern of international specialization because they fail to explain why countries have come to acquire technological supremacy in a certain set of goods. Other models begin with the assumption that technological opportunities are the same throughout the world and trace comparative advantage to other sources. But the assumption of identical technologies seems at odds with casual observation, and it has been rejected frequently on statistical grounds when subjected to careful empirical scrutiny (e.g., see Bowen et al. 1987).

In this chapter and the next we study the determinants of the pattern of trade between two large innovating countries. Our approach to endogenous innovation provides a useful vehicle for examining the evolution of "dynamic comparative advantage." We assume that firms worldwide compete in the industrial research lab and that research successes generate competitive advantages that can be exploited in world product markets. In this setting the momentary technological advantages that induce a particular pattern of trade have more fundamental, dynamic determinants.

The starting point for the analysis in this chapter is the two-sector, two-factor model of section 5.3. As we have discussed before, the two factors may represent resources that are available in relatively fixed supply even in the long run, or they may represent inputs that have attained steady-state levels of supply after periods of accumulation. The two sectors are distinguished by the opportunities that they afford for technological progress and by the intensity with which they employ the two primary inputs.

In section 7.1 we investigate the determinants of endogenous comparative advantage when innovators develop new varieties of horizontally differentiated products. In so doing, we extend to a dynamic setting the static analyses of intraindustry and interindustry trade of Krugman (1981), Dixit and Norman (1980), and Ethier (1982a). At every moment the pattern of trade is determined, inter alia, by the number of blueprints in the hands of each country's firms. Over time the trade pattern evolves in accordance with the number of new discoveries made by entrepreneurs in each country. This in turn depends upon the R&D investments that take place in each location.

Section 7.2 examines the case of international quality competition. Entrepreneurs worldwide strive to improve the products that are momentarily available in the global market. At every moment a single firm is able to manufacture the state-of-the-art product in a particular industry. This firm captures the world market for the product in question, selling its wares both at home and abroad. The direction of trade in any particular product line may reverse itself over time, as the identity of the industry leader changes. In the aggregate the pattern of intersectoral trade is determined, inter alia, by the number of industries in which each country's firms happen to hold the technological lead. This in turn depends upon the countries' prior investments in R&D.

A critical feature of the analysis in this chapter is the assumption that ideas and knowledge flow readily across national boundaries. In the model of expanding variety we specify explicitly that general knowledge capital in each country—which reflects the collective wisdom accumulated from past experience in industrial research—disseminates costlessly and instantaneously to the international research community. In other words, we make K_n a public good at the global level. When innovation takes the form of quality upgrading, the assumption of international knowledge spillovers is deeper ingrained in the structure of the model. International spillovers are introduced implicitly when we allow researchers in each country to seek improvements in the high-technology products that are being manufactured abroad. In both cases the assumption that knowledge spillovers are international in scope restricts the set of country characteristics that can serve as sources of long-run comparative advantage. We find, in particular, that the size of a country and the history of its production structure play no role in the explanation of its long-run trade pattern. In contrast to this, we shall find in chapter 8 that these variables become very important to the determination of long-run trade patterns when knowledge capital is a national public good.[1]

1. The reader will recognize a strong parallel between these claims and the findings of Ethier

Throughout sections 7.1 and 7.2 we impose the restriction that each firm must locate its manufacturing facilities in the same country as its research labs. This assumption might reflect a need for close contact between the engineers who have developed a product and those who are responsible for arranging its production. In any event we identify conditions under which no incentive exists for geographic separation of a firm's production and research operations. In these circumstances even a small amount of extra costs associated with communication between facilities would be enough to ensure that firms set up their manufacturing plants near to their labs. But in some situations profit opportunities will vary across countries in the trading equilibrium. Then an incentive exists for firms to undertake production where that activity is most profitable, no matter where the blueprints may have been developed. In section 7.3 we allow firms to separate their research and production activities and examine a long-run trading equilibrium with an endogenous number of multinational corporations. The final section explores international patent licensing. Licensing arrangements represent another means by which innovators in one country can avail themselves of more favorable manufacturing conditions abroad.

7.1 International Brand Proliferation

We assume that households worldwide share the preferences that were introduced in chapter 5, namely,

$$U_t = \int_t^{\infty} e^{-\rho(\tau - t)}[\sigma \log C_Y(\tau) + (1 - \sigma)\log C_Z(\tau)]\, d\tau, \quad 0 < \sigma < 1. \tag{7.1}$$

As before, C_Z denotes consumption of a traditional good, while C_Y may represent the consumption of a single, high-technology product manufactured from differentiated intermediate inputs, or it may represent an index of consumption when households consume a variety of innovative goods. In the former case the high-tech good is manufactured according to the simple production function $Y = D$, where D is an index of differentiated intermediate inputs; in the latter case we take $C_Y = D$ (a relevant subutility index) as a matter of definition. In either case the utility function implies that households devote constant budget shares to each type of product,

(1979), who studied the implications for the pattern of trade of static external economies that might be either national or international in scope. We will pursue this analogy between the static and dynamic models further below.

with high-tech goods accounting for a fraction σ of household spending. For the time being, we limit the form of D to the CES specification given in (5.2a).

We let E^i represent aggregate spending in country i, $i = A, B$, and write world spending as $E = E^A + E^B$. Prices are normalized so that $E = 1$. Then E^i is the *share* of world spending undertaken by residents of country i. The spending shares of the two countries depend, inter alia, on the possibilities that exist for international trade in financial assets, since net asset positions are a component of national wealth. We treat here the two extreme cases of perfect capital mobility and complete capital immobility. The extent of international capital mobility, it turns out, has no bearing on the long-run pattern of production specialization in our model because the interest rate attains the same long-run level in both countries in any event. With perfect capital mobility, arbitrage in the world bond market ensures that $r^A = r^B = r$, where r^i is the interest rate on bonds issued by firms in country i. In this case our normalization implies that $r = \rho$ at every moment in time. When capital is not mobile, intertemporal optimization requires that

$$\frac{\dot{E}^i}{E^i} = r^i - \rho. \tag{7.2}$$

Then, when countries' shares in world spending approach constants in the long run, their nominal interest rates converge to ρ.

We assume, as before, that competitive firms assemble the traditional good according to a time-invariant, constant-returns-to-scale production function. The technology for producing this good is common to the firms located in either country. If the traditional good is produced in both places, then

$$p_Z = c_Z(w_L^i, w_H^i), \qquad i = A, B, \tag{7.3}$$

where w_L^i and w_H^i are the rewards to unskilled labor and human capital, respectively, in country i, and $c_Z(\cdot)$ represents the cost of producing a unit of good Z. The unit manufacturing cost may exceed the product price in a country that does not produce this good.

The technology for producing differentiated products also exhibits constant returns to scale. We assume for now that these goods must be produced in the country in which they have been developed. Let the unit cost function for each (known) differentiated product be $c_x(w_L^i, w_H^i)$. As we know, manufacturers in this sector practice markup pricing. So all innovative goods assembled in a particular country bear the same price p^i, where

$$p^i = \frac{1}{\alpha} c_x(w_L^i, w_H^i), \qquad i = A, B. \tag{7.4}$$

In each country producers of differentiated products earn profits that are a fraction $(1 - \alpha)$ of their revenues. It is easy to show (e.g., see Helpman and Krugman 1985, ch. 6) that (7.1) and the underlying CES specification in (5.2a) imply that each firm producing a high-technology good in country i captures sales of

$$x^i = \left[\frac{(p^i)^{-\varepsilon}}{n^A (p^A)^{1-\varepsilon} + n^B (p^B)^{1-\varepsilon}} \right] \sigma E, \qquad i = A, B, \tag{7.5}$$

where n^i is the measure of high-technology producers in country i and $\varepsilon = 1/(1 - \alpha)$ is the constant elasticity of demand perceived by each one. Then, with $E = 1$, each high-technology firm in country i earns a flow of profits given by

$$\pi^i = \left[\frac{(p^i)^{1-\varepsilon}}{n^A (p^A)^{1-\varepsilon} + n^B (p^B)^{1-\varepsilon}} \right] (1 - \alpha) \sigma, \qquad i = A, B. \tag{7.6}$$

The cost of inventing a new, differentiated product in country i is $c_\gamma(w_L^i, w_H^i)/K_n^i$, where K_n^i is the stock of knowledge capital in that country. As before, the measure of knowledge capital reflects the amount of general scientific and engineering information that is freely available to researchers when they pursue their innovation efforts. In this chapter we assume that information moves freely and rapidly throughout the world research community. The alternative possibility that there exist impediments to the flow of knowledge across national boundaries forms the basis for our analysis in chapter 8.

With perfect international knowledge spillovers, researchers worldwide draw upon a common knowledge base; that is, $K_n^A = K_n^B = K_n$. As before, we make the knowledge stock proportional to cumulative experience in R&D and choose units so that $K_n = n$, where $n \equiv n^A + n^B$ is the total number of differentiated products available in the world economy. The familiar free-entry condition requires that

$$v^i = \frac{c_\gamma(w_L^i, w_H^i)}{n}, \qquad i = A, B, \tag{7.7}$$

in a steady state with active R&D in both countries, where v^i is the stock-market value of a firm located in country i. If a country engages in no R&D at a moment in time, the value of its existing firms may fall short of the cost of developing new varieties there. As before, the absence of arbitrage opportunities implies that the returns to each equity must be "normal" on the local capital markets; that is, $\pi^i/v^i + \dot{v}^i/v^i = r^i$. In a steady state with constant factor prices and interest rates equalized worldwide at a level ρ, this condition can be expressed as[2]

$$\frac{\pi^i}{v^i} = \rho + g, \qquad i = A, B, \tag{7.8}$$

where $g \equiv \dot{n}/n$ is the rate at which new products are being introduced to the world economy, and also the growth rate of the global knowledge stock.

The market for the traditional good clears when aggregate supply $Z^A + Z^B$ equals aggregate demand. This requires

$$Z^A + Z^B = \frac{1 - \sigma}{p_Z}, \tag{7.9}$$

since households spend a fraction $1 - \sigma$ of their total spending of $E = 1$ on traditional goods. Equilibrium in the market for each differentiated product has been expressed by equation (7.5). Finally, the equality of supplies and demands in the markets for the primary inputs in each country implies that

$$a_\gamma(w_L^i, w_H^i)\xi^i g^i + a_x(w_L^i, w_H^i)X^i + a_Z(w_L^i, w_H^i)Z^i = \begin{bmatrix} L^i \\ H^i \end{bmatrix}, \quad i = A, B, \tag{7.10}$$

where L^i and H^i are the exogenous supplies of unskilled labor and human capital, respectively, in country i and $X^i \equiv n^i x^i$ is the aggregate output of innovative products there. Also $g^i \equiv \dot{n}^i/n^i$ is the rate of product development in country i, and $\xi^i \equiv n^i/n$ is the fraction of differentiated products manufactured there. The vectors $a_j(\cdot)$, $j = x, Z$, and $a_\gamma(\cdot)/n$ represent the unit input coefficients in the two manufacturing sectors and in the R&D activity, respectively.

We investigate the properties of the steady-state equilibrium. In the steady state the allocations of resources to the three activities of research,

2. We verify below that there exists a steady-state equilibrium in which factor prices are constant and firm values decline at the rate of new product development.

manufacturing of traditional goods, and manufacturing of innovative goods remain fixed in each country over time. If firms in both countries undertake research in the steady state, then (7.7) applies for $i = A$ and $i = B$, and these free-entry conditions together with the no-arbitrage conditions (7.8), imply that $\pi^A / c_y(w_L^A, w_H^A) = \pi^B / c_y(w_L^B, w_H^B)$. Substituting for π^A and π^B in this equation using (7.4) and (7.6), we find

$$\frac{c_x(w_L^A, w_H^A)^{1-\varepsilon}}{c_y(w_L^A, w_H^A)} = \frac{c_x(w_L^B, w_H^B)^{1-\varepsilon}}{c_y(w_L^B, w_H^B)}. \tag{7.11}$$

If the three activities of manufacturing traditional goods, manufacturing high-technology goods, and R&D can be uniquely ranked in terms of their factor intensities, then (7.3) and (7.11) can be satisfied simultaneously only if factor prices are the same in both countries. In other words, in the absence of factor intensity reversals, factor price equalization obtains as a long-run proposition in any steady state in which both countries are incompletely specialized.

Trade Equilibrium with Factor Price Equalization

We establish below that a long-run equilibrium with factor price equalization (FPE) always exists when the compositions of the countries' factor endowments are not too dissimilar. Our demonstration of this uses methods popularized by Dixit and Norman (1980). We begin by identifying the long-run equilibrium that would obtain in a hypothetical "integrated world economy," that is, an economy in which goods, factors, capital, and knowledge move freely across international borders. Then we attempt to construct feasible allocations of resources for the two countries that have the same techniques of production in every location as in the integrated equilibrium and that yield the same aggregate outputs of goods and knowledge. When this can be accomplished in a way that satisfies the separate no-arbitrage conditions for the two countries and that has each country producing a number of innovative goods that is consistent with its prior investments in R&D, then the proposed allocations constitute an FPE equilibrium in a trading world economy with separate factor markets in each country.

In Figure 7.1 we have drawn a rectangle with dimensions that represent the global endowments of the two primary factors. The horizontal dimension of the rectangle reflects the world endowment of unskilled labor $L = L^A + L^B$, while the vertical dimension reflects the stock of human

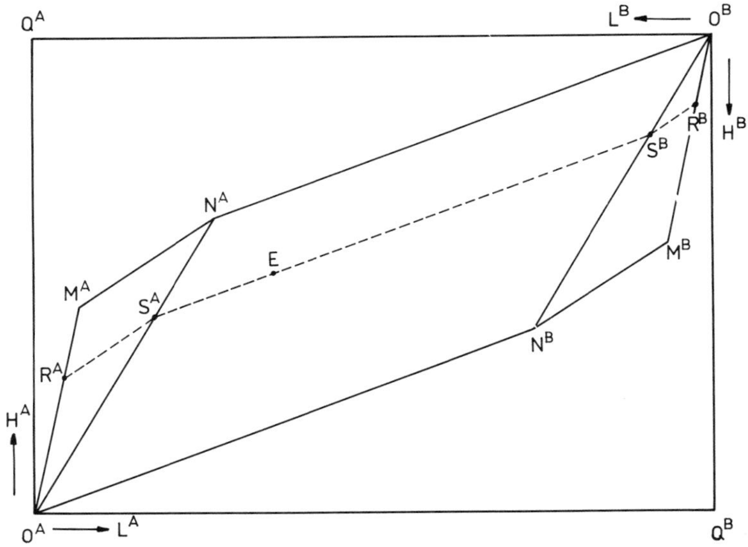

Figure 7.1

capital $H = H^A + H^B$. The line segment O^AM^A in the figure represents the vector of resources that is deployed to R&D in the long-run equilibrium of the integrated world economy. This vector can be found, for example, by solving for the equilibrium allocation of resources in the closed-economy model of section 5.3, using the aggregate resource stocks L and H as factor supplies. Similarly the segment M^AN^A represents the vector of resources that is used in manufacturing differentiated products in the integrated equilibrium, and the segment N^AO^B depicts the resources employed in producing the traditional consumer good. The figure reflects the assumption, which we adopt henceforth, that R&D is the most human capital intensive of the three activities and that traditional manufacturing is the most unskilled labor-intensive activity. Notice that the three employment vectors exhaust the available world supplies of the primary inputs.

The separate resource endowments of the two countries can be depicted in the figure by a point such as E in the interior of the rectangle. The vector O^AE (not drawn) represents the endowment of country A, while EO^B represents that of country B. When point E lies above the diagonal (as drawn), country A is relatively better endowed with human capital. Let us restrict our attention for the time being to endowment points that lie in the interior of the parallelogram $O^AN^AO^BN^B$. This restriction limits the extent of dissimilarity in the endowment ratios of the two countries. Later on we will describe the trade equilibria that obtain when the endowment point lies outside the indicated region.

For an endowment point such as E, we conjecture an equilibrium allocation of resources for each separate country. Suppose that country A employs the vector of factors $O^A R^A$ in R&D in the long run and that country B employs the vector $R^B O^B$ in this activity. With these allocations the aggregate output of blueprints matches that of the integrated equilibrium at every moment, and each country's R&D sector uses the two primary factors in the same proportions as they are employed in this activity in the hypothetical integrated equilibrium. Suppose further that country A devotes the inputs represented by the vector $R^A S^A$ to the production of differentiated products (where S^A lies along the line segment joining O^A and N^A), while country B devotes the vector $S^B R^B$ (parallel to $R^A S^A$) to this activity. Again, the aggregate production of high-tech goods under the proposed allocation matches that of the integrated economy, and the techniques of production are the same. Finally, suppose that the employment vectors in the production of the traditional good are $S^A E$ in country A and ES^B in country B so that the proposed allocation reproduces the aggregate output and techniques of production for this good as well. The resource allocations that we have proposed surely are feasible, inasmuch as employments are nonnegative in every use and the aggregate demands just exhaust each country's available factor supplies.

The next step is to establish that the proposed allocation constitutes an equilibrium for the world economy, when factor prices and commodity prices in each country are the same as in the integrated equilibrium. Equal factor prices require identical techniques of production in each location. Identical techniques indeed are applied by the two countries in the proposed allocation. Also, when factor prices in each country are the same as in the integrated equilibrium, so too are all unit activity costs the same. It follows that the activity of manufacturing traditional goods, which earns zero profits in the integrated equilibrium, must also break even in each country in the proposed trade equilibrium. Differentiated products bear the same prices as in the integrated equilibrium, since each is marked up by $1/\alpha$ over the unit cost of its production. With the same cost of R&D as in the integrated equilibrium, the no-arbitrage condition is satisfied for shares in each country's firms. World spending has been normalized to equal one, just as it was in the integrated equilibrium. Since all demand functions are homothetic, aggregate demand for each product must be the same in the trading world economy as in the integrated economy. But then all product markets must clear, since the proposed allocation reproduces the aggregate output supplies.

It remains to be established only that the rates of product development in the two countries are consistent with the the numbers of goods that each has been assumed able to produce. The ratio of the number of new goods invented in country A per unit time to the number invented in country B, $\dot{n}^A/\dot{n}^B$, is equal to the ratio of the lengths of the vectors O^AR^A and R^BO^B. In the steady state this ratio must equal the ratio of innovative products manufactured in each country, n^A/n^B. Since product prices are the same worldwide, the demands for the individual products manufactured in each country are equal (i.e., $x^A = x^B$; see [7.5]). So the ratio of the number of products manufactured in each country is equal to the ratio of the aggregate outputs of these goods X^A/X^B, which in turn is equal to the ratio of the respective employment vectors in the high-technology sectors. This latter ratio is represented in the figure by the ratio of R^AS^A to S^BR^B. The required equality is established by the similarity of the triangles $O^AR^AS^A$ and $O^BR^BS^B$. It follows that the proposed allocation constitutes a long-run equilibrium for the trading world economy.

Static trade models with three activities and two primary factors typically admit *many* allocations that exhaust the separate endowments of two trading partners (e.g., see Dixit and Norman 1980, pp. 114–119). The patterns of specialization and trade are not uniquely determined in such models. However, in our setting, if each country is incompletely specialized in the long run, the steady-state allocations *must* be exactly as we have described. Uniqueness follows from the aforementioned requirement in the dynamic model that the level of output of innovative products in each country be consistent with the rate of innovation that takes place there. This requirement has no analog in the static trade models. In terms of the figure, point S^A must lie along the line joining O^A and N^A; in other words, the vector of resources devoted to the *composite activity* of inventing and producing innovative goods in each country must be proportional to the vector of resources devoted to this composite activity in the integrated equilibrium.

In the free-trade equilibrium with FPE, each country introduces new innovative products at the same steady-state rate; that is, $g^A = g^B = g$. If this were not so, the share of differentiated products manufactured in the country with slower innovation would eventually approach zero, and thus by (7.10) its allocation of resources to R&D and to the production of high-technology goods would be negligible in the long run. But the equilibrium that we have described has finite allocations of resources to each activity in both countries. The equality of the rates of product innovation notwithstanding, the country with a relative abundance of human capital conducts *relatively* more R&D in the steady state than its trade partner, compared to its relative output of the traditional good ($\xi^A g^A/Z^A > \xi^B g^B/Z^B$). By dint of its relative specialization in research, this country acquires the know-how to produce a relatively wider range of innovative goods ($n^A/Z^A > n^B/Z^B$). Outputs of the representative differentiated product are the same in both countries, so $X^A/Z^A > X^B/Z^B$. These predictions about the pattern of world specialization are, of course, highly reminiscent of those that derive from static theories of factor-endowment-based trade. Cross-country differences in relative resource supplies dictate here the long-run pattern of specialization in production.

What does the predicted pattern of specialization imply about the long-run pattern of international trade? We note first that our model predicts the practice of *intraindustry trade,* with firms in each country exporting the unique brands that they have developed. The basis for this type of trade is the same here as in the static models with differentiated products (see Krugman 1981, Dixit and Norman 1980; Ethier 1982a). Households demand diversity in consumption, which firms can supply only by bearing fixed costs. In the static models the fixed costs are a component of total production costs, whereas here they take the form of up-front research outlays. In either event each partner to trade will have an incentive to import the unique varieties produced abroad rather than incur a second fixed cost to produce these goods locally.

Concerning the pattern of *interindustry trade,* we have two cases to consider. In the event that financial assets are not traded internationally, each country must finance all R&D that takes place within its borders with domestic savings. Since each country's trade account must balance at every moment in time, one country must import the traditional good and export (on net) high-tech products, while the other country has just the opposite pattern of trade. We have seen that the human-capital-rich country (i.e., country *A*) specializes relatively in the production of innovative goods. But this country's residents consume the same share E^A of world output of *every* good. Therefore country *A* must be the one that develops a sectoral trade surplus in high technology. The labor-abundant country *B*, on the other hand, imports differentiated products on net and exports the traditional good. This pattern of intersectoral trade corresponds of course to the predictions of the Heckscher-Ohlin theorem.

If agents may trade their financial assets on international capital markets, on the other hand, countries need only balance the present value of their trade flows. In the steady state a country may run a deficit on trade account balanced by a surplus on service account. In the event the country in deficit may (but need not) become a net importer of *both* differentiated products and the traditional consumer good in the steady state. If a human-capital-rich country imports both goods in the long-run equilibrium, the share of imports in its total consumption of the traditional good will exceed the share of net imports in its total consumption of innovative products. But if an unskilled labor-rich country imports both goods in the steady state, its import penetration ratio for differentiated products will exceed that for traditional goods. Finally, if the long-run trade imbalance is not so large as to cause one country to become a net importer in both sectors, then the steady-state pattern of trade again must conform to the Heckscher-Ohlin prescription.

The predicted pattern of specialization in production also has implications for the relative rates of growth in the two trading economies. The aggregate rate of growth of manufactured output in each country is a weighted average of the rates of productivity growth in the two manufacturing sectors. In forming this weighted average, the shares of the respective sectors in the total value of industrial output serve as weights.[3] Our model predicts equal rates of productivity growth in the sectors that manufacture innovative goods in each country. But high technology comprises a larger share of the national economy in the human-capital-rich country than it does in the unskilled-labor-rich country. It follows that real output growth is faster in the former country than in the latter.[4] Of course both countries experience the same growth rate of real consumption in the

3. In chapter 3 we noted that when new goods are being introduced to the economy, the measurement of growth in manufactured output requires the computation of an appropriate price index. The index must reflect the fact that the prices of some goods (i.e., those newly invented) fall in every period from infinity to a finite level p. Since the price index for aggregate output falls, ceteris paribus, when new products are developed, the corresponding quantity index rises when the same volume of high-tech goods incorporates a greater variety of products.

4. As we discussed in chapter 3, measured growth in manufactured output and measured growth of real GDP do not coincide in the context of our model of expanding product variety because (1) GDP includes not only manufacturing activities but also the R&D activity, and (2) productivity in R&D grows at a different rate than productivity in the high-tech manufacturing sector. Our statements in the text concerning the relative rates of growth of real output apply with equal force to the rates of growth of GDP. The human-capital-rich country experiences a faster growth of real GDP, because the ratio of the value generated in high-tech manufacturing to the value generated in the R&D sector is the same for the two countries, and each of these sectors represents a relatively larger fraction of GDP in the human-capital-rich country than in the unskilled-labor-rich country.

steady state, since the long-run interest rates are the same in both countries and each has access via trade to the entire set of innovative products.

Our prediction of an association between factor endowments and both the direction of trade in high-technology goods and the growth rate of manufactured output would seem to accord well with empirical observation. Grossman (1990), for example, cites evidence that the Japanese economy experienced between 1965 and 1987 a concurrent change in the composition of its national factor endowment (due to a rapid build up of human capital) and a structural transformation of its production sector toward knowledge-intensive output. These events were joined by an increase in the relative share of R&D in GDP, and by a change in the source of Japanese comparative advantage. Concerning the latter, both Grossman (1990) and Balassa and Noland (1989) provide statistical evidence of a much higher R&D intensity of Japanese net exports at the end of this period than at the beginning. Finally, the investments in technology engendered rapid growth in productivity during the period, which contributed to Japan's robust economic performance.

Trade Equilibrium without Factor Price Equalization

Let us examine now the patterns of specialization and trade that result for endowment point outside the parallelogram $O^A N^A O^B N^B$. When the countries' resource compositions are so disparate, there does not exist any decomposition of the aggregate allocations $O^A N^A$ and $N^B O^B$ of the integrated equilibrium into component allocations that separately exhausts the factor supplies of the two countries. That is, with the restriction that each good must be manufactured in the country where it was developed, commodity trade alone is not sufficient to reproduce the integrated equilibrium. The steady-state equilibrium in this case entails unequal factor prices in the two countries. Then at least one of the countries must find itself uncompetitive in the long run either in inventing new products or in producing the traditional manufactured good.[5]

Dixit and Norman (1980, pp. 113–114) describe the patterns of specialization that may arise in a static trade model when there are no factor

5. If a country fails to invent new varieties in the steady-state equilibrium, then its resource input into the production of differentiated products becomes arbitrarily small. Although such a country continues forever to produce those brands that it previously developed, equation (7.5) implies that aggregate demand for any finite number of varieties approaches zero as the total number of varieties available in the world grows large.

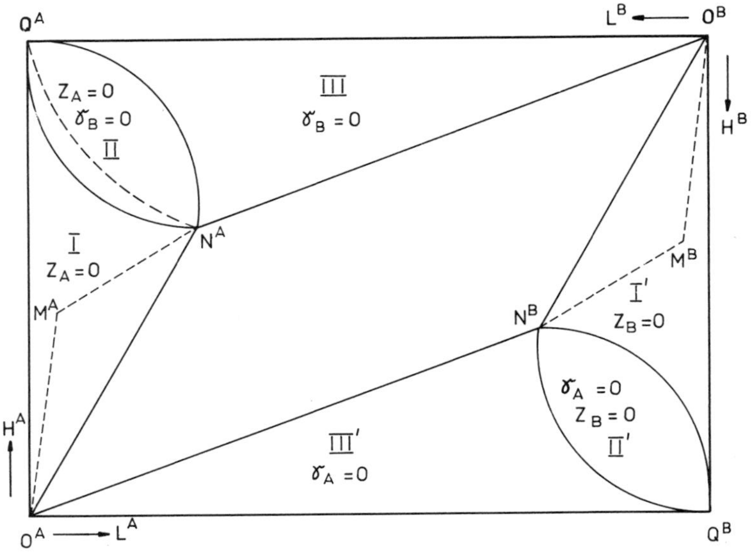

Figure 7.2

intensity reversals and the endowment point lies outside the FPE region. We extend their analysis here to study the long-run patterns of specialization that emerge when technologies are endogenous.[6] In figure 7.2 we have drawn a pair of curves that join point N^A with the upper-left vertex of the rectangle. A symmetric pair of curves join N^B with the lower-right vertex. These curves divide the area outside $O^AN^AO^BN^B$ into six regions, such that a different long-run pattern of specialization obtains in each one.

In the region labeled I, bounded by $O^AN^AQ^A$ (and thus including the triangle $O^AM^AN^A$), both countries engage in product innovation and the production of differentiated goods, but only the labor-rich country *B* produces the traditional manufactured good. In such an equilibrium the return to innovation must be the same in each country; that is, equation (7.11) applies. This means that profits must be higher for manufacturers of high-tech products in the country that has the higher cost of innovation. Country *B* has greater product development costs because the reward to (scarce) human capital is greater there than in country *A*, and R&D is the most

6. We note, however, that Dixit and Norman neglected the possibility that each country may become specialized in the production of a single good. This possibility is realized for a nonnegligible set of factor endowments both in their model (i.e., the standard, two-sector–two-factor model of trade) and in ours.

human capital intensive of the three activities. Therefore country B must enjoy lower costs of manufacturing differentiated products in the long-run equilibrium which enable its firms to capture higher per brand profits.[7]

For endowments in the region labeled II, each country is specialized in its long-run production. The human-capital-rich country devotes resources to R&D and to the production of high-tech goods. The labor-rich country produces traditional goods and a vanishing quantity of the differentiated products that its firms developed before the cessation of R&D there. In the interior of this region, the rate of return on investments in new technology is higher in the steady state in country A, while country B enjoys a cost advantage in the production of good Z.

Finally, for endowments in region III, the labor-rich country B ultimately devotes all but a negligible portion of its resources to the production of traditional goods, as its output of differentiated products asymptotically approaches zero. The human-capital-rich country conducts R&D and manufactures both types of goods in the long run. Since firms in both countries actively produce the traditional good, the cost of manufacturing this competitively priced product must be the same in each location. Then manufacturing costs in the high-technology sector must be lower in country A because the R&D sector makes relatively more intensive use of human capital, which is relatively abundant there. Country A enjoys an even greater relative cost advantage in the research lab, where human capital is used most intensively. It follows that the return to innovation is unambiguously higher in this country.

The remaining regions (labeled I′, II′, and III′) are analogous to those just described, but the identities of the human-capital-rich and labor-rich countries are reversed. In every one of the six regions, only the labor-rich country ever specializes in the production of traditional goods and only the human-capital-rich country ever specializes in R&D and the production of innovative products. In each case therefore the long-run pattern of trade conforms to the Heckscher-Ohlin theorem, unless one country happens to export (on net) both traditional and innovative products, in order to balance a long-run deficit on service account. And in each case the growth rate

7. When manufacturing costs in the two countries are not the same, imitation may be a profitable activity in the low-cost country. Entrepreneurs there who develop clone products can earn positive profits in duopolistic competition with innovators in the high-cost country. If these profits are substantial enough, they may justify the costs of imitation. In this chapter we will rule out the possibility of imitation with reference either to patent protection or sufficiently high costs of imitation. The imitative activities of entrepreneurs in low-wage countries are the focus of chapters 11 and 12.

of manufactured output and of real GDP must be higher in the human-capital-rich country than in the labor-rich country.

7.2 International Quality Competition

Much of the international competition in high technology takes place in the quality dimension. A firm's market share in a high-tech industry often is determined as much or more by its ability to offer products that are more sophisticated and more reliable than those of its foreign (and domestic) rivals as it is by its ability to produce goods at lower cost, or to offer new, horizontally differentiated varieties. We can use our model of quality upgrading to examine the long-run patterns of specialization and trade that emerge when firms in different countries compete in the research lab to introduce products of ever higher quality.

As in section 7.1 our point of departure is the two-sector, two-factor model that was developed in section 5.3. Many components of the two-country model with quality upgrading are the same as for the comparable model with expanding product variety. In particular, we adopt the same utility function as in (7.1), except that C_Y now represents a bundle of quality-differentiated goods, with $C_Y = D$ again but D taken this time from (5.2b). Also the specification of manufacturing costs remains the same as before. So (7.3), which equates the price of the traditional good to the unit cost of producing this good in each country, continues to apply if both countries manufacture the traditional good in the steady-state equilibrium. We use $c_y(w_L^i, w_H^i)$ to denote once again the cost function for R&D, in this case describing the flow cost to a firm located in country i, $i = A, B$, of achieving a probability dt of inventing the next generation of high-tech product for some industry j in every time interval of length dt.

We know from previous discussions that, in the oligopoly equilibrium for product j, the industry leader captures the entire world market by setting a price that is λ times as high as the unit cost of production of its closest competitor on the quality ladder. We must distinguish firms now by their country of origin and by the location of their nearest rival. Let p^{ij} denote the equilibrium price charged by the purveyor of a state-of-the-art product from country i when the competitor that is able to supply the previous generation product resides in country j. Then

$$p^{ij} = \lambda c_x(w_L^j, w_H^j), \qquad i = A, B, j = A, B. \tag{7.12}$$

Such a leader sells $\sigma E/p^{ij} = \sigma/p^{ij}$ units at this price and earns a flow of profits equal to

$$\pi^{ij} = \sigma\left[1 - \frac{c_x(w_L^i, w_H^i)}{\lambda c_x(w_L^j, w_H^j)}\right], \qquad i = A, B, j = A, B. \tag{7.13}$$

Entrepreneurs in each country may target their research efforts at state-of-the-art products manufactured locally, or at those manufactured abroad. It is apparent from (7.13) that all leading firms, regardless of their location, earn higher profits when their nearest competitor resides in the country with higher manufacturing costs. Therefore all entrepreneurs in both countries prefer to improve products that are being assembled in the high-cost country. If one country indeed were to exhibit a higher unit cost in high technology, then over time that country would lose competitiveness in all such goods. This is because all research efforts worldwide would be aimed at improving that country's products, and each success abroad would mean the permanent loss of technological advantage in an additional product line. Such a situation contradicts the hypothesis that both countries are active in both sectors in the steady state. Therefore in a steady-state equilibrium with nonnegligible output of innovative products in each country, we must have

$$c_x(w_L^A, w_H^A) = c_x(w_L^B, w_H^B). \tag{7.14}$$

Equations (7.13) and (7.14) imply that $\pi^{ij} = \pi \equiv (1 - 1/\lambda)\sigma$ for all i and j. It follows that all industry-leading firms located in country i share the same stock market value, which we denote by v^i.

We turn next to the free-entry and no-arbitrage conditions. Free entry implies that

$$v^i = c_y(w_L^i, w_H^i), \qquad i = A, B, \tag{7.15}$$

in a steady state with active R&D in both countries. Arbitrage ensures that, in a steady state, the profit rate for leading firms equals the local interest rate plus a premium reflecting the flow probability of a total capital loss. We let ι^{ji} denote the aggregate research effort by entrepreneurs in country j targeted at a representative state-of-the-art product manufactured in country i. An industry leader in country i faces an instantaneous probability $(\iota^{Ai} + \iota^{Bi})dt$ that one of the research efforts aimed at upgrading its product will succeed. The steady-state, no-arbitrage condition that applies to shares in industry leading firms located in country i is $\pi/v^i = r^i + \iota^{Ai} + \iota^{Bi}$. Recognizing that interest rates will be equalized in the steady state at ρ, and letting $\iota^i \equiv \iota^{Ai} + \iota^{Bi}$ denote the aggregate intensity of world research targeted at a typical product of country i, we have (using [7.15] and the definition of π)

$$\frac{\sigma(1-1/\lambda)}{c_y(w_L^i, w_H^i)} = \rho + \iota^i, \qquad i = A, B. \tag{7.16}$$

Thus profit rates need not be equalized in a long-run equilibrium with active research in both countries, if manufacturers in different locations face different risks of displacement by next-generation products.

The market-clearing conditions that apply here are similar to those for the model of expanding product variety. In fact equation (7.9) still describes equilibrium in the market for the traditional consumer good. But in place of (7.10), we have

$$a_y(w_L^i, w_H^i)(\iota^{iA}n^A + \iota^{iB}n^B) + a_x(w_L^i, w_H^i)X^i + a_Z(w_L^i, w_H^i)Z^i = \begin{bmatrix} L^i \\ H^i \end{bmatrix},$$
$$i = A, B, \tag{7.17}$$

where n^i is the number of industry leading firms in country i, and so $\iota^{iA}n^A + \iota^{iB}n^B$ measures the aggregate amount of R&D undertaken there.

In a time interval of length dt, firms in country A capture the technological lead from firms in country B in a total of $\iota^{AB}n^B$ industries, while firms in country B gain leadership positions in $\iota^{BA}n^A$ new industries at the expense of extant leaders in country A. In a steady state each country maintains leadership in a constant fraction of the total number of high-technology products. Thus the inflows must balance the outflows, or

$$\iota^{AB}n^B = \iota^{BA}n^A. \tag{7.18}$$

Equation (7.18) implies that $\iota^{iA}n^A + \iota^{iB}n^B = \iota^i n^i$, or that the aggregate amount of R&D undertaken in each country matches, in the steady state, the aggregate amount of R&D targeted at the country's leaders. Using this fact and (7.17), we can derive the following factor-market-clearing conditions that apply in a steady state with incomplete specialization:

$$a_y(w_L^i, w_H^i)\iota^i n^i + a_x(w_L^i, w_H^i)X^i + a_Z(w_L^i, w_H^i)Z^i = \begin{bmatrix} L^i \\ H^i \end{bmatrix}, \qquad i = A, B. \tag{7.19}$$

Notice that (7.19) has the same form as (7.10), except that ι^i (the intensity of R&D effort targeted at goods produced in country i) in the former equation has replaced g^i (the rate of new product development in country i) in the latter.[8]

8. In (7.10), ξ^i represents the share of innovative goods manufactured in country i. The variable n^i has this same interpretation in (7.19), since the total measure of goods is one in this case.

In the model of quality competition, as in the model of horizontally differentiated products with international knowledge spillovers, factor prices must be equalized in a steady state with incomplete specialization in each country. Factor price equalization is ensured here by (7.3) and (7.14), which require unit costs to be the same in the two countries in two distinct manufacturing activities. When factor prices are equalized, so too are costs of innovation. Then the no-arbitrage conditions imply that $\iota^A = \iota^B$ (see [7.16]). That is, in an FPE equilibrium, industry leaders in each country face the same risk per unit time of losing their technological leads.

Now the analogy between (7.10) and (7.19) becomes even clearer. In each case techniques of production are the same in the two countries when factor prices are equalized. And in each case the ratio of the vector of resources employed in R&D in country *A* to the vector so employed in country *B* must equal the ratio of the vector of resources employed in manufacturing high-technology goods in country *A* to the vector employed in this sector in country *B*, these ratios all being equal to n^A/n^B. In other words, the activities of improving and producing high-tech products effectively become a joint activity in the steady state of the model with quality improvements just as the activities of inventing and manufacturing differentiated products behaved like a joint activity in the model of expanding variety. From this discussion, it should be apparent that the analysis of the pattern of specialization and trade that we conducted using figure 7.1 in section 7.1 applies with equal force here. That is, a long-run, free-trade equilibrium with factor price equalization obtains when the compositions of the countries' resource endowments are not too dissimilar. The FPE equilibrium reproduces the price structure and aggregate quantities of the steady state for a hypothetical integrated economy with quality upgrading.[9] And in the FPE equilibrium the country with a relative abundance of human capital specializes relatively in R&D, and by dint of its relatively greater number of research successes, captures leadership positions in a relatively larger number of high-technology industries, as compared to its

9. In fact there are multiple FPE equilibria that reproduce the aggregate quantities of the integrated equilibrium. These equilibria differ in the extent to which entrepreneurs in each country target for upgrading products manufactured in their own country versus those manufactured abroad. A continuum of values of ι^{AA}, ι^{AB}, ι^{BA}, and ι^{BB} is consistent with (7.18), $\iota^{AA} + \iota^{BA} = \iota$, and $\iota^{AB} + \iota^{BB} = \iota$, where ι is the intensity of R&D effort targeted at each product in the integrated equilibrium. Any such combination of values can arise in a free trade equilibrium that reproduces the outcome for the integrated economy. However, all of these possible FPE equilibria are observationally equivalent at the macro level. The various equilibria share the same allocation of resources among alternative uses, the same distribution of income across countries, and the same pattern of international trade.

relative output of traditional goods. If trade is balanced in the steady state, then the human-capital-rich country imports the traditional good in the long run, and it exports a greater volume of high-tech goods than it imports. If steady-state trade is not balanced, then one country may import both goods in the long run, but in any event the pattern of trade will be biased in favor of imports of traditional products by the human-capital-rich country. Finally, the human-capital rich country realizes faster growth of (quality-adjusted) manufactured output and (quality-adjusted) real GDP in the long-run equilibrium.

Outside the region of factor price equalization, the possible patterns of specialization also are the same as before. For endowments in regions I and I′ of figure 7.2, the human-capital-rich country conducts R&D and produces vertically differentiated products, while the labor-rich country engages in all three productive activities. The fact that both countries produce innovative goods in the long-run equilibrium implies, by (7.14), that manufacturing costs are the same for these goods in both countries. Then the cost of manufacturing the traditional good is lower in the labor-abundant country, which has the lower wage rate for unskilled labor. The human-capital-rich country, on the other hand, enjoys a cost advantage in product innovation. This advantage is offset by the greater extent to which the country's products are the target of entrepreneur's innovation efforts, so that the expected discounted return to a unit outlay in R&D is the same in every location.

In regions II and II′ of figure 7.2, the unskilled-labor-rich country specializes in the production of traditional manufactures, while the human-capital-rich country specializes in R&D and the production of innovative goods. The cost of manufacturing high-tech products in the labor-abundant country may equal or exceed the cost of producing these goods in the human-capital-rich country for endowment points in these regions. Lastly, for endowments in regions III and III′, both countries produce the traditional good, although only the human-capital-rich country is active in high technology. Trade equalizes the cost of producing good Z in the two countries, which implies that manufacturing costs for high-tech goods are unambiguously higher in the human-capital-poor country. If an entrepreneur from this high-cost country were to succeed in capturing the market for any such good, its product (alone) would be the target of R&D efforts in industrial research laboratories worldwide. But in the steady state, firms in this country perform no R&D and therefore have no leading products to be targeted.

7.3 Multinational Corporations

Let us relax now the restriction that firms must manufacture their innovative products in the same country where their research facilities are located. In a trade equilibrium with factor price equalization, firms have no incentive to move their production away from their research labs because all activities are equally profitable in all locations. Then even a small amount of extra cost associated with the establishment of multinational corporations will be enough to prevent them from forming. But we have seen that factor price equalization does not always obtain in the long-run trading equilibrium. We return now to the cases where it does not, to ask whether firms have an incentive to separate their research and manufacturing operations.

We refer again to Figure 7.2. For endowments in regions I and I′, innovators in the human-capital-rich country surely do have an incentive to move their production activities offshore. In the model of expanding product variety, we have seen that such endowments lead to a trade equilibrium in which the costs of manufacturing innovative products in the human-capital-rich country are higher than those elsewhere. In the model of quality upgrading, on the other hand, an endowment point in one of these regions gives rise to a trade equilibrium in which the manufacturing costs for high-tech goods are the same everywhere. But in this case innovative goods manufactured in the human-capital-rich country are targeted more intensively for improvement than those manufactured in the labor-abundant country. Therefore innovators who produce their goods in the human-capital-rich country face a more rapid loss of their profit-making potential. The prospect of a longer tenure as industry leader motivates these firms to shift their production to the labor-rich country in this case.

Multinational corporations will not form, however, when the endowment point lies in region III or region III′ of figure 7.2. In these regions the trade equilibrium is characterized by a higher cost of high-tech manufacturing in the labor-abundant country. Given the opportunity to shift their production facilities to this country, innovators in the human-capital-rich country will see no advantage from doing so. This is true no matter whether innovation takes the form of brand proliferation or improvements in the quality of a fixed set of goods.

Finally, consider region II (or II′). Figure 7.2 shows a dotted line that divides this region into two parts. On the left side of the dotted line, relative cost conditions in the two countries in the trade equilibrium are more similar to those in region I. On the right side, they are more similar to those in region III. In the model of horizontally differentiated products,

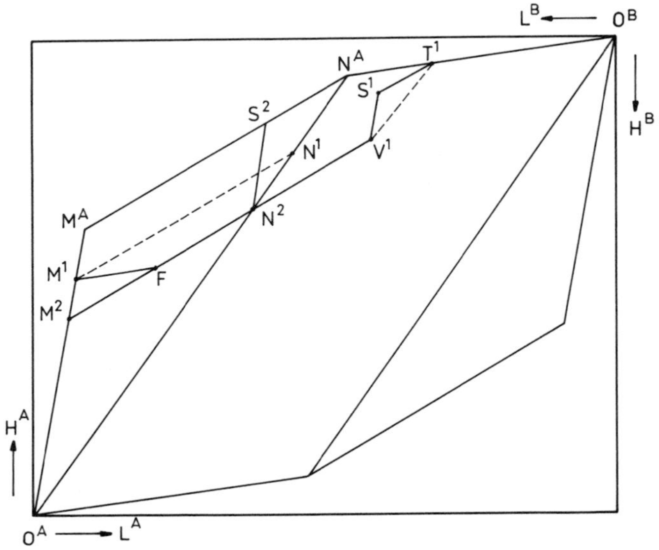

Figure 7.3

this line represents the set of endowments (outside the FPE region, and above the diagonal) that give rise to *equal* manufacturing costs for innovative products in the two countries in a trade equilibrium. In the model of vertically differentiated products, this line represents the border of the set of endowments for which such cost equalization holds. In each case the cost of manufacturing high-tech products is higher in the labor-rich country for all endowments points to the right of the line. It follows that multinationals form when the endowment point lies to the left of the line, but not when it lies to the right.

More can be said about the equilibrium outcome for endowment points that lie in one of the triangles $O^AM^AN^A$ or $O^BM^BN^B$, which are subsets of regions I and I′, respectively. In these cases there exist trade equilibria with multinational corporations that reproduce the aggregate magnitudes of the integrated equilibrium. In fact there are many feasible allocations that accomplish this. All of them are characterized by factor price equalization. Figure 7.3 shows two of the possibilities for the endowment point F. In one possible steady-state equilibrium, country A employs the vector of resources O^AM^1 in research and the vector M^1F in the production of traditional goods. All innovative goods (be they horizontally or vertically differentiated) invented in country A are manufactured in country B. The manufacturing operations of the multinationals make use of the vector of resources $FV^1 = M^1N^1$. Country B also devotes the vector V^1S^1 to indigenous R&D, S^1T^1 to production of goods that have been developed locally, and T^1O^B to the production of traditional goods. In a second possible steady-state equilibrium, country A devotes the resources represented by O^AM^2 to R&D and those represented by M^2F to the production of high-tech goods. The total bundle of resources needed to manufacture the equilibrium output of the innovative goods developed in country A's research labs is represented by M^2N^2. Therefore the vector FN^2 of resources in country B must be employed in multinational firms. In this equilibrium country B devotes N^2S^2 to R&D, S^2N^A to producing high-tech goods developed at home, and N^AO^B to manufacturing the entire world's supply of the traditional good. This particular equilibrium has the property that, among all those that could emerge in the steady state, it minimizes the number of multinational firms and also the level of employment of country B resources in such enterprises. It may have special claim to our attention, therefore, if separation of research and production does involve some (small) extra cost.

For endowments in $O^AM^AN^A$ and $O^BM^BN^B$, an FPE equilibrium is made possible by the separation of research and production activities by at least some entrepreneurs in the human-capital-rich country. This separation relieves the pressures of labor demand that otherwise cause the wage rate in this country to exceed that in the labor-rich country. In the remainder of regions I and I', and in the relevant portions of regions II and II', the same incentives for the formation of multinationals exist. In fact, for some of these endowments, the incentives may be even stronger than in the triangles. But the separation of research and production facilities by some or all firms is not sufficient to eliminate the tendency for factor prices in the two countries to diverge. The equilibrium with multinationals may be characterized either by the property that all entrepreneurs in the human-capital-rich country locate their production facilities abroad or by the property that the profitability of manufacturing innovative goods is the same in all locations.

The long-run pattern of trade in an equilibrium with multinational corporations may differ from that which emerges when research and production cannot be separated. In particular, the human-capital-rich country may import both the traditional good and a greater volume of innovative goods than it exports, even in the absence of international borrowing or lending. The country would show a deficit on trade account offset by a surplus on service account. The surplus would reflect either intracorporate transfers for "technological services rendered" or royalty payments from the foreign subsidiary to the parent patent holder. In other words, the human-capital-abundant country can find itself, in effect, exchanging blueprints for commodities in the long-run equilibrium.

7.4 Patent Licensing

If factor prices differ in the two countries of a trading world economy and if it is costly for firms to establish production facilities offshore, then an innovator may consider a licensing arrangement as an alternative means to capitalize on the prospect of lower manufacturing costs or longer periods of market leadership abroad. Under such an arrangement an innovator extends manufacturing rights to a producer in the foreign country, in exchange for a royalty payment. Needless to say, there may be substantial contracting costs and informational difficulties associated with patent licensing. The innovating firm may find it difficult to describe a new product to potential licensees without revealing the details of the technology. And it may be costly for a licensor to monitor the actions of a licensee in order to collect the agreed upon royalty payments and to ensure the satisfaction of other contract provisions. International agreements may be especially difficult to enforce if legal systems and patent laws vary in different parts of the world.

The potential costs of licensing have been discussed elsewhere in the literature.[10] Here we focus only on the simple and extreme case in which contracting and enforcement costs are negligible. We consider agreements that provide for the (costless) transfer of the technology in exchange for a lump-sum payment. We restrict attention to licensing contracts that grant the licensee an unrestricted right to produce and market the patented good. In principle, the licensor may sign such agreements with several producers, but our assumptions on oligopolistic conduct (i.e., price competition) imply that second bids are always zero.

Let us consider first the case of horizontally differentiated products. A question arises as to whether the licensing contract can include an enforceable covenant of noncompetition. That is, can the innovating firm commit itself to refrain from producing the good that it developed once it concludes the agreement with the licensee? If it cannot make this commitment, then a potential licensee must expect ex post competition from the licensor. Under these conditions the former firm's maximum willingness to pay for the license equals the present value of the profits that it could earn in

10. Caves et al. (1983) discuss the nature of these costs and attempt to measure them.

duopolistic competition with the licensor. Suppose, for concreteness, that manufacturing costs for differentiated products in country A exceed those in country B. In the duopoly equilibrium a licensee in country B would set a price equal to licensor's marginal cost of production.[11] Using the expression for demand that comes from maximizing the CES function in (5.2a) subject to the constraint that total spending on differentiated goods equals σ, we compute maximal profits for the licensee to be

$$\pi^L = (c_x^A - c_x^B)\frac{\sigma(c_x^A)^{-\varepsilon}}{\int_0^n p(j)^{1-\varepsilon}\,dj}, \tag{7.20}$$

where $c_x^i \equiv c_x(w_L^i, w_H^i)$. A steady-state equilibrium with licensing occurs if and only if these profits, when evaluated using the factor prices that prevail in the free-trade equilibrium without licensing, exceed the profits that the licensor could earn by producing the good itself. The monopoly profits available to an innovator in country A are given by

$$\pi^A = c_x^A\left(\frac{1}{\alpha} - 1\right)\frac{\sigma(c_x^A/\alpha)^{-\varepsilon}}{\int_0^n p(j)^{1-\varepsilon}\,dj}. \tag{7.21}$$

A comparison of (7.20) and (7.21) reveals that licensing takes place if and only if the free-trade equilibrium without licensing entails a manufacturing cost difference between the two countries that satisfies

$$\frac{c_x^A - c_x^B}{c_x^A} \geq (1-\alpha)\alpha^{\alpha/(1-\alpha)}. \tag{7.22}$$

For example, if $\alpha = \frac{1}{2}$ so that the elasticity of substitution between every pair of differentiated products is two, then licensing occurs if and only if the manufacturing cost difference exceeds one quarter of the cost of production in the high-cost country. In terms of figure 7.2, licensing may occur in the absence of enforceable noncompetition covenants for endowment points in regions I and II (and symmetrically, in regions I′ and II′) that are not too close to the dotted curve N^AQ^A along which $c_x^A = c_x^B$.

When licensing does take place in the absence of a credible commitment on the part of the licensor not to compete, the ultimate equilibrium cannot

11. We assume here that in the ultimate equilibrium with licensing, the cost difference between the countries is not so large as to make the (unrestricted) monopoly price in the low-cost country fall below the manufacturing cost of the high-cost country. That is, we suppose that $c_x^B(w_L^B, w_H^B)/\alpha > c_x^A(w_L^A, w_H^A)$. For certain endowment points there may exist a licensing equilibrium in which this assumption is violated. Then the actual licensing equilibrium would entail monopoly pricing by licensees and higher profits (and royalty payments) than those described in (7.21).

be characterized by FPE. If factor prices were equalized, the licensee could not earn any profits in the anticipated duopoly competition, and so would not bid a positive amount for the license. Two types of equilibrium outcomes may obtain. First, the constraint on the size of the cost differential such that licensing is profitable may bind. That is, (7.22) may hold in equilibrium as an equality. In this case the equilibrium entails specialization by the human-capital-abundant country in R&D and the production of some locally developed varieties of differentiated products. Firms in the labor-rich country also conduct R&D in this equilibrium, and differentiated products are manufactured there using both indigenously developed technologies and blueprints imported under licensing agreements. The second type of equilibrium arises when all manufacturing of innovative goods developed in the human-capital-abundant country moves offshore without the constraint on the size of the cost differential for profitable licensing ever becoming binding. Then (7.22) holds as a strict inequality, and the human-capital-rich country specializes in the research activity alone. In both cases the equilibrium with licensing may exhibit a different pattern of trade than would be observed without licensing. This point can be seen most clearly in the second example. Absent licensing, the human-capital-rich country exports innovative goods in exchange for traditional manufactures. With licensing, this country imports both commodities and exports only technology.

Now suppose that licensing contracts may include an enforceable covenant of noncompetition. All equilibrium contracts will incorporate such a provision, since the royalty payment that a licensor could extract when the licensee acts as a monopolist exceeds the sum of the maximum royalty payment under duopoly plus the licensor's own duopoly profits. With a covenant of noncompetition, a licensing contract is equivalent to an outright sale of the (enforceable) patent by the inventor. The maximum willingness to pay for this contract equals the present value of the profits that a producer in the low-cost country could earn if it had developed the variety itself. In this case licensing is profitable for the inventor whenever manufacturing costs for differentiated products are lower in the foreign country than they are at home.

It should be apparent that the licensing equilibrium in this case is exactly like the equilibrium with multinational corporations in section 7.3. In particular, if the endowment point lies in triangle $O^A M^A N^A$ of figure 7.2, factor prices will be equalized in a long-run equilibrium with free trade and free licensing. As in the case of multinational corporations, many equilibria are possible when factor prices are equalized, since all activities are equally profitable in every location, and the possibility of licensing affords a degree of freedom as to what is produced where. In the equilibrium with *minimal licensing*, the human-capital-rich country specializes in R&D and the production of innovative goods, while the labor-rich country performs all activities, including some production of innovative goods under licensing contracts. For endowment points outside of $O^A M^A N^A$ but still inside region I of figure 7.2, and for endowments points in region II to the left of the dotted curve $N^A Q^A$, the steady-state equilibrium includes trade in technology, but factor prices are not equalized in the long-run equilibrium with licensing. In all of these cases the human-capital-rich country exports technology services and imports the traditional good in the long-run equilibrium. Its balance of trade in innovative products may be positive or negative.

Let us consider now the implications of costless patent licensing in the model of quality improvements. In this model innovators have an incentive to license their discoveries to rivals even in the absence of cross-country differences in competitive conditions. In an FPE equilibrium without licensing, a successful innovator competes with the manufacturer that has the know-how to produce the previous generation product. The industry leader captures the entire market in the Bertrand equilibrium, but in the process of underpricing its rival, the firm dissipates much of its market power. If the industry leader could license its state-of-the-art technology to the holder of the last-generation patent, and if the two could agree as part of the licensing contract not to compete in the product market, (e.g., only the licensee would produce the new good), then the dissipation of profits could be minimized. The two producers could always find a royalty fee that allowed them to share these gains from reduced competition.

A licensing contract between an industry leader and its most viable competitor, especially one that incorporated a covenant of noncompetition, might well fall in violation of antitrust laws. If we were in any case to introduce these contracts into our model, the qualitative properties of the steady-state equilibrium would change dramatically. Prices for high-technology products would rise with each new discovery. And incentives to innovate would vary across sectors, according to the size of the technological gap between the producer of the state-of-the-art product and its nearest arm's-length competitor. We choose not to pursue this possibility any further here. Instead, we assume henceforth that antitrust laws prevent anticompetitive agreements between patent holders in the same industry.

There remains the possibility that an innovator in the human-capital-rich country might license its state-of-the-art technology to a potential manufacturer in the labor-abundant country that has no ties to the industry in question. Let us consider first the case in which noncompetition clauses are illegal or unenforceable. In the trade equilibrium without licensing, the cost of manufacturing high-tech products in the labor-rich country equals or exceeds the cost of manufacturing these goods in the human-capital-rich country. If the licensor and licensee were to engage in price competition subsequent to any patent sharing, the licensee would earn zero profits in the ensuing Bertrand equilibrium. Therefore, no firm in the labor-rich country would bid a positive amount for a blueprint not accompanied by an exclusive right to market the good. No licensing takes place in this case.

In the event that noncompetition clauses can be enforced, on the other hand, licensing may occur. As in the model of horizontal product differentiation, the equilibrium with patent licensing reproduces the equilibrium with multinational corporations. Licensing is observed when the trade equilibrium without licensing has equal manufacturing costs for high-tech goods in the two countries, that is, for endowments in regions I and I′ and portions of II and II′ in figure 7.2. Entrepreneurs are motivated to license in this case by the prospect that their licensees might enjoy a longer period of industry leadership than they themselves can expect if they produce the innovative good in house. In the equilibrium with licensing, factor price equalization obtains for endowments in the triangles $O^AM^AN^A$ and $O^BM^BN^B$, but not otherwise. In any event it is always the human-capital-rich country that exports technology services when licensing occurs.

In this chapter we have derived orthodox predictions about the long-run patterns of commodity trade and direct foreign investment from a fully specified dynamic model in which technological capabilities are the outgrowth of investments by far-sighted, profit-maximizing entrepreneurs. We have shown that in the absence of opportunities for international borrowing or lending, direct foreign investment, and patent licensing, the Hecksher-Ohlin theorem is valid as a long-run proposition. Financial integration introduces the possibility of long-run trade imbalance, but cannot reverse the pattern of trade from the Heckscher-Ohlin prescription. Direct investment and international licensing may alter the trade pattern, but then these other forms of international exchange are guided by factor-endowment considerations.

Our model adds one important prediction to the list of results that can be derived from static theories of international trade. We find that long-run growth rates of manufactured output and GDP are linked to resource endowments. In all cases in which the R&D sectors of both countries are active in the long run, the steady-state rates of innovation in the high-technology sectors of the two countries are the same. However, the R&D and high-tech manufacturing sectors represent a larger fraction of value added in the human-capital-rich country than they do in the labor-rich country. The latter country specializes relatively in manufacturing traditional goods, where opportunities for technological progress are fewer. As a result the human-capital-rich country experiences a faster rate of growth of output. It is important to stress, however, that despite these differences in output growth, both countries enjoy similar rates of growth of real consumption in a long-run equilibrium with free trade.

Our results in this chapter rely heavily on the assumptions that researchers worldwide share comparable laboratory skills and that the pool of general knowledge is an international one. When engineers are equally able and knowledge spillovers are international in scope, national advantage in R&D can arise only from differences in factor costs. Even when factor prices are equalized in the long-run equilibrium, dynamic comparative advantage arises due to an *incipient* cost advantage in R&D, one that derives from the cross-country differences in relative factor supplies. Ethier (1979) concludes similarly that factor endowments alone determine the pattern of international specialization and trade when (static) externalities generate scale economies in production, but the external effects are international in scope. We turn next in chapter 8 to the case where there exist impediments to trans-border information flows. There we shall find a role for a new set of factors in the determination of the global pattern of specialization and trade.

8 Hysteresis

In chapter 7 we studied the sources of dynamic comparative advantage in a world economy with international spillovers of technical information. Strikingly, we found that long-run patterns of specialization and trade are determined solely by countries' relative factor endowments. In that context neither an economy's size nor its initial conditions has any bearing on its ultimate comparative advantage, or on its long-run rates of innovation and growth.

When all countries share in a common pool of knowledge capital, a national advantage in the research lab can derive only from differences in factor costs. But if knowledge bears some of the characteristics of a *local* public good, then the accumulated wisdom in a particular location can influence the cost of innovation there. This suggests that prior experience may influence the allocation of resources to research activities, and ultimately a country's trade pattern and growth rate. In this chapter we focus on the role of history (i.e., initial conditions) in determining long-run patterns of specialization in production. To do so, we make the opposite extreme assumption about the scope of technological spillovers from the one adopted in chapter 7. We assume that research projects contribute to general knowledge capital *only* in the country where the research is carried out.[1]

We study a world economy comprising two countries that may differ only in size and in their prior research experience. Production in the two manufacturing sectors requires labor as the sole factor input. There are constant returns to scale in all activities and identical input requirements in the two countries. Thus endogenously derived differences in technological

---

1. Reality undoubtedly lies between the extremes that form the basis for our alternative analyses. A plausible specification might include, for example, lags in the diffusion of technology that are shorter within a country than between countries. See Grossman and Helpman (1990) for an analysis of this intermediate case.

capabilities form the only basis for international trade. In this setting we find that initial conditions govern long-run outcomes. Whichever country begins with a greater stock of knowledge capital enjoys an initial advantage in the research lab. In many situations this country accumulates knowledge more quickly than its trade partner, thereby perpetuating and even adding to its productivity lead. The steady-state equilibrium is characterized by concentration of research activity in one country, typically the one that inherits the technological lead.[2] History alone determines the long-run trade pattern and rates of output growth.

An exception to the prescription of "once behind, always behind" arises when the government of a lagging country intervenes in the market to promote local research activity. A sufficiently large subsidy to R&D can be used to overcome the productivity disadvantage that comes from relative inexperience in innovation. Interestingly the requisite subsidy need not be a permanent one. Once the push from policy has enabled an initially lagging country to catch up, the policy can be removed without reversing the process that has been set in motion. This presents a clear case of policy *hysteresis*; a temporary policy can have permanent effects. In the last section we discuss why this is so, and consider whether policies that induce "tipping" can be justified on grounds of national welfare.

8.1 A Benchmark Economy

As a benchmark for the upcoming analysis, we construct a model of trade between economies that differ only in size and in research experience, in a world where technological spillovers are global in reach. The model resembles the one presented in section 7.1, except that labor is the only factor of production. Of course with a single primary factor, economic activities cannot differ in factor intensity, nor can countries differ in the composition of their resource endowments. It is not surprising then to find that nothing pins down the trade pattern. A continuum of long-run equilibria exists for the world economy, with each country playing the part of the exporter of high-tech goods in some cases. The multiple equilibria differ also in the rates of output growth that the two countries achieve in the transition to the steady state and in the long run. In the sections that

2. There always exists one steady-state equilibrium with active research sectors in both countries. But this equilibrium is globally unstable. Given the sizes of the two countries, convergence to such an equilibrium requires a unique set of initial conditions (i.e., a particular ratio of the initial knowledge capital stocks).

follow, where knowledge spillovers are assumed to be national in scope, initial conditions serve to eliminate these indeterminacies.

As in section 7.1 the two countries labeled A and B potentially can produce a homogeneous product and varieties of horizontally differentiated goods. Blueprints for the latter must be developed in the research lab before manufacturing can begin. The technologies for production and innovation exhibit constant returns to scale, and units are chosen to make all input coefficients equal to one. That is, one unit of labor can be used to produce one unit of the traditional good or one unit of any known variety of high-technology product, or to expand the set of producible varieties by K_n brands per unit time (where K_n again is the stock of knowledge capital).

The traditional good Z is manufactured only in the country with the lowest unit production cost, and is priced at the level of the minimum cost. This implies that

$$p_Z = \min(w^A, w^B), \tag{8.1}$$

$$s_Z^i = 0 \qquad \text{when } w^i > w^j,\ i, j = A, B;\ j \neq i, \tag{8.2}$$

where $s_Z^i \equiv Z_i/(Z^A + Z^B)$ is the share of country i in world output of the traditional good and w^i is the wage rate there. Households, who maximize the utility function given in (7.1), devote a fraction $1 - \sigma$ of their spending (normalized to equal one) to traditional goods. Thus, equilibrium in the world market for these goods requires $p_Z(Z^A + Z^B) = 1 - \sigma$, or

$$p_Z Z^i = (1 - \sigma)s_Z^i, \qquad i = A, B. \tag{8.3}$$

High-tech goods are priced at a markup over unit production costs. The demand functions for the individual varieties (see [7.5]) can be used to compute the share s^i of world spending on high-technology products that is devoted to the brands of country i. The prices and demands also allow us to calculate the profits that accrue to manufacturers of high-technology products in either country. All of this gives

$$p^i = \frac{w^i}{\alpha}, \qquad i = A, B, \tag{8.4}$$

$$s^i = \frac{n^i(p^i)^{1-\varepsilon}}{\sum_j n^j(p^j)^{1-\varepsilon}}, \qquad i = A, B, \tag{8.5}$$

$$\pi^i = \frac{(1 - \alpha)\sigma s^i}{n^i}, \qquad i = A, B. \tag{8.6}$$

Market clearing in the high-technology sector implies that

$$p^i X^i = \sigma s^i, \qquad i = A, B, \tag{8.7}$$

where $X^i \equiv n^i x^i$ is aggregate output of differentiated products in country i, as before.

In each country free entry into innovation ensures a value of the representative high-technology firm that is no higher than the cost of product development, and equal to it when R&D actually is taking place. The cost of a new variety is w^i/n in country i, where $n \equiv n^A + n^B$, in view of our assumption that knowledge accumulates in proportion to global research activity. Thus

$$v^i \leq \frac{w^i}{n}, \qquad \text{with equality for } \dot{n}^i > 0,\ i = A, B. \tag{8.8}$$

The familiar no-arbitrage condition requires that

$$\pi^i + \dot{v}^i = \rho v^i, \qquad i = A, B, \tag{8.9}$$

provided that capital is internationally mobile (so that a nominal interest rate of ρ prevails in each country at every moment in time). Finally, the equilibrium conditions for the labor markets take the form

$$\frac{\dot{n}^i}{n} + X^i + Z^i = L^i, \qquad i = A, B. \tag{8.10}$$

We wish to demonstrate that a continuum of equilibria exists for this economy. Let us suppose that wage rates are equalized along the equilibrium trajectory, that each country has active producers in both of the manufacturing sectors, and that each develops new products. With wages equalized at the common level w, and $\dot{n}^i > 0$ for $i = A, B$, the free-entry condition (8.8) becomes

$$v^i = \frac{w}{n}, \qquad i = A, B. \tag{8.11}$$

Thus, wage equalization implies the equalization of the values of high-technology firms.[3] It also ensures that prices and sales of all varieties are the same, irrespective of country of origin. Thus $s^i = n^i/n$; in other words, each country captures spending on high-tech goods in proportion to its share in the total number of differentiated products. Using this fact and the

3. Actually this conclusion does not require the assumption that each country conducts R&D at a positive level. If wages are equalized at every moment, then by (8.4)–(8.6), per brand profits must be equalized as well. But the value of any firm equals the present value of the profits that it earns. It follows that equal wages imply equal firm values.

expression for profits (8.6) in the no-arbitrage condition (8.9), and rearranging terms, we find that

$$\frac{\dot{w}}{w} = \rho + \sum_i s^i g^i - \frac{(1-\alpha)\sigma}{w}, \tag{8.12}$$

where $g^i \equiv \dot{n}^i/n^i$ is the rate of innovation in country i, as before. This equation has the interpretation that the interest rate ρ must equal the sum of the profit rate $\pi^i = (1-\alpha)\sigma/w$, and the rate of capital gain, $\dot{v}^i/v^i = \dot{w}/w - \Sigma_i s^i g^i$. We also use (8.1)–(8.5) and the facts that $w^i = w$ and $s^i = n^i/n$ to rewrite the labor-market-clearing conditions (8.10) as

$$g^i s^i + \frac{\alpha\sigma s^i}{w} + \frac{(1-\sigma)s_Z^i}{w} = L^i, \qquad i = A, B. \tag{8.13}$$

Here the three terms on the left-hand side still represent employment levels in R&D, high-tech manufacturing, and traditional manufacturing, respectively, in country i.[4]

We consider the dynamic evolution of the world economy. The no-arbitrage condition (8.12) relates movements in the (common) wage rate to the aggregate rate of innovation, $g \equiv \dot{n}/n = \Sigma_i s^i g^i$. In figure 8.1 we show combinations of g and w that imply an unchanging wage rate. Above the $\dot{w} = 0$ schedule wages are rising, while below it they are falling. The figure also depicts a resource constraint, labeled RR, that the world economy must respect at every moment in time. This constraint is derived by summing the separate constraints for the two countries (i.e., [8.13] for $i = A$ and $i = B$), and takes the form

$$g + \frac{1-(1-\alpha)\sigma}{w} = \bar{L}, \tag{8.14}$$

where $\bar{L} \equiv L^A + L^B$ is the aggregate world supply of labor.

Point E in the figure represents a steady-state equilibrium with a constant aggregate growth rate and a constant real wage. The world economy diverges from this point unless the initial wage happens to place the economy there to begin with. Arguments similar to those invoked in chapter 3 can be used to establish that only this wage implies an initial value of firms that matches the present value of subsequent profits. We conclude that with rational expectations, the aggregate number of products

4. For example, spending on high-tech goods manufactured in country i equals σs^i, and each such good carries a price of w/α. So $\alpha\sigma s^i/w$ units are produced, each requiring one unit of labor. The interpretation of the third term is similar.

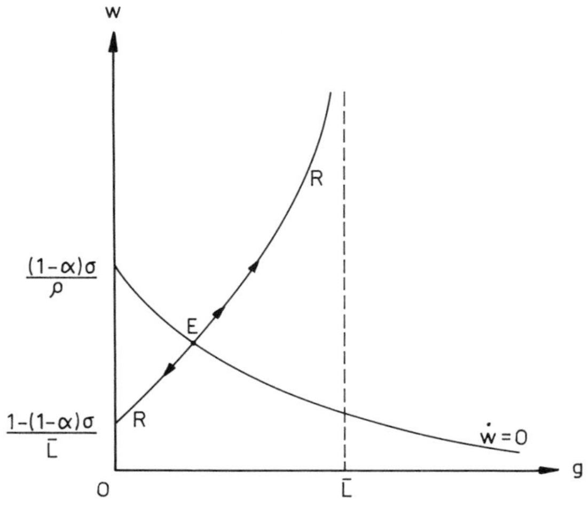

Figure 8.1

in the world economy grows always at the constant rate

$$g = (1-\alpha)\sigma\bar{L} - [1-(1-\alpha)\sigma]\rho \tag{8.15}$$

and that the wage rate in each country is always equal to

$$w = \frac{1}{\bar{L}+\rho}. \tag{8.16}$$

This equilibrium coincides with the one that would be realized by an integrated world economy with a labor force of $\bar{L}$.[5]

What are the allocations of resources in the two separate countries that underlie this equilibrium? There are many possibilities. Let us confine attention to trajectories that converge to a steady state. In a steady state the intersectoral allocation of resources remains fixed in each country. This requires the market shares s^i and s_Z^i to be fixed as well (see [8.13]). Differentiating the expression $s^i = n^i/n$ that applies when wages are equalized, we find that

$$\dot{s}^i = s^i s^j (g^i - g^j), \qquad i = A, B; i \neq j. \tag{8.17}$$

Thus constancy of market shares requires convergence in the rates of innovation.

5. Equation (8.15) represents a generalization of (3.28) for the case of an economy that devotes only a fraction σ of its spending to high-technology products.

In a steady state with $g^A = g^B = g$, and with g and w given by (8.15) and (8.16), respectively, the factor-market-clearing conditions (8.13) for the two countries become

$$[\sigma\bar{L} - (1-\sigma)\rho]s^i + (1-\sigma)(\bar{L}+\rho)s_Z^i = L^i, \qquad i = A, B. \tag{8.18}$$

Now we see that there exist many (positive) values of s^A, s^B, s_Z^A, and s_Z^B that satisfy $s^A + s^B = 1$, $s_Z^A + s_Z^B = 1$, and (8.18), for any given division of the world's resources into component allocations L^A and L^B. Suppose, for example, that $L^A = L^B = \bar{L}/2$ and $\sigma = \frac{1}{2}$. Then (8.18) can be satisfied with $s^A = 1$ and $s_Z^A = \rho/(\bar{L}+\rho)$, or with $s^A = 0$ and $s_Z^A = \bar{L}/(\bar{L}+\rho)$, or by a continuum of market shares in between. If $s^A = 1$, country A becomes a net exporter of high-tech goods in the long run. Also in this case its real output grows at a positive rate. If $s^A = 0$, on the other hand, country A imports high-technology goods in the steady state, and it experiences negligible growth in real output (because its high-technology sector comprises a small fraction of its GDP).

Next we investigate whether initial conditions dictate the steady-state resource allocations to which each of the countries converges. Let us suppose that country A initially can produce $n^A(0)$ varieties of high-tech goods, and that country B can produce a distinct set of $n^B(0)$ varieties. We suppose further that the initial product shares $s^A(0)$ and $s^B(0)$ are among those that are consistent with the aforementioned requirements for a steady-state equilibrium, given the sizes of the two countries. Then one possible equilibrium trajectory for the world economy has the two countries maintaining their initial market shares forever. But this is not the only possibility. Other candidates include all those trajectories with market shares guided by (8.17) that satisfy the resource constraints (8.13) and that have an aggregate rate of innovation given by g in (8.15) at every moment in time.

Alternative equilibrium trajectories can be constructed as follows: Choose any initial allocation such that $g^A(0) > g > g^B(0)$. Then using (8.17) and $g = \Sigma_i s^i g^i$, we have

$$\dot{s}^A = s^A(g^A - g). \tag{8.19}$$

The share of country A in the total number of varieties grows initially. Over time, we gradually reduce g^A and gradually increase g^B, while preserving the relationship $g^A s^A + g^B s^B = g$. The countries' shares in the output of traditional goods then must be adjusted to satisfy (8.13). Provided that the implied shares remain positive, the resulting trajectory represents a feasible equilibrium path.[6] In the long run the two rates of innovation must converge to $g = (1 - \alpha)\sigma\bar{L} - [1 - (1 - \alpha)\sigma]\rho$, whereupon the market shares cease to evolve. The long-run market shares, and hence the long-run allocations of resources in each country, are determined by the (arbitrarily selected) initial divergence in rates of innovation and by the speed with which the two rates are brought together.

We see that there exists a continuum of equilibrium trajectories consistent with given initial conditions.[7] The trajectories lead to different steady states with different patterns of trade. This indeterminacy of the trade pattern has an analog in the static theory of international trade. Economies with static production externalities that are international in scope similarly exhibit multiple trade equilibria, whenever the number of industries exceeds the number of factors of production (see Ethier 1979; Helpman 1984). In both the static and dynamic models the spread of the spillover benefits across national boundaries eliminates any tendency for the increasing returns activity to concentrate in a single location.

6. For some initial conditions and divisions of resources between the countries, it may be impossible to construct an equilibrium trajectory that everywhere reproduces the aggregate values of the integrated economy. For example, suppose that country A is much smaller than country B but that it begins with a large share of the world's high-technology products. In particular, suppose that initially $n^A/(n^A + n^B) > L^A/\alpha\sigma(\bar{L} + \rho)$. Then the resource constraint for country A cannot be satisfied when the the wage rate is as given by (8.16) because at this wage the country's high-tech manufacturers demand more labor than the country's available supply. In this case the equilibrium trajectory involves an initial phase in which country A specializes in the production of differentiated products and country B alone conducts research and produces traditional goods. Once country B has accumulated a large enough share of the world's products, labor is released by the manufacturing enterprises in country A and innovation begins there.

7. It is interesting to note that the multiplicity of equilibrium trajectories disappears, even for the case of international knowledge spillovers, if financial assets cannot be traded. Without capital mobility all R&D in each country must be financed by local savings. The requirement of current account balance pins down for each country a unique trajectory and thus a unique steady state. Take, for example, the case in which the initial product shares are roughly in proportion to the relative sizes of the two countries. In this case factor prices and interest rates are equalized by commodity trade. With equal interest rates and logarithmic preferences, each country saves the same fixed proportion of its aggregate wealth. Wealth includes the value of financial assets $n^i v^i$ and the present value of labor income wL^i/ρ. It follows from (8.11) that the share of country i in aggregate world wealth equals $(\rho s^i + L^i)/(\bar{L} + \rho)$. This must equal the country's share in world innovation $\dot{n}^i/\dot{n}$. Equating these two, we find $g^i/g = (\rho + L^i/s^i)/(\bar{L} + \rho)$. Therefore a country innovates faster than its trade partner if and only if its share of the world labor supply exceeds its share of the high-technology products. In the long run each country innovates at the same rate, and each captures market share in both the traditional and high-technology sectors in proportion to its relative size.

Although the various trajectories entail different rates of output growth and different patterns of trade for each country, it is apparent that the countries should be indifferent as to which one emerges. All equilibria that reproduce the integrated economy share the same wage profile and the same aggregate rate of innovation. In each country, households earn the same returns on their investments and face the same commodity prices in each one. Thus incomes and consumption opportunities are the same. It follows that all equilibria yield the same aggregate level of welfare to each country.

8.2 Steady States

We turn now to a world economy where the knowledge spillovers generated by industrial research are *national* in scope. We begin the analysis by identifying the different types of steady states that may emerge and the structural conditions that are prerequisites for each one. Equilibrium trajectories are described in the following two sections.

Several modifications of the model are necessary in order to capture the specificity of national knowledge stocks. We suppose now that each country accumulates knowledge capital in proportion to its own research activity. Units are chosen so that $K_n^i = n^i$. Then $1/n^i$ units of labor are needed in country i to develop each new variety of the differentiated product. Free entry into R&D implies that

$$v^i \le \frac{w^i}{n^i}, \qquad \text{with equality for } \dot{n}^i > 0,\ i = A, B, \tag{8.8$'$}$$

while the labor-market-clearing conditions become

$$\frac{\dot{n}^i}{n^i} + X^i + Z^i = L^i, \qquad i = A, B. \tag{8.10$'$}$$

The latter conditions can be rewritten, using (8.1), (8.3)–(8.5), and (8.7), as

$$g^i + \frac{\alpha\sigma s^i}{w^i} + \frac{(1-\sigma)s_Z^i}{w^i} = L^i, \qquad i = A, B. \tag{8.13$'$}$$

In the steady state the intersectoral resource allocation in each country remains fixed. We see from (8.13′) that this requires constant wage rates and constant market shares in each country (since the market shares are bounded by zero and one). Several different long-run outcomes are possible.

First, R&D activity may be concentrated in a single country, while firms in both locations engage in the production of traditional goods. With $g^i > g^j = 0$ and relative wages constant in the long run, (8.5) implies that the market share of the innovating country in high technology approaches one; that is, $s^i = 1$. Competitive pricing of traditional goods requires equal unit costs, hence equal wage rates. Then the steady state is characterized by a long-run no-arbitrage condition derived from (8.6), (8.9), and (8.8′), and two labor-market-clearing conditions derived from (8.13′). These are

$$\frac{(1-\alpha)\sigma}{w} = \rho + g^i, \tag{8.20}$$

$$g^i + \frac{\alpha\sigma}{w} + \frac{s_Z^i(1-\sigma)}{w} = L^i, \tag{8.21}$$

$$\frac{s_Z^j(1-\sigma)}{w} = L^j, \tag{8.22}$$

which, together with $s_Z^i + s_Z^j = 1$, determine the long-run wage, the long-run innovation rate, and the long-run market shares in the traditional sector. Solving this system, we find that $s_Z^j \leq 1$ requires that

$$\frac{L^j}{L^i + \rho} \leq \frac{1-\sigma}{\sigma}. \tag{8.23}$$

A second type of steady state with R&D activity concentrated in one country (e.g., country i) is characterized by the concentration of the production of traditional goods in the other country. This requires $w^j \leq w^i$ (see [8.2]). The no-arbitrage and labor-market-clearing conditions become

$$\frac{(1-\alpha)\sigma}{w^i} = \rho + g^i, \tag{8.24}$$

$$g^i + \frac{\alpha\sigma}{w^i} = L^i, \tag{8.25}$$

$$\frac{1-\sigma}{w^j} = L^j. \tag{8.26}$$

From these conditions we find that $w^j \leq w^i$ implies that

$$\frac{L^j}{L^i + \rho} \geq \frac{1-\sigma}{\sigma}. \tag{8.27}$$

This is, of course, just the opposite inequality from (8.23). In a steady state in which one country performs all of the world's R&D, that same country also can produce traditional goods only if it is large in comparison to its trade partner, or if the share of world spending devoted to traditional products is great. Otherwise, the country that performs R&D must specialize its manufacturing activities in high technology.

Two types of steady states involve *equal* rates of innovation in the two countries. In one such long-run equilibrium both countries produce traditional goods. With $g^i = g^j = g$, and $w^i = w^j = w$ (as is required by competition in the traditional-goods sector), we have the steady-state no-arbitrage conditions

$$\frac{(1-\alpha)\sigma s^k}{w} = \rho + g, \qquad k = i, j, \tag{8.28}$$

and the labor-market-clearing conditions

$$g + \frac{\alpha\sigma s^k}{w} + \frac{s_Z^k(1-\sigma)}{w} = L^k, \qquad k = i, j. \tag{8.29}$$

From (8.28) we see that $s^i = s^j = \frac{1}{2}$; that is, the countries come to share evenly the world market for high-technology goods. Then (8.28), (8.29), and $s_Z^i \leq 1$ imply that

$$\frac{L^j - L^i}{L^i + \rho} \leq \frac{2(1-\sigma)}{\sigma}. \tag{8.30}$$

A second configuration that can arise when the countries innovate at the same rates entails the production of traditional goods in one country only (e.g., country j). The steady state is characterized by

$$\frac{(1-\alpha)\sigma s^k}{w^k} = \rho + g, \qquad k = i, j, \tag{8.31}$$

$$g + \frac{\alpha\sigma s^i}{w^i} = L^i, \tag{8.32}$$

$$g + \frac{\alpha\sigma s^j}{w^j} + \frac{1-\sigma}{w^j} = L^j. \tag{8.33}$$

This equilibrium requires $w^j \leq w^i$, which in turn implies that

$$\frac{L^j - L^i}{L^i + \rho} \geq \frac{2(1-\sigma)}{\sigma}. \tag{8.34}$$

The two equilibria in this pair also are mutually exclusive (compare [8.34] and [8.30]). Both countries can produce traditional goods when the difference in their size is relatively small, whereas only the larger country can engage in such production when the size gap is large.

No other type of steady state is possible. In particular, it is not possible for the countries to innovate at positive but unequal rates in the long run. To verify this, let us suppose to the contrary that $g^i > g^j > 0$. In the event the long-run no-arbitrage conditions would imply that $(1-\alpha)\sigma s^i/w^i = \rho + g^i$, $i = A, B$. But the market share of country j in the high-technology sector would shrink to zero, so the no-arbitrage condition for this country would require its wage rate also to approach zero. A wage of zero in country j cannot be consistent with labor market clearing because it implies an unbounded demand for the country's labor by firms that manufacture traditional goods.

Our analysis reveals that for any given parameter configuration, there exist exactly *three* different steady-state equilibria. In one equilibrium country A alone innovates and either both countries produce traditional goods (if [8.23] is satisfied for $i = A$ and $j = B$) or only country B does so (if [8.27] is satisfied for $i = A$ and $j = B$). In a second possible steady state, R&D takes place in country B, and traditional goods are produced either in both countries (if [8.23] is satisfied for $i = B$ and $j = A$) or only in country A (if [8.27] is satisfied for $i = B$ and $j = A$). The third steady state has equal rates of innovation in the two countries, and traditional manufacturing taking place either in both locations (if [8.30] is satisfied for $i = A$ *and* $i = B$) or only in the larger country (if [8.34] is satisfied for $i = A$ *or* $i = B$). We note the analogy with *static*, two-sector trade models with economies of scale in one sector. In the static models it is common for there to exist three equilibria, two with the increasing returns activity concentrated in a single country and one with diversified production in all locations (see Helpman 1984). Typically, the latter type of equilibrium is unstable. Appendix A8.1 establishes that the same is true here. The steady-state outcomes with equal rates of innovation can emerge in the dynamic equilibrium only if the initial product shares in the high-technology sector happen to coincide with the steady-state shares. If in such an equilibrium an exogenous shock were to cause the ratio of the product shares to deviate momentarily from its steady-state level, the world economy would migrate to a different long-run equilibrium with R&D activity concentrated in one location. In recognition of this instability, we focus our attention henceforth on the equilibria with geographic concentration of R&D efforts. Our question becomes, Which country innovates?

8.3 Equal-Wage Trajectories

In this section we study dynamic equilibria that are characterized by factor price equalization. We show that if $L^j/(L^i + \rho) \leq (1 - \sigma)/\sigma$ as in (8.23), and the countries are similar in size, then *exactly* one equilibrium trajectory with FPE emanates from every initial position (i.e., numbers of differentiated products in each country).[8] Along this trajectory the country that inherits the greater stock of knowledge comes to dominate the world market for high-technology goods.

First we note that when countries share a common wage rate, profits per firm are the same in both locations. Therefore, if wage rates are equalized all along the equilibrium trajectory, so too will be the present values of the profit streams and hence the stock market values of firms in each country. This means that a similar reward awaits any innovating firm regardless of its location. With free entry into R&D and a unified world capital market, investors will finance only those firms operating in the country with the lower cost of R&D. But, if wage rates are the same, costs must be lower in the country that has the larger stock of knowledge capital, and thus the greater productivity in the research lab. It follows that all of the world's research will take place in the technologically leading country.

We describe now the equilibrium dynamics along an equal-wage trajectory and find the conditions that are needed for the existence of such a path. Without loss of generality we can assume that country A inherits the lead in technology and, consequently, that all research is conducted there. In the event the world wage rate is guided by the no-arbitrage condition (8.9) that applies to the value of firms in country A. Using (8.6) and $v \equiv w/n^A$, we have

$$\frac{\dot{w}}{w} = g^A + \rho - \frac{(1 - \alpha)\sigma s^A}{w}. \tag{8.35}$$

Summing the resource constraints (8.13′) that apply for $i = A$ and $i = B$ when $g^B = 0$, we find that

$$g^A = \bar{L} - \frac{1 - (1 - \alpha)\sigma}{w}. \tag{8.36}$$

Of course the right-hand side of (8.36) must be positive, or else innovation cannot be sustained with equal wages. Now we combine (8.35) and (8.36)

8. We also require, as usual, that the world economy be large enough to sustain positive growth.

to obtain

$$\dot{w} = w(\rho + \bar{L}) - [1 - (1 - \alpha)\sigma] - (1 - \alpha)\sigma s^A. \tag{8.37}$$

In figure 8.2 the line segment *DE* shows the combinations of the wage and the market share of country *A* in high technology that imply no change in the wage rate, per (8.37). This segment has been drawn only for values of $s^A \geq \frac{1}{2}$ because R&D concentrates in country *A* only when this country suffers no disadvantage in the research lab. Next we substitute (8.36) into (8.17) to derive

$$\dot{s}^A = s^A(1 - s^A)\left[\bar{L} - \frac{1 - (1 - \alpha)\sigma}{w}\right]. \tag{8.38}$$

When $s^A \geq \frac{1}{2}$ and $g^A > 0$, the market share of country *A* always is expanding. Only when it reaches one (the vertical line through point *E* in figure 8.2) does the share become stationary. The arrows in the figure show the direction of movement of the variables w and s^A at every point.

The figure also shows the constraints on the wage and the market share that must be satisfied for there to exist a momentary equilibrium with equal wage rates. Feasibility requires nonnegative allocations of resources to all activities. For $g^A \geq 0$, we need the right-hand side of (8.36) to be nonnegative. This occurs in the region above the horizontal line labeled *FF'*. Provided that $\bar{L}$ is sufficiently large, point *F* lies below point *D*, and this constraint does not bind.[9] For $s_Z^B \geq 0$ and $s_Z^A \geq 0$, we must have

$$0 \leq \frac{wL^B - \alpha\sigma(1 - s^A)}{1 - \sigma} \leq 1, \tag{8.39}$$

in light of the expression for s_Z^B that derives from (8.13′) and $g^B = 0$. The economy must remain within the region bounded by the lines labeled $s_Z^A = 0$ and $s_Z^B = 0$. The former line lies everywhere above point *E* when the inequality (8.23) is satisfied. The latter line lies everywhere below *FF'* (and thus never binds) when the countries are of equal size.

A unique trajectory leads to the steady-state point *E*. Under the conditions outlined this trajectory remains within the feasible region. Thus, given any initial stocks of products such that $n^A(0) \geq n^B(0)$, if the countries are of roughly equal size and the world economy is sufficiently large, there exists an equilibrium growth path with equal wages. Along this path country *A* alone innovates, and firms in that country capture an ever-growing share of the world market for high-technology products.

9. More precisely this requires that $(1 - \alpha)\sigma\bar{L}/2 > [1 - (1 - \alpha)\sigma]\rho$.

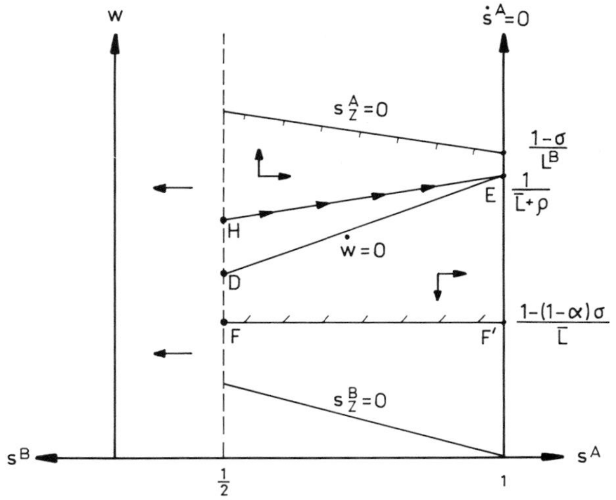

Figure 8.2

We have established conditions under which a productivity lead in R&D is self-perpetuating. Neither country can overcome an initial deficit in research experience along a trajectory that maintains wage equality. Thus the equal-wage trajectories exhibit a strong form of *hysteresis*. Events in history that provide one country with a head start in the accumulation of knowledge have long-lasting effects on the patterns of specialization and trade.[10]

What happens if the countries inherit identical stocks of knowledge capital? In this case, there are two equally plausible trajectories that differ in terms of the identity of the country that performs the world's R&D.[11] If innovators in country *A* begin to conduct research while those in country *B* remain idle, then country *A* immediately takes the lead in research productivity and the world economy embarks along the trajectory labeled *HE*. If, instead, it is country *B* that gets underway first, then that country enjoys forever an advantage in the research lab. The realization of one versus the other of these equilibria depends entirely upon the expectations of agents in the world economy.[12]

10. Markusen (1991) finds a similar result in a two-period model of entry into an increasing returns activity.

11. As we have noted previously, there also exists a third equilibrium trajectory in this case, one in which the countries immediately and forever introduce new products at the same rate. However, this equilibrium is globally unstable: Any momentary departure from it would cause a permanent cessation of R&D activities in one country.

12. Krugman (1991) and Matsuyama (1991) have shown, in different dynamic settings, how

Along the equilibrium trajectory shown in figure 8.2, innovation and output growth accelerate in country A. The rate of innovation rises because the wage rate does, and so the manufacturing sectors release resources that move into R&D ([8.36] gives the inverse relationship between g^A and w). The growth rate rises, both because the pace of product development quickens and because the share of high-technology products in the country's manufactured output expands. These predictions contrast sharply, of course, with those of the neoclassical growth model (see chapter 2), where innovation is exogenous and the growth rate declines over time. Country B, on the other hand, experiences no technological progress here, and no growth in real output. Over time its trade pattern shifts toward ever greater net imports of high-technology products.

It should be emphasized, however, that despite the evident asymmetries in rates of innovation and the pattern of trade, residents of either country fare equally well in the dynamic equilibrium with FPE. When wage rates are equalized, labor incomes follow the same path in both places. Also with global capital markets, all households face a similar set of investment opportunities. Finally, international trade allows residents of every country to consume the full range of innovative products. Thus any two households that begin with the same wealth will experience the same levels of utility along an equal-wage trajectory regardless of their country of residence. Growth rates of domestic output provide misleading measures of national welfare in this instance.

8.4 Unequal-Wage Trajectories

It is not always possible for the world economy to traverse a path to a steady state that preserves cross-country wage equality at every moment in time. As we have just seen, an equilibrium with FPE is highly asymmetric, inasmuch as one country performs all of the world's R&D and also produces a disproportionate share of the world's high-technology products, while the other country uses its labor mostly (and increasingly) to produce traditional goods. Only for certain parameter values will it be possible to find a path for the wage rate that allows these differences in labor demand to match the exogenous differences in labor supply.

We use figure 8.3 to analyze the relationship between underlying parameter values and the likelihood that wages must diverge somewhere along

history can dictate the long-run outcome for some initial conditions, while expectations will be determinative for others. It is noteworthy that their models share with this one the feature that increasing returns characterize production in one of two manufacturing sectors.

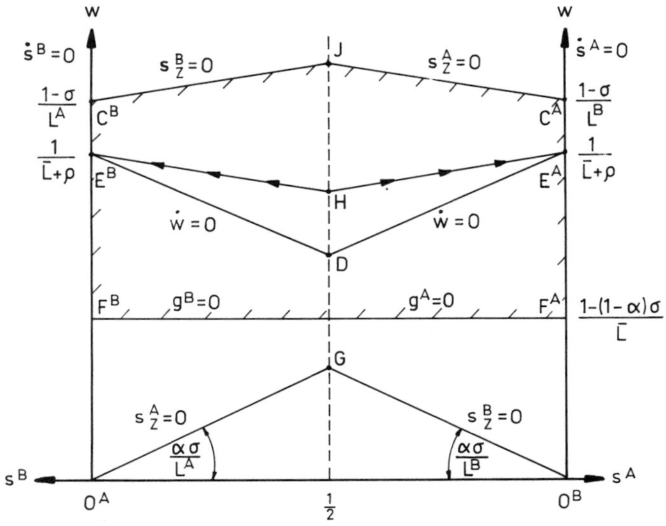

Figure 8.3

the equilibrium path. The figure reproduces the relevant curves from figure 8.2 and includes the corresponding curves that apply when $s^A < \frac{1}{2}$ and country B alone engages in product development. The trajectories marked HE^A and HE^B represent the dynamic equilibria when (8.23) is satisfied and the countries are of equal size. The economy travels along HE^A if $n^A(0) > n^B(0)$, and along HE^B otherwise.

Let us consider what happens when we vary the spending shares, while maintaining the assumption that the countries are of equal size. An increase in the budget share of high-tech goods shifts down the points labeled C^A and C^B. When σ becomes large, these points must lie below the points labeled E^A and E^B. Then wage rates must differ in the steady state because a single country cannot perform R&D, supply the world market for virtually all differentiated products, and also produce traditional goods. For large σ the high-tech manufacturing sector eventually comes to demand vast amounts of labor in the innovating country. Once the traditional sector has released all of its resources (at the point where HE^A hits JC^A, or HE^B hits JC^B), further expansion in labor demand that results from the development of new goods induces an increase in the relative wage of the innovating country.[13]

13. An increase in the budget share of high-tech goods also raises the point labeled G in the figure. However, this point must fall below the F^BF^A curve when the countries are of equal size, and so the nonnegativity constraint on the share of the noninnovating country in the traditional sector never binds in this case.

An increase in the budget share of traditional goods, on the other hand, causes the F^BF^A line to shift upward. For large enough values of $1 - \sigma$, the line must pass above the point labeled H. Then R&D will be unprofitable even for the technologically leading country if wages are equal and market shares in high technology are close to even.

Next we examine variations in the relative sizes of the two countries. We consider different cross-country distributions of a fixed world resource endowment $\bar{L}$. A transfer of labor from country B to country A shifts the point labeled C^B downward, and that labeled C^A upward. This increases the likelihood of there existing a long-run equilibrium with FPE and country A engaged in both R&D and the production of both types of goods, but it reduces the likelihood of such an equilibrium with country B diversified in its manufacturing activities. When the relative size of the innovating country is small, it becomes increasingly difficult for that country to supply the world with an expanding range of high-technology products and still have resources to spare for the production of traditional goods. The traditional sector in a small, innovating country eventually disappears, whereupon further product development brings about a rise in that country's relative wage.

A change in the cross-country distribution of labor also shifts the lines labeled O^AG and O^BG. As country A becomes larger relative to country B, it becomes more likely that O^BG will cut the trajectory labeled HE^A. Then, if the larger country A inherits only a slightly greater number of differentiated products than country B, wages cannot be equalized during an initial phase of the dynamic equilibrium. The small country initially is unable to meet the world's demand for its unique varieties while maintaining a nonnegative output of traditional goods. Therefore the wage and price in the small country must begin above those in the larger country.

What are the properties of the equilibrium trajectory when wage rates must differ across countries? We begin to answer this question by investigating a world economy comprising two countries of equal size. For such a world economy we can establish that the country with the larger initial stock of knowledge eventually performs all of the world's industrial research. Thus initial conditions determine the countries' fates again in this case.

To establish that R&D activity must, in the long run, be concentrated in the country that begins with the greater number of differentiated products, let us suppose to the contrary that an initially lagging country (e.g., country B) can overcome a deficit in research experience. We argue first that the wage rate in country B cannot be lower than that in country A

during the final moments of the phase when $n^B < n^A$. If country B is to eliminate its knowledge deficit, it must be that $g^B > g^A$ at the moment when $n^A - n^B$ is positive but small. At that moment country B must have greater employment in R&D. It also must have greater employment in the sector producing high-tech goods because labor demand by this sector equals $\alpha\sigma s^i/w^i$ in country i, and $s^B/w^B \geq s^A/w^A$ when $w^B < w^A$ and the numbers of products are nearly the same (see [8.5]). Finally, if $w^B < w^A$, then employment in traditional manufacturing is positive in country B but zero in country A. Thus, with $n^A - n^B$ positive but small, $w^B < w^A$ implies that country B employs more labor than country A in every activity. This contradicts the fact that the countries are of equal size.

So we must have $w^B \geq w^A$ during the final moments of the catch-up phase. Then entrepreneurs in country B, facing both higher factor prices and a lower research productivity, experience greater costs of product development than their counterparts in country A. The former entrepreneurs can attract financing under these conditions only if their prospective reward from research is greater; that is, if $v^B > v^A$. The value of firms in country B can exceed that of firms in country A only if per firm profits are higher in the former country than in the latter for some finite interval of time. During this interval, which must occur after country B has taken over the technological lead, $\pi^B > \pi^A$ implies that $w^B < w^A$. Then country B will experience greater derived demand for its labor by both traditional and high-tech manufacturers. Again, this situation cannot be consistent with the clearing of both labor markets, given our assumption that the countries are of equal size and the hypothesis that country B conducts more research. Thus our supposition that country B can overturn its knowledge deficit leads to a contradiction. With similarly sized economies the country that inherits the greater stock of knowledge always comes to dominate the world market for high-technology products.

In figure 8.4 we construct an example of an equilibrium trajectory with unequal wages. In the example, cross-country wage differences persist in the long run. The figure applies to the case when $L^B/(L^A + \rho) > (1 - \sigma)/\sigma$ as in (8.27), so that point C^A in figure 8.3 lies below point E^A. Then the equal-wage trajectory HE^A is not feasible because it crosses the boundary JC^A where s_Z^A turns negative.

Let us hypothesize that $w^A > w^B$, and that country A alone develops new products while country B alone produces traditional goods. Using the no-arbitrage condition (8.9) and free-entry condition (8.8′) that apply to the value of firms in country A, and the measure of per firm profits in (8.6), we can derive an expression for the evolution of the wage rate in the innovating country:

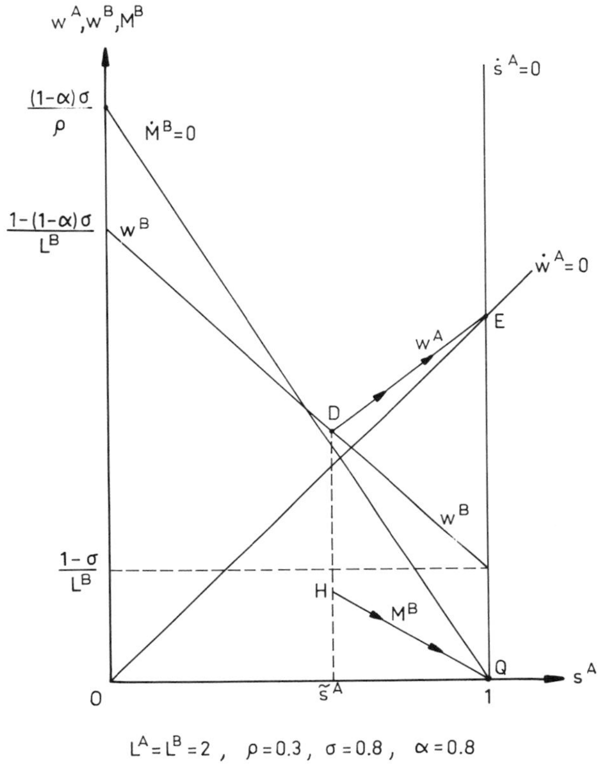

Figure 8.4

$$\frac{\dot{w}^A}{w^A} = g^A + \rho - \frac{(1-\alpha)\sigma s^A}{w^A}. \tag{8.40}$$

Then we can substitute for g^A using the labor-market-clearing condition (8.13′) that applies when $s_Z^A = 0$. This gives

$$\dot{w}^A = w^A(L^A + \rho) - \sigma s^A. \tag{8.41}$$

We use (8.41) in figure 8.4 to plot the combinations of the wage rate and the market share of the innovating country that imply a constant value for w^A. Above the line labeled $\dot{w}^A = 0$ the wage in country A rises, while below the line it falls.[14]

Next we determine the evolution of market shares. By differentiating (8.5) and imposing $g^B = 0$, we derive

14. Figure 8.4 has been drawn for a particular set of parameter values. These are $L^A = L^B = 2$, $\rho = 0.3$, $\sigma = 0.8$, and $\alpha = 0.8$.

$$\dot{s}^A = s^A(1 - s^A)\left[g^A - \frac{\alpha}{1-\alpha}\left(\frac{\dot{w}^A}{w^A} - \frac{\dot{w}^B}{w^B}\right)\right].$$

The labor market constraint for country B implies that $\dot{w}^B = -\alpha\sigma\dot{s}^A/L^B$ when $g^B = 0$, while the labor market constraint for country A implies that $g^A = L^A - \alpha\sigma s^A/w^A$. Substituting these and (8.41) into the expression for $\dot{s}^A$, we find that

$$\dot{s}^A = \frac{s^A(1-s^A)[1-\sigma+\alpha\sigma(1-s^A)]}{(1-\alpha)(1-\sigma)+[1-\alpha(1-s^A)]\alpha\sigma(1-s^A)} \times \left[\frac{\alpha\sigma s^A}{w^A} + \frac{(1-2\alpha)L^A}{\alpha} - \rho\right]. \tag{8.42}$$

When $(1-\alpha)L^A > \alpha\rho$, as is required for an equilibrium with sustained growth, the term in brackets on the far right-hand side of (8.42) is positive at all points above the $\dot{w}^A = 0$ locus. Then the market share of country A is rising in this region, for all $s^A < 1$. The figure shows a trajectory DE that leads to the steady-state point E.

The trajectory DE is a candidate for the equilibrium. We must now check that the properties of this path are consistent with the assumptions that we used in constructing it. First, we must confirm that $w^A > w^B$, as we supposed. The labor market condition for country B implies that

$$w^B = \frac{(1-\sigma)+\alpha\sigma(1-s^A)}{L^B}. \tag{8.43}$$

The line labeled w^B in the figure represents the wage in country B. For $w^A > w^B$ we need the equilibrium path to remain everywhere above this line. Thus our hypothesis concerning the configuration of wages is valid if and only if the market share of country A exceeds $\tilde{s}^A$.

Second, we have assumed that $g^B = 0$. Thus it must not be profitable for entrepreneurs in country B to invest in research, even though factor costs are lower there and per brand profits are higher. This requires country A to hold a productivity advantage that more than compensates for its higher factor prices. More precisely, entrepreneurs in country B will refrain from innovating when $v^B < w^B/n^B$, or when $M^B < w^B$, where $M^B \equiv n^B v^B$ is the aggregate value of shares in country B firms. The value of shares in the typical firm located in country B evolves according to the no-arbitrage condition (8.9), where profits are given in (8.6). Since the number of such firms does not change in a regime with no R&D in country B, we have

$$\frac{\dot{M}^B}{M^B} = \rho - \frac{(1-\alpha)\sigma(1-s^A)}{M^B}. \tag{8.44}$$

Figure 8.4 shows the combinations of market shares and stock market values for which the aggregate share value is constant. Above the $\dot{M}^B = 0$ line the aggregate stock market value rises, while below the line it falls. Since the value of firms must remain finite when s^A approaches one, it follows that M^B converges to zero along a trajectory such as the one labeled HQ in the figure. The figure has been drawn for parameter values that locate the HQ trajectory everywhere below the w^B line for $s^A \geq \tilde{s}^A$. In the event $M^B < w^B$, and thus R&D is not profitable in country B.

We conclude that if country A inherits a fraction of the world's differentiated products that afford it an initial market share in excess of $\tilde{s}^A$, then the path labeled DE satisfies the requirements for a dynamic equilibrium. Moreover, if $n^A(0) > n^B(0)$, there can exist no equilibrium trajectory that leads to a steady state other than at point E. Along DE, and in the long run, only country A performs research, while only country B manufactures traditional goods. The long-run trade pattern involves an exchange of high-technology products by country A for the traditional goods (and the initially inherited high-technology products) of country B.

When country A inherits a fraction of differentiated products that imply an initial market share of less than $\tilde{s}^A$, the constraint that $w^A \geq w^B$ initially binds. Then the two wage rates must be equal during an initial phase of the dynamic equilibrium. As long as the share of country B in the existing varieties of differentiated products remains reasonably high, this country cannot supply its unique brands to the world market in the desired quantities and also satisfy the entirety of world demand for traditional goods. Instead, the world economy travels along an equal-wage trajectory, with innovation occurring only in country A but production of traditional goods taking place in both locations. Over time country A comes to produce a growing fraction of the world's innovative products. Resources shift from traditional manufacturing into the high-technology sector in that country, and in the opposite direction in country B. Eventually the world economy reaches point D, whereupon a regime switch takes place.[15] Wage rates

15. Note that a regime change must occur exactly at point D. Otherwise, there would be a discrete change in the wage rate in one country and therefore a discrete change in the value of firms. But this implies the existence of forseeable, infinitely large capital gains or losses. Such is not consistent with the assumption of rational expectations. The requirement that both economies attain the wage rate at D when s^A reaches $\tilde{s}^A$ pins down the initial wage rate along the equal-wage trajectory.

diverge from that point onward (w^A rises, while w^B falls), and country A engages in no further production of traditional goods.

For parameter values different from those that underlie figure 8.4, it may happen that the M^B trajectory crosses the w^B line to the right of $\tilde{s}^A$. Then the unequal-wage trajectory described above will not be feasible during an initial phase of the dynamic equilibrium because the associated wage rates, interest rate, and firm values make R&D a strictly profitable activity in country B. Instead, the economy passes through an initial phase where innovation takes place in both countries, though at a faster rate in country A than in country B. During this phase the lower factor costs prevailing in country B, and the greater profits that accrue to innovators there, offset the country's relative lack of knowledge capital. But over time the advantage of researchers in country A grows larger, making it more and more difficult for researchers in country B to compete. Eventually the research sector in country B shrinks to zero, and the world economy enters into a regime such as the one depicted by DE in figure 8.4.

We turn finally to the case of differently sized economies. A new possibility arises when the country that trails in the research race (i.e., the country that inherits the smaller stock of knowledge) happens to be one with a substantially larger endowment of labor. Rather than present a detailed analysis of this case, we describe informally the qualitative nature of the new outcome that can obtain.

Recall that a country that suffers a productivity disadvantage in the research lab can profitably conduct research only if its wage rate is lower than that abroad. A low wage rate gives this country a competitive advantage in traditional manufacturing, which places certain demands on its labor force. With equally sized countries, these demands preclude the undertaking of substantial R&D by the initially lagging country. But if the lagging country is quite large in relation to its trade partner, and if the budget share of traditional goods is relatively small, then the country might be able to overcome a modest deficit in knowledge capital. The large country would need to invest heavily in R&D despite allocating substantial resources to the production of traditional goods, while the small country would devote most (or perhaps all) of its resources to the production of existing varieties. The result would be faster innovation in the larger country, which would enable it to eliminate the technology gap and ultimately to capture the world market for high-tech goods. What makes this a possibility here is the fact that, all else equal, large countries tend to enjoy a comparative advantage in performing activities that are subject to increasing returns to scale (see Helpman 1984).

We can summarize the findings of this section as follows. When structural parameters preclude an equilibrium trajectory with equal wages at every moment, several different outcomes are possible. If the trade partners are of roughly equal size, then all outcomes are characterized by the eventual concentration of R&D activity in the country that begins with the larger stock of knowledge capital. The long-run equilibrium may be reached by a path that has R&D investment and the production of traditional goods taking place only in distinct locations, or there may be an initial phase with incomplete specialization in one country or the other. If the trade partners are of disparate sizes, on the other hand, then a large country might be able to overcome a modest deficiency in knowledge capital if the share of spending devoted to traditional goods is relatively small.

8.5 R&D Subsidies

In the preceding sections we have seen that when knowledge spillovers are geographically concentrated, initial conditions determine the long-run trade pattern. Often it is the country that inherits the technological lead that comes to dominate the world market in high technology. A country's fate need not be sealed, however, if its government can provide local entrepreneurs with adequate incentive to conduct industrial research. In this section we show how government intervention might be used to "tip" the world economy from one steady state to another. We also discuss the normative implications of this potential use of government policy.

Let us suppose that the government of country A offers to pay the fraction ϕ of R&D costs, at a time when its researchers lag behind in the international technological competition. We focus our attention on an equilibrium trajectory that is characterized by factor price equalization. When wages are equalized, so too are profits and the value of firms in either location. Then entrepreneurs in country A can obtain the reward v by bearing the (subsidized) cost of product development. With the subsidy in place, value maximization by these entrepreneurs ensures that

$$v \leq \frac{(1-\phi)w}{n^A}, \qquad \text{with equality for } \dot{n}^A > 0. \tag{8.45}$$

All research activity takes place in country A, rather than in the technically more advanced country B, whenever the private costs of R&D are lower in the former location than in the latter, that is, when $(1-\phi)/n^A < 1/n^B$. Thus a subsidy rate can always be found that generates research activity in a country suffering from a deficiency of technical knowledge.

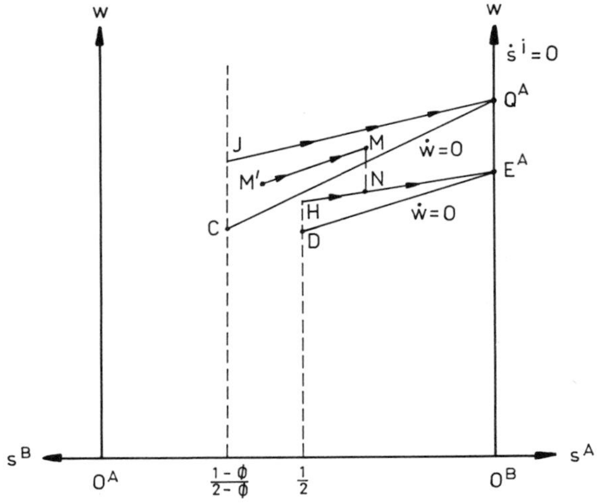

Figure 8.5

We consider a subsidy sufficiently large to locate research activity in country A. Then (8.45) implies that $\dot{v}/v = \dot{w}/w - g^A$, and the no-arbitrage condition becomes

$$\frac{\dot{w}}{w} = g^A + \rho - \frac{(1-\alpha)\sigma s^A}{w(1-\phi)}. \tag{8.46}$$

We can substitute for g^A, using the labor-market-clearing conditions (8.13′), to derive

$$\dot{w} = w(\rho + \bar{L}) - [1 - (1-\alpha)\sigma] - \frac{(1-\alpha)\sigma s^A}{1-\phi}, \tag{8.47}$$

a differential equation for w that is analogous to (8.37).

In figure 8.5 we depict as the line segment CQ^A the combinations of wage rates and market shares that imply that $\dot{w} = 0$. The line has been drawn only for market shares greater than $s^A = (1-\phi)/(2-\phi)$ because the hypothesis that R&D takes place in country A is not justified for market shares smaller than this.[16] The differential equation for the market share (8.38) and the nonnegativity constraints on g^A and s_Z^i, $i = A, B$, are the same as they were in the absence of the subsidy. Thus, if the subsidy remains permanently in place, the economy traverses the trajectory leading

16. Recall that $s^A = n^A/(n^A + n^B)$, when wage rates are equalized. Using this fact, it is easy to see that $(1-\phi)/n^A > 1/n^B$ implies that $s^A > (1-\phi)/(2-\phi)$.

to the point Q^A. In the dynamic equilibrium country A overcomes its knowledge deficiency and captures the world market for high-technology goods.

We see that policy intervention can be used by a government to tip the equilibrium from one steady state (at E^B) to another (at Q^A). We show now that the intervention that accomplishes this purpose need not be invoked on a permanent basis. Consider a temporary subsidy that is implemented at time 0, with termination preannounced to occur at date T. As long as the subsidy remains in place, (8.47) guides the movements of the wage. Then, after the subsidy has been removed, (8.37) applies instead. No jump in firm value can take place at time T; otherwise, agents would stand to reap infinite capital gains.[17] Therefore the wage rate common to the two countries must fall by ϕ percent at time T in order to preserve equality between firm value and private R&D costs in the moments following the removal of the subsidy.

Figure 8.5 can be used to describe the evolution of the economy. The point M' in the figure represents the product share of country A when the subsidy is introduced at time 0. The economy moves along the trajectory $M'M$ as long as the subsidy remains in effect. Country A attains the market share at M by the time that the subsidy is eliminated at time T. For the subsidy to "work," in the sense of tipping the equilibrium, this share must exceed $s^A = \frac{1}{2}$. At time T the wage rate falls by ϕ percent, taking the economy to the point labeled N. This point lies along the trajectory labeled HE^A, which is identical to the similarly labeled path in figure 8.2. Finally, the economy proceeds along the path NE^A until country A dominates high technology at the steady state at E^A. The requirement of a ϕ percent fall in the wage rate at time T and the requirement that the fall leave the economy somewhere along the trajectory HE^A, are enough to determine what the wage rate must be when the trajectory begins at time $t = 0$.

Clearly a temporary policy has permanent effects here. The lagging country gains research experience with its government's support until the accumulated stock of knowledge surpasses that of its trade partner. Once this has been accomplished, the subsidy is no longer needed to ensure an adequate incentive for continued research. Evidently government policy can turn a stagnant economy into a growing one, and an importer of high-technology products into an exporter of these goods.

17. Put differently, the value of a firm always equals the present discounted value of expected profits. So long as a policy change is fully anticipated, this value must be a continuous function of time.

Does such a use of policy serve to raise national welfare? The answer to this question depends upon the context. In the present one with equal wage rates and perfectly mobile capital, an R&D subsidy often *reduces* the welfare of a country that lags in the technology race. The subsidy induces an increase in the resource cost of product development inasmuch as it shifts R&D activity from a more efficient location to a less efficient one. This effect surely harms the residents of both countries. The subsidy also alters the rate of innovation. The welfare implications of this are ambiguous because the innovation rate may rise or fall. The subsidy directly promotes product development, but it also reduces the efficiency with which that activity is performed. If on net the number of new products that are introduced per unit time falls, then households will suffer from the exacerbation of an existing distortion.[18] But even if the subsidy speeds product development, households in the policy active country may lose because they must bear the full cost of the government transfers, while they gain only a fraction of the benefits that derive from faster innovation.

How can we account for the fact that a policy that increases the national growth rate so dramatically fails to raise the level of national welfare? Here, as before, international trade in goods and assets severs the link between consumption opportunities and gross *domestic* product. Residents of a country that specializes in the production of traditional goods still benefit from innovations that are made abroad because they invest their savings in foreign assets and import the novel goods that emerge from foreign labs.

There do, however, exist circumstances in which a subsidy to R&D in the lagging country might be justified on grounds of national welfare. We mention two such possibilities without conducting a complete welfare analysis. First, in situations where the structural parameters do not permit a steady-state equilibrium with wage equalization, the country that conducts the world's R&D also enjoys the higher wage rate in the long run. Then policy that succeeds in capturing the R&D activity for local entrepreneurs can generate a welfare-enhancing increase in labor income for local residents. A similar argument for policy has been made in the context of static models of increasing returns where similar countries may realize different levels of income and utility depending upon which one comes to specialize in the increasing returns activity (see Ethier 1982b). Second,

18. Recall from chapter 3 that a one-sector economy introduces new varieties more slowly than is optimal because private agents neglect the positive spillovers from their research efforts. Innovation also is too slow here, both for this same reason and because the noncompetitive pricing of differentiated products implies excessive employment in the traditional sector.

when capital is less than perfectly mobile, some domestic investors may be constrained to find local outlets for their accumulated savings. Then a country may gain by promoting local research because this raises the return on R&D investments.

In this chapter we have studied the determinants of patterns of specialization and trade in a world economy with national spillovers of technical knowledge. We have found that history plays a prominent role in deciding long-run outcomes. A country that begins with a head start in the accumulation of knowledge often widens its productivity lead over time. Then this country becomes increasingly an exporter of the goods that make use of new technologies. Exceptions to this rule arise only when the trailing country is much larger than its trading partner, or when the government of the laggard uses policy intervention to eliminate its initial disadvantage in the research lab.

The analysis here complements that in chapter 7. In reality technological spillovers are neither perfectly global nor completely local in reach. Also differences in national factor endowments make certain locations better suited for certain activities, even when initial conditions suggest otherwise. In general, both history and comparative advantage emanating from differences in factor composition have a role to play in determining where different activities will be undertaken and with what consequences for the welfare of residents of every country.

APPENDIX

A8.1 Instability of Equilibria with Equal Rates of Innovation

In section 8.2 we established that there always exists a steady-state equilibrium in which both countries innovate at a common rate. This equilibrium may involve wage equality and production of the traditional good in both countries, or it may entail unequal wages and concentration of the production of the traditional good in one country. In this appendix we prove that in either case the equilibrium with equal rates of innovation is unstable.

We begin with the steady state with unequal wages. Recall that this equilibrium exists when inequality (8.34) is satisfied. Let country B be the one with the higher wage so that $s_Z^B = 0$ and $s_Z^A = 1$ in the steady state. We consider the equilibrium dynamics along a hypothetical trajectory that leads to this steady state. Equation (8.12′) gives the labor-market-clearing conditions that apply at every moment in time. Since both countries engage in R&D, the free-entry condition (8.8′) holds as an equality for each one. Combining this condition with the no-arbitrage condition (8.9) and the expression for profits (8.6), we obtain

$$\frac{\dot{w}^i}{w^i} = \rho + g^i - \frac{(1-\alpha)\sigma s^i}{w^i}, \qquad i = A, B. \tag{A8.1}$$

Then substituting (8.12′) into (A8.1), we find that

$$\dot{w}^A = (\rho + L^A)w^A - \sigma s^A - (1-\sigma), \tag{A8.2}$$

$$\dot{w}^B = (\rho + L^B)w^B - \sigma(1 - s^A). \tag{A8.3}$$

Next we differentiate (8.5), noting (8.4), to derive

$$\dot{s}^A = s^A(1 - s^A)\left[g^A - g^B + \frac{\alpha}{1-\alpha}\left(\frac{\dot{w}^B}{w^B} - \frac{\dot{w}^A}{w^A}\right)\right].$$

After substituting (8.12′), (A8.2), and (A8.3) into this expression, we obtain

$$\dot{s}^A = \frac{s^A(1-s^A)}{1-\alpha}\left[(1-2\alpha)(L^A - L^B) + \frac{(2\alpha-1)(1-\sigma)}{w^A} + \alpha^2\sigma\left(\frac{s^A}{w^A} - \frac{1-s^A}{w^B}\right)\right]. \tag{A8.4}$$

Equations (A8.2)–(A8.4) constitute an autonomous system of differential equations for w^A, w^B, and s^A, with steady-state values

$$\bar{w}^A = \frac{1-\sigma}{L^A - L^B}, \quad \bar{w}^B = \frac{\sigma}{\rho + L^B} - \frac{1-\sigma}{L^A - L^B}, \quad \bar{s}^A = \frac{\rho + L^B}{L^A - L^B}\frac{1-\sigma}{\sigma}, \tag{A8.5}$$

where $L^A > L^B$ and, by (8.34), $(L^A - L^B)/(\rho + L^B) > 2(1-\sigma)/\sigma$. To linearize this system, we take a linear approximation to (A8.4) about the steady state. This yields

$$\begin{bmatrix} \dot{w}^A \\ \dot{w}^B \\ \dot{s}^A \end{bmatrix} = \begin{bmatrix} \rho + L^A & 0 & -\sigma \\ 0 & \rho + L^B & \sigma \\ a_{31} & a_{32} & a_{33} \end{bmatrix} \begin{bmatrix} w^A - \overline{w}^A \\ w^B - \overline{w}^B \\ s^A - \overline{s}^A \end{bmatrix}, \tag{A8.6}$$

where

$$a_{31} = -\frac{\overline{s}^A(1-\overline{s}^A)}{1-\alpha}\frac{\alpha^2\sigma^2}{\overline{w}^A\overline{w}^B}\left(1 + \frac{2\alpha - 1}{\alpha^2}\frac{L^A - L^B}{\rho + L^B}\right)\left(1 - \frac{\rho + L^B}{L^A - L^B}\frac{1-\sigma}{\sigma}\right),$$

$$a_{32} = \frac{\overline{s}^A(1-\overline{s}^A)}{1-\alpha}\frac{\alpha^2\sigma^2}{\overline{w}^A\overline{w}^B}\frac{\rho + L^B}{L^A - L^B}\frac{1-\sigma}{\sigma},$$

$$a_{33} = \frac{\overline{s}^A(1-\overline{s}^A)}{1-\alpha}\frac{\alpha^2\sigma^2}{\overline{w}^A\overline{w}^B}\frac{\sigma}{\rho + L^B}.$$

The first- and second-order principal minors of the 3×3 matrix on the right-hand side of (A8.6) are positive. The determinant of the matrix is given by

$$\frac{\overline{s}^A(1-\overline{s}^A)}{1-\alpha}\frac{(1-\alpha)^2\sigma^2}{\overline{w}^A\overline{w}^B}\left(1 - \frac{\rho + L^B}{L^A - L^B}\frac{1-\sigma}{\sigma}\right)(L^A - L^B) > 0.$$

Since all principal minors are positive, the matrix is positive definite and thus all of its characteristic roots are real and positive (see Perlis 1952, th. 9–25). It follows that the steady-state equilibrium cannot be approached from any direction. Unless the economy happens to begin with the wage rates and market shares given in (A8.5), the economy must diverge to a different long-run equilibrium.

We turn now to the steady-state equilibrium in which both countries innovate at the same positive rate and both produce traditional goods. The existence of this equilibrium requires that inequality (8.30) be satisfied. From (8.28) and (8.29) we compute the following steady-state values of the (common) wage rate and the market shares in the high-technology industry:

$$\overline{s}^i = \frac{1}{2} \qquad \text{for } i = A, B, \tag{A8.7}$$

$$\overline{w} = \frac{1}{L^A + L^B + 2\rho}. \tag{A8.8}$$

Substituting these expressions back into (8.29), we obtain the steady-state labor-market-clearing conditions,

$$\overline{g} + \frac{\alpha\sigma}{2}(L^A + L^B + 2\rho) + (1-\sigma)\overline{s}_Z^k(L^A + L^B + 2\rho) = L^k, \qquad k = A, B. \tag{A8.9}$$

Together with the constraint that $\overline{s}_Z^A + \overline{s}_Z^B = 1$, these equations yield a solution for innovation rate and the market shares in the traditional sector.

We have already established in section 8.3 that the steady state described by (A8.7)–(A8.9) cannot be approached along a trajectory with equal wage rates. When wages are equalized all along an equilibrium growth path, only the country that begins with the larger stock of knowledge capital ever conducts research. Unless the countries happen to begin with equal stocks of knowledge capital, the equal-wage trajectory must lead to an equilibrium with R&D activity concentrated in one country.

It remains to be shown that there cannot exist a trajectory with unequal wage rates that converges in the long-run to the steady state with wage equality. Let us suppose, to the contrary, that such a trajectory exists, with $w^A < w^B$ along the approach to the steady state. Both w^A and w^B must evolve continuously as long as both countries conduct research; otherwise, there would be a jump in firm values, leaving open the possibility for arbitrage gains. It follows that both wage rates must tend smoothly to $\bar{w}$. Since n^i does not jump, (8.4) and (8.5) imply that the equilibrium market shares in the high-technology industry also must converge smoothly to their steady-state values. But as long as the wage rates differ, the country that has the lower wage manufactures all of the traditional goods. It follows that the hypothesized trajectory involves a jump at the last moment in the market shares in the traditional sector. This abrupt change in resource allocation must be matched in each country by an offsetting change in the level of R&D activity.

At the last moment before this "jump," the wage rates will have nearly converged to $\bar{w}$. With $w^A < w^B$, $s_Z^A = 1$, $s_Z^B = 0$, and

$$g^A = L^A - \frac{\alpha\sigma}{2}(L^A + L^B + 2\rho) - (1-\sigma)(L^A + L^B + 2\rho), \tag{A8.10}$$

$$g^B = L^B - \frac{\alpha\sigma}{2}(L^A + L^B + 2\rho), \tag{A8.11}$$

where we have used (8.29) and (A8.8) in writing (A8.10) and (A8.11). Observe that (A8.9)–(A.8.11) imply that

$$g^A = g^B - (1-\sigma)(L^A + L^B + 2\rho)2\bar{s}_Z^B < g^B \qquad \text{for } \bar{s}_Z^B > 0.$$

Therefore the hypothesized trajectory entails a higher rate of innovation in country B at the moment before the jump. But, since both countries innovate at that moment, the no-arbitrage condition (A8.1) must be satisfied for both. This requires that $\dot{w}^A/w^A < \dot{w}^B/w^B$, since $g^A < g^B$, and the wage rates and market shares are nearly equal. We have then a contradiction because the wage rates cannot converge to the common value $\bar{w}$ if the country that has the lower wage also has the smaller rate of wage increase at the moment before convergence. It follows that there does not exist a trajectory with unequal wages that leads to the steady state with equal wages and equal rates of innovation. This steady state can only be attained if the countries begin with equal wages and with equal numbers of differentiated products.

9 Trade and Growth

In chapters 7 and 8 we extended our models of endogenous innovation to include international transactions of various kinds. We examined a world economy comprising two large countries, each one capable of conducting frontier research. The analysis in those chapters focused on the sources of dynamic comparative advantage and the determination of long-run patterns of investment and trade. It is time now to return to our main line of inquiry, namely, the relationship between the economic environment and long-run growth performance. In chapter 6 we began to investigate the links between a country's international economic relations and its rate of technological progress. There we treated only the case of a small economy that does not affect world prices or world technology. While useful as a starting point, such an analysis is limited by its neglect of the important feedbacks that occur from policies and events in one country to the world market environment in which it operates. In this chapter and the next, we reconsider the issues that were raised in chapter 6, this time treating the case of an economically large country.

This chapter addresses the relationship between trade, innovation, and growth. In order to highlight the implications of international trade for long-run performance, we conduct a sequence of comparisons of a country's equilibrium growth path under the alternative scenarios of economic isolation and international integration. We identify and discuss four distinct mechanisms by which a country's external relationships might affect its growth performance. First, international exchange opens channels of communication that facilitate the transmission of technical information. This mechanism is the focus of section 9.1. Second, international competition encourages entrepreneurs in each country to pursue new and distinctive ideas and technologies. As a result trade alleviates duplication of research effort. We study the implications of this for long-run growth rates in section 9.2. A third effect of international integration is to enlarge the size of the market in which the typical firm operates. This has opposing implications for the incentives faced by potential innovators. On the one hand, a larger market means more sales and greater profits for a given market share. On the other hand, a firm in a larger market may find itself facing a greater number of competitors. In section 9.3 we analyze the net impact of these conflicting forces. Finally, in section 9.4 we discuss the reallocation of resources that attends the opening of trade between dissimilar countries. When countries' research experiences differ in a world of national knowledge capital stocks, or when the composition of their endowment bundles differ, economic integration induces a particular pattern of specialization that has implications for output growth in each of the trading partners.

9.1 Diffusion of Knowledge

We argued in section 6.5 that the most important benefit to a country from participating in the international economy might be the access that such integration affords to the knowledge base in existence in the world at large. Countries that trade in world markets invariably learn a great deal about innovative products and about the novel methods that are being used to produce older goods. While it is true that agents in an economically isolated country might also acquire some such information by reading professional journals, speaking to foreign experts, or inspecting prototype products, it seems that the contacts that develop through commercial interaction play an important part in the international exchange of information and ideas. At the least participation in world markets would seem to accelerate greatly a country's acquisition of foreign knowledge.

Despite the argument that, *in practice*, the international transmission of knowledge cannot easily be separated from the international exchange of goods and services, the growth effects of knowledge spillovers and those of commodity trade are *conceptually* distinct. It is instructive to begin by considering the extent to which cross-country knowledge flows promote faster world growth, before introducing the further influences of product market integration.[1] We adopt for this purpose a simple version of our model of expanding product variety. We assume that each country manufactures a range of differentiated products from a single primary input. The designs for new products are developed using this input and knowledge capital. General knowledge accumulates as a by-product of industrial

1. This pedagogic device is adopted from Rivera-Batiz and Romer (1990). Our analysis in this section and the next parallels theirs.

research, and its stock is proportional to the total number of goods developed in the past. In short, we take as our starting point the basic, one-sector model of endogenous growth of section 3.2.

We will consider knowledge flows between two countries indexed by i, $i = A, B$. These countries share common preferences and a common discount rate, ρ. The technologies for developing new blueprints and for manufacturing known varieties also are the same in the two countries, but the sizes of their labor forces may differ. Without loss of generality, we take $L^A \geq L^B$.

Recall from section 3.2 the autarky outcomes. Nominal spending is normalized so that $E^i(\tau) = 1$ for all τ. Then the nominal interest rate $r^i(\tau)$ is equal to the discount rate ρ. Each variety of differentiated product bears a price

$$p^i = \frac{w^i}{\alpha}, \qquad i = A, B, \tag{9.1}$$

where w^i is the wage rate in country i, and also the marginal and average cost of a unit of output manufactured there. In an equilibrium with ongoing R&D, the value of the representative firm must be equal to

$$v^i = \frac{w^i a}{n^i}, \qquad i = A, B, \tag{9.2}$$

where n^i is the measure of products previously developed in country i and also the local stock of knowledge capital (see [3.24]). Arbitrage equates the total return on equity claims to the interest rate ρ, or

$$\frac{1-\alpha}{n^i v^i} + \frac{\dot{v}^i}{v^i} = \rho, \qquad i = A, B. \tag{9.3}$$

Finally, equilibrium in the labor market requires that

$$\frac{a}{n^i}\dot{n}^i + \frac{1}{p^i} = L^i, \qquad i = A, B, \tag{9.4}$$

which is equality between the sum of the demands for labor by R&D and manufacturing enterprises and the exogenous factor supply.

In a steady state the aggregate value of the stock market and its inverse $V^i \equiv 1/n^i v^i$ turn out to be constant. Then the value of a representative firm declines at the rate of new product development; that is, $\dot{v}^i/v^i = -\dot{n}^i/n^i \equiv -g^i$. The no-arbitrage condition that applies in the steady state can be written as

$$(1-\alpha)V^i = \rho + g^i, \qquad i = A, B. \tag{9.5}$$

Next, from the pricing equation (9.1) and the free-entry condition (9.2), we obtain $p^i = 1/\alpha a V^i$. In the steady state (9.4) becomes

$$g^i + \alpha V^i = \frac{L^i}{a}, \qquad i = A, B. \tag{9.6}$$

Equations (9.5) and (9.6) can be used to solve for the steady-state value of each country's stock market and the long-run rates of innovation. The solution is depicted in figure 3.2 for the case in which $L^i/a > \rho\alpha/(1-\alpha)$. This parameter restriction, we recall, ensures positive growth in the long run. We can also calculate from (9.5) and (9.6) an explicit solution for the long-run rate of innovation, namely,

$$g^i = (1-\alpha)\frac{L^i}{a} - \alpha\rho, \qquad i = A, B. \tag{9.7}$$

Manufactured output grows at the rate $g^i(1-\alpha)/\alpha$.

Now suppose that communication channels open between the two countries, while their product markets remain segmented and mutually impenetrable. Let us assume for simplicity (as we did in chapter 7) that the international exchange of information takes place instantaneously and costlessly. Researchers in each country learn now not only from the R&D projects undertaken locally but also from the *novel* experiments that are carried out abroad. However, research endeavors that are common to the two countries contribute only once to the world stock of knowledge.

With international diffusion of technical information, the knowledge stock in country i is given by $K_n^i = n^i + \psi^i n^j, j \neq i$, where ψ^i is the fraction of products available in country j that are not available in country i. Notice that $K_n^A = K_n^B = K_n$, where K_n represents the number of distinct research projects that have been conducted somewhere in the world. A question that arises immediately is: What determines ψ^i? That is, how much overlap is there in the inventive activities of the two communities of researchers? Within a single economy entrepreneurs surely have an incentive to avoid duplicating the efforts of others. This is because all blueprints are equally costly to develop, and unique products yield strictly higher profits than do goods with competing producers. Economic forces tend to reduce (or, in our simple economy, eliminate) duplication of research effort when innovators compete in an integrated market. However, with separate product markets in the two countries of the world economy, the mechanisms that ensure nonredundancy in research do not operate. Entrepreneurs are indifferent as to whether their blueprints are novel in the world at large or merely novel in their own local market. In fact no economic argument can be used to pin down a value for ψ^i nor to limit its fluctuations over time.

Since the time series for ψ^i must be taken as arbitrary, we may as well concentrate on a special case that illustrates both the growth-enhancing role of international communication and the mitigating effects of redundancy in research. Let us suppose that a constant fraction $(1 - \psi)$ of the new products developed in country B (the smaller country) replicate products that are already available in country A (the larger country), while the products introduced in country A are always unique. Then the knowledge stock in each country equals $K_n = n^A + \psi n^B$, $0 \leq \psi \leq 1$.

Entrepreneurs in country i introduce new varieties at a cost of $w^i a/K_n$ per product, and so free entry implies that

$$v^i = \frac{w^i a}{n^A + \psi n^B}, \qquad i = A, B. \tag{9.8}$$

Also the international diffusion of knowledge reduces the input requirements for R&D in each country. The labor-market-clearing conditions become

$$\frac{a}{n^A + \psi n^B}\dot{n}^i + \frac{1}{p^i} = L^i, \qquad i = A, B. \tag{9.9}$$

Two further conditions characterize a steady state of the world economy with international knowledge diffusion. First, as before, the value of the stock market in each country remains constant. Second, the ratio of the numbers of products available in each location, n^A/n^B, is constant. A constant ratio of products ensures a constant allocation of resources to each country's research sector when each has a constant rate of innovation. It requires convergence of the long-run innovation rates in the two countries; that is, $g^A = g^B = g$. Then the steady-state no-arbitrage condition (9.5) implies that

$$(1 - \alpha)V = \rho + g, \tag{9.10}$$

where V denotes the inverse of the aggregate stock market value in each country (i.e., $V = V^A = V^B$).

We can use (9.1), (9.8), and the definition of V^i to calculate the steady-state levels of employment in the manufacturing sector of each country. They are

$$\frac{1}{p^i} = a\alpha V \frac{n^i}{n^A + \psi n^B}, \qquad i = A, B. \tag{9.11}$$

Equation (9.11) implies that the ratio of the numbers of manufacturing jobs in the two countries is equal in the long run to the ratio of the numbers of different brands available in each. We substitute (9.11) into (9.9) and use $g = g^A = g^B$ to derive

$$a(g + \alpha V)\frac{n^i}{n^A + \psi n^B} = L^i, \qquad i = A, B. \tag{9.12}$$

Dividing this equation, as it applies to country A, by the same equation applied to country B, we find that the ratio of the numbers of products available in each country is equal in the long run to the ratio of the sizes of the two labor forces.

We are ready, finally, to derive the long-run rate of innovation in the world economy with international knowledge spillovers but no commodity trade. Using (9.12), we calculate

$$L^A + \psi L^B = a(g + \alpha V). \tag{9.13}$$

Equations (9.10) and (9.13) can be solved for g and V, which gives

$$g = (1 - \alpha)\frac{L^A + \psi L^B}{a} - \alpha\rho. \tag{9.14}$$

When we compare (9.14) with (9.7), we see that the opening of international channels of communication accelerates innovation and growth in both countries. Research in any location contributes now to a global stock of knowledge, which accumulates more rapidly than would the local stocks of knowledge in isolated research communities. The more rapid accumulation of knowledge implies a more rapid reduction in the cost of product development in each country, and so entrepreneurs introduce new varieties at a faster pace. At the same time it is clear from (9.14) that the benefits from international communication are attenuated by any duplication of research effort. The greater the extent of overlap in the research projects of the two countries (i.e., the smaller the ψ), the lower are the common long-run rates of innovation and growth.

9.2 Trade between Similar Countries

Next we allow for the integration of world product markets. We ask whether international trade between similar economies contributes to the growth performance of each one above and beyond the gains that derive from the transmission of technical information. Our starting point is the equilibrium of the preceding section, where the two economies derive spillover benefits from one another's research but where each maintains a closed market to imports from the other.

One important effect of trade is to introduce competition between innovators in different countries. Such competition gives entrepreneurs in each location a strong incentive to invent products that are unique in the world economy. In our simple model the integration of world commodity markets suffices to eliminate research redundancy. Each new product invented in either country in an equilibrium with world trade is a novel one. Thus each R&D project contributes fully to the global stock of knowledge capital.

Integration has two further effects here. First, the opportunity to sell abroad enlarges the size of the market available to any producer. By itself this effect of trade tends to increase the profit opportunity available to any innovator. But working against this is the fact of intensified competition. In a world of free trade, each producer must compete for sales with a wider range of varieties. Such competition tends to reduce the profits available to any single firm. While both of these effects are present here, they are more the focus of the discussion in section 9.3.

We must modify some of the equations from the last section in order to reflect the integration of world commodity markets. Aggregate spending in the world economy equals $E(\tau) = E^A(\tau) + E^B(\tau)$. This we normalize to be equal to one at every moment in time. The normalization guarantees a nominal interest rate of ρ in each country in a steady state with constant spending shares.[2] Demand for the products manufactured in country i varies now with the terms of trade. Households allocate the budget share

$$s^i = \frac{n^i(p^i)^{1-\varepsilon}}{\sum_j n^j(p^j)^{1-\varepsilon}}, \qquad i = A, B, \tag{9.15}$$

to goods produced in country i (see [8.5]). Since $E = 1$, s^i represents also aggregate spending on goods emanating from country i.

The advent of trade also alters the stock market value of profit-making firms. Each firm continues to set its price at a constant markup over marginal cost (see [9.1]). But sales per firm now are given by s^i/n^ip^i. So profits per firm are $(1-\alpha)s^i/n^i$, and the no-arbitrage condition becomes

2. Moreover, if world financial markets are integrated, then a nominal interest rate of ρ obtains at every moment in time. See the discussion of this point in chapter 7.

$$\frac{(1-\alpha)s^i}{n^i v^i} + \frac{\dot{v}^i}{v^i} = \rho, \qquad i = A, B. \tag{9.16}$$

With international spillovers of knowledge capital and no redundancy in research effort, entrepreneurs have access to the global knowledge stock $K_n = n$, where $n \equiv n^A + n^B$. Therefore the cost of developing a new product in country i equals $w^i a/n$, and free entry ensures that

$$v^i = \frac{w^i a}{n}, \qquad i = A, B. \tag{9.17}$$

Finally, the expansion in knowledge capital reduces the labor requirements for achieving a given rate of innovation. Manufacturers also demand less labor (at a given level of aggregate spending) due to the increased extent of market competition. The labor-market-clearing condition now reads

$$\frac{a}{n}\dot{n}^i + \frac{s^i}{p^i} = L^i, \qquad i = A, B. \tag{9.18}$$

Once again, we concentrate on the steady state, which has a fixed division of resources between R&D and manufacturing in each country. We will see that the steady state again is characterized by constant aggregate values of each nation's stock market and by constant shares of each country in the total number of differentiated varieties.[3] For the value of each stock market to be constant, the share price of a typical firm must fall at the local rate of innovation. Constancy of the relative numbers of products requires convergence in long-run innovation rates. Thus the no-arbitrage condition (9.16) becomes

$$(1-\alpha)s^i V^i = \rho + g, \qquad i = A, B, \tag{9.19}$$

where g again denotes the *common* long-run rate of innovation in each country. Equation (9.19) implies that in the long run $s^i V^i$ is the same for both countries; in other words, the value of each country's stock market is proportional to the share of world spending devoted to its goods.

To solve for g, we need a second equation relating the rate of innovation to $s^i V^i$. This equation can be derived as follows: Substitute (9.1) and (9.17) into the labor-market-clearing condition (9.18), and note that $\dot{n}^i/n^i = g$ in the steady state. This gives

3. If the product ratio were not constant, the input requirements for a given rate of innovation would vary over time with a country's share in the total number of products.

$$\xi^i(g + \alpha s^i V^i) = \frac{L^i}{a}, \qquad i = A, B, \tag{9.20}$$

where $\xi^i \equiv n^i/n$ is the share of country i in the total number of differentiated products. Since $s^i V^i$ is the same for both countries, (9.20) implies that the ratio of the number of goods produced in each country again reflects the relative sizes of the two labor forces; that is, $n^A/n^B = L^A/L^B$. We can apply (9.20) for $i = A$ and $i = B$, and sum the results, to obtain

$$g + \alpha s^i V^i = \frac{L^A + L^B}{a}, \qquad i = A, B. \tag{9.21}$$

The steady-state rate of innovation in the world economy with both knowledge diffusion and international trade can be calculated from (9.19) and (9.21). We find that

$$g = (1 - \alpha)\frac{L^A + L^B}{a} - \alpha\rho. \tag{9.22}$$

When we compare this rate to the steady-state growth rate for an economy that does not engage in commodity trade but nonetheless captures all available international knowledge spillovers (see [9.14]), we find that the marginal contribution of trade to long-run growth stems entirely from the elimination of duplicative research. If there happens to be no research redundancy in the equilibrium without trade ($\psi = 1$), the integration of product markets will have no effect on the long-run growth rate in either country. Evidently, the expansion of market size that attends the opening of world trade has no net impact on long-run growth.[4] This is because when products are being developed at the same rate in each of two trading economies, the extra demand that each producer enjoys in a larger world market exactly matches the loss of sales that each suffers due to the expansion in the number of competing varieties.

One should not conclude from this discussion that the expansion of market size and the intensification of monopolistic competition provide no benefits to the parties engaged in trade. Welfare gains from these two

4. In fact in our model with international knowledge flows if we happen to have $\psi = 1$, then an unanticipated opening of commodity trade does not affect even the short-run growth rate. After the opening of trade, the world economy jumps immediately to a new growth path with the same rate of innovation as before. This claim follows from the fact that there is only one state variable in our model, namely the fraction of differentiated products produced in each location. And, when $\psi = 1$, the equilibrium value for ξ^i is the same in the steady state with and without trade.

sources come as "level effects" rather than as "growth effects." The existence of static gains from trade can be seen most clearly for the case where $\psi = 1$. Then, since an (unanticipated) opening of world trade does not change the *rate* of introduction of new products in any location, the total number of varieties in existence in the world economy is the same at every moment as would have existed in the continued absence of trade. Yet, with trade, consumers in each location are able to purchase the full complement of n brands rather than the smaller number n^i of national products. This expansion of variety affords a permanent increase in the *level* of utility for every household.

9.3 Trade with Uneven Innovation[5]

When a country becomes integrated into world product markets, its entrepreneurs find their incentives to innovate affected by the change in market size. We have already seen in the last section that there are offsetting implications of a larger market for the profitability of R&D. On the one hand, aggregate demand for manufactured products increases when the market expands to include both foreign and domestic households. On the other hand, the share of the market captured by any given firm shrinks when its set of rivals grows to include both foreign and domestic producers. In this section we explore in more detail the net impact of these opposing influences on the incentives to innovate.

In the economy of section 9.2, international spillovers of technical information created a common pool of knowledge capital, which made entrepreneurs worldwide equally capable of generating technological advances. The equilibrium was characterized by convergence in the rates of innovation in the two countries. Since the shares of each country's firms in aggregate demand became constant in the long run, and these shares were equal to the share of the country in the total size of the world market, it followed that trade introduced additional competitors for the representative firm exactly in proportion to its expansion of the number of potential customers. The offsetting influences of the increase in market size on the profitability of R&D just canceled in every country.

This need not be the case, however, if circumstances dictate unequal rates of product development in the two countries. A country with more rapid technological progress might capture an ever growing share of the world market for innovative products. Then this country might realize

5. The issues addressed in this section were first raised by Feenstra (1990a).

through trade a greater incentive to introduce new products, whereas its trade partner might find the incentive to innovate diminished. We have already seen an example of this in chapter 8, where a technologically lagging country could be driven by trade to specialize in the production of traditional goods. In that context not only the size of the market and the extent of foreign competition influenced the equilibrium outcome but also the possibility that resources might be reallocated between different types of manufacturing sectors. Here we wish to isolate the implications of greater market size and foreign competition, while leaving the effects of intersectoral resource reallocations for consideration in the next section. Accordingly, we consider an economy similar to the one in chapter 8, except that now there is only a single manufacturing sector, which produces differentiated goods.

We assume now, as in chapter 8, that knowledge spillovers are national in scope. The absence of (perfect) international knowledge spillovers allows the research sectors in the two countries to realize different long-run rates of innovation. The world economy has the same structure as the one in section 9.2, except that $K_n^i = n^i$ now, for $i = A, B$. With this change in specification, the labor-market-clearing condition becomes

$$ag^i + \frac{s^i}{p^i} = L^i, \qquad i = A, B, \tag{9.24}$$

where $g^i \equiv \dot{n}^i/n^i$ in (9.24) has replaced $\dot{n}^i/n$ in (9.18), in view of the different labor requirements for product development that apply. Also free entry into R&D implies that

$$v^i = \frac{w^i a}{n^i}, \qquad i = A, B, \tag{9.25}$$

in place of (9.17). The no-arbitrage condition (9.16) takes the same form as before.

From the markup pricing equation (9.1), the free-entry condition (9.25), and the no-arbitrage condition (9.16), we can calculate the following expression for the rate of change of wages in each country:

$$\frac{\dot{w}^i}{w^i} = \rho + g^i - \frac{(1-\alpha)s^i}{aw^i}, \qquad i = A, B.$$

After substituting for s^i/aw^i from (9.24) and using the expression for the autarky innovation rate in (9.7), this equation becomes

$$\frac{\dot{w}^i}{w^i} = \frac{g^i - \bar{g}^i}{\alpha}, \qquad i = A, B, \tag{9.26}$$

where $\bar{g}^i \equiv (1 - \alpha)L^i/a - \alpha\rho$ denotes the autarky rate of product development in country i.

The discussion above suggests that we should track the evolution of market shares in each country. By differentiating the definition of s^i (the share of country i in aggregate world demand) given in (9.15), we find that

$$\frac{\dot{s}^i}{s^i} = (1 - s^i)\left[(g^i - g^j) + (1 - \varepsilon)\left(\frac{\dot{p}^i}{p^i} - \frac{\dot{p}^j}{p^j}\right)\right], \qquad i, j = A, B; j \neq i.$$

The constancy of markups in (9.1) implies that $\dot{w}^i/w^i = \dot{p}^i/p^i$. So in light of (9.26) market shares evolve according to

$$\frac{\dot{s}^i}{s^i} = (1 - s^i)[(1 - \varepsilon)(g^i - g^j) + \varepsilon(\bar{g}^i - \bar{g}^j)], \quad i, j = A, B; j \neq i. \tag{9.27}$$

Finally, we compute from (9.24) how the rates of product development vary over time. Using (9.1) and (9.26), we find that

$$\dot{g}^i = \left(\frac{L^i}{a} - g^i\right)\left[\frac{1}{\alpha}(g^i - \bar{g}^i) - \frac{\dot{s}^i}{s^i}\right], \qquad i = A, B. \tag{9.28}$$

To begin the analysis of the long-run dynamics, let us conjecture that the larger country comes to dominate the market for innovative goods (i.e., $s^A \to 1$). Later we will verify that this must be the case. If the share of country A in aggregate demand tends to one in the long run, $\dot{s}^A/s^A$ must approach zero. The resource constraint (9.24) requires $L^i/a > g^i$. Therefore (9.28) implies that g^A tends to $\bar{g}^A$ from above.[6] In other words, country A (the large country) grows at exactly the same rate in the long-run equilibrium with free trade as it does in autarky. However, its growth is faster with trade than without during (at least) the final stages of the transition to the steady state.

What about the smaller country? This country sees its share in world demand falling through time. Although s^B tends to a constant value (namely, zero) as s^A approaches one, the rate of change in the small country's

6. Since s^A tends to one from below, $\dot{s}^A$ must be positive in the final approach to the steady state. Suppose that $g^A < \bar{g}^A$ during this approach. Then (9.28) would imply that $\dot{g}^A < 0$. The rate of innovation would fall farther and farther from the autarky rate, which would contradict the assumption of convergence to a steady state with a fixed allocation of resources. Feenstra (1990a) has shown that the assumption of convergence to a steady state is in fact justified by the equilibrium dynamics no matter what the initial conditions are.

market share does not approach zero. From (9.27) we calculate

$$\frac{\dot{s}^B}{s^B} = (1 - \varepsilon)(g^B - g^A) + \varepsilon(\bar{g}^B - \bar{g}^A), \tag{9.29}$$

in a long-run equilibrium with $s^A = 1$. Substituting this expression into (9.28) and setting $\dot{g}^B = 0$, we compute the steady-state rate of innovation for country B,

$$g^B = \bar{g}^B - \frac{\alpha(1-\alpha)}{1-\alpha(1-\alpha)}(\bar{g}^A - \bar{g}^B). \tag{9.30}$$

Equation (9.30) implies that the smaller country innovates *less rapidly* in a long-run equilibrium with international trade than it does in autarky. The disparity between the free trade and autarky growth rates varies directly with the difference in the sizes of the two economies.

It cannot be concluded, however, even in this case of a diminished growth rate for country B, that trade is harmful to this country. There are two reasons why country B might gain from trade despite the decline in its rate of innovation. First, the country enjoys static utility gains from having access to imported goods that are differentiated from local products. Second, its households can enjoy, thanks to trade, a faster rate of increase in product variety than they can in autarky. The number of products available in the world market grows in the long run at rate $\bar{g}^A$ in a free-trade equilibrium, whereas consumers in country B see new products being introduced at the lower rate $\bar{g}^B$ in an equilibrium without trade. But there does remain the *possibility* of losses from trade. Trade causes a long-run reallocation of resources from R&D to manufacturing in the smaller country, from an initial situation in which the level of research activity is already too low. Thus trade exacerbates an existing market failure and so may reduce welfare.[7]

Let us explore further the reasons why the integration of world product markets has the effect of temporarily accelerating innovation in the larger country and eventually slowing innovation in the smaller one. We have seen that the relatively greater stock of knowledge capital in the larger economy allows it to introduce new products at a faster rate. As a result of its more rapid innovation, this country captures a growing share of the total number of differentiated varieties and also a growing share of world

---

7. Feenstra (1990a) shows formally that the opening of trade has ambiguous implications for the utility of the representative household in the smaller of two trading economies. See also the discussion of this point in chapter 8.

aggregate demand. The growth in demand puts upward pressure on wages there. Equation (9.26) reveals in fact that wages in country A are rising all along the final approach to the steady state (recall that g^A approaches $\bar{g}^A$ from above). The rising path of wages offers the prospect of capital gains, and so entrepreneurs in the larger country find a greater incentive to introduce new products. Of course, once the large country comes to dominate the world market, there can be no further expansion in its market share, and the incentive to innovate settles back to what it would have been in autarky.

The process is just the opposite in the small country. Its falling market share exerts downward pressure on the wage rate. Entrepreneurs foresee capital losses and so are less willing to invest in R&D. Even in the long run the wage rate and the market share in the smaller country continue to decline. Trade reduces the profitability of R&D in this country because it places local entrepreneurs in competition with a rapidly expanding set of imported, differentiated products.

Before leaving this section, we must confirm that no other steady-state equilibrium exists besides the one that we have described. Suppose we were to hypothesize that the share of country B tends to one in the long run. Then arguments similar to those invoked above would imply that $g^B = \bar{g}^B$ in a steady state with trade. Also we would have a formula identical to (9.30) for the long-run rate of innovation in country A, except that the labels A and B would be reversed. Using this formula and the expression for $\dot{s}^A/s^A$ in (9.27), we would find that $\bar{g}^A > \bar{g}^B$ implies that $\dot{s}^A > 0$ in the long run. But the market share of country B cannot approach one, as we have just assumed, if the share of country A is growing through time. In short, the hypothesis that country B can come to dominate the world market for innovative goods leads to a contradiction.

A final possibility is that the market shares might converge to constants between zero and one. With $\dot{s}^i = 0$, (9.28) implies that $g^i = \bar{g}^i$, for $i = A, B$. But this can be consistent with $\dot{s}^i = 0$ in (9.27) only if $\bar{g}^A = \bar{g}^B$. A long-run equilibrium cannot be characterized by constant market shares between zero and one unless the countries happen to be of equal size. In that case, and that alone, the expansion of market size that results from the opening of trade has no net impact on the profitability of R&D in either of the trading economies.

9.4 Trade between Dissimilar Countries

A further impact of trade on growth arises when trading partners are dissimilar in some respect and when, due to their dissimilarities, each specializes (relatively or completely) in a different manufacturing activity. Of course, for this effect of international trade to materialize, there must exist at least two manufacturing sectors that differ in some fundamental way. Accordingly we turn our attention to a two-sector world economy that produces a variety of differentiated, high-technology products and a homogeneous, traditional good.

We have already studied in chapters 7 and 8 the patterns of specialization that are induced by economic integration in some two-sector economies. Here we draw out the implications of trade for countries' long-run growth rates in situations where integration causes resources to reallocate between different manufacturing sectors. Consider again the economy of chapter 8 where a single factor is used to produce both high-technology and traditional products (and also to perform R&D) and where technological spillovers are confined to the country in which they are generated. This economy is similar to the one that we studied in the previous section except that now there is a possibility that resources might shift out of high technology altogether in the face of international technological competition. We recall from chapter 8 that if trade partners are similar in size, a country with an initial lead in the accumulation of knowledge capital comes to dominate world research and world production of high-technology goods, while an initially lagging country specializes eventually in the production of traditional goods. Thus we have an example where the opening of trade dramatically reduces long-run output growth in one country as a result of the induced resource reallocation. A country that would experience technological progress in an autarky equilibrium finds itself with stagnant productivity and real output when it engages in international trade. Due to the country's relative inexperience in R&D when trade opens, its researchers cannot compete successfully in the world technology race. Consequently market forces drive the country's resources into an alternative activity.[8]

Let us return now to the two-factor economy of chapter 7 where unskilled labor and human capital are used in the two manufacturing sectors and in the research lab in different combinations. We know from chapter 7 that if knowledge spillovers are global in reach, the country that is rela-

8. We recall from chapter 8 that in some cases a large country can overcome an initial deficiency in knowledge capital to attain long-run competitiveness in the R&D activity. As the size of the traditional sector shrinks to zero, the conditions for this become automatically satisfied. This reconciles the findings of chapter 8 with those in the previous section where we saw that regardless of its initial relative standing in terms of accumulated knowledge, a larger country never suffers a slowdown in the rate of its innovation.

tively well endowed with human capital specializes relatively in R&D and the production of high-technology products, while the country that is relatively well endowed with unskilled labor specializes relatively in traditional manufacturing. What then are the implications of the opening of trade for the growth rates in each country? To answer this question, we need some further analysis.

Our discussion in the remainder of this chapter applies both to the model of expanding product variety and the model of ongoing product improvements.[9] We recall that in an isolated, two-sector economy, the traditional good Z and the differentiated products $x(j)$ are priced according to

$$p_Z^i = c_Z(w_L^i, w_H^i), \tag{9.31}$$

$$p_x^i = \frac{1}{\delta} c_x(w_L^i, w_H^i), \tag{9.32}$$

where $\delta = \alpha$ in the model of horizontal product differentiation and $\delta = 1/\lambda$ in the model of vertical product differentiation. Given Cobb-Douglas preferences and the normalization of spending so that $E^i(\tau) = 1$, commodity-market-clearing requires that

$$p_Z^i Z^i = 1 - \sigma, \tag{9.33}$$

$$p_x^i X^i = \sigma, \tag{9.34}$$

where Z^i denotes the output of the homogeneous good in country i, X^i is the aggregate output of innovative goods there ($X^i = n^i x^i$), and σ represents the share of spending devoted to high-tech products. The conditions for equilibrium in the two factor markets can be written as

$$a_\gamma(w_L^i, w_H^i)\gamma^i + a_x(w_L^i, w_H^i)X^i + a_Z(w_L^i, w_H^i)Z^i = \begin{bmatrix} L^i \\ H^i \end{bmatrix}, \tag{9.35}$$

while the (steady-state) no-arbitrage and free-entry conditions imply that

$$\frac{(1-\delta)\sigma}{c_\gamma(w_L^i, w_H^i)} \le \rho + \gamma^i. \tag{9.36}$$

9. Up to this point we have restricted attention in this chapter to the model of expanding variety. This is because the model of quality upgrading does not readily lend itself to distinguishing the separate influences of international communication and commodity trade. While it is possible to consider an equilibrium in that model in which firms can improve upon goods developed abroad but households cannot import those goods, the dynamics of this artificial equilibrium are rather complicated, and they do not show transparently the various effects of trade that we have described.

In (9.35) and (9.36), γ^i represents either the rate of new product development g^i in the model of expanding variety or the arrival rate of quality improvements ι^i in the model of quality upgrading. Equality obtains in (9.36) whenever firms in country i engage in R&D in the long-run equilibrium. Finally, we suppose as before that R&D is the most human-capital intensive of the three activities and that the production of traditional manufactures is the least so.

What happens when the countries engage in trade? In chapter 7 we saw that factor price equalization obtains in the long-run equilibrium when the two trading economies have somewhat similar endowment bundles. If factor prices are equalized, the two countries experience equal rates of innovation, and the trade equilibrium reproduces the aggregate magnitudes of an integrated world economy. To find the effects of trade on output growth, we need to know how the long-run innovation rate in the integrated economy compares to the long-run rates in the two isolated economies and also how the composition of output varies between the trade and autarky equilibria in each country.

The effects of the integration on the innovation rate in either country can be analyzed in this case by considering the implications of an expansion of resources from an initial level equal to the country's national endowment to a final level equal to the world endowment. One major conclusion that emerged from section 5.3, where we studied the effects of resource expansions, was that factor accumulation need not stimulate innovation and growth. In particular, we found that an increase in the supply of the factor used least intensively in research (i.e., unskilled labor) leads in some circumstances to a slowing of long-run innovation. It stands to reason therefore that a country entering into trade with a partner well endowed with unskilled labor might suffer a similar fate. The mechanism is the following: In the trade situation the world economy has a relatively greater abundance of unskilled labor than the human-capital-rich country has when it operates in isolation. As a result the integrated economy undertakes more of the activity that uses unskilled labor intensively. To do so, it draws resources from the remaining activities. Thus the scale of industrial research activities may shrink in the human-capital-rich country despite the productivity gains that result from any international spillovers of knowledge and despite the fact that the country has a comparative advantage in this activity.

To demonstrate the possibility that the opening of trade might lead the innovation rate in the human-capital-rich country to fall, we construct a simple numerical example. The example illustrates an extreme case, inasmuch as the human-capital-rich country innovates at a positive rate in the autarky equilibrium, but the world economy stagnates when trade takes place.

Example 9.1
Suppose that no substitution of unskilled labor for human capital is possible in R&D or in manufacturing. The fixed unit input coefficents are as follows:

$$a_Y = \begin{bmatrix} 0 \\ 1 \end{bmatrix}, \quad a_x = \begin{bmatrix} 1 \\ 1 \end{bmatrix}, \quad a_Z = \begin{bmatrix} 1 \\ 0 \end{bmatrix}.$$

This means, for example, that a unit of activity in R&D requires one unit of human capital and zero units of labor, and so on. The factor endowments in the two countries are given by

$$\begin{bmatrix} L^A \\ H^A \end{bmatrix} = \begin{bmatrix} 7 \\ \frac{5}{2} \end{bmatrix}, \quad \begin{bmatrix} L^B \\ H^B \end{bmatrix} = \begin{bmatrix} 21 \\ \frac{3}{2} \end{bmatrix}.$$

The remaining parameter values are

$$\rho = \tfrac{19}{2}, \quad \delta = \tfrac{1}{2}, \quad \sigma = \tfrac{1}{2}.$$

Autarky Equilibria We use (9.31)–(9.36) to calculate the steady states for the two countries when they operate in isolation. In country A the rate of innovation is $\gamma^A = \frac{1}{2}$. The autarky values for the other variables of interest are

$$X^A = 2, \quad p_x^A = \tfrac{1}{4}, \quad w_H^A = \tfrac{1}{40},$$

$$Z^A = 5, \quad p_Z^A = \tfrac{1}{10}, \quad w_L^A = \tfrac{1}{10}.$$

Country B does not innovate in the steady state of an autarky equilibrium; that is, $\gamma^B = 0$. Its autarky prices and quantities are given by

$$X^B = \tfrac{3}{2}, \quad p_x^B = \tfrac{1}{3}, \quad w_H^B = \tfrac{11}{78},$$

$$Z^B = \tfrac{39}{2}, \quad p_Z^B = \tfrac{1}{39}, \quad w_L^B = \tfrac{1}{39}.$$

At these factor prices the profit rate in the high-technology sector is $\pi^B/v^B = 39/22$, which falls short of the long-run interest rate $r = \rho = 19/2$. Therefore R&D is not viable.

Trade Equilibrium To compute the trade equilibrium, we conjecture that factor prices are equalized by trade. After solving for the equilibrium allocations in an integrated economy with an endowment equal to the combined endowments of the two trading partners, we check that the aggregate quantities can be reproduced in a trade equilibrium with segmented factor markets.

The integrated economy has the endowment

$$\begin{bmatrix} L \\ H \end{bmatrix} = \begin{bmatrix} 28 \\ 4 \end{bmatrix}.$$

The steady-state equilibrium for such an economy involves no R&D; that is, $\gamma = 0$. The equilibrium outputs and prices are

$$X = 4, \quad p_x = \tfrac{1}{8}, \quad w_H = \tfrac{1}{24},$$

$$Z = 24, \quad p_Z = \tfrac{1}{48}, \quad w_L = \tfrac{1}{48}.$$

At these factor prices the interest rate of $\rho = 19/2$ exceeds the profit rate of $\pi/v = 6$.

It remains to be shown that the integrated equilibrium can be reproduced with commodity trade. If factor and commodity prices are the same in the trade equilibrium as they are in the integrated equilibrium, and $X^A = 5/2$, $X^B = 3/2$, $Z^A = 9/2$, and $Z^B = 39/2$, then factor markets clear separately in each country, with nonnegative values for all factor prices and sectoral outputs.[10] We conclude that the integrated equilibrium is also a free-trade equilibrium and that trade reduces to zero the growth rate in country A.

Let us move on from this specific example to some more general points that can be made about the likelihood that trade between differently endowed countries will retard the pace of innovation and growth in one country or the other. We note first that the rate of innovation cannot fall in the country that is relatively poorly endowed with human capital. This country integrates into a world economy that has greater access to human capital, both in absolute terms and relative to the supply of unskilled workers. As we have seen in chapter 5, an increase in the quantity of human capital that is not accompanied by a decline in the relative abundance of this factor leads to faster innovation in the long run. Still, the labor-rich country can experience a decline in its growth rate of real output, since its resources shift in accordance with comparative advantage from the production of high-technology goods to the production of traditional goods. That is, the country specializes in the stagnant manufacturing activ-

10. In the trade equilibrium with factor price equalization, the ratio of the number of differentiated products manufactured in each country equals the ratio of the countries' aggregate outputs of high-tech goods. In our example, $n^A/n^B = X^A/X^B = 5/3$.

ity, even as it enjoys faster technological progress in its dynamic manufacturing sector. But whereas the unskilled labor-abundant country might suffer a decline in its rate of output growth, this country *cannot* experience a fall in the growth rate of its consumption index. Its real consumption grows at the same rate as world output, which is a faster rate of growth than the country experiences in autarky.

Second, we note that when technological spillovers are global in reach, international trade between countries with similar factor compositions must increase the rates of innovation and growth in each one. This claim follows from another result in chapter 5. We showed that an equiproportionate expansion in the endowments of all factors necessarily spurs technological progress and long-run growth.

In the appendix to chapter 5 we established that the rate of innovation responds positively to an expansion in the supply of unskilled labor when the elasticity of substitution between human capital and unskilled labor exceeds one in both manufacturing sectors. This result implies that trade must stimulate innovation in the present context when substitution possibilities in production are sufficiently great. If the rate of innovation does in fact decline when the human-capital-rich country begins to trade, the rate of growth of its *consumption* index will fall as well, but the growth rate of its manufactured *output* may rise as the country increases its specialization in high-tech manufacturing.

Finally, we note that even when the human capital-rich country experiences a decline in its rate of innovation relative to the autarky situation, the residents of this country may benefit from trade. When available product variety or average product quality is less than it would have been had the country chosen to remain isolated, the losses that the households suffer in the long run may be more than offset by short-run trading gains. All households benefit from having access to imported goods that are horizontally or vertically differentiated from their local products. Specialization in manufacturing according to comparative advantage affords an additional source of static trading gains. But, as in section 9.3, the fact that economic integration can slow innovation in one of the countries does suggest a possibility of losses from trade.

In this chapter we have examined a number of distinct channels through which international trade might affect long-run innovation and growth. We began by noting that growth rates will be faster when the technical knowledge that contributes to productivity in industrial research flows readily across international borders, compared to a situation in which all such information must be generated locally. This finding bears on the growth effects of trade because information may be exchanged when business associates meet to arrange commercial transactions. Integration of world product markets also places innovators in different parts of the world in competition with one another, and so gives them an incentive to pursue ideas that are novel in the world economy. For this reason trade tends to reduce duplication of research effort and thus to increase the aggregate productivity of resources employed in R&D.

There are several cases in which trade may dampen the incentives for research in one of a pair of trading economies. First, when knowledge spillovers are national in reach and countries differ in size, a small country may find its share of the world market declining over time. Then firms in this country will face increasingly intense competition from abroad, which reduces the profitability of their investments in knowledge. Second, international competition with a technologically advanced country can bring about a slowing of innovation and growth in a country that begins with a disadvantage in research productivity. This outcome requires also that technological spillovers be geographically concentrated and arises when a relatively stagnant manufacturing sector absorbs resources displaced from high technology. Third, a country that is well endowed with unskilled labor may be led by trade to specialize in traditional manufacturing, in which case the overall growth rate of manufactured output may fall even as the pace of technological progress in high technology rises. Finally, a human-capital-rich country may find that integration into the world economy raises so much the reward to its human capital that the incentive for R&D is reduced. As a result the country may innovate more slowly in the trade equilibrium than in autarky. If the share of high-technology goods in total manufactured output does not increase greatly, its rate of output growth may decline as well.

We noted, however, that even when a country suffers a slowing of output growth due to the opening of trade, it may nonetheless gain from engaging in that trade. Benefits arise from two distinct sources. First, international trade affords households in each country the opportunity to consume innovative goods that are developed abroad. Second, trade provides the usual static efficiency gains, as countries specialize in accordance with comparative advantage.

Our analysis in this chapter has focused only on the extreme cases of total isolation or completely free trade. In practice, of course, a country's choice of trade regime is not limited to these two extremes. In the next chapter we will study the effects on long-run growth of a variety of policies that the government of an open economy might adopt that are less extreme than the sealing of its borders.

10 International Transmission of Policies

In earlier chapters we have studied how various policies affect long-run rates of innovation and growth. R&D subsidies were treated in the context of a closed economy in chapters 3 and 4, and in the context of a small open economy in chapter 6. In chapter 6 we also examined the effects of barriers to trade in final goods in an economy that produces these goods from nontraded, differentiated components. Now we continue and broaden our analysis of the implications of government intervention.

The present investigation extends our previous analysis in several different directions. First, by incorporating two distinct manufacturing sectors, we allow for a wider range of reallocative responses to government policy than could arise in the one-sector models of chapters 3 and 4. Second, in contrast to chapter 6, we analyze production subsidies and trade policies that operate directly on the incentives faced by manufacturers of high-technology products. Third, and perhaps most important, we focus here on the international transmission of policy influences. When policies are introduced in a country that is part of the world trading system, these are bound to effect resource allocations abroad. Also the equilibration of world markets following a policy intervention has implications for the growth response in the policy-active country. In this chapter we pay special attention to the spillover of policy effects from an interventionist country to the rest of the world and identify situations in which the overall growth effects of a given policy differ from what one would expect by extrapolating results that apply to a closed economy.

The chapter is organized by type of policy. In section 8.2 we study subsidies to R&D; in section 8.3, subsidies that promote production in one of the two manufacturing sectors; and in section 8.4, measures that impede or promote international trade. Before all of this, we develop in section 8.1 a graphical presentation of the model that will serve as the basis for the subsequent analysis.

10.1 Quality Upgrading: A Graphical Treatment

The details of policy analysis differ somewhat for the two distinct models of endogenous innovation that we have used so far in this book. However, many of the same mechanisms operate irrespective of whether innovation entails an expansion in the variety of a set of horizontally differentiated products or a continual upgrading of the qualities of a fixed set of goods. For this reason we choose to conduct the formal analysis for only one of these cases, namely, the two-country model with quality ladders. In a few places we will indicate that the model of expanding product variety would generate somewhat different conclusions.

The basic two-sector model of quality ladders was introduced in section 5.3 and extended to include two countries and international trade in section 7.2. Here we restrict the specification slightly. As before we assume that two inputs, human capital and unskilled labor, are used in producing a traditional good and a set of vertically differentiated (high-tech) products, and in an R&D activity that generates quality improvements in the high-technology sector. Now, however, we suppose that unit input coefficients are fixed in all activities. We let a_{ij} represent the unit requirement of factor i, $i = H, L$, for manufacturing any high-technology product ($j = x$), for manufacturing the traditional good ($j = Z$), and in the research lab ($j = \gamma$).

A number of pricing and market-clearing equations describe the allocation of resources in each country in the free-trade equilibrium. These must be combined in a suitable way if we are to develop a useful, graphical apparatus for the upcoming policy analysis. Fortunately the assumption of fixed-coefficient technologies introduces enough linearity into the system of equilibrium relationships to allow this combination to proceed.

We begin with the steady-state, factor-market-clearing conditions, which (see [7.19]) now take the form

$$a_{L\gamma}n^i\iota^i + a_{Lx}X^i + a_{LZ}Z^i = L^i, \qquad i = A, B, \tag{10.1}$$

$$a_{H\gamma}n^i\iota^i + a_{Hx}X^i + a_{HZ}Z^i = H^i, \qquad i = A, B. \tag{10.2}$$

Recall that ι^i is the intensity of research targeted at the typical high-technology product manufactured in country i, and that n^i is the number of goods for which a manufacturer in country i holds the industry lead. Therefore $n^i\iota^i$ is the aggregate amount of research activity targeted at products emanating from country i. In a steady state in which the two countries' firms maintain leadership in a constant fraction of the total number of high-technology industries, $n^i\iota^i$ also measures the aggregate extent of R&D activity undertaken in country i.[1]

With the assumption of fixed input-output coefficients, these equations allow us to solve for the aggregate output levels X^i and Z^i as functions of the factor supplies in country i and the extent of R&D activity undertaken there. We find that

$$X^i = \bar{X}^i + b_X n^i \iota^i, \qquad i = A, B, \tag{10.3}$$

and

$$Z^i = \bar{Z}^i + b_Z n^i \iota^i, \qquad i = A, B, \tag{10.4}$$

where

$$\bar{X}^i = (H^i a_{LZ} - L^i a_{HZ})/(a_{Hx}a_{LZ} - a_{Lx}a_{HZ}),$$
$$\bar{Z}^i = (L^i a_{Hx} - H^i a_{Lx})/(a_{Hx}a_{LZ} - a_{Lx}a_{HZ}),$$
$$b_X = (a_{HZ}a_{L\gamma} - a_{LZ}a_{H\gamma})/(a_{Hx}a_{LZ} - a_{Lx}a_{HZ}),$$
$$b_Z = (a_{H\gamma}a_{Lx} - a_{L\gamma}a_{Hx})/(a_{Hx}a_{LZ} - a_{Lx}a_{HZ}).$$

We assume, as before, that R&D is the most human-capital intensive of the three activities and that the manufacturing of traditional consumer goods is the least so. This ranking of factor intensities implies that $b_X < 0$ and $b_Z > 0$. In other words, aggregate output of the traditional good in country i increases and that of high-tech products declines when there is an expansion of the R&D sector there. These Rybczynski effects reflect the fact that an increase in research activity places especially heavy demands on a country's limited stock of human capital, and so the more human-capital intensive of the manufacturing sectors must contract. In the process the more labor-intensive sector expands.

We sum the pair of equations that result from applying (10.3) for $i = A$ and $i = B$ to obtain

$$X = \bar{X} + b_X \gamma, \tag{10.5}$$

where $X \equiv X^A + X^B$ denotes the aggregate world output of high-tech goods, $\bar{X} \equiv \bar{X}^A + \bar{X}^B$, and $\gamma = n^A\iota^A + n^B\iota^B$ measures the rate of innovation in the world economy at large.[2] Equation (10.5) relates the global

1. See the discussion following equation (7.18).

2. γ is the rate of arrival of product improvements per unit time when n^A products are targeted with intensity ι^A and n^B products are targeted with intensity ι^B. Applying familiar properties of the Poisson distribution, we note that an index of consumption of innovative goods grows at rate $\gamma \log \lambda$.

output of innovative products to the aggregate rate of technological progress. Similarly we derive

$$Z = \bar{Z} + b_Z\gamma \tag{10.6}$$

by summing the pair of equations in (10.4), where $Z \equiv Z^A + Z^B$ and $\bar{Z} \equiv \bar{Z}^A + \bar{Z}^B$.

Next we recall the commodity-market-clearing conditions,

$$p_x X = \sigma, \tag{10.7}$$

$$p_Z Z = 1 - \sigma, \tag{10.8}$$

and the equilibrium pricing relationships,

$$p_x = \lambda(w_L^i a_{Lx} + w_H^i a_{Hx}), \qquad i = A, B, \tag{10.9}$$

$$p_Z = w_L^i a_{LZ} + w_H^i a_{HZ}, \qquad i = A, B. \tag{10.10}$$

Notice that we have not attached any country superscript to the price of innovative goods p_x in (10.7) and (10.9). This reflects the fact (see the discussion preceding equation [7.14]) that the cost of manufacturing high-technology products must be the same in the two countries in a steady state with positive output from this sector in both nations. The equality relationship in (10.10) for $i = A$ and $i = B$ similarly requires an assumption that both countries are active in the traditional sector. In all that follows, we focus only on long-run equilibria in which both countries remain diversified in their production activities.

By substituting equation (10.5) into (10.7) and (10.6) into (10.8), we can express the commodity prices in terms of the factor supplies and the innovation rate. Then (10.9) and (10.10) can be used to eliminate the output prices altogether. This gives

$$w_L^i a_{Lx} + w_H^i a_{Hx} = \frac{\sigma}{\lambda(\bar{X} + b_X\gamma)}, \qquad i = A, B, \tag{10.11}$$

$$w_L^i a_{LZ} + w_H^i a_{HZ} = \frac{1 - \sigma}{\bar{Z} + b_Z\gamma}, \qquad i = A, B. \tag{10.12}$$

These two linear equations show once again what we know to be true, namely, that factor prices are equalized in a free-trade equilibrium with incomplete specialization in each country. The equations allow us to solve for the common equilibrium factor rewards in terms of world resource endowments and the rate of technological progress. A graphical solution is

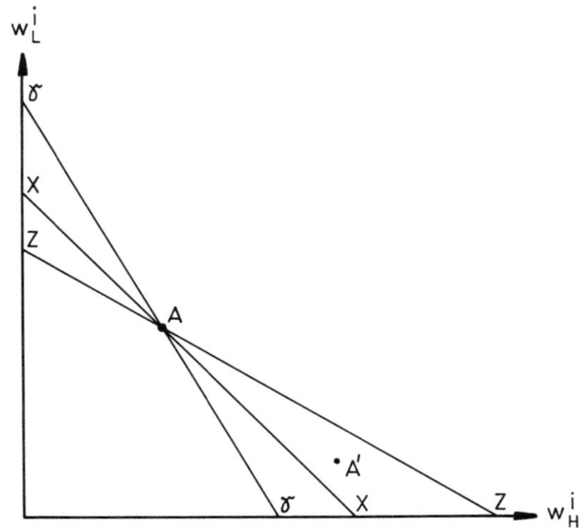

Figure 10.1

presented in figure 10.1. In the figure the line XX depicts equation (10.11), representing equilibrium in the markets for high-tech goods for a given rate of innovation γ. An increase in either factor price raises the cost of producing innovative goods, which causes their price to rise and demand to fall. When the available inputs are fully employed, factor endowments and the innovation rate fully determine the equilibrium output of these goods. So the remaining factor reward must fall to alleviate the price hike, stimulate demand, and restore equilibrium. The line ZZ, representing the equilibrium condition for traditional goods in (10.12), has a similar interpretation. This line is flatter than the XX line because the traditional manufacturing sector makes relatively more intensive use of unskilled labor.

The point of intersection of the two lines identifies the equilibrium factor rewards that correspond to the given rate of innovation. We can easily see how these rewards vary with the rate of innovation. An increase in γ shifts the XX line out and the ZZ line in, establishing a new intersection at a point such as A'. Greater rates of innovation are associated therefore with larger rewards to human capital and smaller rewards to unskilled labor.

Ultimately we will need to know the nature of the relationship between the rate of innovation and the cost of R&D. This too can be derived from figure 10.1. In the figure we have drawn a line through point A, which depicts combinations of factor rewards that give rise to the same unit cost of research as at A. Points on this line, which we have labeled $\gamma\gamma$, satisfy

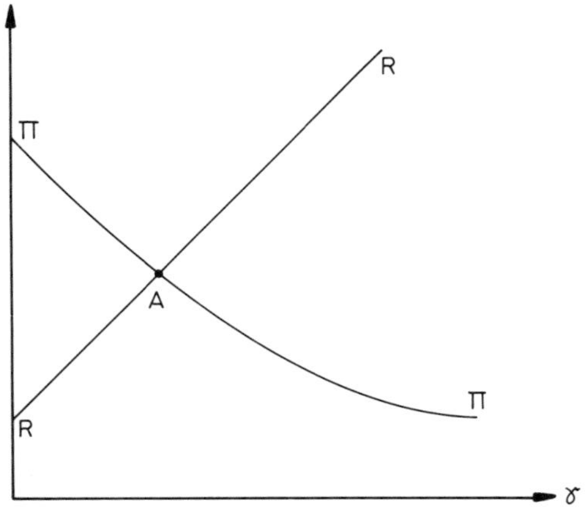

Figure 10.2

$$w_L^i a_{L\gamma} + w_H^i a_{H\gamma} = c, \qquad i = A, B. \tag{10.13}$$

This line has a steeper slope than either XX or ZZ because R&D is the most human capital intensive of the three activities. Since point A' lies above the $\gamma\gamma$ line, we may conclude that looking across steady states, a higher rate of innovation is associated with a higher cost of innovation. We denote this relationship by the increasing function $c(\gamma)$.

Next, we make use of the steady-state no-arbitrage conditions. These take the form

$$\frac{(1-\delta)\sigma}{w_L^i a_{L\gamma} + w_H^i a_{H\gamma}} = \rho + \iota^i, \qquad i = A, B; \delta = \frac{1}{\lambda}. \tag{10.14}$$

In view of our discussion in the preceding paragraph, they can be rewritten as

$$\frac{(1-\delta)\sigma}{c(\gamma)} = \rho + \iota^i, \qquad i = A, B. \tag{10.15}$$

Now we multiply (10.15) by n^i, and sum across countries, to derive

$$\frac{(1-\delta)\sigma}{c(\gamma)} = \rho + \gamma. \tag{10.16}$$

The left-hand side of (10.16) represents the steady-state profit rate. It declines with the rate of innovation γ because increases in γ raise the cost of R&D. This relationship is depicted by ΠΠ in figure 10.2. The right-hand side of (10.16) represents the required return on equities, reflecting the cost of capital and the risk of total capital loss. This risk rises with the rate of innovation, and hence so too does the required return. We represent this relationship by the upward-sloping line *RR* in the figure. The equilibrium rate of innovation in the world economy is shown at point *A*.

10.2 R&D Subsidies

Suppose now that the government of country *A* implements a subsidy to R&D (fincanced by lump-sum taxation), while that of country *B* continues to pursue a policy of laissez faire. Let ϕ^i denote the share of research expenses borne by the government in country i so that $0 < \phi^A < 1$ and $\phi^B = 0$. With the subsidy in place, free entry into research in country *A* implies that $v^A = (1 - \phi^A)(w_L^A a_{L\gamma} + w_H^A a_{H\gamma})$, and the no-arbitrage condition becomes

$$\frac{(1-\delta)\sigma}{(1-\phi^i)(w_L^i a_{L\gamma} + w_H^i a_{H\gamma})} = \rho + \iota^i, \qquad i = A, B. \tag{10.14'}$$

This is the only change introduced by the policy intervention into the system of equilibrium relationships.

The R&D subsidy in country *A* does not disturb the long-run equalization of factor prices, provided that both countries remain incompletely specialized in the new steady state. As before, factor price equalization obtains in the course of the equalization of manufacturing costs in the high-technology sectors and traditional sectors of the two countries. The equalization of these manufacturing costs is, as we have seen, necessary for the long-run survival of these activities in each country. But the equality of factor prices implies of course that innovation costs are the same in the two countries. Thus we may proceed to derive the innovation cost function $c(\gamma)$ just as we did before. By inserting this function into (10.14′), we obtain

$$\frac{(1-\delta)\sigma}{(1-\phi^i)c(\gamma)} = \rho + \iota^i, \qquad i = A, B. \tag{10.17}$$

One effect of the R&D subsidy is immediate from (10.17). The new long-run equilibrium is characterized by $\iota^A > \iota^B$. Firms in each country earn the same profits upon achieving a research success, but the private cost of R&D is lower in country *A*. If investment is to be viable in each country, it must be the case that successful entrepreneurs in country *B* expect to retain their monopoly position for a longer spell than those in country *A*. This requires that the intensity of research targeted at a typical

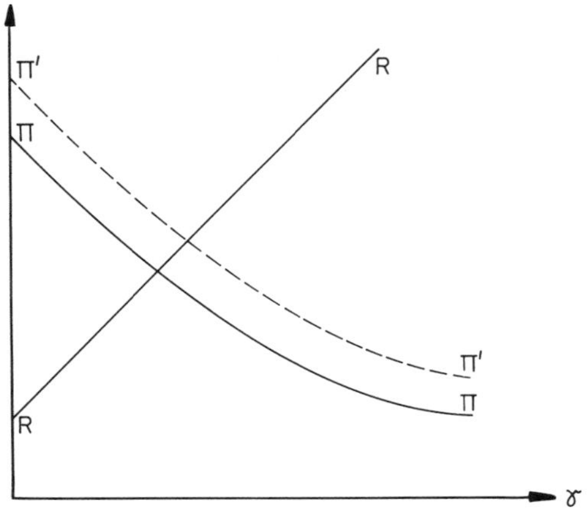

Figure 10.3

product manufactured in country A exceed that targeted at a product assembled in country B. In the new equilibrium the ex ante expected rate of return on any R&D investment is the same in either location.

Next we can multiply (10.17) by n^i and sum the resulting equations for $i = A$ and $i = B$, as we did before, to derive

$$\frac{(1-\delta)\sigma}{c(\gamma)}\left[\frac{n^A}{1-\phi^A} + n^B\right] = \rho + \gamma. \tag{10.18}$$

This equation provides the basis for the diagrammatic analysis presented in figure 10.3. In the figure we have reproduced from figure 10.2 the ΠΠ curve and the RR curve that apply in the absence of any policy intervention (when $\phi^A = 0$). Before the subsidy the term in the brackets on the left-hand side of (10.18) equals one. When the subsidy is introduced, the bracketed term rises above one.[3] This shifts the ΠΠ curve up to Π'Π', as illustrated in the figure. The RR curve is not affected. The figure shows that an R&D subsidy in either country raises the aggregate rate of innovation in the world economy.[4]

Next we investigate the effect of the R&D subsidy on the sizes of the research sectors in the two economies. The size of the research sector reveals the contribution that each country makes to world technological

3. A simple calculation using $n^B = 1 - n^A$ reveals that the bracketed term is equal to $1 + \phi^A n^A/(1-\phi^A)$, which exceeds one for $0 < \phi^A < 1$.

4. It can further be shown that a marginal increase in the subsidy rate from any arbitrary initial level accelerates global innovation. See Grossman (1990).

progress. By applying (10.17) for $i = B$ and noting the rise in the cost of innovation (recall that $c'(\gamma) > 0$), we find that the subsidy in A reduces the intensity of research targeted at a typical high-technology product of country B (i.e., ι^B falls). Since $\gamma = n^A\iota^A + (1 - n^A)\iota^B$ rises, and $\iota^A = \iota^B$ before the subsidy, it follows that ι^A must rise.[5] Then from (10.5) we see that the subsidy reduces aggregate world output of high-tech goods. Each of these goods is equally priced and the total measure of such goods is equal to one. So the fall in X implies also a fall of the same magnitude in $x^i(j) = x$. Rewriting (10.3) for $i = B$ as

$$n^B(x - b_X\iota^B) = \bar{X}^B, \tag{10.19}$$

and noting the decline in the term in parenthesis (recall that $b_X < 0$), we conclude that n^B must rise. Finally, since

$$n^Ax = \bar{X}^A + b_X n^A\iota^A \tag{10.20}$$

by application of (10.3) for $i = A$, and both n^A and x fall, it follows that the size of the R&D sector in country A (as measured by $n^A\iota^A$) expands.

It is not surprising that a subsidy to R&D should cause the research sector to expand in the policy-active country. The international transmission of the policy is more interesting, however. In the appendix to this chapter we show that $n^B\iota^B$ must fall in response to the introduction of a small R&D subsidy in country A.[6] By promoting its own research sector, a country causes the corresponding sectors in its trading partners to contract. Here the negative international spillover can never be so large as to cause the overall rate of innovation in the world economy to decline. But in Grossman and Helpman (1990) we have constructed an example based on the model of expanding product variety where this surprising outcome occurs. That is, we have shown that a subsidy to research by a country that has comparative disadvantage in performing this activity may (but need not) cause a sufficiently severe contraction in R&D activity abroad to effect an overall *decline* in the global rate of technological progress.

One additional implication of the subsidy that was noted in passing warrants further discussion. We saw that a subsidy to research in country

5. Strictly speaking, this argument establishes only that ι^A rises in response to a *small* research subsidy. Algebraic methods can be used to extend the result to include large subsidies.

6. Somewhat tedious calculations can be used to establish that any marginal increase in the rate of an R&D subsidy in country A also causes the size of the research sector in country B to shrink.

A actually leads in the long run to a reduction in the fraction of high-technology products assembled there (n^B rises, and thus n^A falls). Since output per product is the same in both countries, it follows that the relative size of the high-technology sector in the policy-active country declines as well. This result may seem paradoxical because research successes are a prerequisite to competitive advantage in the high-technology industries. The paradox can be resolved in two ways. First, viewed from the vantage of the resource constraint, if relatively more of country A's factor inputs, and especially its human capital, are deployed in the research lab, then relatively fewer of these inputs will be available for use in manufacturing. Second, considering the issue of competitiveness, while it is true that the research sector expands in country A and contracts in B, it is also true that a shift occurs in the targeting of the global research effort. Researchers devote relatively more effort to improving products manufactured in country A than they do to products manufactured in country B. Even though entrepreneurs in country A achieve a greater number of R&D successes per unit time with the subsidy than without, the successes lead the country to capture fewer *new* industries.

10.3 Production Subsidies

Many countries promote their high-technology sector by implicit or explicit subsidies to production. For example, government procurement practices often serve to subsidize local output of innovative products with defense applications. At the same time traditional sectors sometimes collect subsidies in the guise of adjustment assistance or otherwise. In this section we study the effects of such output subsidies on long-run rates of innovation and growth.

Let us begin with government policies that encourage production of high-tech goods. We let ϕ_x^i denote the ad valorem rate of subsidy paid by the government of country i to the manufacturer of any such product. Suppose that country B again follows a policy of laissez faire; that is, $\phi_x^B = 0$. Notice first that the subsidy drives a wedge between the private costs of manufacturing high-tech products in the two locations. An innovator who competes with a manufacturer of the previous generation product located in country A sets a limit price (excluding any subsidy) of $\lambda(w_L^A a_{Lx} + w_H^A a_{Hx})/(1 + \phi_x^A)$ in the duopoly competition. If it charged a price higher than this, it would leave an opening for the rival to undercut its price, since the latter could then make a positive profit after collecting the payment from its government. On the other hand, a successful innovator who displaces a producer in country B continues to charge a net-of-subsidy price of $\lambda(w_L^B a_{Lx} + w_H^B a_{Hx})$. In a long-run equilibrium with active high-technology producers in each country, it must be equally attractive to target goods produced in either location. This requires that the net-of-subsidy prices be the same no matter where the competitor is located, or that

$$p_x = \frac{\lambda(w_L^i a_{Lx} + w_H^i a_{Hx})}{1 + \phi_x^i}, \qquad i = A, B. \tag{10.9'}$$

At this price sales per product are given by $x = \sigma(1 + \phi_x^i)/\lambda(w_L^i a_{Lx} + w_H^i a_{Hx})$, and (10.11) becomes

$$w_L^i a_{Lx} + w_H^i a_{Hx} = \frac{\sigma(1 + \phi_x^i)}{\lambda(\bar{X} + b_X \gamma)}, \qquad i = A, B. \tag{10.11'}$$

It is apparent from (10.11′) and (10.12) that the output subsidy causes a divergence of factor prices in the two locations. Consequently the R&D costs in the two countries come to differ. Using (10.11′), (10.12), and (10.13), we obtain the cost of innovation in country i, which depends now on the aggregate rate of innovation and on the local subsidy rate. We denote this dependence by $c(\gamma, \phi_x^i)$.

The output subsidy also alters the profitability of manufacturing high-tech goods in country A. Producers in that country receive gross-of-subsidy revenue of $(1 + \phi_x^A)p_x$ for each unit of output that they sell. Using (10.9′) and the expression for sales per brand, we find that per firm profits in country i are equal to $\pi^i = (1 + \phi_x^i)(1 - \delta)\sigma$. So the new no-arbitrage condition reads

$$\frac{(1 + \phi_x^i)(1 - \delta)\sigma}{c(\gamma, \phi_x^i)} = \rho + \iota^i, \qquad i = A, B. \tag{10.21}$$

We can proceed now, as we have done before, by multiplying this equation by n^i and summing the expressions for $i = A$ and $i = B$. This gives

$$(1 - \delta)\sigma\left[\frac{(1 + \phi_x^A)n^A}{c(\gamma, \phi_x^A)} + \frac{n^B}{c(\gamma, 0)}\right] = \rho + \gamma. \tag{10.22}$$

From (10.22) we see that the effect of an output subsidy on the global rate of innovation hinges on a comparison of the term $(1 + \phi_x^A)/c(\gamma, \phi_x^A)$ with the pre-subsidy term $1/c(\gamma, 0)$. That is, it depends upon the subsidy's impact on the profitability of R&D relative to its cost. To investigate this matter

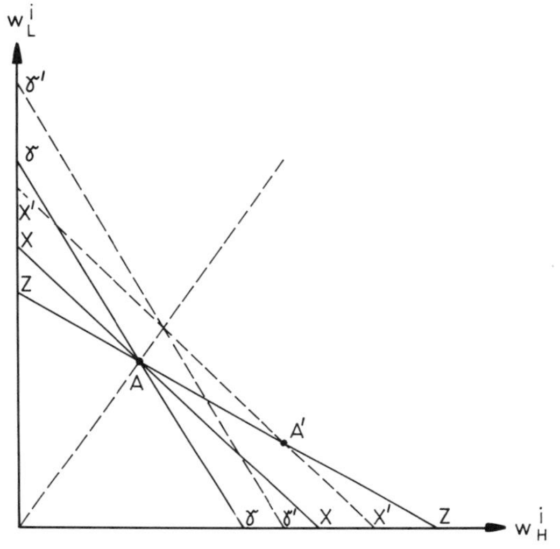

Figure 10.4

further, we turn to figure 10.4. In this figure we have reproduced from figure 10.1 the *XX*, *ZZ*, and $\gamma\gamma$ curves that depict equations (10.11), (10.12), and (10.13), respectively. Equation (10.11′) indicates that when firms receive an inducement to produce high-technology goods, this shifts the *XX* line radially outward by an amount that is proportional to the the rate of the subsidy. The new line is represented by *X′X′*, and the new factor prices that are consistent with the initial rate of innovation are those at *A′*. The line $\gamma'\gamma'$ depicts combinations of factor rewards that imply a cost innovation higher than at *A* by a percentage amount equal to the size of the subsidy. Since *A′* lies outside this line, it is clear that at the initial rate of innovation, R&D costs rise *more than in proportion to the subsidy rate.* It follows that the subsidy has an adverse effect on the rate of return to R&D.

Now it is a simple matter to show the long-run impact of the subsidy on the global rate of innovation. Since the proportional rise in $c(\gamma, \phi_x^A)$ exceeds the size of the subsidy ϕ_x^A, the introduction of the subsidy causes the term in brackets in (10.22) to fall below its laissez-faire level.[7] In terms of figure 10.3, the policy effects an inward shift in the ΠΠ curve, that is, a shift in the opposite direction from that caused by an R&D subsidy. Since the

7. Initially the term in brackets is equal to $1/c(\gamma, 0)$. After the policy is introduced, this term is a weighted average of this same amount and $(1 + \phi_x^A)/c(\gamma, \phi_x^A)$, with weights of $1 - n^A$ and n^A, respectively. Since $(1 + \phi_x^A)/c(\gamma, \phi_x^A) < 1/c(\gamma, 0)$ as we have just seen, the policy reduces the size of the bracketed term.

incentive to innovate is diminished by the production subsidy, the rate of technological progress falls.

It is perhaps surprising to find that a subsidy to manufacturers of high-tech products would slow the rate of innovation in the world economy. But the conclusion makes intuitive sense once the general equilibrium ramifications of the policy have been properly considered. A policy of promoting high-tech manufacturing generates additional activity in this sector at every moment in time, at the expense of production of traditional goods. This reorientation of manufacturing necessitates a reallocation of resources. But the expansion of the high-technology sector requires a greater input of human capital relative to unskilled labor than can be accommodated by resources released from traditional manufacturing. So high-tech manufacturing must draw additional human capital away from the research activity. Of course the factor price movements support this reallocation. The subsidy to producers of high-tech goods causes the reward to human capital to rise, and thereby increases the cost of R&D. This cost hike induces research firms to release the requisite resources.

The other long-run effects of the output subsidy are also opposite to those of a subsidy to R&D. The R&D sector in the policy-active country contracts, while that in the trade partner expands. Output of each high-tech good rises in both countries, and the policy-active country comes to enjoy competitive advantage in a larger fraction of the high-tech industries. Together, these effects imply an expansion of the aggregate size of the high-technology sector in the country that promotes this activity, whereas the high-technology sector in its trade partner contracts.

We investigate next the effects of policies that promote production in the traditional manufacturing sector. Here we can be brief. We let the subsidy rate in country i be ϕ_Z^i, with $\phi_Z^B = 0$. With this policy in place, (10.10) must be replaced by

$$p_Z = \frac{w_L^i a_{LZ} + w_H^i a_{HZ}}{1 + \phi_Z^i}. \tag{10.10$'$}$$

Equations (10.9), (10.10′), and (10.13) can be used to derive the cost of innovation in country i, $c(\gamma, \phi_Z^i)$. To see the nature of the dependence of these costs on the subsidy rate, we combine (10.6), (10.8), and (10.10′) to obtain

$$w_L^i a_{LZ} + w_H^i a_{HZ} = \frac{(1-\sigma)(1+\phi_Z^i)}{\bar{Z} + b_Z \gamma}, \qquad i = A, B. \tag{10.12$'$}$$

From this equation we see that the introduction of a subsidy to traditional manufactures in A causes the ZZ curve of figure 10.1 to shift out. This effects an increase in the reward to unskilled labor, a decline in the reward to skilled labor, and a fall in the cost of R&D at the initial rate of innovation γ. Thus the incentive to invest in research rises when a subsidy is introduced for traditional manufacturing. Technological progress accelerates as a result.

Evidently the long-run growth effect of a particular industrial policy is not a matter of whether the targeted sector uses technology intensively. Rather, this effect hinges on the relationship between the targeted sector and the R&D activity in the general-equilibrium production structure. Here the sector that assembles high-tech goods acts as a substitute in production for R&D because this manufacturing sector uses a bundle of factors that is more similar in composition to the one required in the research lab than is the bundle employed in producing traditional manufactures. For this same reason the traditional manufacturing sector and the R&D activity do not compete intensively in factor markets, and so these two sectors behave as complements in the general-equilibrium production structure.

10.4 Trade Policies

We consider, finally, government policies that serve to impede or promote international trade. We are interested both in policies that alter the incentives to trade high-technology products and those that impinge upon exchange in the traditional manufacturing sector. It is not necessary, however, to analyze these two types of interventions separately. The well-known Lerner (1936) symmetry theorem implies the equivalence of a policy that subsidizes exports of all high-tech goods and taxes imports of these same products and an export-tax-cum-import-subsidy applied to traditional manufactures. In the formal analysis we introduce a policy parameter that corresponds to a tariff on imports of traditional goods in country A if this country imports these goods in the free-trade equilibrium, and to a subsidy to exports of these goods otherwise. The subsequent discussion interprets the results for the case of trade interventions in the high-technology industries.

A policy that taxes imports or subsidizes exports of traditional products raises the local price of these goods in country A above the level of world prices. We let τ^A represent the ad valorem rate of the trade policy. Then the internal price of good Z in country i becomes $(1 + \tau^i)p_Z$, with $\tau^B = 0$. On the supply side the policy intervention replicates the effects of a production subsidy. So we can use (10.10′) for the pricing of traditional goods, after replacing ϕ_Z^i by τ^i. This gives

$$p_Z = \frac{w_L^i a_{LZ} + w_H^i a_{HZ}}{1 + \tau^i}, \qquad i = A, B. \tag{10.10''}$$

The additional effects of the trade policy come from the demand side. Consumers in country A pay $p_Z(1 + \tau^A)$ for the traditional good and purchase $(1 - \sigma)E^A/p_Z(1 + \tau^A)$ units of this good when the trade policy is in effect.[8] Market clearing now requires that

$$p_Z Z = (1 - \sigma)\left[\frac{E^A}{1 + \tau^A} + E^B\right]. \tag{10.8'}$$

Using (10.6), (10.8′), and (10.10″), we can derive the modified version of (10.12), which reads

$$w_L^i a_{LZ} + w_H^i a_{HZ} = \frac{(1 - \sigma)(1 + \tau^i)}{\bar{Z} + b_Z \gamma}\left[\frac{E^A}{1 + \tau^A} + E^B\right], \quad i = A, B. \tag{10.12''}$$

Then (10.11) and (10.12″) combine to give the cost of innovation in each country. These costs now vary with the spending shares and the size of the policy intervention, in addition to the usual dependence on the rate of innovation. Moreover the functional relationship between R&D costs and these various variables differs in the two countries. So we write $c^i(\gamma, E^A, E^B, \tau^A)$ to represent the cost of innovation in country i. As before, R&D costs increase in each country with the aggregate rate of innovation.

Substituting the new innovation cost functions into the no-arbitrage conditions in the usual way, we derive

$$\frac{(1 - \delta)\sigma}{c^i(\gamma, E^A, E^B, \tau^A)} = \rho + \iota^i, \qquad i = A, B. \tag{10.23}$$

After multiplying (10.23) by n^i and adding the respective expressions for $i = A$ and $i = B$, we obtain

$$(1 - \delta)\sigma\left[\frac{n^A}{c^A(\gamma, E^A, E^B, \tau^A)} + \frac{n^B}{c^B(\gamma, E^A, E^B, \tau^A)}\right] = \rho + \gamma. \tag{10.24}$$

We are ready now to investigate how the trade policy influences the global rate of innovation. For ease of exposition we concentrate on the effects of

8. Recall that E^i denotes the share of country i in nominal world spending. With $E = 1$ by our normalization, E^i represents also the level of spending in country i.

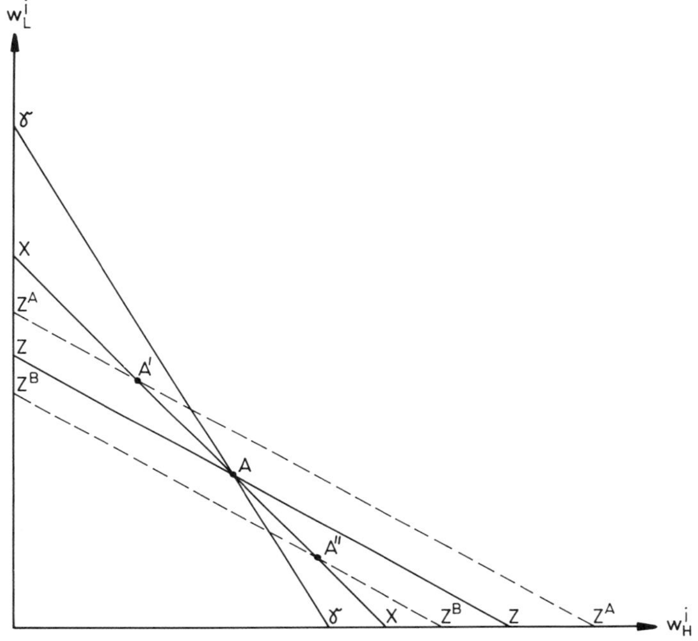

Figure 10.5

small departures from free trade. Consider first the effect of τ^A on c^A. Holding the spending shares and γ constant for the moment, we see from (10.12″) that raising τ^A from zero to $d\tau^A$ moves the ZZ line in figure 10.5 out to Z^AZ^A. The extent of this shift, measured radially, is proportional to $E^Bd\tau^A$. Clearly the cost of innovation at the initial spending shares and innovation rate falls in country A, since the new intersection point at A' lies inside the $\gamma\gamma$ line. The percentage reduction in the cost of R&D also is proportional to $E^Bd\tau^A$. Now consider the effect of τ^A on c^B. Again referring to (10.12″), the ZZ line shifts in for country B by an amount that is proportional to $E^Ad\tau^A$. The new line is depicted by Z^BZ^B in figure 10.5. At the initial τ, E^A, and E^B, the cost of innovation rises in the passive country. The percentage increase in c^B is proportional to $E^Ad\tau^A$, and the factor of proportionality is the same as applies to the decline in c^A.

Next observe from (10.12″) that the ensuing adjustment of the spending shares has no further influence on the cost of innovation in either country, when the initial equilibrium is one of free trade.[9] So we have fully ac-

9. Since $E^A + E^B = 1$, the partial effect on the bracketed term in (10.12″) of a change in spending shares equals $-\tau^A dE^A/(1 + \tau^A)$. Evaluated at $\tau^A = 0$, this effect vanishes.

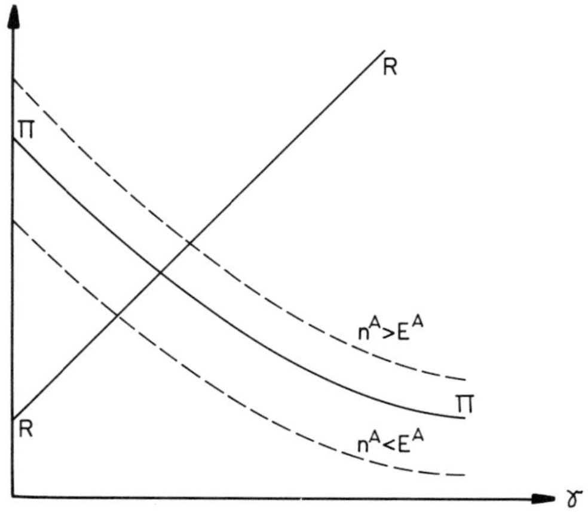

Figure 10.6

counted for the changes in R&D costs at the initial rate of innovation γ. We proceed to figure 10.6, which shows the $\Pi\Pi$ and RR curves that apply with free trade. The trade intervention shifts the $\Pi\Pi$ curve in the direction indicated by the sign of the change in the bracketed term in (10.24). This term increases when τ^A rises slightly above zero, if and only if the product-share-weighted average cost of innovation falls. Therefore the $\Pi\Pi$ curve shifts outward if $n^A E^B > n^B E^A$ (or $n^A > E^A$), and it shifts inward otherwise.[10] We conclude that the rate of innovation rises with the imposition of a small tariff or export subsidy on traditional products in country A if and only if this country's free-trade share of the world market for high-tech products exceeds its share in world spending.

In some situations the condition $n^A E^B > n^B E^A$ and its opposite, $n^A E^B < n^B E^A$, reflect the pattern of international comparative advantage. The former condition always implies that country A exports a greater volume of high-technology products than it imports in the free-trade equilibrium, while the latter condition makes country A a net importer of these goods.[11]

10. The derivative of the term in square brackets in (10.24), evaluated at the point where $c^A = c^B = c$, equals $-(n^A dc^A + n^B dc^B)/c^2$. The argument in the previous paragraph has established that $dc^A = -kE^B d\tau^A$ and $dc^B = kE^A d\tau^A$, for some $k > 0$.

11. The value of aggregate output in the high-technology sector of country i is $n^i p_x x$. Homothetic preferences imply that each country consumes the same proportion of world output of every good. Households in country i spend $E^i p_x x$ on each high-technology product, which represents also the country's aggregate spending on all innovative goods. Therefore country i exports high-tech goods on net if and only if $n^i > E^i$, which is equivalent to $n^i E^j > n^j E^i$, $j \neq i$, because $n^j = 1 - n^i$ and $E^j = 1 - E^i$.

If neither country imports both goods (on net) in the steady state, as must be the case in the absence of international capital flows, then the market share exceeds the spending share if and only if country *A* enjoys comparative advantage in manufacturing high-tech goods (i.e., if and only if it is relatively well endowed with human capital). In this case a trade intervention in the traditional manufacturing sector accelerates world innovation and growth if the intervention takes the form of a tariff in the importing country. If, on the other hand, the policy represents a subsidy in the exporting country, then the growth rate falls in the long-run equilibrium.

We extend our findings now to include policies that apply to trade in innovative products. An export subsidy for traditional products corresponds by Lerner symmetry to a tax on exports of high-technology products coupled with an import subsidy for these goods. Therefore world innovation accelerates when a country that is a net importer of innovative goods extends a small subsidy to its exporters of these goods and protects its local market with a small import tariff. When the same policies are pursued by a country that has an aggregate trade surplus in high-technology products, the global rate of innovation falls. In the event that no country runs a long-run trade deficit in both sectors, promotion of the high-technology sector via trade policy enhances world growth performance if and only if the intervention is undertaken by the country with comparative *disadvantage* in R&D.[12]

Why should the growth effects of trade policy differ from those of a production subsidy? And why should they vary with the identity of the country that introduces the policy? Clearly the reasons must have to do with the fact that besides subsidizing production, trade policies also tax consumption. We have seen that a subsidy to manufacturers of high-tech goods contracts the amount of R&D activity in the policy-active country. At the initial relative prices, the magnitude of this effect is proportional to the size of the country's high-technology sector. A consumption tax, on the other hand, reduces demand for high-tech goods in the policy-active country. Taken by itself, such a policy would cause resources to be released from the high-technology sectors in both countries. Much of the human capital thus released would find its way into the research lab. Therefore a consumption tax on high-technology products would tend to promote growth. This component of the effect of trade policy is proportional in magnitude to the quantity of high-tech goods consumed in the policy-

12. In Grossman and Helpman (1990) we report a similar result for the effects of trade policy in a model of expanding product variety.

active country. The net impact of trade policy combines these offsetting influences. The former dominates for a country that produces more than it consumes of the innovative goods, while the latter dominates for a country that consumes more than it produces.

Let us return to the case of an import tariff or export subsidy applied to traditional manufactures, to explore in more detail the effects of these policies on resource allocation in each country. If the innovation rate rises in response to a small positive $d\tau^A$, then the total impact on the cost of R&D in country B must be positive. Then from (10.23), ι^B must fall. On the other hand, if the innovation rate declines with the introduction of trade policy, then the cost of R&D in country A also declines. In this event (10.23) implies a rise in ι^A. In the former case (10.19) requires an increase in n^B, if x happens to fall, while in the latter case (10.20) dictates a fall in n^A if x happens to rise. But (10.5) indeed implies an inverse relationship between the innovation rate and the aggregate or per firm output of high-technology products. So we have in either case the same implication. A trade policy that supports a country's traditional manufacturing sector reduces the number of its leading-edge industries. Of course the opposite is true of trade policy that supports the high-technology sector.

Now the impact on the size of each country's R&D sector is evident for some cases. When a tariff on imports of traditional goods causes the world innovation rate to rise, both the number of active producers of high-tech goods in country A and output by the representative one of these producers falls. Then (10.20) implies an expansion of this country's R&D sector. This expansion in research activity is necessary to employ the human capital released from the high-tech manufacturing sector. Similarly, in the event that a subsidy to exports of traditional goods causes the world rate of innovation to fall, then the high-tech manufacturing sector in country B expands at both the intensive and extensive margins (i.e., x and n^B both increase). In this case the R&D sector in country B clearly contracts. The appendix shows these results are more general. No matter what the initial pattern of specialization, a small trade policy that supports a country's traditional manufacturing sector also promotes its research sector. At the same time the international transmission of policy implies an opposite reallocation of resources abroad. Once again these results reflect the fact that traditional manufacturing and R&D are complements in production.

This chapter has examined the international transmission of various policy instruments. We have discovered that when policies serve to promote innovation and growth in the country that introduces them, they often achieve these goals at the expense of innovation and growth in trade partner countries. A subsidy to R&D, or a trade policy that protects a country's labor-intensive producers, will spur technological progress at home while impeding innovation abroad. The net effect of these policies on world growth may be adverse.

The analysis has also highlighted the importance of the general equilibrium relationships between different productive sectors. Activities that use similar bundles of inputs substitute for one another on the production side. We found, for example, that a subsidy to R&D may cause a country to export fewer high-tech goods and import more of them. The subsidy draws skilled labor into the research lab and leaves less of this factor for manufacturing innovative products. If the high-tech manufacturing sector uses skilled labor relatively more intensively than the traditional manufacturing sector, then the result follows. Similar arguments apply to policies that promote production in the high-technology sector. These policies can have a detrimental impact on innovation and growth because they serve to boost the cost of innovation.

APPENDIX

A10.1 Comparative Steady States

In this appendix we calculate the long-run effects of policy interventions in country A on the size of the research sector in each country. We begin with the case of a small subsidy to R&D. Similar, but more tedious, calculations could be used to establish that qualitatively similar results apply for any marginal increase in the subsidy rate, irrespective of the initial level of the policy instrument.

When the initial conditions are those of laissez faire, the initial equilibrium is characterized by $\iota^A = \iota^B = \gamma$. By differentiating the definition of $\gamma \equiv n^A\iota^A + n^B\iota^B$, we find therefore that

$$d\gamma = n^A d\iota^A + n^B d\iota^B.$$

Then from (10.5) we derive $dX = b_X(n^A d\iota^A + n^B d\iota^B)$. Combining this expression for dX with (10.3), and noting that $X^i = n^i X$, gives

$$dn^i = \frac{b_X n^A n^B}{X - b_X\gamma}(d\iota^i - d\iota^j), \qquad i = A, B; j \neq i. \tag{A10.1}$$

It follows from (A10.1) that

$$d(n^i\iota^i) = \frac{n^i}{X - b_X\gamma}[(X - b_X\gamma n^i)\, d\iota^i - b_X\gamma n^j\, d\iota^j], \qquad i = A, B; j \neq i. \tag{A10.2}$$

The fact that $b_X < 0$ implies that $X - b_X\gamma > 0$. Hence the direction of change in the scale of R&D activity in country i is given by the sign of the term in the square brackets. We note in passing that (A10.2) applies for any small departure from laissez faire, not only for an R&D subsidy. This expression will be equally applicable when we come to derive the allocative effects of a small trade intervention below.

We have already shown in the main text that a small subsidy to R&D in country A spurs innovative activity in that country; that is, $d(n^A\iota^A)/d\phi^A > 0$ at $\phi^A = 0$. Our objective here is to calculate the effect on $n^B\iota^B$. To this end we combine (10.11), (10.12), and (10.13), to derive

$$c + \frac{b_X\sigma}{\lambda(\bar{X} + b_X\gamma)} + \frac{b_Z(1-\sigma)}{\bar{Z} + b_Z\gamma} = 0. \tag{A10.3}$$

Together with (10.18), which we can rewrite in the form of

$$\frac{(1-\delta)\sigma}{c}\left(\frac{n^A}{1-\phi^A} + n^B\right) = \rho + \gamma, \tag{A10.4}$$

this gives us two equations with which to calculate the response of c and γ to a change in the subsidy rate (starting from $\phi^A = 0$). The result of this calculation is

$$\frac{dc}{d\phi^A} = \frac{cn^A\Lambda}{1 + \Lambda}, \tag{A10.5}$$

where[13]

$$\Lambda \equiv \frac{(1-\delta)\sigma}{c^2}\left[\frac{b_X^2\sigma}{\lambda X^2} + \frac{b_Z^2(1-\sigma)}{Z^2}\right].$$

Next we use (10.17) and (A10.5) to calculate the induced changes in the intensity of research targeted at firms in each country. We obtain

$$\frac{d\iota^A}{d\phi^A} = \frac{(1-\delta)\sigma}{c}\,\frac{1+n^B\Lambda}{1+\Lambda} > 0, \tag{A10.6}$$

$$\frac{d\iota^B}{d\phi^A} = -\frac{(1-\delta)\sigma}{c}\,\frac{n^A\Lambda}{1+\Lambda} < 0. \tag{A10.7}$$

Substituting these results into (A10.2), we find that employment in the R&D sector of country B declines in response to an R&D subsidy in country A if and only if $X\Lambda + b_X\gamma > 0$. But note that

$$X\Lambda + b_X\gamma > \frac{(1-\delta)\sigma}{c^2}\,\frac{b_X^2\sigma}{\lambda X} + b_X\gamma = \frac{\rho+\gamma}{c}\,\frac{b_X^2\sigma}{\lambda X} + b_X\gamma,$$

where the equality relationship follows from (10.18). Hence, using (A10.3), we have

$$X\Lambda + b_X\gamma > \frac{b_X\gamma}{c}\left(c + \frac{b_X\sigma}{\lambda X}\right) = -\frac{b_X\gamma}{c}\,\frac{b_Z(1-\sigma)}{Z} > 0. \tag{A10.8}$$

It follows that $d(n^B\iota^B)/d\phi^A < 0$ at $\phi^A = 0$; in other words, a small R&D subsidy in country A reduces employment in the R&D sector of country B.

Now we perform a similar exercise with regard to trade policy. We consider the long-run effect on the sizes of the two R&D sectors of a small import tariff or export subsidy applied by country A to trade in traditional manufactures.

Let τ^i be the ad valorem rate of the trade policy in country i, with $\tau^A = 0$ initially, and $\tau^B \equiv 0$. From (10.11), (10.12″), and (10.13) we obtain

$$c^i + \frac{b_X\sigma}{\lambda(\bar{X} + b_X\gamma)} + \frac{b_Z(1-\sigma)}{\bar{Z} + b_Z\gamma}\left(\frac{E^A}{1+\tau^A} + E^B\right)(1+\tau^i) = 0, \quad i = A, B. \tag{A10.9}$$

Next we write (10.24) in the form of

$$(1-\delta)\sigma\left(\frac{n^A}{c^A} + \frac{n^B}{c^B}\right) = \rho + \gamma. \tag{A10.10}$$

Then from (A10.9) and (A10.10) we can derive

$$\frac{dc^A}{d\tau^A} = -\frac{b_Z(1-\sigma)}{Z(1+\Lambda)}(n^B\Lambda + E^B) < 0, \tag{A10.11}$$

13. In writing the definition of Λ, we make use of (10.5) and (10.6).

$$\frac{dc^B}{d\tau^A} = \frac{b_Z(1-\sigma)}{Z(1+\Lambda)}(n^A\Lambda + E^A) > 0, \tag{A10.12}$$

where we have used (10.6), the definition of Λ (following [A10.5]), and the fact that $\tau^A = 0$ in the initial equilibrium.

Equation (A10.2) gives once again the change in the sizes of the R&D sectors in response to a small policy intervention. We can substitute in this equation for $d\iota^i = -(1-\delta)\sigma dc^i/c^2$, which follows from differentiating (10.23). Combining the result with (A10.11) and (A10.12), we find that

$$\frac{d(n^A\iota^A)}{d\tau^A} > 0 \qquad \text{if and only if } T^A > 0,$$

and

$$\frac{d(n^B\iota^B)}{d\tau^A} < 0 \qquad \text{if and only if } T^B > 0,$$

where

$$T^A \equiv (X - b_X n^A\gamma)(n^B\Lambda + E^B) + b_X n^B\gamma(n^A\Lambda + E^A),$$

$$T^B \equiv (X - b_X n^B\gamma)(n^A\Lambda + E^A) + b_X n^A\gamma(n^B\Lambda + E^B).$$

Rearranging terms and recognizing that $n^BE^A - n^AE^B = E^A - n^A = n^B - E^B$, we have

$$T^A = n^B(X\Lambda + b_X\gamma) + (X - b_X\gamma)E^B > 0, \tag{A10.13}$$

$$T^B = n^A(X\Lambda + b_X\gamma) + (X - b_X\gamma)E^A > 0, \tag{A10.14}$$

where the inequalities follow from the fact that $b_X < 0$ and that $X\Lambda + b_X\gamma > 0$ (see [A10.8]). We conclude that a small tariff on traditional manufactures promotes activity in the R&D sector in country A and contracts activity in the corresponding sector of country B.

11 Imitation

The diffusion of technology has played a central role in our analysis of innovation and growth. We have argued that the process of knowledge accumulation may exhibit diminishing returns if innovators cannot benefit from the far-reaching advances in applied science that are achieved by their counterparts in other laboratories. And we have seen that the extent to which information disseminates across international borders figures prominently in the determination of long-run patterns of trade and in the relationship between trade and growth.

Our analysis thus far has maintained a sharp distinction between two types of outputs from investments in learning. Blueprints that are necessary for manufacturing new goods have been treated as proprietary information, whereas "knowledge capital" that affects productivity in the research lab has been assumed a public good. This formulation limits knowledge dissemination to the spread of general scientific principles and excludes any spillovers of more product-specific information. But in reality both types of diffusion take place. Not only do entrepreneurs apply abstract concepts in new and different contexts, but many times they undertake to copy closely the designs and processes that rivals have developed.[1] In this chapter and the next we examine the determinants and the consequences of technological *imitation.*

For imitation to be profitable, two things must be true. First, a successful imitator must be able to earn positive profits in competition with the original inventor of a new product or process. And second, the enforcement of any applicable patents must not be so strict as to make imitation prohibitively expensive. These conditions may sometimes be satisfied in a

1. For example, in a study of 48 product innovations in the chemical, drug, electronics, and machinery industries, Mansfield et al. (1981) found that 34 new products had been imitated during the sample period. The sample period varied by product between five and twenty years.

closed economy if oligopolistic conduct is not very competitive and if the nature of the product makes it possible to "invent around the patent."[2] But they are more likely to be satisfied in an open world economy when imitation may take place in countries where manufacturing costs are low. If firms operating in low-cost countries gain the ability to assemble "clones," they can capture market share and quasi-rents by underpricing rivals in the technologically advanced countries. Also the governments of nations with little indigenous R&D activity may be lax in their enforcement of patent rights and may afford especially little protection to the intellectual property of foreign nationals.[3] It should not be surprising then to find that imitation has played a major role in the transfer of technology to the newly industrializing countries or that the manufactured exports of these countries are dominated by goods that were once produced in the "North."

These arguments suggest that international trade with certain types of partners may increase an innovating country's exposure to the risk of imitation. This has obvious implications for the incentives that entrepreneurs have to invest in R&D in the first place. Yet imitation also serves to spread the use of a given technology and so allows the public good characteristics of knowledge to be more fully exploited. If low- and middle-income countries have an abundance of the factors used intensively in manufacturing, or if they have a comparative disadvantage in the creation of knowledge, then the transfer of technology to these countries may cause resources to be released from the manufacturing sectors in high-income countries which then find their way into industrial research labs. Our purpose here is to explore carefully the nature of the relationship between innovation and imitation in a context in which both of these activities result from the investment decisions of farsighted entrepreneurs.

In this chapter we restrict our attention to a world economy that innovates by developing new varieties of horizontally differentiated products.[4]

---

2. Segerstrom (1991) develops a model of imitation, based on Grossman and Helpman (1991a), in which the innovator and the latecomer share positive industry profits as a result of their ability to engage in tacit collusion.

3. The protection of foreign intellectual property rights constitutes a major item of contention in North–South trade relations. Benko (1987) and the United States International Trade Commission (1988) outline the discrepancies between national and international treatment of intellectual property for a sample of (mostly) developing countries.

4. Krugman (1979) studies innovation and imitation in the context of North–South trade. He, like us, adopts the Dixit-Stiglitz specification for utility and posits that each new, differentiated product is first produced in the North before the technology eventually diffuses to the South. However, Krugman takes the rates of innovation and imitation to be

We leave to chapter 12 the interesting possibility that clones themselves might be displaced from the market by a new generation of improved goods. In contrast to much of our previous analysis, the two models of product innovation yield rather different predictions about the relationship between key economic variables and long-run rates of innovation and growth.

11.1 A Model of Imitation

We return to our simplest model of expanding product variety. Households in the North and South consume a variety of differentiated products (and only these goods) manufactured from a single primary input. Preferences, which are represented by (3.1) and (3.2), are characterized by a constant elasticity of substitution between every pair of goods and a unitary elasticity of intertemporal substitution. Then (3.3) gives the demand for each variety. Spending in each region grows at a rate equal to the difference between the interest rate and the subjective discount rate. World spending is normalized to equal one at every moment in time so that interest rates equal ρ in a steady state with constant regional shares in aggregate world demand.[5]

Once a firm in either region has mastered the technology for some product, the good can be manufactured with one unit of labor per unit of output. Then marginal costs are w^N for firms that produce in the North, and w^S for those that operate in the South. All firms with the capacity to manufacture a given brand compete as price-setting oligopolists. The equilibrium price of each variety depends upon the market structure prevailing in the industry. We consider several alternatives in turn.

A Northern firm that is uniquely able to produce some innovative good faces competition only from other, horizontally differentiated brands. Such a firm sees the demand in (3.3) and maximizes profits by setting its price at a fixed markup over unit cost. This gives the pricing equation

$$p^N = \frac{w^N}{\alpha}, \tag{11.1}$$

where p^N represents the price of a brand produced by a typical Northern

exogenous parameters, whereas we focus our analysis on the endogenous determination of these rates.

5. As before, we need not take any stand on the feasibility of international asset trade. In the event of perfect capital mobility, the interest rate equals the discount rate at every moment in time.

monopolist. The monopolist realizes sales of x^N and earns operating profits

$$\pi^N = (1 - \alpha)p^N x^N \tag{11.2}$$

per unit time.

When two Northern firms compete in the market for the same brand, each sets a price equal to w^N and each earns zero operating profits. Thus the second firm to have mastered the technology (i.e., the imitator) earns no return on its R&D investment. Our assumptions about market conduct again rule out costly imitation in the region where the innovators are located.

Next we consider the outcome when a Southern producer competes with the Northern firm whose product it targeted for imitation. To find the Nash equilibrium of this competition, we take as given for the moment the price set by the Northern firm and concentrate on the profit maximizing response by its rival. If the Southern firm charges a price less than that of the Northern firm, it captures the entire market for the product. The demand function (3.3) gives the resulting sales. If the Southern firm's price is greater than that of the Northern firm, the former competitor makes no sales. Finally, if the Southern firm chooses a price that is just equal to that of its rival, then it may sell any quantity between zero and the total of industry demand. The kinked curve *BCD* in figure 11.1 depicts the demand facing the Southern firm when its rival's price is p_1^N. From this we can derive the (discontinuous) marginal revenue curve *BCER*.

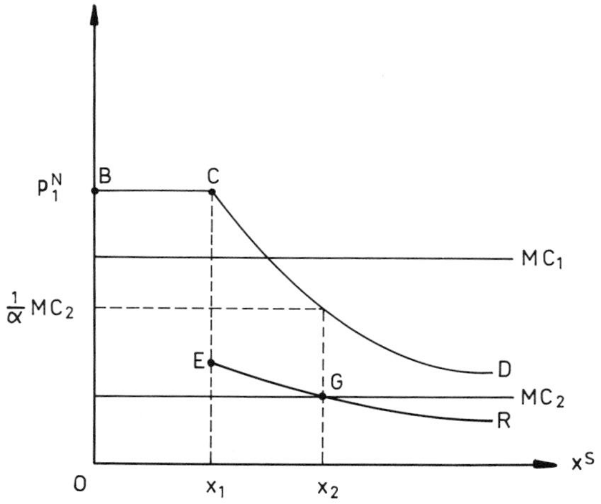

Figure 11.1

There are now three different scenarios to consider. First, if the unit cost of the Southern firm, w^S, happens to be above the price p_1^N, then the Southern firm cannot profitably enter the market. Second, if the Southern firm's marginal cost curve passes between C and E (as does the one labeled MC_1 in the figure), then the imitator maximizes profits by charging a price a shade below p_1^N. Sales in this case are given by x_1 in the figure, and profits total $(p_1^N - w^S)x_1$. Finally, if the Southern wage gives rise to a marginal cost curve that passes below point E (e.g., MC_2), then the Southern firm chooses the optimal price $p_2^S = w^S/\alpha$ that it would set if it faced no competition from the Northern innovator. This monopoly price yields sales of x_2, and profits equal to $(1 - \alpha)p_2^S x_2$.

Similar arguments apply to the strategic choices of the Northern firm. It follows that in a Nash equilibrium the Northern firm would capture the entire market if its marginal production cost (the Northern wage) were less than its rival's cost (the Southern wage). This outcome would leave the Southern firm with zero operating profits and thus would fail to provide the imitator with a positive return on its investment. In a long-run equilibrium with ongoing imitation, this situation cannot arise. This leaves two further possibilities. In what we will call the *narrow-gap case*, the Southern producer enjoys a relatively small cost advantage over its Northern rival. In this case, if the Southern firm were to charge the monopoly price w^S/α, the Northern firm could profitably undercut and force the Southern firm's sales to zero. The equilibrium outcome instead has the Southern firm setting a "limit price" at the level of (or just below) its competitor's cost.[6] Then the Southern brand's price and profits are

$$\left.\begin{aligned} p^S &= w^N && (11.3a) \\ \pi^S &= \left(1 - \frac{w^S}{w^N}\right)p^S x^S && (11.4a) \end{aligned}\right\} \text{ for } w^N > w^S > \alpha w^N.$$

Alternatively, the manufacturing cost differential might be sufficiently large so that the Southern firm could charge its monopoly price without fear of reprisal from the Northern rival. The price and profits that obtain in this *wide-gap case* are

$$\left.\begin{aligned} p^S &= \frac{w^S}{\alpha} && (11.3b) \\ \pi^S &= (1 - \alpha)p^S x^S && (11.4b) \end{aligned}\right\} \text{ for } \alpha w^N > w^S.$$

6. This limit-pricing equilibrium should be familiar from the model of quality upgrading in chapter 4 and subsequently.

The final market structure that we need to consider is one where two or more Southern producers have imitated the same Northern brand. This creates another situation of Bertrand competition that leaves each producer without operating profits. Since we assume that learning is costly for every successive imitator, it will not pay for a Southern entrepreneur to become the second local producer of any variety.

We turn next to the innovation and imitation activities. In the North product development proceeds as before. The knowledge capital stock is given by $K_n = n$ (see [3.22]) and new blueprints require a/K_n units of labor. There are no barriers to entry into R&D, so value maximization implies that

$$v^N \leq \frac{w^N a}{n}, \qquad \text{with equality whenever } \dot{n} > 0, \tag{11.5}$$

where v^N is the value of a Northern brand that has not been copied.

We assume that the South does not innovate. This is in keeping with the stylized fact that most new products are designed and developed in high-income countries.[7] At the same time we treat imitation as an investment activity similar to new product development. In reality imitation requires managerial talent, scientists, and technicians, much like any other type of research. Pack and Westphal (1976, p. 105), for example, describe case studies of firms in less developed countries that have gained mastery over products and processes that are new to their local economies. They note that such learning requires "effort to apply existing knowledge in new circumstances," and that the effort takes the form of "investment in technological capability."[8] We assume here that an entrepreneur in the South can gain the ability to produce an existing variety by devoting a_m/K_m units of

7. If, instead of merely ruling out Southern innovation, we had wished to derive its absence from more primitive assumptions, we could have done so in one of three ways. First, we could have assumed that even with comparable stocks of knowledge, researchers in the South would require more labor to invent new goods than researchers in the North. In other words, we could have endowed the North with a comparative advantage in product development. Second, we could have posited the existence of location specific knowledge capital, and supposed that $K_n^S \ll K_n^N$. Then the North's "head start" in science and technology would be perpetuated in the long run (see chapter 8). Finally, we could have assumed that the North and the South are endowed with different primary inputs (e.g., Northern labor might be skilled, Southern labor not), and that the Northern factor is the one that performs better in the research lab. Any one of these approaches would yield an equilibrium similar to the one described below.

8. In the survey cited above, Mansfield et al. (1981) found that copying costs averaged 65 percent of the cost of the original innovation.

labor to the task of imitation. Here K_m represents a stock of knowledge capital in the South that is useful in assimilating and adapting foreign technologies.

The South accumulates public knowledge due to spillovers from local investments in technology. The knowledge stock K_m varies with cumulative experience in imitation, which is measured by n^S, the number of technologies that the South has already acquired. The productivity of Southern imitators might also depend upon the number of products n^N that Northern firms are uniquely able to produce. There are two reasons why this might be so. First, n^N measures a body of research that has been carried out in the North but not yet assimilated by the South. If some technical information spills across international borders, then the novel Northern research projects might contribute to the South's stock of general knowledge. Second, it might be relatively easier for a Southern entrepreneur to copy a Northern product when the number of potential targets is larger. In the main text we concentrate on the simplest specification that excludes international knowledge spillovers and ignores any effect of the size of the target group on the cost of imitation. We posit the linear relationship

$$K_m = n^S. \tag{11.6}$$

An appendix treats the more general case with $K_m = K_m(n^S, n^N)$.

Southern entrepreneurs can enter freely into the activity of imitation. Entrepreneurs decide how many products to copy and which ones. Since all clone products yield identical profits, we will assume that imitators choose randomly from among the stock of n^N Northern products that have not previously been copied. Optimization with respect to the scale of investment implies that

$$v^S \le \frac{w^S a_m}{n^S}, \qquad \text{with equality whenever } \dot{n}^S > 0, \tag{11.7}$$

where v^S is the value of a typical Southern brand. This relationship, like the analog for innovation (11.5), limits the value of a firm to the cost of market entry.

Our next task is to relate the returns on different assets. Once a Southern firm has mastered the technology for some product, it earns an infinite stream of oligopoly profits. The owners of the firm collect profits $\pi^S dt$ in a time interval of length dt and also realize a capital gain (or loss) of $\dot{v}^S dt$. The total return on equity claims must equal the opportunity cost, r^S of the invested capital, which implies the no-arbitrage condition

$$\frac{\pi^S}{v^S} + \frac{\dot{v}^S}{v^S} = r^S. \tag{11.8}$$

A Northern firm holding the blueprint for a product that has not yet been copied earns profits $\pi^N dt$ during an interval of length dt. This firm faces an ongoing risk that its product will be selected by a Southern entrepreneur as the target for imitation. In an interval of length dt, $\dot{n}^S dt$ products will be copied. With random selection a given firm will lose its monopoly position during such an interval with probability $\dot{n}^S dt/n^N$. In the event that this occurs, the owners of the firm suffer a capital loss of size v^N. Otherwise, they gain (or lose) $\dot{v}^N dt$. It follows that the total expected return on shares in a Northern firm equals

$$\pi^N dt - \frac{\dot{n}^S dt}{n^N} v^N + \left(1 - \frac{\dot{n}^S dt}{n^N}\right) \dot{v}^N dt.$$

We equate this to the return on a loan of size v^N, divide the resulting equation by $v^N dt$, and take the limit as dt becomes small to derive

$$\frac{\pi^N}{v^N} + \frac{\dot{v}^N}{v^N} - \frac{\dot{n}^S}{n^N} = r^N, \tag{11.9}$$

where r^N is the yield on a Northern bond. This no-arbitrage condition is similar to the one that applies in our model of quality upgrading where producers similarly face an ongoing risk of displacement from the market.

Finally, we require that all factor markets clear. From (3.3) we calculate per brand sales for firms located in each country. This gives

$$x^i = \frac{(p^i)^{-\varepsilon}}{n^S(p^S)^{1-\varepsilon} + n^N(p^N)^{1-\varepsilon}}, \qquad i = S, N. \tag{11.10}$$

In the North manufacturing enterprises demand $n^N x^N$ units of labor, while $a\dot{n}/n$ units are employed in research. Labor market equilibrium requires that

$$\frac{a}{n}\dot{n} + n^N x^N = L^N, \tag{11.11}$$

where L^N is the supply of labor in the North. Similarly $n^S x^S$ units of Southern labor are used in manufacturing, while $a_m \dot{n}^S/K_m = a_m \dot{n}^S/n^S$ units are engaged in imitation. Market clearing implies that

$$\frac{a_m}{n^S}\dot{n}^S + n^S x^S = L^S, \tag{11.12}$$

where L^S is the size of the Southern labor force.

11.2 Steady-State Equilibrium

We solve for a steady-state equilibrium with a fixed intersectoral allocation of labor in each country. Let $\xi^i \equiv n^i/n$, $i = N, S$, be the share of region i in the total number of differentiated products. In the long run ξ^N and ξ^S must approach constants. This requires convergence in the growth rates of the number of varieties manufactured in each region; that is, $g^N = g^S$, where $g^i \equiv \dot{n}^i/n^i$, $i = N, S$. Since $n = n^N + n^S$, we have $g = \xi^N g^N + \xi^S g^S$. It follows that $g = g^N = g^S$ in a steady state.

It proves useful to define the rate of imitation $m \equiv \dot{n}^S/n^N$. This variable represents the proportion of Northern products that are copied per unit of time. From the definitions $m = g^S\xi^S/(1 - \xi^S)$. In the steady state, when $g^S = g$,

$$\xi^S = \frac{m}{g + m}. \tag{11.13}$$

The higher the rate of imitation relative to the rate of innovation, the larger is the fraction of varieties manufactured in the South in the long run.

We can develop a diagrammatic representation of the steady state. It will be necessary of course to distinguish between the wide-gap and narrow-gap cases. But note that this distinction matters only for the behavior of firms in the South. We begin our analysis by deriving a relationship that reflects market clearing in the North and that is applicable therefore to either regime.

As before, it turns out that the aggregate value of the Northern stock market is constant in the steady state. That is, the value of the typical firm falls at the rate of product development. This, plus the fact that $r^N = \rho$ in the long run, allows us to write the steady-state, no-arbitrage condition (11.9) as

$$\frac{\pi^N}{v^N} = \rho + g + m. \tag{11.14}$$

Substituting the pricing equation (11.1) and the labor-market-clearing condition (11.11) into the expression for profits (11.2), we find that

$$\pi^N = \frac{(1 - \alpha)w^N}{\alpha(1 - \xi^S)n}(L^N - ag). \tag{11.15}$$

Then, combining (11.13), (11.14), (11.15), and the free-entry condition (11.5), we have (for the case of $g > 0$) the following relationship between

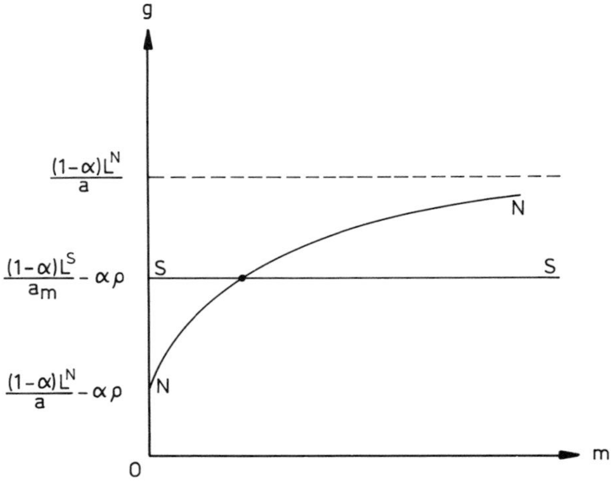

Figure 11.2

the long-run rates of innovation and imitation that is implied by market clearing in the North:

$$\frac{1-\alpha}{\alpha}\left(\frac{L^N}{a} - g\right)\frac{g+m}{g} = \rho + g + m. \tag{11.16}$$

This equation is depicted by the curve *NN* in figure 11.2.

The shape of *NN* is critical to the analysis that follows. Let us discuss therefore why it slopes upward. Comparing steady states with different rates of innovation, the one with the larger g has a higher real cost of capital (right-hand side of [11.16]) because the rate of capital loss for the typical Northern firm is higher in this case. At the same time the profit rate is lower in the equilibrium with the higher g (see [11.15]) because sales per brand are smaller. This is so for two reasons. Greater innovation means more employment in R&D, which leaves fewer workers for manufacturing. And it means a larger steady-state share of the North in the total number of varieties (smaller ξ^S), which implies that the labor employed in manufacturing will be spread more thinly. Now we compare two steady states with different rates of imitation. The one with the larger m has the higher real cost of capital because an increase in the rate of imitation raises the risk of market displacement for the typical Northern firm. On the other hand, an increase in m raises the typical firm's profit rate. The higher the rate of imitation, the smaller is the steady-state share of products manufactured in the North (see [11.13]) and so the greater are the sales of each Northern firm for a given total number of products n. With the CES specification of demand, it turns out that the effect of m on the profit rate is proportionately greater than the effect on the cost of capital. It follows that a higher rate of innovation must be matched by a *higher* rate of imitation in order to preserve equality between the two sides of equation (11.16).

It is necessary now to distinguish between the alternative types of equilibria. We discuss the wide-gap and narrow-gap cases in turn and postpone until section 11.4 a discussion of the conditions that give rise to each regime.

Wide-Gap Equilibrium

In a wide-gap equilibrium Southern firms charge their monopoly price, ignoring potential competition from Northern innovators. Equation (11.4b) gives the profits of the typical Southern firm. After combining this equation with the pricing formula (11.3b), the labor-market-clearing condition (11.12), and $g^S = g$, profits can be expressed as

$$\pi^S = \frac{(1-\alpha)w^S}{\alpha n^S}(L^S - a_m g). \qquad (11.17)$$

In a steady state the aggregate value of all Southern firms, like that of Northern firms, remains constant. The value of the typical Southern brand falls at the rate $g^S = g$. Using this fact together with the free-entry condition (11.7), the expression for profits (11.17), and $r^S = \rho$, the no-arbitrage condition (11.8) that applies in a long-run equilibrium with ongoing imitation becomes

$$\frac{1-\alpha}{\alpha}\left(\frac{L^S}{a_m} - g\right) = \rho + g, \qquad \text{in the wide-gap case.} \qquad (11.18)$$

This equation, which is analogous to (11.16), gives combinations of the long-run rates of innovation and imitation that are consistent with pricing behavior, the absence of arbitrage opportunities, and labor market clearing in the South. The equation is depicted by the horizontal line *SS* in figure 11.2. The line is horizontal because a change in g alters both the profit rate (because it changes employment in manufacturing, hence sales per firm) and the required return on capital (because it changes the steady-state rate of capital loss on a typical Southern firm), whereas a change in the rate of imitation does not affect either of these magnitudes. A rise in m does increase the share of products manufactured in the South, which causes profits per firm to shrink. But in the steady state per firm profits fall exactly in proportion to the decline in firm value, which results from the expansion of Southern knowledge (at given n) and thus the reduction in imitation costs.

When $L^N/a < L^S/a_m < L^N/a + \alpha\rho/(1-\alpha)$, the SS and NN curves intersect in the positive orthant.[9] Then, if the wage rates implied by the point of intersection satisfy the inequality requirements for a wide-gap equilibrium (an issue to which we will return in section 11.4), the intersection point represents a steady-state equilibrium with positive rates of innovation and imitation. Solving (11.18) for g, we find that

$$g = (1-\alpha)\frac{L^S}{a_m} - \alpha\rho. \tag{11.19}$$

Notice that in this case the long-run rate of innovation is proximately determined by conditions in the South. This result rests on the particular specification of Southern knowledge accumulation that we have used. In appendix A11.1 we show that the SS curve is not horizontal when the Southern stock of knowledge capital takes the more general form $K_m = K_m(n^S, n^N)$. Then structural features of both the North and South interact to determine the long-run innovation rate.

Narrow-Gap Equilibrium

In the narrow-gap case Southern firms price their goods just low enough to prevent their Northern rivals from entering the market. This case arises when the difference across regions in the cost of manufacturing is not too large. Dividing one labor-market-clearing condition (11.11) by the other (11.12) and using $g^S = g$, we find that

$$\frac{x^N}{x^S} = \frac{\xi^S}{1-\xi^S}\left(\frac{L^N - ag}{L^S - a_m g}\right). \tag{11.20}$$

The expression for demand in (11.10) allows us to express relative sales as a function of relative prices; that is, $x^N/x^S = (p^S/p^N)^\varepsilon$. But $p^S/p^N = \alpha$, by the pricing relations (11.1) and (11.3a) that apply in the narrow-gap case. Substituting these expressions into (11.20) and noting that the steady-state relationship (11.13) implies that $\xi^S/(1-\xi^S) = m/g$, we obtain

9. The requirement for such an intersection is less restrictive in the case in which the knowledge capital stock in the South varies with the number of products produced by the North; see appendix A11.1.

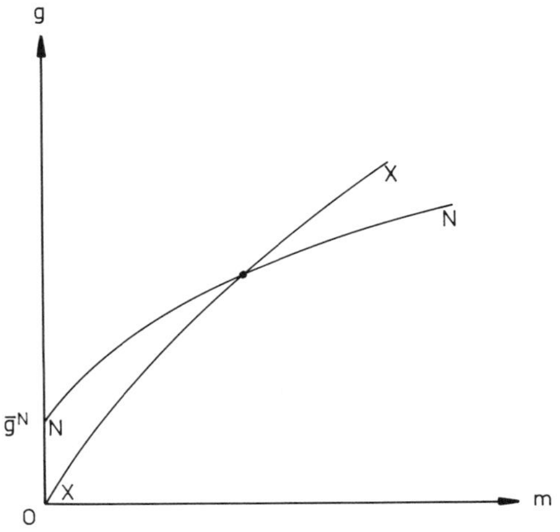

Figure 11.3

$$\alpha^{\varepsilon} = \frac{m}{g}\left(\frac{L^N - ag}{L^S - a_m g}\right), \qquad \text{in the narrow-gap case.} \qquad (11.21)$$

In figure 11.3 we have reproduced the *NN* curve, which applies also to the narrow-gap case. The curve *XX* represents equation (11.21). It depicts combinations of the rates of innovation and imitation that are consistent with the clearing of product and labor markets in each region. The curve slopes upward because the rates of imitation and innovation have opposing implications for the relative outputs of the typical Northern and Southern brands, whereas the relative sales are fixed on the demand side by the constancy of relative prices ($p^S/p^N = \alpha$).[10] We show in appendix A11.2 that the *XX* curve intersects the *NN* curve exactly once, and that it does so from below. Provided that the wage rates associated with the point of intersection satisfy $w^S > \alpha w^N$, this point represents a narrow-gap equilibrium.

In the next section we will examine how structural features of the world economy affect steady-state outcomes in an equilibrium with innovation and imitation. The discussion there treats separately the wide-gap and narrow-gap cases. In section 11.4 we address the issue of what parame-

10. It is easy to check that the right-hand side of (11.21) decreases with g, provided that $L^S/a_m > L^N/a$. We will see below that this latter condition is necessary for the narrow-gap case to arise.

ters and policies give rise to each type of equilibrium. Since the applicability of either regime depends on relative manufacturing costs, our analysis in section 11.4 focuses on the determination of relative wage rates. As such, the analysis is interesting in its own right.

11.3 Determinants of Innovation and Imitation

In successive subsections we consider how long-run rates of innovation, imitation, and growth in the two regions of the world economy are affected by (1) participation in international trade, (2) the sizes of the two trading blocs, and (3) the extent to which governments use policies to promote research activity.

International Integration

What are the implications of international trade for growth rates in countries that are at different stages in their economic development? And how does the exposure to imitation by the South affect the incentives to innovate in the North? We can answer these questions by comparing the equilibrium described above with the autarky outcomes for the individual regions.

Let us begin with the North. In the absence of trade, this region introduces new products at the rate $\bar{g}^N$, where (see [3.28]),

$$\bar{g}^N = (1 - \alpha)\frac{L^N}{a} - \alpha\rho. \tag{11.22}$$

We recognize this as the point of intersection of the *NN* curve in figure 11.2 (or figure 11.3) with the vertical axis. In other words, the growth rate of the North would be the same in free trade as it is under autarky if the former equilibrium happened to be characterized by $m = 0$. When the rate of imitation instead is positive, the trade equilibrium lies along the *NN* curve, above and to the right of its intersection with the vertical axis. It follows that the North grows faster when it trades with the South than when it remains economically isolated.

Clearly the explanation for this finding is the same as that for the shape of the *NN* curve. Exposure to imitation shortens the expected duration of monopoly rents for the typical Northern innovator. But, in the equilibrium with imitation, Northern producers enjoy higher rates of profits during their tenure as monopolists. Each surviving Northern firm benefits when a Southern producer takes over manufacturing from a rival Northern brand because it then is able to hire some of the laid-off workers and thereby expand its sales and profits. And, as we have seen, the positive effect of imitation on the profit rate outweighs the adverse effect on the cost of capital.

In the South, imitation is the vehicle for technological progress. Real output grows in an equilibrium with imitation and trade because new technologies are being assimilated from the North. If the South has little or no capacity to invent new products on its own, then (trivially) the South grows faster with imitation and trade than without. But even if the South could develop varieties from scratch, it is quite likely to grow faster in the trade equilibrium. In the wide-gap case, for example, new products are introduced to the economy at the rate $g^S = g$, where g is given in (11.19). Real output grows at the rate $g^S(1-\alpha)/\alpha$. By contrast, the autarky rate of innovation in the South, assuming that it had the ability to invent new goods, would be given by

$$\bar{g}^S = (1-\alpha)\frac{L^S}{a^S} - \alpha\rho, \tag{11.23}$$

where a^S is a parameter analogous to a, reflecting the productivity of Southern labor in product development. Surely $a^S > a^m$; that is, with a comparable stock of knowledge capital, more labor is needed to invent a new good than to copy an existing one. Then $g^S > \bar{g}^S$. The potential for imitation allows the South to introduce new varieties at lesser resource cost than if it had to develop the varieties from scratch. This resource savings translates into more rapid innovation and faster growth.

The narrow-gap case requires a more subtle analysis. But ultimately the conclusions are similar. In the trade equilibrium the number of products manufactured by the South grows at the rate $g^S = g$, where g now is the solution to (11.16) and (11.21). More transparent perhaps is the expression that comes from combining the pricing relation (11.3a), the expression for profits (11.4a), the free entry condition (11.7), the no-arbitrage condition (11.8), and the labor-market-clearing condition (11.11). Noting that $r^S = \rho$ and that $\dot{v}^S/v^S = -g^S$ in a steady state, this combination yields

$$g^S = \left(1 - \frac{w^S}{w^N}\right)\frac{L^S}{a_m} - \left(\frac{w^S}{w^N}\right)\rho. \tag{11.24}$$

Since $w^S/w^N > \alpha$ in a narrow-gap equilibrium, $g^S < (1-\alpha)L^S/a_m - \alpha\rho$. Then, if the input requirements for imitation are not very different from the input requirements for product development in the South (i.e., $a_m \approx a^S$), it seems that the region could grow less rapidly with trade than in autarky.

But there are good reasons to doubt the likelihood of this outcome. If it were true that $\bar{g}^S > g^S$, it must also be the case that $\bar{g}^S > \bar{g}^N$; that is, the autarky rate of innovation in the South would exceed that in the North.[11] This requires $L^S/a^S > L^N/a$. If the South indeed were larger than the North in this sense, a free trade equilibrium might well have the South active in product development. This would certainly be the outcome with international spillovers of general knowledge capital (see section 9.2). Such an outcome might also obtain in the absence of such spillovers if the North's initial lead in product development were not too large. Since we have assumed above that the South undertakes no innovation, we require either that the North has a greater capacity for inventing new goods in autarky or that the South initially is far behind in terms of its stock of knowledge capital and lacks the ability to exploit an international pool of knowledge in order to catch up. Only in the latter situation can we construct an example where trade with the North retards long-run growth in the South, and then only if the resource requirements for inventing new goods are not very much greater than those for copying existing varieties. Surely the most plausible scenario has the South benefiting from the opportunity to engage in imitation.

It is interesting to consider what the growth rate in the South would be if entrepreneurs there were able to copy Northern products without the country actually engaging in international trade. With imitation but no commodity exchange, the number of products available in the South grows in the long run at the rate

$$\tilde{g}^S = (1 - \alpha)\frac{L^S}{a_m} - \alpha\rho. \tag{11.25}$$

This rate of growth in technological capability matches the one that the region achieves in a wide-gap equilibrium (compare [11.19]) and exceeds the rate that is achieved in a narrow-gap equilibrium (compare [11.24], noting that $w^S/w^N > \alpha$). We see that it is the transfer of technology associated with the opening of trade, and not the integration of product markets per se, that contributes to a more rapid pace of progress in the South. There is of course a strong parallel between this finding and similar ones in chapter 9 concerning the growth effects of trade between large, innovating economies.

11. The North innovates more rapidly with trade than without. So $g > \bar{g}^N$. Since $g^S = g$ in the steady state, $\bar{g}^S > g^S$ implies that $\bar{g}^S > \bar{g}^N$.

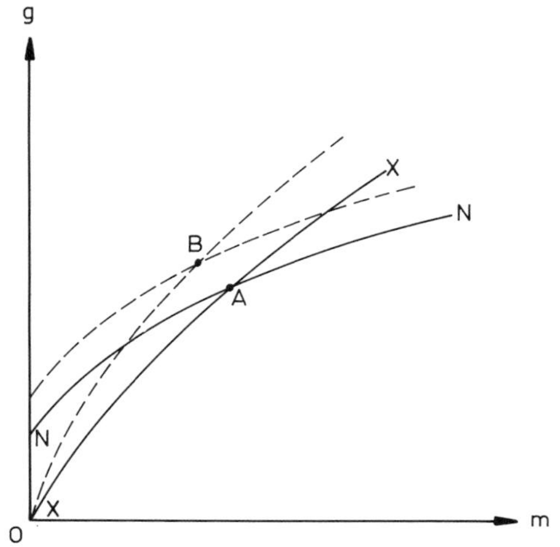

Figure 11.4

Region Size

We ask now how the sizes of the two regions influence the long-run rates of imitation and innovation. Referring back to figure 11.2, an increase in the labor force of the North shifts the *NN* curve upward, while leaving the *SS* line in place. The equilibrium point shifts inward along the latter schedule. We conclude that the size of the North has no bearing on the long-run rate of innovation in a wide-gap equilibrium.[12] A larger North does imply a lower rate of imitation and a greater steady-state share of the North in the total number of differentiated products (see [11.13]).

In the narrow-gap case an increase in L^N shifts both the *NN* and the *XX* curves up and to the left, as illustrated in figure 11.4. From the initial equilibrium point at *A*, the *NN* curve shifts to the left by more.[13] It follows that the rate of innovation is higher at the new equilibrium point *B* than at the old. The rate of imitation declines with an expansion in the size of the North, just as it does in the wide-gap case. This is because the upward shift

12. We emphasize again that this result depends critically on the particular production function for knowledge capital in the South that we have specified in (11.6). In the appendix we show that an increase in L^N generally increases the equilibrium rate of innovation when $K_m = K_m(n^S, n^N)$, for an arbitrary linearly homogeneous function, $K_m(\cdot)$.

13. The *XX* curve shifts to the left by $m/(L^N - ag)$ per unit increase in L^N. Using (11.16), this shift equals $(1 - \alpha)(g + m)m/a\alpha g(g + m + \rho)$. The leftward shift in the *NN* curve amounts to $(1 - \alpha)(g + m)^2/\alpha g\rho$ per unit increase in L^N, which is larger.

of the XX curve relative to the initial point of equilibrium exceeds that of the NN curve.[14]

An expansion in the size of the South causes the SS curve in figure 11.2 to shift up. The NN curve is not affected. Clearly the long-run rates of innovation and imitation both rise in the wide-gap case. When the labor force of the South expands, the region devotes more resources to imitation and also manufactures a greater share of the world's differentiated varieties. The increase in the rate of imitation boosts the Northern profit rate by relatively more than it raises the real cost of capital. This strengthens the incentives for product development, and so the innovation rate rises.

Similar results apply in the narrow-gap case. When L^S increases, the XX curve in figure 11.3 shifts down and to the right. The equilibrium moves to a higher point along the original NN curve. Again, the rates of imitation and innovation both increase. Since the rate of imitation grows proportionately more (i.e., m/g rises), the fraction of the total number of varieties manufactured in the South rises in the long run.[15]

Government Policy

Let us consider now the long-run effects of policies that the governments might use to encourage local accumulation of knowledge. The most direct way for a government to promote learning would be for it to subsidize the cost of this activity. A research subsidy in the North would be relatively straightforward to implement. In the South the government would need to share in the expense of a diverse set of activities, including reverse engineering, the adaptation of foreign technologies to local conditions, and so forth. An alternative approach that might have similar consequences would involve a relaxation of patent protection laws as applied to foreign intellectual property. Such a change in enforcement practice would encourage imitation by reducing the cost to a Southern entrepreneur of inventing around existing patents.

14. From (11.21) we calculate that the vertical shift in the XX curve per unit increase in L^N exceeds $1/ag$. From (11.16) we find that the NN curve shifts up by less than this amount.

15. Differentiating (11.16) totally, we find that

$$\frac{(1-\alpha)(L^N - ag)}{\alpha ag}(\hat{m} - \hat{g}) = \left[1 + \frac{(1-\alpha)(g+m)}{\alpha g}\right]dg + dm,$$

where $\hat{m} = dm/m$ and $\hat{g} = dg/g$. Thus m/g rise as we move up and to the right along a given NN curve.

We use ϕ^N to denote the fraction of product development costs borne by the government of the North. With this subsidy in place, the private cost of introducing a new variety becomes $w^N(1 - \phi^N)a/n$. Since the value of a Northern firm cannot exceed this amount, we have a new expression for v^N to use in computing the profit rate in (11.14). This gives a modified equation for the *NN* curve, which now takes the form

$$\frac{1}{1-\phi^N}\frac{1-\alpha}{\alpha}\left(\frac{L^N}{a} - g\right)\frac{g+m}{g} = \rho + g + m. \tag{11.16$'$}$$

We see from (11.16′) that an increase in the subsidy rate shifts the *NN* curve up and to the left. That is, for a given rate of imitation, a higher rate of innovation is needed to maintain parity between the profit rate and the cost of capital. Neither the *SS* curve of the wide-gap case nor the *XX* curve of the narrow-gap case is affected by the subsidy.

In the wide-gap case a subsidy shifts the equilibrium point inward along the *SS* curve. The steady-state rate of imitation falls, but the rate of innovation remains unchanged. The policy causes the North to accumulate a greater share of the total number of differentiated products. This implies a lower *rate* of imitation for any given allocation of resources to this activity in the South. The fall in m reduces the profitability of R&D in the North, offsetting the direct stimulus to innovation provided by the subsidy. Since a particular value for g is required for long-run market clearing and the absence of arbitrage opportunities in the South, the opposing influences on the long-run incentives for product development ultimately cancel. Thus the pace of innovation rate returns to its pre-subsidy rate.

In the narrow-gap regime the subsidy shifts the equilibrium point up and to the right along a fixed *XX* curve. In this case the subsidy encourages product development in the long run. Interestingly the effect of the subsidy on the rate of imitation is just the opposite from that in the wide-gap case.

We turn next to policies that might be used to promote learning in the South. Suppose that policy reduces the private cost of imitation by the fraction ϕ^S. This might be the result of a direct subsidy to imitators, or it might reflect an easing of patent enforcement policy. In any event the value of the typical firm is reduced when the cost of imitation falls, and so the equation for the *SS* curve becomes

$$\frac{1}{1-\phi^S}\frac{1-\alpha}{\alpha}\left(\frac{L^S}{a_m} - g\right) = \rho + g. \tag{11.18$'$}$$

The *XX* and *NN* curves remain as before.

If the world economy begins in a wide-gap equilibrium, then a policy-induced fall in private cost of imitation shifts the *SS* curve up along a fixed *NN* curve. This causes an increase in both the rate of imitation and the rate of innovation. Imitation activity responds to the cost reduction. Then entrepreneurs in the North expand their research efforts because the more rapid pace of copying implies greater expected profits for the typical new variety.

In a narrow-gap equilibrium the fall in private imitation costs has no lasting impact on research activities in either country. In such an equilibrium the terms of trade that result from firms' strategic interaction are independent of relative wages. Then so too are the relative sales of typical Northern and Southern brands. This fixes a relationship between m and g that is independent of investment incentives in the South (see [11.21]). The *NN* curve is another such relationship, inasmuch as it derives only from market conditions in the North. It follows that structural features outside the research sector of the South fully determine both m and g, and in fact the complete (long-run) allocation of resources in both countries. In the long run a change in the cost of imitation affects only relative wages.

We might think to investigate other forms of government intervention besides technology policy. Production subsidies and trade instruments quickly come to mind. However, these policies do not influence the allocation of resources here (see Grossman and Helpman 1991d), much as production subsidies failed to affect innovation in the one-sector model of chapter 3. In a one-sector economy policies that seek to promote manufacturing are fully offset by changes in factor rewards. Such policies *would* have a role to play in determining growth rates in a world economy with two manufacturing sectors. Then the analysis could proceed along similar lines to our study of trade and industrial policies in chapter 10. But the task of introducing a second manufacturing sector proves cumbersome here and adds few insights to the previous analysis. We have chosen therefore to leave this extension to the interested reader.

11.4 Determinants of Relative Wages

We have put off until now any discussion of the conditions that give rise to one type of equilibrium or the other. Recall that the applicability of the wide-gap case or the narrow-gap case hinges on relative manufacturing costs in the two regions. When the cost differential is large, firms in the South can set monopoly prices without fear of competition from Northern rivals. Smaller cost differentials force Southern firms to limit price in order to guarantee their place in the market. These considerations lead us to examine the economic forces that determine relative wages.

Our starting point is equation (11.20), which expresses the ratio of the outputs of typical producers in the North and the South as a function of the shares of these regions in the total number of varieties and the allocation of labor to manufacturing in each one. This equation applies to both equilibrium regimes. Combining it with (11.13) and the relationship between relative demands and relative prices that is implied by (11.10), we have

$$\left(\frac{p^S}{p^N}\right)^{\varepsilon} = \frac{m}{g}\left(\frac{L^N - ag}{L^S - a_m g}\right). \tag{11.26}$$

Now we conjecture the existence of a wide-gap equilibrium and investigate the consistency of this hypothesis. In a wide-gap equilibrium $p^S/p^N = \omega$, where $\omega \equiv w^S/w^N$ is the relative wage of the South compared to that of the North. Substituting for the terms of trade in (11.26), we find that

$$\omega^{\varepsilon} = \frac{m}{g}\left(\frac{L^N - ag}{L^S - a_m g}\right). \tag{11.27}$$

Figure 11.5 shows two curves in (m, g) space, labeled $\omega^1\omega^1$ and $\omega^2\omega^2$, along which the relative wage rates determined by (11.27) are equal to the constants ω_1 and ω_2, respectively. From (11.27) we see that ω rises when m is increased while g is held constant. Therefore $\omega_2 > \omega_1$. Note that the curves lie on opposite sides of the *XX* schedule defined by (11.21). It follows that $\omega_2 > \alpha$ and $\omega_1 < \alpha$.

Suppose that the *SS* curve had the location represented by the curve labeled S^1S^1. This curve intersects the *NN* curve at the point *A*.[16] Point *A*, which is our candidate for a wide-gap equilibrium, implies a relative wage of ω_1. Since this relative wage satisfies the requirement for the wide-gap case (i.e., that $w^S < \alpha w^N$, or $\omega < \alpha$), our hypothesis that there exists a wide-gap equilibrium would be confirmed in this case. Now suppose that the *SS* curve instead were represented by S^2S^2, which intersects the *NN* curve at point *B*. Since the implied relative wage this time is ω_2, the requirement for the wide-gap case would be violated. Evidently a wide-gap equilibrium exists if and only if the *SS* curve intersects the *NN* curve below the point of intersection of the latter curve with the *XX* schedule.

16. We have drawn the *NN* curve to be flatter than every iso-wage curve at their common points of intersection. In appendix A11.2 we show that this must be the case.

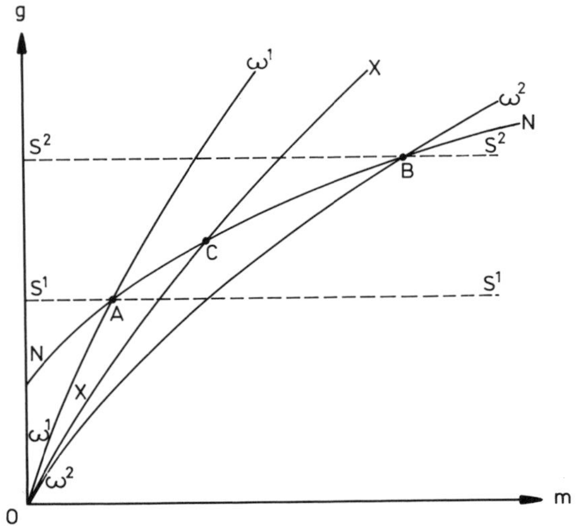

Figure 11.5

Next we conjecture that there exists a narrow-gap equilibrium. In the event relative wages are given not by (11.27) but rather by (11.24). Noting that $g^S = g$ in a steady-state equilibrium, we can determine ω implicitly from

$$g = (1 - \omega)\frac{L^S}{a_m} - \omega\rho. \tag{11.28}$$

Clearly the iso-relative-wage loci are horizontal lines in this case. Suppose once again that S^1S^1 gave the location of the SS curve. Point C at the intersection of XX and NN would be our candidate for a narrow-gap equilibrium. But this point lies above point A, which (by [11.19]) has $g = (1 - \alpha)L^S/a_m - \alpha\rho$. It follows that $\omega < \alpha$ at point C if the latter is taken to represent a narrow-gap equilibrium. But this violates the requirements of the narrow-gap case. Consequently our hypothesis that there exists a narrow-gap equilibrium must be rejected for this SS curve.

We return finally to a scenario in which S^2S^2 depicts the SS schedule. The candidate equilibrium at point C now falls below the intersection of the SS line and the NN curve at B. The latter point again has $g = (1 - \alpha)L^S/a_m - \alpha\rho$ (but of course for different values of the parameters than the ones that gave rise to S^1S^1). So in this case the relative wage at C is greater than α. The condition for the existence of a narrow-gap equilibrium is satisfied in this case, and point C represents such an equilibrium.

To summarize, a wide-gap equilibrium exists if and only if the intersection of the SS curve and the NN curve falls *below* the intersection of the NN curve with the XX curve, whereas a narrow-gap equilibrium exists if and only if the former intersection point lies *above* the latter intersection point.[17] We are left with the task of relating the locations of the various curves to the underlying structural parameters.

For the sake of brevity, we analyze only two of the many determinants of relative wage rates. These are the sizes of the two regions and the technology policies of the two governments. Consider first the size of the labor force in the South. An increase in L^S shifts the SS curve upward and the XX curve down and to the right. The NN curve is not affected. The intersections of NN with both the SS and XX schedules move up, but the former point moves up by more.[18] It follows that an expansion in the size of the South makes a narrow-gap outcome more likely.

We can readily calculate the effects of an increase in L^S on the relative wage within each regime. From (11.27) we see that there are three potential channels of influence in the wide-gap case. First, there is the direct effect of L^S on relative wages that comes about due to the change in the relative supplies of the two types of labor. Through this channel an increase in L^S tends to depress the relative wage of the South. Second, there is an effect that comes about due to any changes in the demands for labor in the two research sectors. When the rate of innovation increases by dg, labor demand in the North grows by $a\,dg$, while that in the South expands by $a_m dg$. Finally, there is an effect associated with the change in the relative numbers of products manufactured in each region ($n^S/n^N = \xi^S/\xi^N = m/g$). When m/g rises, the relative demand for labor in the South increases, ceteris paribus, as a result of the relative expansion in the size of the South's manufacturing sector. This tends to push up wages in the South relative to those in the North.

17. If $L^S/a_m < L^N/a$, the SS curve lies everywhere below the NN curve. Then there exists no steady state with ongoing imitation by the South. Instead, the equilibrium has the South imitating for a while, then producing a fixed set of goods. Recall that $L^S/a_m > L^N/a$ is necessary and sufficient for the XX curve to slope upward. It follows that this condition will be satisfied in any equilibrium with ongoing imitation.

18. Using (11.16) and (11.21), we can calculate the upward movement of the intersection point of XX and NN. Noting (11.13), this gives

$$\frac{dg}{dL^S} = \frac{\rho a_m(\xi^N)^2\alpha^{\varepsilon+1}}{\rho a_m(\xi^N)^2\alpha^{\varepsilon+1} + L^N - ag - \xi^N\xi^S\alpha a\rho}.$$

From (11.19) we see that the SS line moves up by $(1-\alpha)/a_m$ for every unit increase in L^S. It is straightforward to show, using (11.16), (11.21), and $L^S/a_m > L^N/a$, that the latter shift is greater.

We have already seen that an expansion in the size of the South increases the rates of imitation and innovation, and expands the fraction of differentiated products that are manufactured in the South. Thus the various influences on the relative wage are in opposition to one another. To resolve the conflict, we substitute (11.16) and (11.18) into (11.27) to derive

$$\omega^{\varepsilon} = \frac{am(\rho + g + m)}{a_m(g + m)(\rho + g)}. \tag{11.29}$$

The right-hand side of (11.29) increases when m, g, and m/g all rise. We conclude that an expansion in the size of the South boosts that region's relative wage, in a wide-gap equilibrium. It turns out that the same result applies to the narrow-gap case.[19]

We inquire next into the effects of changes in the size of the North. An increase in L^N shifts both the *NN* and *XX* curves up and to the left. The point of intersection of these two curves rises (see figure 11.4), while the *SS* curve remains in place. Thus the likelihood of a wide-gap equilibrium increases. In such an equilibrium growth in L^N reduces m but has no effect on g. Using (11.29), it is easy to show that the relative wage of the South must decline. In other words, the direct effect of the increase in the supply of Northern labor is more than offset by the induced shift in the relative demand for labor caused by the expansion in the share of differentiated products emanating from the North. Similarly in the narrow-gap case an increase in L^N shrinks the relative wage of the South. This can be established directly from (11.28) after noting that $dg/dL^N > 0$ in this regime.

We have found then that the long-run relative wage of a region varies directly with the size of that region and inversely with the size of its trade partner. This result may be surprising to readers versed in the neoclassical growth model, and it stands in sharp contrast to the findings reported by Krugman (1979). Krugman investigated the effects of country size on relative factor rewards in a dynamic model with constant and exogenous rates of innovation and imitation. In that context the only channel of influence is what we have called the direct effect of relative supplies on relative factor rewards. But in our analysis we have allowed the rates of innovation and imitation to adjust to any changes in resource supplies. We find that the indirect effects on factor demands induced by these changes in rates of innovation and imitation outweigh the direct

19. This can be established by substituting the expression for dg/dL^S in footnote 18 into the total differential of (11.28).

effects in the long run. The fact that countries enjoy relatively higher wages when they are of relatively larger size reflects the dynamic scale economies that are present in our model.

We conclude this chapter by examining how technology policies influence relative factor rewards. An R&D subsidy in the North shifts the *NN* curve up and to the left, without affecting either the *SS* or the *XX* curve. This makes the realization of a wide-gap equilibrium more probable. In a wide-gap equilibrium the subsidy reduces the rate of imitation (the long-run rate of innovation does not change), and so by (11.27) it reduces the relative wage of the South. The same is true in the narrow-gap case where the subsidy accelerates innovation. The result follows directly from inspection of (11.28). In the wide-gap case the rise in the relative wage of the North is due to the expansion in relative labor demand by Northern manufacturers. In the narrow-gap case it is the growth of the North's research sector that accounts for the relative increase in demand for Northern labor.

The relative wage effects of a policy-induced fall in the private costs of Southern imitation are the opposite of those described in the preceding paragraph. In the wide-gap case the *SS* schedule shifts upward. This moves the equilibrium up along a fixed *NN* curve. The new point of equilibrium falls on a lower iso-relative-wage curve (see figure 11.5). Recall that lower curves in the figure correspond to higher relative wages in the South. In the narrow-gap case we have seen that the Southern technology policy (i.e., a subsidy to imitation or a relaxation of laws protecting foreign intellectural property) affects neither the rate of innovation nor the rate of imitation in the long run. To find the effect on relative wages, we need to modify equation (11.28). When we derive this equation in the same manner as before, but recognize that $v^S = (1 - \phi^S)\omega\alpha_m$ due to the effects of policy, we find that

$$g^S = \frac{1 - \omega}{1 - \phi^S} \frac{L^S}{a_m} - \omega\rho. \tag{11.28'}$$

Since the steady-state rate of expansion in the set of Southern varieties does not change after the policy is introduced, the relative wage ω must rise in response to an increase in ϕ^S. We conclude that government policies to promote local learning activities improve the relative plight of workers in the policy-active country. This is true no matter whether the policy is undertaken by the innovating North or the imitating South.

This chapter has introduced imitation into our model of expanding product variety. We have studied a two-region world economy with an industrialized North and a middle-income South. In the former, more advanced region product development takes place just as in previous chapters. In the less advanced region, by contrast, entrepreneurs devote resources to the tasks of learning and adapting technologies that have been developed in the North. In this setting product imitation represents an alternative means of international dissemination of research results, one that is additional to any spillovers of general technical information that may occur.

Perhaps surprisingly, we find a positive feedback relationship between the processes of innovation and imitation. When the South copies Northern products, this reduces the expected duration of monopoly power for any Northern innovator. But the direct, adverse effect of imitation on the incentive to innovate is offset by an indirect, positive one. Imitation serves to thin the ranks of Northern competitors for any given firm. If production of competing brands moves offshore, surviving monopolists can hire more labor and produce more output than otherwise. For this reason imitation raises the profit rate for Northern firms during their stay in the market. We have found that the positive effect dominates the negative one in our model of expanding product variety. In other words, an increase in the rate of imitation raises ex ante expected profits for a typical new variety and so strengthens the incentive to innovate. This is a strong result. But it is one that relies heavily on the particulars of the specification, as we shall discover presently in chapter 12.

APPENDIX

A11.1 Accumulation of Knowledge Capital in the South

The main text dealt with a simple case where only local experience in imitation contributes to the South's stock of knowledge capital. In this appendix we analyze a more general case where imitators benefit also from having a larger stock of products in the North. As we noted in the text, productivity in Southern research might increase with n^N either because there are international spillovers of knowledge capital (i.e., the unique research projects in the North contribute to the understanding of scientific principles in the South) or because the costs of copying decline when there is a longer list of potential targets to choose from.

We replace (11.6) in the text by

$$K_m = K_m(n^S, n^N), \tag{A11.1}$$

for some $K_m(\cdot)$ that is linearly homogeneous and increasing in both arguments. With this new function free entry into imitation implies that

$$v^S \leq \frac{w^S a_m}{K_m(n^S, n^N)}, \tag{A11.2}$$

and the labor-market-clearing condition becomes

$$\frac{a_m}{K_m(n^S, n^N)} \dot{n}^N + n^S x^S = L^S. \tag{A11.3}$$

In a steady state in which $\dot{K}_m/K_m = \dot{n}^S/n^S = g$ and $r^S = \rho$, the South's no-arbitrage condition (11.8) its free entry condition (A11.2), its labor-market-clearing condition (A11.3), and its pricing and profit relations (11.3b) and (11.4b) imply that

$$\left(\frac{1-\alpha}{\alpha}\right)\left(\frac{L^S}{a_m}\right) K_m\left(1, \frac{g}{m}\right) = \rho + \frac{g}{\alpha} \quad \text{in the wide-gap case.} \tag{A11.4}$$

This is the general form of the *SS* curve, of which (11.18) is a special case.

The more general specification of $K_m(\cdot)$ does not affect the shape or location of the *NN* curve. Thus a wide-gap equilibrium can be represented in figure A11.1 by the intersection of this curve and one depicting (A11.4). In the figure we have drawn the latter curve (labeled *SS*) for the case in which $K_m(\cdot)$ has constant elasticities with respect to each of its arguments (i.e., it has a Cobb-Douglas form). In general, the *SS* curve slopes upward at points that have $g/\beta^N(\alpha\rho + g) < 1$, where β^N is the elasticity of $K_m(\cdot)$ with respect to n^N.

A sufficient condition for the *NN* curve to intersect the *SS* curve along a downward sloping portion of the latter curve is

$$(1-\alpha)\frac{L^N}{a} > \frac{\alpha\rho}{1-\beta^N}. \tag{A11.5}$$

This will be satisfied whenever the autarky rate of innovation is positive in

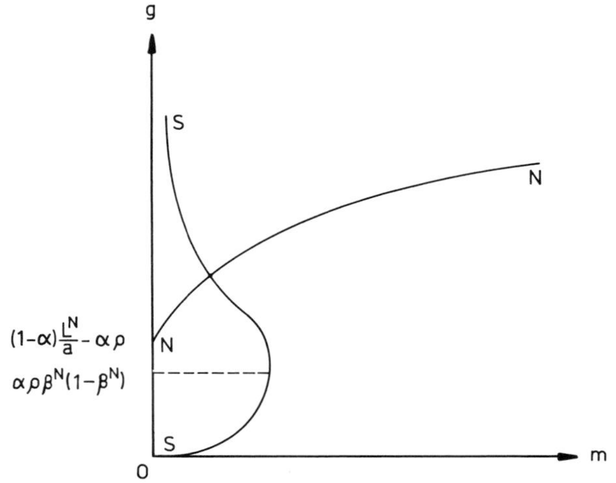

Figure A11.1

the North (i.e., $[1-\alpha]L^N/a > \alpha\rho$) and β^N is not too large. Then an expansion of the North's labor force or a subsidy to research in the North, which shift the *NN* curve up and to the left, will give rise to higher rates of innovation and lower rates of imitation. Even if the *SS* curve slopes upward, there will be a positive effect of increases in L^N and ϕ^N on the long-run rate of innovation.

In the narrow-gap case the *XX* curve—which is given by (11.21) for the special case of $K_m = n^S$—now takes the more general form

$$\alpha^{\varepsilon} = \frac{m}{g}\left(\frac{L^N - ag}{L^S K_m(1, g/m) - a_m g}\right). \tag{A11.6}$$

Provided that β^N is not too large, the analysis of this case follows along similar lines to those in the main text.

A11.2 Intersections of Iso-Relative-Wage Curves and *NN*

We verify here that the curves in (m,g) space defined implicitly by

$$\omega^{\varepsilon} = \frac{m}{g}\left(\frac{L^N - ag}{L^S - a_m g}\right), \tag{A11.7}$$

for some constant value of ω, intersect the *NN* curve from below. From (11.16) we calculate the slope of the *NN* curve. We find that

$$\left.\frac{dm}{dg}\right|_{NN} = \frac{m}{g} + \frac{m}{g - \bar{g}^N} + \frac{m}{(1-\alpha)L^N/a - g}, \tag{A11.8}$$

where $\bar{g}^N$ represents the autarky rate of innovation in the North. The slope of a typical iso-relative-wage curve is given by

$$\left.\frac{dm}{dg}\right|_{\omega\omega} = \frac{m}{g} - \frac{m}{L^S/a_m - g} + \frac{m}{L^N/a - g}. \tag{A11.9}$$

Let $\Delta(g) \equiv (dm/dg)|_{NN} - (dm/dg)|_{\omega\omega}$ be the difference in the slopes of the two curves at a point that is common to each one. Using (A11.8) and (A11.9), we calculate

$$\Delta(g) = \frac{1}{g - \bar{g}^N} + \frac{1}{L^S/a_m - g} + \frac{\alpha L^N/a}{[(1-\alpha)L^N/a - g](L^N/a - g)}. \tag{A11.10}$$

Since $g \geq \bar{g}^N$ all along the NN curve, the first term on the right-hand side of (A11.10) is positive. The remaining terms are positive as well because $L^S/a_m > L^N/a > g$ in an equilibrium with $m > 0$ (see footnote 10) and $(1-\alpha)L^N/a > g$ for all points along the NN curve.[20] It follows that $\Delta(g) > 0$, which proves that the $\omega\omega$ curves intersect the NN curves from below.

The XX curve (see [11.21]) is a special case of (A11.7) with $\omega = \alpha$. Thus our proof establishes also that this curve intersects NN from below. Since both the NN and the XX curves are everywhere upward sloping, the intersection point of these two curves is unique.

20. From (11.16), $(1-\alpha)L^N/a - g = \alpha g\rho/(g+m) > 0$.

12 Product Cycles

In a much celebrated article Vernon (1966) described a "product cycle" for the typical innovative commodity. Most new goods, he claimed, are developed in the industrialized North and manufactured there until their designs have been perfected and production techniques standardized. Then the innovating firms move the locus of production to the less developed South where wage rates and perhaps materials prices are lower. In a final stage of the product's life, new and superior goods may impinge upon its market share and ultimately render it obsolete.

In Vernon's conception of the product cycle, the transfer of technology takes place under the auspices of the innovating firm. A Northern innovator might establish an offshore production facility via direct foreign investment, or it might license the technology to a local producer in the South. This view of technological diffusion describes well, for example, the events in the consumer electronics industry and the office machinery industry in the early 1960s (see Hirsch 1967). But more recently the rapid advances in the technical capabilities of engineers and entrepreneurs in the newly industrialized countries (or NICs) have made imitation a more common vehicle for technology transfer.[1] Thus the product cycle of the personal computer in the 1980s has been characterized not only by increasing offshore production by the multinational firms that originally developed the product but also (and perhaps more so) by the introduction of "clones" by arm's-length competitors of these innovating firms.

In chapter 11 we specified a model of interrelated innovation and imitation processes that gave rise to a product cycle for the typical commodity. As in Vernon (1966), our model predicted the migration of innovative

1. Lockwood (1954, ch. 6) recounts the role that "technological borrowing and assimilation" played in the post-Meiji growth and development experience of Japan. Rhee, Ross-Larson, and Purcell (1984) describe a similar process of learning by imitation that is taking place in South Korea.

goods from North to South. But it could not capture the reversals in patterns of specialization and trade that often take place when mature and standardized products eventually become obsolete with the invention of a new generation of goods. In the personal computer industry, for instance, the clones of the original IBM PC ultimately lost their place in the market to superior machines based on the 80286 microprocessor chip (i.e., the IBM AT and Compaq 286), which themselves were later copied by the South and then upgraded once more by firms in the North. In this chapter we analyze a model that generates such ebbs and flows in market share as an outgrowth of ongoing imitation and innovation *in the same industries*. Our approach involves an extension of the model of rising product quality to include imitation activities in a low-wage region.

The concerns of the present chapter are similar to those of the preceding one. We are interested in the nature of the feedbacks between innovation and imitation and the effects of North–South trade on growth in each region. An important difference between the two analyses can be traced to the fact that in chapter 11 innovation in a particular product line ceased at the moment that a new good was introduced, whereas here it remains an ongoing process. In the present context not only must entrepreneurs in the North look ahead to their ultimate displacement from the market by imitators in the South, but so too must Southern firms foresee their own eventual demise in the wake of further technological advances in the North. This new element of our model introduces a second link between innovation and imitation that was not present in the previous analysis. We will see that the difference in specification bears significantly on some central issues in North–South trade.

12.1 Imitation with Rising Product Quality

Recall the setting of chapter 4. A fixed set of goods potentially can be produced in an unlimited number of vertically differentiated varieties or "qualities." A "state of the art" describes the highest quality of each good producible by some firm at a given moment in time. Improvements in the state of the art require the allocation of resources to R&D. When successful in the research lab, an innovator discovers a new commodity that provides λ times as many services as the commodity of the previous generation in the same product line.

We represent preferences again by (4.1) and (4.2). These preferences apply to households in both the North and the South. They yield the aggregate demands in (4.3), where $E(t)$ now denotes aggregate world spending. Once again, we normalize spending to equal one at every moment in time so that the interest rates equal the subjective discount rate in a steady state with constant shares of each region in world demand.

Labor is the only primary factor of production in each region. It can be used for manufacturing or research. In manufacturing, one unit of labor is needed to produce every unit of output. This makes the marginal cost of all known varieties equal to w^N in the North and to w^S in the South. Once again, oligopolistic conduct takes the form of price competition. Then profitable imitation in the South requires $w^S < w^N$. We concentrate on parameter values that yield a steady-state equilibrium with this property.

We distinguish three types of profit-making firms that may operate in equilibrium. These firms earn different rates of profit and face different risks of loss of their places in the market. They are (1) Northern firms that have exclusive ability to produce some state-of-the-art product and that compete with other Northern firms that can produce the second-to-top quality, (2) Northern firms that have exclusive ability to produce a state-of-the-art product and that compete with Southern firms that can produce the second-to-top quality, and (3) Southern firms that have mastered, via imitation, the technology for producing a state-of-the-art variety. We denote the measure of firms in each of these categories by n^{NN}, n^{NS}, and n^S, respectively. We will find that the three categories exhaust the possibilities for profitable enterprises and that each good in the continuum has exactly one producer. It follows that $n^{NN} + n^{NS} + n^S = 1$.

Let us derive now the profit rate for each category of firm and show at the same time that no other type of firm can earn positive profits. Consider, first, a firm in the South that is the only one in that region to have successfully copied the top-of-the-line variety in some product line. This firm competes with the Northern inventor of the product that it imitated.[2] In the duopoly equilibrium the Southern firm perceives a perfectly elastic demand when it charges a price of w^N (the unit production cost of its rival), zero demand at prices above this level, and unit elastic demand at prices below it. The firm maximizes profit by setting a limit price of w^N, which enables it to capture all of industry demand (see the discussion of this point in chapter 4). When the price is w^N, sales are given by $1/w^N$ (see [4.3] and recall that $E = 1$), and instantaneous profits equal

2. In principle, the Southern firm might also face competition from another Southern producer of a previous generation product. But we will find that a long-run equilibrium with positive rates of innovation and imitation must be characterized by $w^N < \lambda w^S$. This makes the Northern firm with the know-how to produce the state-of-the-art product a more formidable competitor for the Southern imitator than any Southern firms with the ability to produce previous generation products.

$$\pi^S = \frac{w^N - w^S}{w^N}. \tag{12.1}$$

In the same industry no other firm (be it the Northern developer of the state-of-the-art product or a firm in any location with the ability to produce a lower-quality product in the same line) earns positive profits.

If two Southern firms have mastered the technology for the same state-of-the-art product, each sets a price equal to its marginal cost w^S in the Bertrand competition. Then each earns zero profits. As in chapter 11, such a market outcome does not arise in the dynamic equilibrium because no Southern firm is willing to invest resources to become the second regional producer of any product.

We consider next the competitive situation facing a Northern firm that has successfully improved upon a product most recently manufactured in the South. Let us suppose for the moment that the Southern competitor has the ability to manufacture the good of the previous generation (i.e., it is only one step behind on the quality ladder). Later we shall verify that this is always the case in the dynamic equilibrium. The Northern leader can charge a premium over the price offered by its rival in view of the superiority of its product. Since the rival cannot profitably price below its unit production cost of w^S, the innovator can capture the entire market by charging anything less than λ times this amount. The optimal strategy again calls for a limit price, this time at the level λw^S, which yields sales of $1/\lambda w^S$ and instantaneous profits equal to

$$\pi^{NS} = \frac{\lambda w^S - w^N}{\lambda w^S}. \tag{12.2}$$

Of course, if $\lambda w^S < w^N$, the Southern producer would win the industry competition rather than the Northern technological leader. In this event no Northern firm would be willing to invest in improving a product emanating from the South. Then, in a dynamic equilibrium with ongoing imitation, the South would ultimately capture all of the products. But such a situation surely would violate the labor-market-clearing condition in the North. We conclude that $\lambda w^S > w^N$ in an equilibrium with active innovation and imitation.

When a Northern firm with the exclusive ability to produce a top-of-the-line product faces competition instead from a Northern rival that has the ability to manufacture the previous generation product, the leader's profit-maximizing limit price is given by λw^N. This price ensures the leader of all sales in the product line. With an output of $1/\lambda w^N$ units, the leader earns profits equal to

$$\pi^{NN} = \frac{\lambda w^N - w^N}{\lambda w^N}. \tag{12.3}$$

Finally, when two Northern firms have the ability to produce the same state-of-the-art product, each earns zero profits in the Bertrand competition. It follows that costly imitation cannot be a profitable activity in the North.

We describe next the process of innovation. We treat research investments as risky ventures, just as in chapter 4. A Northern firm that devotes resources to R&D purchases a probability of success per unit time that is proportional to the scale of its efforts. In a modest departure from our previous specification, we distinguish now between productivities in the research labs of firms that have invented the most recent top-of-the-line products and those in the labs of their would-be successors. A firm that has successfully developed the state of the art may have accumulated along the way some product specific information that would help it to achieve a further advance in technology. Since outsiders can observe only the final product and not the process that led to its discovery, they may need to invest greater resources in order to attain a similar probability of a breakthrough. We specify that "leaders"—namely, firms that have invented the current state-of-the-art product in some industry j—can achieve a probability ιdt of a research success in a time interval of length dt by devoting $a_L \iota$ units of labor to research during that interval. Whereas a "follower"—which is a firm that developed a previous generation product, participated unsuccessfully in some past technology race, or is a new entrant into the research competition—must devote $a_F \iota$ units of labor to research for the interval dt to achieve this same probability ιdt of success, where $a_F > a_L$.

With this research technology it is apparent that only leaders will undertake efforts to recapture markets held by firms in the South. A firm that is successful in its attempt to upgrade a Southern product earns a reward that is independent of its identity as a leader or a follower. But leaders enjoy an advantage in the research lab. Moreover the research technology exhibits constant returns to scale. Since all firms face the same cost of capital, leaders will crowd followers out of the market for investments aimed at improving Southern products.

We concentrate on symmetric equilibria in which all Northern leaders that have lost their markets to Southern imitators conduct R&D with equal intensity. This is a natural assumption to make because the same profit opportunity awaits any firm that manages to recapture its market, irrespective of the product line or the quality of its good. Northern firms with products that have been copied by the South can reap an expected gain of $v^{NS}\iota^S dt$ at cost $w^N a_L \iota^S dt$ by undertaking R&D at intensity ι^S, where v^{NS} denotes the value of a typical firm that has a Southern producer as its nearest competitor. Maximization of expected value implies that

$$v^{NS} \leq a_L w^N, \qquad \text{with equality for } \iota^S > 0, \tag{12.4}$$

where ι^S represents now the scale of the research effort targeted at every Southern product.

A Northern leader whose product has escaped Southern imitation similarly enjoys a cost advantage in the research lab relative to any Northern followers that might think to develop the next generation of product in the same line. But, as we have seen before, a follower stands to gain more from a research success in this situation than do leaders. The reward to a successful follower is the expected value of a stream of profits given by (12.3) that continues until another improvement or imitation is achieved in the same product line. Successful leaders, on the other hand, capture only the increment between these profits and the higher profits that accrue to a firm with a two-step lead over its nearest rival.[3] In view of the differences on both the cost and benefits side, either leaders or followers might have the greater incentive to undertake research aimed at improving Northern-based goods. In appendix A12.1 we show that such research will be undertaken only by followers, provided that $a_F/a_L < 2 - 1/\lambda$. We henceforth adopt this parameter restriction and leave the alternative case to the interested reader. Since extant leaders make no efforts to widen their technological leads, the gap between any leader and its nearest rival never exceeds a single quality step.

We let v^{NN} represent the value of a Northern firm that has another Northern firm as its closest competitor. Value maximization by followers ensures that

$$v^{NN} \leq a_F w^N, \qquad \text{with equality for } \iota^N > 0, \tag{12.5}$$

where ι^N is the aggregate intensity of research effort targeted at the typical Northern-based product.

---

3. As we discussed in chapter 4, leaders might think to undertake research as a means to deter rivals from targeting their products for improvement. Such an investment strategy could be profitable if R&D outlays were observable. As before, we wish to avoid the complications associated with deterrent research, and so we assume that the size of a firm's research operation cannot be observed by its rivals.

Research activities undertaken in the South are confined to the assimilation and adaptation of Northern technologies. In other words, we assume that Southern entrepreneurs are unable to develop next-generation products.[4] We model imitation as a risky venture similar to innovation. A Southern firm that devotes $a_m m$ units of labor to the task of imitation for a time interval of length dt will succeed in its efforts to develop a marketable copy of the targeted product with probability mdt. Such an investment yields the firm an expected gain of $mv^S dt$ at a cost of $w^S a_m mdt$, where v^S represents the value of a typical Southern brand. Again, we impose symmetry by assuming that every Northern brand is targeted by would-be imitators to the same aggregate extent. Value maximization this time implies that

$$v^S \leq a_m w^S, \qquad \text{with equality for } m > 0, \tag{12.6}$$

where m is the per brand intensity of imitative activity in the South.

The values of the various categories of firms are guided by familiar no-arbitrage relationships. A Northern producer—be it one that faces competition from another Northern firm as its closest rival or one that competes with a Southern firm as its closest rival—may forfeit its earnings stream in one of two ways. Its product might be improved upon by another Northern entrepreneur, or it might be successfully copied by a firm in the South. The probabilities of these events occurring in a small interval of time of length dt are $\iota^N dt$ and mdt, respectively. In either case the owners suffer a capital loss equal to the total value of their holdings in the firm.[5] Equating in the usual way the sums of the profit rates and the expected rates of capital gain (or loss) to the opportunity cost of funds in the North, we obtain

4. Just as in chapter 11, it would be possible for us to derive an absence of innovative research in the South from more primitive assumptions. We might, for example, extend our model to include two or more factors of production, and assume that the South is poorly endowed with the factor used intensively in quality upgrading. Or we might model knowledge spillovers that are (partly) specific to the region in which they are generated.

5. There is one difference between these two occurrences. An extant leader that loses its market to a Southern imitator retains its superior technology for developing the next-generation product, whereas a firm that is displaced by a Northern innovator re-enters the pool of potential followers. But in either event, the value of a leading firm falls to zero at the moment that its profit stream subsides. This is because the stock market places zero value on the *option* to invest in R&D after imitation has taken place. This investment opportunity, like all others, yields only a normal return when capital markets are in equilibrium.

$$\frac{\pi^{NS}}{v^{NS}} + \frac{\dot{v}^{NS}}{v^{NS}} - (\iota^N + m) = r^N \tag{12.7}$$

and

$$\frac{\pi^{NN}}{v^{NN}} + \frac{\dot{v}^{NN}}{v^{NN}} - (\iota^N + m) = r^N, \tag{12.8}$$

where r^N is the interest rate there.

Each Southern firm faces a probability $\iota^S dt$ of displacement from the market in a time interval of length dt. This event will be realized if a Northern leader succeeds in improving upon the product that the Southern firm previously copied, in which case the value of the Southern brand goes to zero. The hypothesis that Southern equities yield normal rates of return implies that

$$\frac{\pi^S}{v^S} + \frac{\dot{v}^S}{v^S} - \iota^S = r^S, \tag{12.9}$$

where r^S is the interest rate in the South.

We turn finally to the labor markets. As always, these must clear in each country at every moment of time. In the North a measure n^S of firms each employs $a_L \iota^S$ units of labor in research aimed at recapturing markets from Southern imitators. Northern followers demand $a_F \iota^N$ units of labor for R&D targeted at each of n^N Northern products. The n^{NN} Northern leaders that have a Northern firm as their closest competitor require $1/\lambda w^N$ units of labor apiece for production purposes. Finally, there are n^{NS} Northern firms with Southern firms as nearest rivals that each demands $1/\lambda w^S$ units of labor for manufacturing. Equating the sum of these various components of labor demand to the exogenous supply L^N, we have

$$a_L \iota^S n^S + a_F \iota^N n^N + \frac{n^{NN}}{\lambda w^N} + \frac{n^{NS}}{\lambda w^S} = L^N. \tag{12.10}$$

In the South the activity of imitation employs $a_m m n^N$ units of labor, since n^N products are targeted with intensity m. The manufacturing sector demands n^S/w^N units of labor to produce $1/w^N$ units of each of n^S brands. Thus market clearing requires that

$$a_m m n^N + \frac{n^S}{w^N} = L^S, \tag{12.11}$$

where L^S denotes the size of the labor force in the South.

This completes the description of the model. In the dynamic equilibrium the various industries experience stochastic product cycles. An individual product might be manufactured for a while in the North before a Southern firm succeeds in its efforts to learn the technology. Then production would shift to the South until the product were made obsolete by further technological developments in the North. Alternatively, there might occur a succession of quality upgrades in the same product line without the manufacturing base ever shifting from North to South. Despite the variations that are possible in the histories of the individual industries, the world economy experiences aggregate rates of innovation and imitation that are nonrandom and that are constant in the long run. In the next section we derive the conditions that characterize a steady state.

12.2 Steady-State Equilibrium

In the steady state, allocations of resources to the various activities remain fixed through time. A fixed allocation requires constant numbers of goods in the different product categories, constant rates of innovation and imitation, and constant relative prices. The last condition ensures that the incentives facing the various agents remain unchanged.

For relative prices to be constant, all nominal variables must grow at the same rate. As before, this implies a rate of growth in the values of all firms equal to the rate of growth in nominal spending. Since our normalization makes $E(t) = 1$ for all t, the values of profit-making entities do not change in the steady state. The normalization also implies that $r^N = r^S = \rho$ in the long run. Using these facts, we combine each value-maximization conditions with the corresponding no-arbitrage condition (e.g., [12.4] and [12.7]) to derive the following steady-state relationships:

$$\frac{\pi^{NS}}{a_L w^N} \leq \rho + \iota^N + m, \qquad \text{with equality for } \iota^S > 0, \tag{12.12}$$

$$\frac{\pi^{NN}}{a_F w^N} \leq \rho + \iota^N + m, \qquad \text{with equality for } \iota^N > 0, \tag{12.13}$$

$$\frac{\pi^S}{a_m w^S} \leq \rho + \iota^S, \qquad \text{with equality for } m > 0. \tag{12.14}$$

In the steady state the measure of products emanating from each region stays fixed, as does the composition of Northern industries. Southern entrepreneurs master new technologies at the rate mn^N, since each of

$n^N \equiv n^{NS} + n^{NN}$ Northern goods is targeted for imitation with intensity m. The South loses product lines at the rate $\iota^S n^S$, as technological advances are made in the n^S labs of displaced Northern leaders. The measure of Southern products remains constant if and only if

$$mn^N = \iota^S n^S. \tag{12.15}$$

Within the group of Northern-based product lines, the subset of industries that have a Northern firm as closest competitor expands whenever a follower achieves a research success in an industry where a Southern firm formerly was second to top. Such research successes take place at the rate $\iota^N n^{NS}$. The subset of industries with Northern firms in second place shrinks, however, whenever a Southern firm copies one of these n^{NN} products. A constant composition of Northern industries requires that the inflows into each category match the outflows, or that

$$\iota^N n^{NS} = mn^{NN}. \tag{12.16}$$

The above conditions admit several types of steady-state equilibria. These equilibria differ in terms of which innovation and imitation activities are viable in the long run. The constellation of parameter values determines which regime applies. For example, a stationary equilibrium with no innovation or imitation may obtain if both of these learning activities are quite costly to perform. Alternatively, we might have an equilibrium with active innovation but no imitation if a_m were large compared to a_L and a_F. Since our main interest lies in the interaction between the two learning processes, we focus our attention on parameter values that give rise to a long-run equilibrium with ongoing technological progress in both regions.

Even so, there are two different regimes to consider. If leaders enjoy a relatively large productivity advantage over followers in the research lab, then only leaders will engage in R&D in the steady state. In this case the dynamic equilibrium involves alternating phases of Northern and Southern production in each industry, with active R&D by Northern firms whose products have been copied and active imitation by Southern entrepreneurs aimed at newly improved products. In a second type of equilibrium, both leaders and followers undertake R&D. This case arises when followers are relatively efficient at innovation, though still less so than leaders. In this type of equilibrium, the history of any product line may be complex because at any moment the position of leadership in the market may pass from one Northern firm to another or from North to South.

In an equilibrium with "efficient followers," conditions (12.12) through (12.14) all hold with equality. They can be used together with the other equilibrium relationships to derive a useful reduced-form system. The reduced form focuses on the variables of interest, namely, $\iota \equiv \iota^N n^N + \iota^S n^S$, the aggregate rate of product improvement, $\mu \equiv mn^N$, the aggregate rate of technology transfer to the South, and $\omega \equiv w^S/w^N$, the relative wage of the South. First, we rewrite the labor-market-clearing conditions (12.10) and (12.11), using these definitions and the steady-state relationships (12.15) and (12.16). This gives

$$a_F(\iota - \mu) + a_L\mu + \frac{n^N(1 - \mu/\iota)}{\lambda w^N} + \frac{\mu n^N}{\iota\lambda\omega n^N} = L^N, \tag{12.17}$$

$$a_m\mu + \frac{1 - n^N}{w^N} = L^S. \tag{12.18}$$

Then we combine the profit expressions (12.1)–(12.3) with the no-arbitrage conditions (12.12)–(12.14) and the steady-state relationships (12.15) and (12.16) to derive

$$\frac{(1 - 1/\lambda\omega)n^N}{w^N} = a_L(\rho n^N + \iota), \tag{12.19}$$

$$\frac{(1 - 1/\lambda)n^N}{w^N} = a_F(\rho n^N + \iota), \tag{12.20}$$

$$\frac{(1/\omega - 1)(1 - n^N)}{w^N} = a_m[\rho(1 - n^N) + \mu]. \tag{12.21}$$

Using (12.19) and (12.20), we can solve immediately for the relative wage rate that prevails in an equilibrium with efficient followers. We find that

$$\frac{\lambda\omega - 1}{(\lambda - 1)\omega} = \frac{a_L}{a_F}. \tag{12.22}$$

In this case the steady-state relative wage does not vary with the sizes of the two regions. The relative wage of the North is higher the more productive are leaders relative to followers in the research lab.

In the regime with "inefficient followers," $\iota^N = 0$. Then (12.15) and (12.16) imply that $n^{NN} = 0$ and $\mu = \iota$; that is, the measure of products that are improved in the North in a unit interval of time equals the measure of products that the South learns to produce during this period. Using these facts, we can simplify the reduced-form labor market conditions (12.17) and (12.18) to read

$$a_L\imath + \frac{n^N}{\lambda\omega n^N} = L^N, \tag{12.23}$$

$$a_m\imath + \frac{1 - n^N}{w^N} = L^S. \tag{12.24}$$

As for the no-arbitrage relationships, (12.13) holds now as an inequality. After substituting for π^{NN} and π^S using (12.1) and (12.3), the remaining conditions (12.12) and (12.14) become

$$\frac{(1 - 1/\lambda\omega)n^N}{w^N} = a_L(\rho n^N + \imath), \tag{12.25}$$

$$\frac{(1/\omega - 1)(1 - n^N)}{w^N} = a_m[\rho(1 - n^N) + \imath]. \tag{12.26}$$

The following two sections analyze the relationship between region size and long-run rates of innovation and imitation in the two regimes. We also study the international transmission of technology policies in each setting.

12.3 Efficient Followers

Let us consider first the regime in which both leaders and followers are active in the research lab. Leaders invest in R&D in order to recapture their markets from clones. Followers target their efforts at the products of Northern rivals, hoping to gain market leadership with newly improved products.

We recall first the findings of chapter 11 where we studied an economy in which imitators target an expanding set of horizontally differentiated products. In that setting North–South trade generally contributes to faster growth in both regions, and an increase in the size of *either* region causes new technologies to be mastered at a faster rate in both. Similarly R&D subsidies in either the North or the South were found to spur technological progress worldwide. To address the same issues in the present context, we need to analyze the reduced-form system comprising equations (12.17)–(12.21). This system does not readily lend itself to a diagrammatic treatment, so we must resort to algebraic methods. Appendix A12.2 contains the details, while the main text focuses on the results.

The answers to several of our questions may hinge upon a particular property of the labor demand schedule in the North. Consider the effects of an increase in the per brand intensity of research by followers, with the wage rates in both regions, the division of products between North and

South, and the per brand intensities of research by leaders and imitators all held constant. The direct effect of this increase in ι^N would be to raise demand for Northern labor (i.e., the left-hand side of [12.17]) in proportion to the resources required per unit of research activity by followers. But an indirect effect operates in the opposite direction. When ι^N increases with n^N constant, the long-run composition of Northern industries shifts in favor of product lines in which the closest competitor to the leader is another Northern firm (see [12.16]). Per brand sales of such products are smaller than those of products with a Southern firm as nearest competitor because the former goods bear a higher price. Therefore the change in the composition of Northern industries generates a reduction in the labor demanded by Northern manufacturing establishments. The total impact on the demand for Northern labor is ambiguous. To keep our discussion from becoming taxonomic, we shall henceforth assume that the direct effect dominates.[6] The appendix shows that where we invoke this assumption, it is never a necessary condition for any specific result.

Consider now the effects of an expansion in the size of the South. As in the model of expanding product variety, we find that this quickens the pace of technological progress there (i.e., μ rises) and increases the intensity of imitation targeted at the typical Northern good (i.e., m rises). The latter variable plays a similar role to the rate of imitation in chapter 11. It measures the instantaneous probability of a shift in the location of a good's production from North to South, and its inverse gives the expected length of a product cycle.

We find, as before, that there are offsetting implications of a larger South for the incentives to innovate in the North. On the one hand, the induced increase in the rate of imitation implies a shorter period of profitability for the typical Northern innovator. On the other hand, leaders may enjoy greater returns during their tenure in the market when the rate of imitation is higher. In chapter 11 we found that with innovation aimed at generating greater product diversity, the latter effect must dominate. Here this need not be the case. When innovators seek to improve a fixed set of commodities, an expansion in the size of the South might increase or decrease the long-run rate of innovation in the North.

For similar reasons it is no longer possible to make a definitive statement about the net effect of trade with the South on the rate of innovation in the North. Such trade opens the North to technological imitation that would

6. More precisely we assume that $a_F \iota > (1/\omega - 1) n^N \mu / \iota \lambda w^N$. This assumption is not required for any of our conclusions regarding the aggregate rate of innovation ι.

not otherwise occur. The risk of having an innovation copied reduces an entrepreneur's incentive to engage in R&D. At the same time trade may raise the profit rate for firms that are lucky enough to escape imitation. In the model of quality upgrading, either effect can dominate, and trade with the South may speed or slow Northern growth.

What are the implications here of an expansion in the size of the North? In the steady state a larger North means more employment in the research sector, hence a higher aggregate rate of innovation. The Northern manufacturing sector also grows with an increase in L^N as the fraction of products emanating from this region increases. In the South the labor released from the manufacturing sector finds alternative employment in performing research activities. As a result the region experiences an acceleration of its acquisition of new technological capabilities. Since an increase in L^N causes an expansion in the scale of the Southern imitation effort, on the one hand, and growth in the number of potential Northern targets for Southern imitators, on the other, the average length of a product cycle may rise or fall.

Next we examine subsidies to imitation and innovation. As before, we introduce parameters ϕ^N and ϕ^S to represent the share of R&D costs that are borne by the governments of the North and the South, respectively.[7] With these policies in place, the various no-arbitrage conditions must be modified to reflect the fact that entrepreneurs pay only a fraction of the cost of research. Accordingly we multiply the right-hand sides of (12.19) and (12.20) by $1 - \phi^N$, and the right-hand side of (12.21) by $1 - \phi^S$, to derive a new reduced-form system.

The introduction of a small subsidy to Northern research unambiguously strengthens the incentives for R&D for both leaders and followers. The aggregate rate of innovation increases as a result. But as the North devotes more resources to research, its manufacturing sector shrinks, and with it the fraction of goods that are produced in this region. Employment in manufacturing expands in the South at the expense of resources devoted to learning. Thus the Northern subsidy indirectly slows the long-run pace of technological progress in the South.

A small subsidy to imitative research in the South has just the opposite effects from those of a subsidy to innovative research in the North. The subsidy causes employment in imitation to rise and the aggregate rate of innovation in the North to fall. Evidently the international transmission of

7. Recall that the technology policy of the South might also be interpreted as an easing of the patent protection afforded to foreign goods.

technology policies places the two governments in conflict in their efforts to promote domestic growth. This conclusion stands in contrast to the findings of chapter 11 where we showed that a subsidy to research in either region hastens technological progress in both.

We conclude this discussion by noting that the subsidization of learning activities in the South might paradoxically extend the average length of a product cycle. Although the subsidy does augment the scale of the Southern effort to assimilate Northern technologies, the set of Northern products may grow as well. If so, it is possible for the intensity of imitation targeted at the typical Northern brand to fall.

12.4 Inefficient Followers

In the event of inefficient followers, $\iota^N = 0$, hence $\iota = \iota^S n^S$. Then (12.15) implies convergence of the aggregate rate of innovation in the North and the rate at which new technologies are assimilated by the South (i.e., $\iota = \mu$). With the simplification that this provides, it is possible to develop a diagram to illustrate the equilibrium.

To this end we substitute the two labor-market-clearing conditions (12.23) and (12.24) into the North's reduced-form, no-arbitrage condition (12.25), and rearrange terms to derive

$$\left(\frac{L^S - a_m\iota}{m - \iota} - \frac{L^N - a_L\iota}{\iota}\right)\frac{m}{a_L} = \rho + m. \tag{12.27}$$

Similarly we substitute (12.23) and (12.24) into the South's no-arbitrage condition (12.26) to find

$$\left[\frac{\lambda(L^N - a_L\iota)}{\iota} - \frac{L^S - a_m\iota}{m - \iota}\right]\frac{m}{a_m} = \rho + \frac{\iota m}{m - \iota}. \tag{12.28}$$

The left-hand sides of (12.27) and (12.28) represent the profit rates for Northern and Southern firms, respectively, while the right-hand sides of these equations represent the risk-adjusted interest rates that apply to each type of firm. The risk factors reflect the probabilities per unit time of the firms suffering displacement from the market.

Close inspection of (12.27) and (12.28) reveals that the respective risk factors appear on both sides of the equations. Canceling these terms, we can rewrite the equilibrium conditions as

$$\left(\frac{L^S - a_m\iota}{m - \iota} - \frac{L^N}{\iota}\right)\frac{m}{a_L} = \rho, \tag{12.29}$$

$$\left[\frac{\lambda(L^N - a_L \iota)}{\iota} - \frac{L^S}{m - \iota}\right]\frac{m}{a_m} = \rho. \tag{12.30}$$

We depict the combinations of ι and m that satisfy (12.30) by the curves labeled *SS* in figures 12.1 and 12.2. The *SS* curve slopes upward because the left-hand side of (12.30) increases with the rate of innovation and declines with the rate of imitation. The curve *NN* depicting combinations of ι and m that satisfy (12.29) may slope in either direction. Figure 12.1 shows the downward-sloping case. If the curve slopes upward, as drawn in figure 12.2, then it must be more steeply sloped than the *SS* curve (see appendix A12.3). In each figure the point representing the initial steady-state equilibrium has been labeled *A*.

Now suppose that L^N increases. This moves both the *SS* curve and the *NN* curve to the left, as illustrated by the dotted curves in figures 12.1 and 12.2. In appendix A12.3 we prove that, at constant ι, the *SS* curve must shift by more. Then, as the figures show, the net result must be an increase in the rate of innovation. The rate of imitation may rise or fall, though it necessarily falls if the *NN* curve slopes downward.

An expansion of the resource base of the South shifts both curves to the right. The rightward shift of the *NN* curve exceeds that of the *SS* curve, as we show in the appendix. In this case the long-run rates of both innovation and imitation rise. The rate of assimilation of new technologies by the

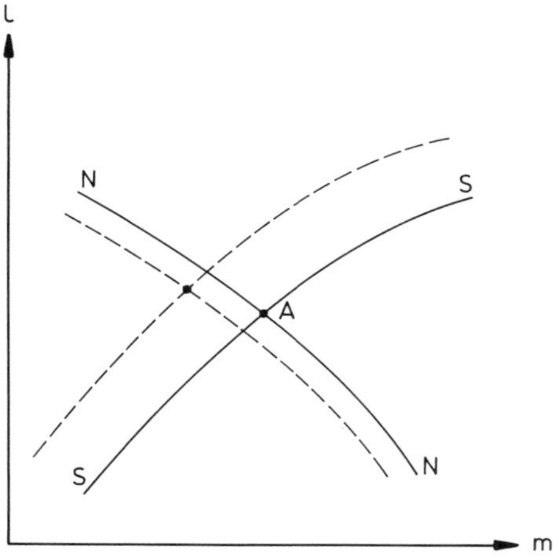

Figure 12.1

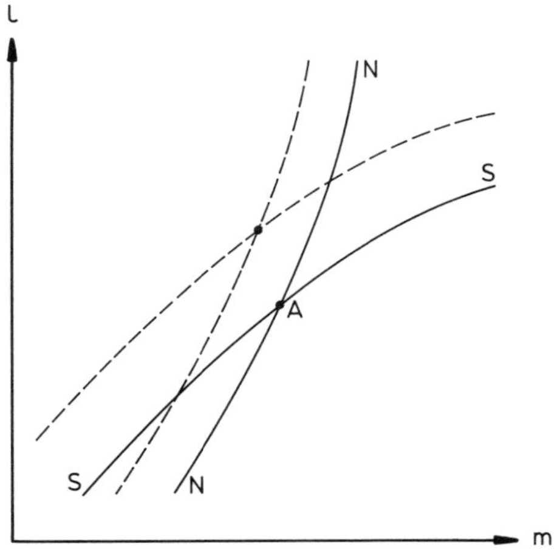

Figure 12.2

South matches the rate of innovation in the North, so the pace of technological progress accelerates in both regions. The length of the average product cycle falls as a consequence of the increased intensity of imitative efforts targeted at every Northern product.

Subsidies to research alter the no-arbitrage conditions as before. When the government of the North bears the fraction ϕ^N of the cost of innovation, the right-hand side of (12.27) must be multiplied by $1 - \phi^N$. A small increase in the rate of subsidy from $\phi^N = 0$ causes the *NN* curve to shift to the right, without affecting the location of the *SS* curve. The result is an increase in both the rates of innovation and of imitation. Similarly, when the government of the South subsidizes local investments in knowledge at the rate ϕ^S, the right-hand side of (12.28) must be multiplied by $1 - \phi^S$. Then a small subsidy shifts the *SS* curve to the left, while the *NN* curve remains in place. The rate of innovation rises, implying a faster pace of technological advance in both regions. The rate at which products flow from one region to the other may rise or fall, depending upon the slope of the *NN* curve. We note, finally, that a subsidy to R&D in the North increases the steady-state relative wage of Northern workers, whereas the subsidization of learning in the South has the opposite effect on long-run relative wages (see appendix A12.3).

We recognize a striking similarity between many of the findings for the case of inefficient followers and the corresponding results that were established in chapter 11. There is in both cases a positive feedback relationship between the processes of innovation and imitation. For example, the rates of technological progress increase worldwide whenever there is an expansion in the resource base of either region. Similarly a government subsidy to learning promotes this activity not only at home but also abroad. Also in both cases the length of the (average) product cycle varies positively with the relative size of the North. Finally, in both cases the relative wage of a region increases when its government begins to promote research.

This chapter has extended the model of rising product quality to include imitation in a low-wage region. We have distinguished two different types of equilibria that may arise depending upon parameter values. In one regime a fixed set of firms conducts all innovative research in the world economy. Although new firms potentially can enter the technology race, their disadvantage in the research lab relative to the firms that have access to private information about the state-of-the-art technology is sufficiently large to preclude the newcomers from attracting capital. In the alternative regime the productivity gap between the current generation of innovators and their would-be successors still exists, but its more modest size allows both leaders and followers to be active in research.

The regime with inefficient followers yields results that parallel those in chapter 11. Technological progress in both regions responds positively to an expansion in the resource base of either one and to the introduction of a research subsidy by either government. But the regime with efficient followers shows the limited generality of these conclusions. In this case an expansion in the size of the South may slow the rate of innovation in the North, and policies that might be used to promote domestic productivity gains spill over abroad with adverse consequences for the foreign rates of technological progress.

APPENDIX

A12.1 Who Improves Northern Products?

We have noted the different advantages that leaders and followers have when it comes to improving products that have escaped imitation. Leaders may be more productive in the research lab if they enjoy access to private information generated in the course of developing the most recent state of the art. Followers, on the other hand, stand to gain more from a research success because the profits they can earn by taking over leadership in an industry exceed the incremental profits that a leader can capture by widening an existing technological lead. In this appendix we will show that if $a_F/a_L < 2 - 1/\lambda$, the followers will have the greater steady-state incentive to undertake research aimed at improving Northern products.

The proof consists of two parts. First, we show that no Northern leader whose closest competitor is another Northern firm (an *NN* firm) attempts to improve upon its own product. Then we show that the same is true for a Northern firm whose nearest rival is a Southern firm (an *NS* firm).

We let v^{2N} represent the stock market value of a hypothetical Northern firm that has captured a two-step quality lead over its nearest Northern rival. Such a firm sets a limit price of $\lambda^2 w^N$ in the duopoly equilibrium and earns profits equal to $\pi^{2N} = 1 - 1/\lambda^2$. The no-arbitrage condition that would apply to shares in this firm, and that for shares in *NN* firms, together imply that in a steady state with constant firm values, $v^{2N} = \pi^{2N} v^{NN}/\pi^{NN}$. Then, noting (12.3), we have

$$v^{2N} - v^{NN} = \frac{v^{NN}}{\lambda} \tag{A12.1}$$

in a steady state.

An *NN* firm achieves an expected gain of $v^{2N} - v^{NN}$ per unit of research activity undertaken for a unit interval of time. The cost of such research is $w^N a_L$. Now, if $a_F/a_L < 2 - 1/\lambda$, then $a_L > a_F/\lambda$. But (A12.1) and (12.5) imply that $v^{N2} - v^{NN} \leq w^N a_F/\lambda$. It follows that R&D cannot be profitable for *NN* firms.

Now consider an *NS* firm. If this firm were to improve upon its own product, it would acquire a two-step lead over its nearest (Southern) rival. Such a firm would have a stock market value of v^{2S} and earn profits equal to $\pi^{2S} = 1 - w^N/\lambda^2 w^S$ by setting a price of $\lambda^2 w^S$. Using (12.2), we calculate

$$\pi^{2S} - \pi^{NS} = \left(1 - \frac{1}{\lambda}\right)\left(\frac{w^N}{\lambda w^S}\right). \tag{A12.2}$$

An *NS* firm gains $v^{2S} - v^{NS}$ in expected value per unit of research activity carried out for a unit interval of time. Using the steady-state, no-arbitrage condition that would apply to shares in a 2*S* firm, and that which applies to shares in *NS* firms, we find that

$$v^{2S} - v^{NS} = (\pi^{2S} - \pi^{NS})\frac{v^{NS}}{\pi^{NS}}. \tag{A12.3}$$

Also (12.2) and (12.4) imply that

$$\frac{v^{NS}}{\pi^{NS}} = \frac{w^N a_L}{1 - w^N/\lambda w^S}, \tag{A12.4}$$

since we must have $\iota^S > 0$ in an equilibrium with a positive measure of *NS* firms. Combining (12.2), (12.3), (12.12), and (12.13), we obtain

$$1 - \frac{w^N}{\lambda w^S} \geq \left(1 - \frac{1}{\lambda}\right)\left(\frac{a_L}{a_F}\right)$$

in a steady state with $\iota^S > 0$. But this inequality and $a_F/a_L < 2 - 1/\lambda$ imply that

$$\left(1 - \frac{1}{\lambda}\right)\left(\frac{w^N}{\lambda w^S}\right) < 1 - \frac{w^N}{\lambda w^S}. \tag{A12.5}$$

Finally, (A12.2)–(A12.5) imply that $v^{2S} - v^{NS} < a_L w^N$. Thus, under the maintained assumption, research is not profitable for *NS* firms.

A12.2 Efficient Followers: Comparative Steady States

In this appendix we compute the long-run responses of ι and μ to changes in the sizes of the two regions and to the introduction of a small research subsidy in either one. For this purpose we make use of equations (12.17)–(12.19) and (12.21) that describe a steady-state equilibrium in the regime with efficient followers. As noted in the main text (see footnote 6), we will assume that

$$b = a_F - \frac{(1/\omega - 1)n^N \mu}{\iota^2 \lambda w^N} > 0$$

at the initial equilibrium point.

Before proceeding with the calculations, we must modify the system to reflect the prevailing research subsidies. As we have noted before, this requires us to multiply the right-hand sides of (12.19) by $(1 - \phi^N)$ and the right-hand side of (12.21) by $(1 - \phi^S)$. Then we can totally differentiate the system about the point where $\phi^N = \phi^S = 0$ to find

$$A \begin{bmatrix} d\iota \\ d\mu \\ dn^N \\ \dfrac{dw^N}{(w^N)^2} \end{bmatrix} = \begin{bmatrix} dL^N \\ dL^S \\ b_N d\phi^N \\ b_S d\phi^S \end{bmatrix}, \tag{A12.6}$$

where $b_N \equiv a_L(\rho n^N + \iota)$, $b_S \equiv a_m(\rho n^S + \mu)$,

$$A \equiv \begin{bmatrix} b & \dfrac{(a_F - a_L)\rho n^N}{\iota} & \dfrac{\beta}{\lambda w^N} & -\dfrac{\beta n^N}{\lambda} \\ 0 & a_m & -\dfrac{1}{w^N} & -n^S \\ a_L & 0 & -\dfrac{a_L \iota}{n^N} & \left(1 - \dfrac{1}{\lambda\omega}\right) n^N \\ 0 & a_m & \dfrac{a_m \mu}{n^S} & \left(\dfrac{1}{\omega} - 1\right) n^S \end{bmatrix},$$

and $\beta \equiv 1 + (1/\omega - 1)\mu/\iota > 0$. Using the first column of A to develop the determinant, it is straightforward to establish that $\Delta \equiv \det A < 0$.

Next we use (A12.6) to calculate

$$\frac{d\iota}{dL^N} = -\frac{a_m}{\Delta}\left[\frac{a_L \iota}{\omega}\frac{n^S}{n^N} + \left(1 - \frac{1}{\lambda\omega}\right) n^N \left(\frac{1}{w^N} + \frac{a_m \mu}{n^S}\right)\right] > 0, \tag{A12.7}$$

$$\frac{d\iota}{dL^S} = \frac{\rho n^N}{\Delta}\left\{(a_F - a_L)\left[\left(\frac{1}{\omega} - 1\right) a_L \frac{n^S}{n^N} + \left(1 - \frac{1}{\lambda\omega}\right)\frac{a_m \mu}{\iota}\frac{n^N}{n^S}\right] - a_m a_L \frac{\beta}{\lambda}\right\} \lesseqgtr 0, \tag{A12.8}$$

$$\frac{d\iota}{d\phi^N} = \frac{a_m b_N}{\Delta}\left\{\frac{\beta}{\lambda}\left[\left(1 - \frac{1}{\omega}\right)\frac{n^S}{w^N} - a_m \mu \frac{n^N}{n^S} - \frac{1}{w^N}\right] + (a_L - a_F) n^N n^S \frac{\rho^2}{\iota}\right\} > 0, \tag{A12.9}$$

$$\frac{d\iota}{d\phi^S} = \frac{\rho b_S}{\Delta}\left\{\frac{\beta}{\lambda} a_m a_L n_N + (a_F - a_L)\left[a_L n^S + \left(1 - \frac{1}{\lambda\omega}\right)\frac{(n^N)^2}{\iota w^N}\right]\right\} < 0, \tag{A12.10}$$

$$\frac{d\mu}{dL^N} = -\frac{1}{\Delta}(a_L a_m \rho n^S) > 0, \tag{A12.11}$$

$$\frac{d\mu}{dL^S} = -\frac{1}{\Delta}\left\{\frac{a_m \mu n^N}{n^S}\left[\frac{a_m \beta}{\lambda} + b\left(1 - \frac{1}{\lambda\omega}\right)\right] + \left(\frac{1}{\omega} - 1\right) n^S \left[\frac{a_m \beta}{\lambda w^N} + \frac{b a_L \iota}{n^N}\right]\right\} > 0, \tag{A12.12}$$

$$\frac{d\mu}{d\phi^N} = \frac{1}{\Delta}(b_N b a_m \rho n^S) < 0, \tag{A12.13}$$

$$\frac{d\mu}{d\phi^S} = -\frac{b_S}{\Delta}\left\{\frac{a_L \beta}{\lambda w^N} + b\left[\frac{a_L \iota n^S}{n^N} + \left(1 - \frac{1}{\lambda\omega}\right)\frac{n^N}{w^N}\right]\right\} > 0, \tag{A12.14}$$

where we have used (12.19) in the derivation of (A12.7) and (A12.9), and (12.21) in the derivation of (A12.9), (A12.11), and (A12.13).

From the same system we find that

$$\frac{dn^N}{dL^S} = \frac{n^N}{\Delta}\left[b a_m \left(1 - \frac{1}{\lambda\omega}\right) + a_L \left(\frac{1}{\omega} - 1\right) n^S (a_F - a_L)\frac{\rho}{\iota} + a_L a_m \frac{\beta}{\lambda}\right] < 0.$$

Since an increase in L^S raises μ while reducing n^N, it follows that the rate of imitation $m = \mu/n^N$ varies directly with the size of the South.

A12.3 Inefficient Followers: Comparative Steady States

In this appendix we derive several properties of the *SS* and *NN* curves that were used in section 12.4. We also examine the long-run responses of the product shares and the relative wage to changes in the sizes of the regions, and to the introduction of research subsidies in each one.

Using (12.30), we calculate the slope of the *SS* curve,

$$\left.\frac{d\iota}{dm}\right|_{SS} = \frac{\iota}{m}\left[\frac{\lambda(L^N - a_L\iota)/\iota^2 + L^S/(m-\iota)^2}{\lambda L^N/\iota^2 + L^S/(m-\iota)^2}\right]. \tag{A12.15}$$

Since $L^N - a_L\iota > 0$ (see [12.23]), we have

$$0 < \left.\frac{d\iota}{dm}\right|_{SS} < \frac{\iota}{m}.$$

Next we calculate the slope of *NN* from (12.29). We find that

$$\left.\frac{d\iota}{dm}\right|_{NN} = \frac{\iota}{m}\left[\frac{(L^S - a_m\iota)/(m-\iota)^2 + L^N/\iota^2}{(L^S - a_m m)/(m-\iota)^2 + L^N/\iota^2}\right]. \tag{A12.16}$$

Here the numerator is positive because (12.24) implies that $L^S - a_m\iota > 0$. If $L^S - a_m m > 0$, then the denominator is also positive, and the *NN* curve slopes upward. Even if $L^S - a_m m < 0$, the denominator may still be positive. But we cannot rule out the possibility that the denominator is negative, in which case the *NN* curve slopes downward. Finally, since $m > mn^N = \iota$, the slope of the *NN* curve when it is positive always exceeds ι/m. We conclude that

$$\left.\frac{d\iota}{dm}\right|_{NN} < 0 \quad \text{or} \quad \left.\frac{d\iota}{dm}\right|_{NN} > \frac{\iota}{m}.$$

These two possibilities are depicted in figures 12.1 and 12.2, respectively.

Although it is theoretically possible for the *NN* curve to slope downward, the upward-sloping case seems more plausible on empirical grounds. As we have seen, a sufficient condition for the *NN* curve to slope upward is $L^S > a_m m$. But this condition is equivalent to $n^N > a_m\iota/L^S$ because $\iota = mn^N$. Thus the *NN* curve slopes upward whenever the fraction of innovative products manufactured in the North exceeds the share of the Southern labor force employed in research activities. A casual reading of the evidence suggests that this condition is satisfied.

Now let us consider the effects of an increase in L^N. From (12.30) we calculate the horizontal shift of the *SS* curve, that is, the change in m at the initial value of ι. We obtain

$$\left.\frac{dm}{dL^N}\right|_{SS} = -\frac{\lambda m/\iota^2}{\lambda(L^N - a_L\iota)/\iota^2 + L^S/(m-\iota)^2} < 0. \tag{A12.17}$$

We similarly derive the horizontal shift of the *NN* curve from (12.29) and find that

$$\left.\frac{dm}{dL^N}\right|_{NN} = -\frac{\lambda m/\iota^2}{\lambda(L^S - a_m\iota)/(m-\iota)^2 + \lambda L^N/\iota^2} < 0. \tag{A12.18}$$

The difference between the denominator of (A12.18) and the denominator of (A12.17) equals

$$\lambda\left[\frac{(1-1/\lambda)L^S - a_m\iota}{(m-\iota)^2} + \frac{a_L}{\iota}\right].$$

This must be positive because by (12.24) and (12.26),

$$\left(1-\frac{1}{\lambda}\right)L^S - a_m\iota = (1-n^N)\left[\frac{a_m\rho}{\lambda} + \frac{1}{w^N}\left(1-\frac{1}{\lambda\omega}\right)\right] > 0.$$

We conclude that the leftward shift of the *SS* curve in response to an increase in L^N exceeds that of the *NN* curve.

Next we calculate the magnitude of the horizontal shifts of these curves in response to an increase in L^S. We find that

$$\left.\frac{dm}{dL^S}\right|_{SS} = \frac{m/\iota(m-\iota)}{\lambda(L^N - a_L\iota)/\iota^2 + L^S/(m-\iota)^2} > 0, \tag{A12.19}$$

$$\left.\frac{dm}{dL^S}\right|_{NN} = \frac{m/\iota(m-\iota)}{(L^S - a_m\iota)/(m-\iota)^2 + L^N/\iota^2} > 0. \tag{A12.20}$$

Both curves shift to the right. The difference between the denominators of (A12.19) and (A12.20) is equal to

$$\frac{(1-1/\lambda)L^N - a_L\iota}{\iota^2/\lambda} + \frac{a_m\iota}{(m-\iota)^2}.$$

From (12.23) we obtain

$$\begin{aligned}\left(1-\frac{1}{\lambda}\right)L^N - a_L\iota &= \frac{1}{\lambda}\left[\left(1-\frac{1}{\lambda}\right)\frac{n^N}{\omega w^N} - a_L\iota\right] \\ &> \frac{1}{\lambda}\left[\left(1-\frac{1}{\lambda\omega}\right)\frac{n^N}{w^N} - a_L\iota\right] \\ &= \frac{\rho n^N a_L}{\lambda} > 0.\end{aligned}$$

The first inequality follows from the fact that $\omega < 1$, while the last equality follows from (12.25). This shows that the denominator of (A12.19) is the larger of the two. Thus an increase in L^S causes the *NN* curve to shift by more than the *SS* curve.

Next we modify the system of equations comprising (12.23)–(12.26) to reflect the presence of research subsidies. This requires us to multiply the right-hand side of (12.25) by $(1-\phi^N)$ and the right-hand side of (12.26) by $(1-\phi^S)$. Now we are ready to compute the responses of relative wages and product shares to changes in the sizes of the two regions and to the introduction of small subsidies in each one. We obtain the following system of equations for the comparative statics calculations:

$$\begin{bmatrix} a_L & -\dfrac{n^N}{\lambda w^N} & \dfrac{1}{\lambda \omega w^N} & -\dfrac{n^N}{\lambda \omega} \\ a_m & 0 & -\dfrac{1}{w^N} & -n^S \\ -a_L & \dfrac{n^N}{\lambda w^N} & \dfrac{a_L \iota}{n^N} & \left(\dfrac{1}{\lambda \omega} - 1\right) n^N \\ -a_m & -\dfrac{n^S}{w^N} & -\dfrac{a_m \iota}{n^S} & \left(1 - \dfrac{1}{\omega}\right) n^S \end{bmatrix} \begin{bmatrix} d\iota \\ \dfrac{d\omega}{\omega^2} \\ dn^N \\ \dfrac{dw^N}{(w^N)^2} \end{bmatrix} = \begin{bmatrix} dL^N \\ dL^S \\ -b_N d\phi^N \\ -b_S d\phi^S \end{bmatrix}, \qquad \text{(A12.21)}$$

where $b_N \equiv a_L(\rho n^N + \iota)$ and $b_S \equiv a_m(\rho n^S + \iota)$. We denote the determinant of the matrix on the left-hand side of (A12.21) by $\tilde{\Delta}$. A direction calculation reveals that $\tilde{\Delta} < 0$.

Using (A12.21), it can be shown that an increase in the size of a region increases the fraction of products manufactured there. The effects of changes in labor supply on relative wages are ambiguous. This result contrasts with that in chapter 11 where we found that an increase in size of either labor force raises the relative wage of the expanding region.

As for the effects of small subsidies to R&D, we find

$$\left.\frac{dn^N}{d\phi^N}\right|_{\phi^N=\phi^S=0} = \frac{a_L(n^S)^2 b_N}{w^N\tilde{\Delta}} < 0,$$

$$\left.\frac{d\omega}{d\phi^N}\right|_{\phi^N=\phi^S=0} = \frac{\omega^2 a_m b_N(\rho a_L n^S + n^S/\lambda\omega^2 w^N + L^S n^N/\lambda\omega w^S)}{\tilde{\Delta}} < 0,$$

$$\left.\frac{dn^N}{d\phi^S}\right|_{\phi^N=\phi^S=0} = -\frac{a_m(n^N)^2 b_S}{\lambda w^N\tilde{\Delta}} > 0,$$

$$\left.\frac{d\omega}{d\phi^S}\right|_{\phi^N=\phi^S=0} = -\frac{\omega^2 a_L b_S(\rho a_m n^N/\lambda\omega + n^N/w^N + L^N n^S/n^N)}{\tilde{\Delta}} > 0.$$

Thus an R&D subsidy in the North shrinks the fraction of products emanating from that region (because the North devotes more resources to research, hence fewer to manufacturing) while raising the North's relative wage. A subsidy to imitation activities in the South has the opposite effects on product shares and the relative wage.

13 Lessons about Growth

In this concluding chapter we review some of the lessons that have emerged from our analysis of endogenous growth. The chapter is not intended as a comprehensive survey of results. Rather, we focus attention on a few central issues. The discussion highlights the theory's capacity to address topical concerns about the processes of growth in interdependent economies. Moreover it shows how the answers to important questions depend upon the details of the economic environment.

What Are the Forces That Drive Economic Growth in the Long Run?

Growing economies produce an ever-increasing quantity, quality, and variety of goods and services. Growth can derive from the accumulation of inputs or from increases in the productivity of a given set of resources. Traditionally economic theory has focused on factor accumulation as the driving force behind growth, although it has long been recognized that productivity gains might be needed to sustain private incentives for investment in the long run. In this book we have elaborated a theory of economic growth based on continuing industrial innovation. Technological progress often has been treated as an exogenous process in long-run economic analysis. This treatment would be appropriate for studying the growth of modern industrial economies if advances in industrial know-how followed automatically from fundamental scientific discoveries and if basic research was guided mostly by nonmarket forces. In the context of growth in the developing economies, technological advancement would be largely exogenous if knowledge diffused inevitably from the industrialized North to the lagging South and if the pace of innovation in the North were little affected by events in the South. But neither of these descriptions of the learning process seems in accordance with the available evidence. Scientific advances no doubt facilitate invention. But substantial investments are needed to transform abstract ideas into commercially viable products. And the ability to borrow from an existing knowledge base surely benefits Southern entrepreneurs. Still, the development of production capability in the South requires additional outlays for technical adaptation and assimilation.

We take the view that technological progress results from the intentional actions of economic agents responding to perceived profit opportunities. Firms and entrepreneurs devote resources to R&D when they see prospects for reaping returns on their investments. Returns come most often in the form of economic rents in imperfectly competitive product markets. Thus monopoly profits provide the impetus for growth, just as in the Schumpeterian process of "creative destruction."

We adopt a general-equilibrium framework for studying growth. When forward-looking entrepreneurs make their investment decisions, they compare anticipated streams of monopoly profits with expected costs of product development. Both the costs of R&D and the rewards that innovators stand to gain are affected by conditions in product, factor, and capital markets. Since prices in these markets are simultaneously determined, a general-equilibrium perspective is needed to impose internal consistency on the analysis.

Our focus on knowledge accumulation forces us to address the peculiar characteristics of information as a commodity. Unlike ordinary tangible commodities, the use of a bit of information by one economic agent does not preclude the simultaneous use of the same information by others. Moreover it is sometimes difficult for inventors to define their intellectual property and to enforce the rights that would prevent others from using it. These attributes of knowledge play an important role in the theory of growth that we articulate.

In particular, we recognize that most industrial R&D generates two distinct types of output. The first type consists of product-specific information that enables a firm to manufacture a particular new good (or an old good by a new and cheaper process). The second output comprises more general technical information, which may facilitate the undertaking of subsequent innovations. In many cases the innovator will be able to appropriate the returns to the product-specific information, either because patents protect product designs or because details of the production process can be hidden from rivals. But the additions to general knowledge are more difficult to appropriate. Problems will arise in the enforcement of property rights when the exact nature of the scientific contribution cannot be delineated. And it may be infeasible for an inventor to hide the contribution to general knowledge if the information becomes apparent upon inspection of his or her product. In the light of these features of knowledge creation, we assign a prominent role to technological spillovers in our modeling of industrial innovation.

In neoclassical models of capital accumulation, growth often peters out unless *exogenous* productivity gains preserve the incentives for investment. By contrast, investment incentives in the economies we study are endogenously maintained by technological spillovers. These spillovers allow successive generations of researchers to achieve technological breakthroughs using fewer resources than their predecessors. The resulting declines in the real cost of invention counteract any tendency for profits to fall. In short, the process of knowledge accumulation generates *endogenously* the productivity gains that sustain growth in the long run.

What Are the Links between the Growth Processes in Different Advanced Economies?

Technological competition in progressive industries increasingly plays out in a global arena. Firms located in different countries race to bring out more sophisticated products, or they strive to differentiate their offerings from those manufactured abroad. To the extent that innovation serves as the engine of growth, the outcomes of these global competitions may be critical to a country's dynamic performance. Our general-equilibrium approach to endogenous innovation allows us to analyze the interdependence of growth processes in different countries.

Countries that are integrated into the world economy interact with one another in several dimensions. They trade goods on world product markets, borrow and lend on world capital markets, and exchange information through market and nonmarket channels. Many of these global interactions generate forces that accelerate growth in every country. But several suggest reasons why international integration might impede growth.

The international exchange of technical information contributes to growth in every country. Some technological spillovers occur naturally within the scientific community. Researchers gain insights by reading foreign journals and by interacting with their counterparts in international forums. The knowledge they acquire by these means raises productivity in the research lab. With greater international transmission of knowledge capital, the cost of research is smaller in every location.

Not all international knowledge flows are independent of economic activities. The transmission of knowledge often takes place when business associates meet to engage in commerce. For example, foreign buyers of local products may provide information about manufacturing techniques, while foreign sellers may suggest ways that their products can be used more effectively. If these channels of communication are empirically important, countries that opt for economic isolation will forfeit many spillover benefits. In short, international commerce can spur innovation by facilitating the process of industrial learning.

Commodity trade has implications for innovation that are distinct from its influence on the dissemination of knowledge. For one thing, international trade introduces forces that improve the efficiency of global research. In the absence of international competition, researchers working in different countries have little incentive to avoid duplication of effort. But when innovators must compete in integrated product markets, they have reason to pursue distinctive ideas. Hence trade induces entrepreneurs to differentiate their inventions and thereby contributes to the global accumulation of knowledge.

International trade also plays a role in determining equilibrium allocations to industrial research. Economic integration may divert a country's resources away from R&D if local entrepreneurs fare poorly in the global technological competition. This outcome obtains in at least two situations. First, a country that has a comparative disadvantage in research, for example, due to a paucity of highly skilled labor, will find that integration induces relative specialization in other (perhaps stagnant) activities. Then, even with the benefits of any technological spillovers, its output may grow more slowly than in autarky. Second, when technological spillovers are national in reach, a country that is small in size, or one that historically has conducted little research, may be driven to specialize in manufacturing activities. In the event technological progress may cease altogether in a country that would continue to innovate if it were economically isolated.

A final link between trade and innovation operates through national factor markets. Economic integration invariably causes the expansion of some manufacturing sectors and the contraction of others. In the process factor rewards adjust to effect the associated resource movements. But as factor prices change, so do the costs of industrial innovation. Thus trade may diminish R&D activity in a country that exports human-capital-intensive manufactures. On the other hand, a country that has a dearth of skilled labor may find that trade eases derived demand for that locally scarce resource. Then inputs released by the importables sector can find new employment generating innovations.

What Determines the Trade Pattern When Comparative Advantage Is Endogenously Generated?

When countries engage in technological competition, comparative advantage evolves over time. Research successes create export opportunities as innovators learn to produce goods that are better than, different from, or less costly than those manufactured abroad. In the long run a country's pattern of trade reflects, inter alia, the resources that it devotes to industrial research.

How is the resource allocation determined? The answer to this question depends upon the economic context. Suppose, for example, that technological spillovers are global in scope so that innovators share access to a common pool of knowledge. History may dictate the initial pattern of specialization as countries produce with the blueprints they inherit. But relative factor endowments must eventually be determinative, just as they are in a static economy. A country that is well endowed with human capital specializes relatively in performing (human-capital-intensive) R&D and develops a comparative advantage in high-tech manufacturing. At the same time a country with an abundance of unskilled labor devotes relatively few resources to industrial research and ultimately finds itself importing high-technology goods.

Initial conditions can matter for the long-run trade pattern when technological spillovers are geographically concentrated. In an extreme case in which trade partners are similar in size and their endowments consist of a single primary factor, a country that inherits even a small technological lead comes to dominate world markets for high-technology products. A productivity differential is self-perpetuating in this case because the technological leader conducts relatively more research and thereby extends its initial advantage.

In more general circumstances factor composition, country size, and research experience interact to determine long-run resource allocations. Large size, an abundance of human capital, and a sizable knowledge base contribute to a country's competitiveness in research. Such competitiveness is reflected in the long-run trade pattern and also in cross-country comparisons of growth rates.

Government policies too can influence the long-run patterns of specialization and trade. The implications of technology policy are perhaps the most interesting. In situations where local experience affects research productivity, a national policy to encourage R&D, even if used only temporarily, can dramatically alter the course of economic history. By strengthening the incentives for private research, the government of a technologically lagging country can "level the playing field." Then a nation that would otherwise specialize in traditional manufacturing can be transformed into an exporter of high-technology goods.

Technology policies have quite a different effect on trade flows when technological spillovers are global in scope. Consider, for example, an economy endowed with human capital and unskilled labor, where R&D is the most human-capital-intensive activity and the manufacturing of traditional products is the least so. In such an economy expansion of R&D comes at the expense of high-tech manufacturing, as these activities compete for the limited human capital stock. Then an R&D subsidy that accelerates innovation also deteriorates the balance of high-technology trade. A sufficiently large (and permanent) subsidy can even make a net importer of a country that would otherwise export innovative products. We conclude that the links between policy and the trade pattern depend upon the nature of the general-equilibrium environment.

Is the Equilibrium Growth Path Socially Efficient?

In a perfectly competitive economy that experiences exogenous technological progress, the equilibrium growth path exhibits productive efficiency. Government intervention can improve social welfare in such a case only when it furthers distributional objectives or generates terms-of-trade gains. But policy prescriptions are not so clearcut for economies that tolerate monopoly power to reward R&D investments and that realize technological spillovers from industrial research. Let us consider first the case of a closed, innovating economy. There are several reasons why the market allocation may differ from the social optimum. First, the extent of monopoly power may vary across sectors. Then the volume of output will be inefficiently small in industries with especially high price–cost markups. Second, potential innovators may fail to consider the consumer surplus that they generate when they introduce new products. Third, private research decisions often fail to reflect any spillover contributions to the public knowledge stock. Finally, innovators generally neglect their adverse impact on the profits earned by extant producers. The fact that consumers and researchers may derive external benefits from invention suggests that innovation will be suboptimally slow in the market equilibrium. But the external harm that befalls rival producers suggests that the opposite outcome might also be possible.

In general, it is impossible to say whether the market allocation to research is too great or too small. There exist circumstances, such as when innovators invent symmetric products and utility functions are characterized by constant elasticities of substitution, where the economy grows more slowly than is optimal. Under these conditions a suitable subsidy to R&D can be used to raise social welfare. But in other cases, such as when innovators race to bring out higher-quality products, a normative evaluation of the equilibrium growth path yields ambiguous results. In any event there is an optimal growth rate for every economy. The R&D sector should never be expanded beyond the point where the future benefits justify the current loss in consumption.

Analysis of a small open economy brings another point into focus. That is, even if the free-market growth rate is clearly too slow, policies that spur innovation need not raise social welfare. R&D subsidies generally do provide benefits because they directly address a market failure. But other policies that have a beneficial effect on R&D may have harmful repercussions elsewhere in the economy. This complication in the formulation of public policy is well known from the theory of the second best. Consider, for example, the potential desirability of a trade intervention that happens to reduce the cost of human capital. Such a policy induces a fall in the cost of research and thereby encourages industrial innovation. But the change in factor prices also affects incentives in the manufacturing sectors. If outputs contract in industries with high price–cost markups, then the subsidy exacerbates a static inefficiency. Social welfare may decline as the result of the intervention, even though policy has alleviated a dynamic distortion.

In an integrated world economy with several large countries, government policies influence the cross-country distribution of innovative activities. Generally, when one country subsidizes R&D, this reduces the profitability of innovation abroad. If research contracts in a country with comparative advantage in this activity, there may be a slowing of aggregate (world) innovation. In the event the policy may reduce welfare levels worldwide.

But even if the global innovation rate does not fall in the long run, a country may suffer for its attempts to capture world research activity. Consider again a world economy with national stocks of knowledge, where an historical leader is destined to dominate high technology. If the government of a lagging country subsidizes R&D for a while, its productivity disadvantage can be overcome. It may seem at first glance that such a policy would be desirable because it generates national productivity growth where otherwise there would be none. But in fact the policy induces a waste of world resources during (at least) the period of technological catch-up. The inefficiency in world research implies a loss of world output, and in general every country finds itself sharing in the loss. Thus welfare may decline in a country that subsidizes R&D, even if the policy succeeds in creating a competitive research environment.

Our analysis reinforces an obvious truth that is sometimes lost in public policy discussions. That is, it is not the growth rate of domestic output that matters for welfare in an integrated world economy but rather the level and growth of consumption opportunities. Commodity trade allows households residing in a particular country to benefit from the products that are developed elsewhere. By using their savings to finance foreign investments, they also can share in the profits generated by foreign innovations. Still, a country may prefer to have R&D take place locally, for any one of several reasons. First, long-run wage rates may be higher in a country that captures increasing returns activities. Second, there may exist institutional impediments to international capital flows, in which case welfare will be affected by the profitability of local investments. Finally, some R&D projects may hold prospects for supernormal returns. Then a country may benefit from strategic initiatives that capture the rents for its national firms.

What Are the Links between Innovation in the Industrialized North and Imitation in the Developing South?

Historically trade between the industrialized North and the less developed South has entailed the exchange of capital-intensive and human-capital-intensive manufactures by the former region for the labor-intensive manufactures and primary commodities of the latter. But in recent decades the product cycle has featured more prominently in North–South trade. In product-cycle trade innovative goods developed in the North are exported to the South for a while. But the trade pattern later reverses, as the South takes over the production of these goods and Northern manufacturers move on to a new set of products. Formerly, when technical abilities in the South were severely limited, foreign investments by Northern-based multinationals were the primary vehicle for technology transfer. But more recently, many entrepreneurs in the South have developed the capacity to emulate Northern technologies. Now imitation accounts for much of the South's technological progress, as well as for many trade frictions between the South and the North.

An immediate question that arises in the context of product-cycle trade is, What are the implications of Southern imitation for the strength of incentives to innovate in the North? It may appear at first glance that the answer is obvious. Entry into a market by a Southern imitator puts an end to the monopoly position enjoyed by an innovator. If this were the only effect of imitation felt in the North, then innovation surely would slow in response to faster Southern learning. But our general-equilibrium perspective suggests another possibility. The greater the rate of Southern imitation, the smaller is the share of innovative products manufactured in the North. Therefore Northern producers who are fortunate enough to escape imitation find fewer competitors in local factor markets. Accordingly their earnings are higher during their stay in the market. Moreover there are circumstances where this profit effect dominates, where higher rates of imitation cause innovators' expected profits to rise even as the average tenure of monopolists falls. Take, for example, an economy in which horizontally differentiated goods account for the bulk of household spending. In this case an increase in the rate of imitation, caused either by an expansion of Southern capacity to copy or by an explicit policy of the South to promote learning activities, induces an increase in the ex ante return to invention. Then the migration of manufacturing from North to South causes an increase in inventive activity in the North.

However, the opposite result also is possible. Imitation can diminish innovation incentives if the North produces traditional as well as innovative goods. Then the Northern resources released from industries targeted by the South may find their way into alternative manufacturing activities. Also greater rates of imitation may impede innovation when the North is engaged in quality upgrading. In this latter case a negative feedback can operate also in the opposite direction. That is, Southern entrepreneurs may invest less in learning when they perceive a more rapid pace of technological obsolescence. Then policies that promote innovation in the North may retard the catching-up process in the South.

Questions relating to productivity and international competitiveness will remain prevalent in public policy discussions for many years to come. Hopefully we have convinced the reader that these issues are amenable to rigorous analysis. Of course we have by no means exhausted the possible elaborations of the theory, nor have we undertaken the important task of confronting the theory with data. Still, our book does take an initial step toward bringing industrial innovation under the purview of the theories of international trade and economic growth.

References

Abegglen, James C., and Stalk, George Jr. 1985. *Kaisha, The Japanese Corporation.* New York: Basic Books.

Abramovitz, Moses. 1956. "Resource and Output Trends in the United States Since 1870." *American Economic Review* 46 (Papers and Proceedings): 5–23.

Adams, James D. 1990. "Fundamental Stocks of Knowledge and Productivity Growth." *Journal of Political Economy* 98: 673–702.

Agency of Industrial Science and Technology. 1989. *Trends of Principle Indicators on Research and Development Activities in Japan.* Technology Research and Information Division, Tokyo.

Aghion, Philippe, and Howitt, Peter. 1990. "A Model of Growth Through Creative Destruction." NBER Working Paper No. 3223. Cambridge, MA.

Arrow, Kenneth J. 1962a. "Economic Welfare and the Allocation of Resources for Inventions." In R. R. Nelson (ed.), *The Rate and Direction of Inventive Activity.* Princeton: Princeton University Press for the NBER.

Arrow, Kenneth J. 1962b. "The Economic Implications of Learning by Doing." *Review of Economic Studies* 29: 155–173.

Arrow, Kenneth J., and Kurz, Mordechai. 1970. *Public Investment, the Rate of Return and Optimal Fiscal Policy.* Baltimore: Johns Hopkins University Press.

Azariades, Costas, and Drazen, Allan. 1990. "Threshold Externalities in Economic Development." *Quarterly Journal of Economics* 105: 501–526.

Balassa, Bela, and Noland, Marcus. 1989. "The Changing Comparative Advantage of Japan and the United States." *Journal of the Japanese and International Economies* 3: 174–187.

Barro, Robert J. 1974. "Are Government Bonds Net Wealth?" *Journal of Political Economy* 82: 1095–1117.

Barro, Robert J. 1989a. "Economic Growth in a Cross Section of Countries." NBER Working Paper No. 3120. Cambridge, MA.

Barro, Robert J. 1989b. "A Cross-Country Study of Growth, Saving, and Government." NBER Working Paper No. 2855. Cambridge, MA.

Barro, Robert J. 1990. "Government Spending in a Simple Model of Endogenous Growth." *Journal of Political Economy* 98: S103–S125.

Baumol, William J., Batey Blackman, Sue Anne, and Wolff, Edward J. 1989. *Productivity and American Leadership: The Long View*. Cambridge: MIT Press.

Benko, Robert P. 1987. *Protecting Intellectual Property Rights*. Washington: American Enterprise Institute.

Bernstein, Jeffrey I., and Nadiri, M. Ishaq. 1988. "Interindustry R&D Spillovers, Rates of Return, and Production in High-Technology Industries." *American Economic Review* 78 (Papers and Proceedings): 429–434.

Bernstein, Jeffrey I., and Nadiri, M. Ishaq. 1989. "Research and Development and Intra-Industry Spillovers: An Empirical Application of Dynamic Duality." *Review of Economic Studies* 56: 249–268.

Blanchard, Olivier J., and Fischer, Stanley. 1989. *Lectures on Macroeconomics*. Cambridge: MIT Press.

Bowen, Harry P., Leamer, Edward E., and Sveikauskas, Leo. 1987. "Multicountry, Multifactor Tests of the Factor Abundance Theory." *American Economic Review* 77: 791–809.

Bresnahan, Timothy. 1986. "Measuring the Spillovers from Technical Advance: Mainframe Computers in Financial Services." *American Economic Review* 76: 742–755.

Caballero, Richard J., and Lyons, Richard K. 1989. "The Role of Externalities in U.S. Manufacturing." NBER Working Paper No. 3033. Cambridge, MA.

Cass, David. 1965. "Optimum Growth in an Aggregative Model of Capital Accumulation." *Review of Economic Studies* 32: 233–240.

Caves, Richard E., Crookwell, Harold, and Killing, J. Peter. 1983. "The Imperfect Market for Licensing." *Oxford Bulletin of Economics and Statistics* 45: 249–267.

Corbo, Vitorio, Krueger, Anne O., and Ossa, F. (eds.). 1985. *Export-Oriented Development Strategies*. Boulder: Westview Press.

Denison, Edward F. 1967. *Why Growth Rates Differ*. Washington: Brookings Institution.

Dixit, Avinash, and Stiglitz, Joseph E. 1977. Monopolistic Competition and Optimum Product Diversity." *American Economic Review* 67: 297–308.

Dixit, Avinash, and Norman, Victor. 1980. *Theory of International Trade*. Cambridge: Cambridge University Press.

Domar, Evsey D. 1946. "Capital Expansion, Rate of Growth, and Employment." *Econometrica* 14: 137–147.

Dosi, Giovanni. 1988. "Sources, Procedures and Microeconomic Effects of Innovation." *Journal of Economic Literature* 26: 1120–1171.

Dowrick, Steve, and Nguyen, Duc-Th. 1989. "OECD Comparative Economic Growth 1950–1985: Catch-up and Convergence." *American Economic Review* 79: 1010–1030.

Ethier, Wilfred J. 1979. "Internationally Decreasing Costs and World Trade." *Journal of International Economics* 9: 1–24.

Ethier, Wilfred J. 1982a. "National and International Returns to Scale in the Modern Theory of International Trade." *American Economic Review* 72: 389–405.

Ethier, Wilfred J. 1982b. "Decreasing Costs in International Trade and Frank Graham's Argument for Protection." *Econometrica* 50: 1243–1268.

Feder, Gershon. 1982. "On Exports and Economic Growth." *Journal of Development Economics* 12: 59–73.

Feenstra, Robert. 1990a. "Trade and Uneven Growth." NBER Working Paper No. 3276. Cambridge, MA.

Feenstra, Robert. 1990b. "New Goods and Index Numbers: U.S. Import Prices." Unpublished manuscript. University of California, Davis.

Feller, William. 1968. *An Introduction to Probability Theory and its Applications.* 3d ed. New York: Wiley.

Findlay, Ronald, and Kierzkowski, Henryk. 1983. "International Trade and Human Capital: A Simple General Equilibrium Model." *Journal of Political Economy* 91: 957–978.

Graham, Frank D. 1923. "Some Aspects of Protection Further Considered." *Quarterly Journal of Economics* 37: 199–227.

Green, Jerry R., and Scotchmer, Susanne. 1989. "Antitrust Policy, the Breadth of Patent Protection and the Incentive to Develop New Products." Harvard Institute for Economic Research Discussion Paper No.1467. Cambridge, MA.

Griliches, Zvi. 1973. "Research Expenditures and Growth Accounting." In B. R. Williams (ed.), *Science and Technology in Economic Growth.* London: Macmillan.

Griliches, Zvi. 1979. "Issues in Assessing the Contribution of Research and Development in Productivity Growth." *Bell Journal of Economics* 10: 92–116.

Grossman, Gene M. 1990. "Explaining Japan's Innovation and Growth: A Model of Quality Competition and Dynamic Comparative Advantage." *Bank of Japan Monetary and Economic Studies* 8: 75–100.

Grossman, Gene M., and Helpman, Elhanan. 1990. "Comparative Advantage and Long-Run Growth." *American Economic Review* 80: 796–815.

Grossman, Gene M., and Helpman, Elhanan. 1991a. "Quality Ladders in the Theory of Growth." *Review of Economic Studies* 58: 43–61.

Grossman, Gene M., and Helpman, Elhanan. 1991b. "Quality Ladders and Product Cycles." *Quarterly Journal of Economics* 106: 557–586.

Grossman, Gene M., and Helpman, Elhanan. 1991c. "Trade, Knowledge Spillovers, and Growth." *European Economic Review* 35 (Papers and Proceedings), forthcoming.

Grossman, Gene M., and Helpman, Elhanan. 1991d. "Endogenous Product Cycles." *The Economic Journal* 101, forthcoming.

Hall, Robert E. 1988. "The Relation between Price and Marginal Cost in U.S. Industry." *Journal of Political Economy* 96: 921–947.

Harrod, Roy F. 1939. "An Essay in Dynamic Theory." *The Economic Journal* 49: 14–33.

Helpman, Elhanan. 1984. "Increasing Returns, Imperfect Markets, and Trade Theory." In R. W. Jones and P. B. Kenen, (eds.), *Handbook of International Economics*. Amsterdam: North Holland.

Helpman, Elhanan, and Krugman, Paul R. 1985. *Market Structure and Foreign Trade*. Cambridge: MIT Press.

Hirsch, Seev. 1967. *Location of Industry and International Competitiveness*. Oxford: Oxford University Press.

Inada, Kenichi. 1964. "Some Structural Characteristics of Turnpike Theorems." *Review of Economic Studies* 31: 43–58.

Jones, Larry E., and Manuelli, Rodolfo. 1990. "A Convex Model of Equilibrium Growth." *Journal of Political Economy* 98: 1008–1038.

Jones, Ronald W. 1965. "The Structure of Simple General Equilibrium Models." *Journal of Political Economy* 73: 557–572.

Jorgenson, Dale W., Gollop, Frank M., and Fraumeni, Barbara M. 1987. *Productivity and U.S. Economic Growth*. Cambridge: Harvard University Press.

Judd, Kenneth L. 1985. "On the Performance of Patents." *Econometrica* 53: 567–586.

Kaldor, Nicholas. 1961. "Capital Accumulation and Economic Growth." In F. Lutz (ed.), *The Theory of Capital*. London: Macmillan.

Kendrick, John W. 1961. *Productivity Trends in the United States*. Princeton: Princeton University Press.

Kendrick, John W. 1981. "Why Productivity Growth Rates Change and Differ." In H. Giersch (ed.), *Towards an Explanation of Economic Growth.* Tübingen: J. C. B. Mohr, Paul Siebeck.

King, Robert G., and Rebelo, Sergio. 1990. "Public Policy and Economic Growth: Developing Neoclassical Implications." *Journal of Political Economy* 98: S126–S150.

Koester, Reinhard B., and Kormendi, Roger C. 1989. "Taxation, Aggregate Activity and Economic Growth: Cross-Country Evidence on Some Supply Side Hypotheses." *Economic Inquiry* 27: 367–386.

Koopmans, Tjalling C. 1965. "On the Concept of Optimal Economic Growth." In *The Economic Approach to Development Planning.* Amsterdam: North Holland.

Krueger, Anne O. 1978. *Foreign Trade Regimes and Economic Development.* Cambridge, MA: Ballinger.

Krugman, Paul R. 1979. "A Model of Innovation, Technology Transfer, and the World Distribution of Income." *Journal of Political Economy* 87: 253–266.

Krugman, Paul R. 1981. "Intraindustry Specialization and the Gains from Trade." *Journal of Political Economy* 89: 959–973.

Krugman, Paul R. 1987. "The Narrow Moving Band, the Dutch Disease, and the Competitive Consequences of Mrs. Thatcher: Notes on Trade in the Presence of Dynamic Scale Economies." *Journal of Development Economics* 27: 41–55.

Krugman, Paul R. 1991. "History vs. Expectations." *Quarterly Journal of Economics* 106: 651–667.

Kuznets, Paul W. 1988. "An East Asian Model of Economic Development: Japan, Taiwan, and South Korea." *Economic Development and Cultural Change* 36 (suppl.): S11–S43.

Lach, Saul, and Schankerman, Mark. 1989. "Dynamics of R&D and Investment in the Scientific Sector." *Journal of Political Economy* 97: 880–904.

Landau, David. 1983. "Government Expenditure and Economic Growth: A Cross-Country Study." *Southern Economic Journal* 49: 783–792.

Leamer, Edward. 1984. *Sources of International Comparative Advantage.* Cambridge: MIT Press.

Lee, Tom, and Wilde, Louis L. 1980. "Market Structure and Innovation: A Reformulation." *Quarterly Journal of Economics* 94: 431–436.

Lerner, Abba P. 1934. "The Concept of Monopoly and the Measure of Monopoly Power." *Review of Economic Studies* 1: 157–175.

Lerner, Abba P. 1936. "The Symmetry between Import and Export Taxes." *Economica* 11: 306–313.

Little, Ian M. D., and Mirrlees, James A. 1969. *Manual of Industrial Policy in Developing Countries*. Paris: Organization for Economic Cooperation and Development.

Lockwood, William W. 1954. *The Economic Development of Japan: Growth and Structural Change. 1868–1938*. Princeton: Princeton University Press.

Lucas, Robert E., Jr. 1988. "On the Mechanics of Economic Development." *Journal of Monetary Economics* 22: 3–42.

Maddison, Angus. 1979. "Per Capita Output in the Long Run." *Kyklos* 32: 412–429.

Maddison, Angus. 1987. "Growth and Slowdown in Advanced Capitalist Economies." *Journal of Economic Literature* 25: 649–698.

Management and Coordination Agency. 1988. *Report on the Survey of Research and Development*. Japan Statistics Bureau, Tokyo.

Mansfield, Edwin. 1985. "How Rapidly Does New Industrial Technology Leak Out?" *Journal of Industrial Economics* 34: 217–223.

Mansfield, Edwin, Rapoport, J., Romeo, A., Wagner, S., and Beardsley, G. 1977. "Social and Private Rates of Return from Industrial Innovation." *Quarterly Journal of Economics* 91: 221–240.

Mansfield, Edwin, Schwartz, Mark, and Wagner, Samuel. 1981. "Imitation Costs and Patents: An Empirical Study." *The Economic Journal* 91: 907–918.

Markusen, James R. 1991. "First Mover Advantages, Blockaded Entry, and the Economics of Uneven Development." In E. Helpman and A. Razin (eds.), *International Trade and Trade Policy*. Cambridge: MIT Press.

Matsuyama, Kiminori. 1991. "Increasing Returns, Industrialization and Indeterminacy of Equilibrium." *Quarterly Journal of Economics* 106: 617–650.

Michaely, Michael. 1977. "Exports and Growth: An Empirical Investigation." *Journal of Development Economics* 40: 49–53.

Mowery, David C., and Rosenberg, Nathan. 1989. *Technology and the Pursuit of Economic Growth*. Cambridge: Cambridge University Press.

National Science Foundation. 1989. *National Patterns of R&D Resources*. Washington: National Science Foundation.

OECD. 1986. *OECD Science and Technology Indicators No.2: R&D, Invention and Competitiveness*. Paris: Organization for Economic Cooperation and Development.

OECD. 1989. *OECD Science and Technology Indicators No.3: R&D, Production and Diffusion of Technology*. Paris: Organization for Economic Cooperation and Development.

Ohyama, Michihiro. 1989. "Human Capital and Endogenous Economic Growth." Keio Economic Society Discussion Paper Series No. 8902. Tokyo.

Pack, Howard, and Westphal, Larry E. 1986. "Industrial Strategy and Technological Change: Theory versus Reality." *Journal of Development Economics* 22: 87–128.

Perlis, Sam. 1952. *Theory of Matrices.* Reading, MA: Addison Wesley.

Ramsey, Frank P. 1928. "A Mathematical Theory of Savings." *The Economic Journal* 38: 543–559.

Rebelo, Sergio. 1990. "Long Run Policy Analysis and Long Run Growth." *Journal of Political Economy* 99: 500–521.

Rhee, Yung Whee, Ross-Larson, Bruce, and Pursell, Garry. 1984. *Korea's Competitive Edge: Managing the Entry into World Markets.* Baltimore: Johns Hopkins University Press for The World Bank.

Rivera-Batiz, Luis A., and Romer, Paul M. 1990. "Economic Integration and Endogenous Growth." Unpublished manuscript. University of California, San Diego.

Romer, Paul M. 1986. "Increasing Returns and Long-Run Growth." *Journal of Political Economy* 94: 1002–1037.

Romer, Paul M. 1987. "Crazy Explanations for the Productivity Slowdown." In S. Fischer (ed.), *NBER Macroeconomics Annual.* Cambridge: MIT Press.

Romer, Paul M. 1989a. "Capital Accumulation in the Theory of Long Run Growth." In R. Barro (ed.), *Modern Business Cycle Theory.* Cambridge: Harvard University Press.

Romer, Paul M. 1989b. "Human Capital and Growth: Theory and Evidence." NBER Working Paper No. 3173. Cambridge, MA.

Romer, Paul M. 1989c. "What Determines the Rate of Growth and Technical Change?" The World Bank Policy, Planning and Research Working Paper No. WPS 279. Washington, DC.

Romer, Paul M. 1990. "Endogenous Technological Change." *Journal of Political Economy* 98: S71–S102.

Samuelson, Paul A. 1965. *Foundations of Economic Analysis.* 2d ed. Cambridge: Harvard University Press.

Sargent, Thomas J. 1979. *Macroeconomic Theory.* Cambridge: Harvard University Press.

Scherer, F. M. 1982. "Interindustry Technology Flows and Productivity Growth." *Review of Economics and Statistics* 64: 627–634.

Schmookler, Jacob. 1966. *Invention and Economic Growth.* Cambridge: Harvard University Press.

Schumpeter, Joseph. 1942. *Capitalism, Socialism and Democracy*. New York: Harper.

Scott, Maurice FitzGerald. 1989. *A New View of Economic Growth*. Oxford: Oxford University Press.

Segerstrom, Paul S. 1991. "Innovation, Imitation and Economic Growth." *Journal of Political Economy*, forthcoming.

Segerstrom, Paul S., Anant, T. C. A., and Dinopoulos, Elias. 1990. "A Schumpeterian Model of the Product Life Cycle." *American Economic Review* 80: 1077–1092.

Shell, Karl. 1967. "A Model of Inventive Activity and Capital Accumulation." In K. Shell (ed.), *Essays on the Theory of Optimal Economic Growth*. Cambridge: MIT Press.

Sheshinski, Eitan. 1967. "Optimal Accumulation with Learning by Doing." In K. Shell (ed.), *Essays on the Theory of Optimal Economic Growth*. Cambridge: MIT Press.

Solow, Robert M. 1956. "A Contribution to the Theory of Economic Growth." *Quarterly Journal of Economics* 70: 65–94.

Solow, Robert M. 1957. "Technical Change and the Aggregate Production Function." *Review of Economics and Statistics* 39: 312–320.

Summers, Robert, and Heston, Alan. 1988. "A New Set of International Comparisons of Real Product and Price Levels: Estimates of 130 Countries." *The Review of Income and Wealth* 34: 1–25.

Syrquin, Moshe, and Chenery, Hollis. 1989. "Three Decades of Industrialization." *World Bank Economic Review* 3: 145–181.

Trajtenberg, Manuel. 1990. "Product Innovations, Price Indices, and the (Mis)-measurement of Economic Performance." NBER Working Paper No. 3261. Cambridge, MA.

U.S. Department of Labor. 1989. *The Impact of Research and Development on Productivity Growth*. Bureau of Labor Statistics, Bulletin 2331. Washington, DC.

U.S. International Trade Commission. 1988. *Foreign Protection of Intellectual Property Rights and the Effect on U.S. Industry and Trade*. USITC Publication No. 2065. Washington, DC.

Vernon, Raymond. 1966. "International Investment and International Trade in the Product Cycle." *Quarterly Journal of Economics* 80: 190–207.

Index